The Tri-State
Gardener's
Guide

Published by Cool Springs Press, a Thomas Nelson Company, P.O. Box 141000, Nashville, Tennessee 37214.

Snodsmith, Ralph, 1939–
  The tri-state gardener's guide : New York, New Jersey, Connecticut / Ralph Snodsmith.
    p. cm.
  Includes bibliographical references (p.).
  ISBN 1-888608-45-5
  1. Landscape plants—New York (State). 2. Landscape plants—New Jersey. 3. Landscape plants—Connecticut. 4. Landscape gardening—New York (State). 5. Landscape gardening—New Jersey. 6. Landscape gardening—Connecticut. I. Title.
SB407 .S654 2001
635.9'0974—dc21

                                                        00-050875

First printing 2001
Printed in the United States of America
10 9 8 7 6 5 4 3 2 1

Managing Editor: Billie Brownell
Horticultural Editor: Charles Cresson
Copyeditor: Jan Keeling
Designer: Sheri Ferguson
Production Artist: S. E. Anderson

On the Cover: Forsythia, photographed by Thomas Eltzroth

The Tri-State
Gardener's
Guide

Ralph Snodsmith

COOL
SPRINGS
PRESS

Nashville, Tennessee

Dedication

I dedicate this book to my wife Mary, my daughter Elizabeth, my cat Dude, and last but not least, my miniature schnauzer Pepper (who was so patient in allowing me to get to the end of the page before he insisted on going outside once more).

Acknowledgments

My biggest thank you is to my wife, Mary, for transcribing my notes and making, as we used to say in Mt. Vernon, Illinois, "a silk purse out of a sow's ear." Without Mary and the miracles of the computer age, this book would still be in my mind's eye.

Looking back, I wish to acknowledge two of the finest friends and gentlemen, both who have probably forgotten more than I will ever know in my lifetime, who gave me the confidence to not only write this book but to guest-lecture at the New York Botanical Garden. They are my mentor, Pascal P. Pirone, Ph.D., author of *Tree Maintenance* and *Diseases and Pests of Ornamental Plants*, and the late Thomas H. Everett, author of the three-million-word, ten-volume *New York Botanical Garden Illustrated Encyclopedia of Horticulture*. Dr. "Pat" Pirone was the Director of Education at the New York Botanical Garden who engaged me as instructor of "Fundamentals of Gardening" over one-third of a century ago.

I also wish to thank Roger Waynick, Hank McBride, Billie Brownell, and the staff of Cool Springs Press for working with me in the production of this book. I appreciate their confidence in my horticultural background and my interest in communicating with gardeners and you, the reader.

And I can never say thank you enough to all of the callers to the Garden Hotline® Radio programs heard over the years (approximately 9,000 on-air hours) on the nationwide WOR Radio Network, ABC Talkradio Network, and on WRKL and WRCR, Rockland County, New York. These callers have been, and continue to be, great listeners, and I want them to know how important they have been in the selection of the plants for this book.

Table of Contents

Welcome
to Gardening
in the Tri-State

Many of you already know about the resident of Rockland County who bought bare-root Poplars in early spring, planted them, and saw them *all* die. But for everyone's enjoyment, let me tell the story once again:

When I was the Horticultural Agent for Cornell Cooperative Extension of Rockland County, New York, a call came into my office one day with a cry for help. The caller explained the problem with his new trees and related that the "guarantee" (which we'll call the "death certificate") read: "If a county agent or a professional nurseryman will sign the certificate, we (the mail-order nursery) will replace any or all plants that do not become established or that die." Immediately I was sure I knew what had gone wrong: the plants had dried out while in transit to the home. No telling how long they were in the mail or how long they were in the warehouse before shipping.

When you order bare-root Poplars for early spring planting, you receive three-foot-long, leafless whips or stems with roots growing from one end. The bundles of stems are tied together, the roots packed in moist peat moss or wood shavings, and all is wrapped in a shipping sleeve and mailed to you.

I told the caller what I thought the problem was, but he pleaded with me to come look at them and sign the certificate. I relented. On my way home that night, I dropped by to take a look.

The community was a brand-new suburban development of split-level and high-ranch homes. Back in the late 1960s and early '70s, developments were often stripped of all vegetation, including trees, before the houses were built, and then they were planted with new landscapes. (Apparently builders in those days did not realize the value of older trees to the community.)

I pulled into the driveway and had to bite my lip to keep from laughing. All along one side of the property line were newly planted Poplars. All across the back property line were newly planted Poplars. And all up the other property line (you guessed it) were newly planted Poplars. There was only one problem. They were all planted upside down! The homeowner thought that the roots were branches. Of course they were dead, and I did sign the "death certificate." I understand that the mail-order nursery replaced the Poplars, and the homeowner attended the very next session of my class, *Fundamentals of Gardening*, at the New York Botanical Garden.

Plan Before You Plant

Whether positioning a new flowering tree or shrub in the landscape or an evergreen tree to screen an objectionable site; whether planning to grow a rosebush for producing flowers or to establish a ground cover where grass doesn't grow; whether planting a bulb garden along a walkway or starting a perennial bed at the base of a stone wall; whether selecting annuals for summer color or establishing a new lawn to present the greenest grass in the neighborhood: *you must plan before you plant*.

Not only must you know which end goes up as with bulbs, bare-root transplants, and sod, but it is also important to know about plant physiology. If the plant cannot manufacture enough food for growth, the plant begins to decline, and if left unattended, the declining plant might die. The roots take up water and dissolved minerals from the soil and move both to the green leaves through the vascular system of the plant, which is often likened to our blood vessels and arteries. In *photosynthesis*, cells containing green chlorophyll manufacture food. The manufactured food is moved back to the leaf and flower buds, stems, and roots, completing the cycle of growth.

It is necessary for you to plant the right plant in the right place, provide nutrition and water, and give it good ol' TLC (tender loving care).

Soils

Of any single component over which you have control, improving soil will provide the longest-lasting results. To make improvements to soil in containers, in a raised bed, in the lawn, or around the foundation landscape, you need to know the soil conditions that exist.

Scoop up a handful of soil in the palm of your hand. Rub your hands together. If the soil feels gritty, it probably contains sand. If the soil feels slick, it probably contains silt and/or clay particles. If the palms of your hands are blackened when you rub them together, there is organic matter in the form of humic acid (the end product of decaying organic matter).

Humic acid is the glue that holds soil particles together as well as apart. It provides the dark, rich color and increases the nutrient-holding capacity of soil. If you garden along the Jersey Shore or the Long Island Sound, you know the importance of adding organic matter to sandy soil. It improves the soil's moisture-holding capacity

while a new tree, shrub, or perennial is becoming established. If you garden inland in New Jersey, on the North Shore of Long Island, or in upstate New York or Connecticut, you're confronted with clay and rocks. Organic matter is also the solution to this problem. Well-rotted compost or milled sphagnum peat moss, spaded in as deeply as possible, will become humic acid and improve aeration and drainage over time.

The only part of the Tri-State area where it is not necessary to add organic matter to soil is the black-dirt region of Pine Island, New York. The soil there is pure organic matter, real black dirt!

Knowing the soil acidity or alkalinity—the soil pH—is mandatory. If you test for soil pH, record the results in your garden recordkeeper. (Good gardeners keep good records.) The information will tell you what improvements need to be made to the soil before planting.

I have asked of audiences, "How many of you have added lime to your garden?" Maybe sixty percent or more will raise their hands. Then I ask how many have ever done a pH test. There might be three or four, if I'm lucky. This tells me that we often do without knowing what we really should do. Just because your neighbor applies lime to his or her lawn or garden does not mean that you should apply lime, too. I'm sure you are not guilty of this, but just in case you are, remember: "Plan before you plant." Do the soil test.

If you spend time researching a plant before you plant it, you will not make the mistake of planting a beautiful plant in the wrong environment. I've often referred to the value of a "fifty-cent plant in a five-dollar hole." If you plant that way, you'll have a "five-dollar plant" shortly. By the same token, if you plant a "five-dollar plant" in a "fifty-cent environment," you'll have a dead plant shortly.

Adding organic matter and altering soil pH is best done before planting. Once the plant is in the ground, it takes great effort to improve the soil.

The Soilless Potting Mix

If you are a container gardener, your growing medium is likely a "soilless mix." By soilless mix I mean the potting mixes made of milled sphagnum peat moss, perlite, and vermiculite. There may be other ingredients as well, depending on the proposed use. From experience I have learned it is better to purchase a prepared soilless planter mix instead of trying to concoct your own with garden soil, potting soil, topsoil, milled sphagnum peat moss, sand, perlite, vermiculite, and a multitude of other ingredients. Many commercial growers have tried making their own, some with success, but I wonder how many plants they killed while trying to figure out how best to water and feed a particular plant growing in their homemade mix.

One of the first commercially prepared mixes used in starting seedlings and growing transplants for the garden was the Cornell mix, developed by Cornell University. What a step forward! Today there are many soilless brands and blends available. Some people unwisely purchase the cheapest mix without looking at its ingredients. I think the key to success in container growing is using the right mix consistently with the same plants. Remember that some plants must have a well-drained soil and some require a soil with more moisture-holding capacity.

There are so many types of soilless mixes, including Cactus mix, African Violet mix, Orchid mix, tropical plant mix, and on and on. In a Cactus mix you'll find a gritty, sharp sand along with a small amount of organic matter. In an African Violet mix you may find well-rotted organic matter or milled sphagnum peat moss for holding moisture, and sand and/or perlite for aeration and drainage.

To identify the ingredients of a mix, take a close look. Probe through the particles. You'll likely find fibers that are bits of peat moss or milled sphagnum peat moss and, in some cases, well-rotted compost. The organic matter provides the body for the mix. You may even find finely shredded hardwood bark or coconut fibers. In some of the least expensive mixes you might find small, pea-sized, pure white, soft, spongy balls, which are used as filler and to add bulk. They are made of styrofoam, which never breaks down. I don't like to use this type of mix, as the styrofoam balls work to the surface every time you water. Grainy or gritty white particles of various sizes are particles of perlite, a bleached volcanic ash used to provide and improve aeration and drainage. The "gold"-looking flecks are not gold but vermiculite, heat-treated mica used to improve the moisture-holding capacity of a soilless mix. (In 1962, when gold was removed as the standard for the United States dollar, I received hundreds of samples from gardeners wanting to know what the "gold" flecks were in their potting mixes! Without exception, all samples were accompanied by letters requesting that, if it is gold, please return the sample.)

Formulators have added crystals of moisture-holding polymers to a few of the newest blends of soilless mixes. These polymers absorb water, creating little reservoirs, holding hundreds of times their weight in water. After planting and watering, the water held by the crystals is released back into the soil to be absorbed by the plant's roots as the soil dries.

A commercially prepared soilless mix contains nutrients and is probably pH balanced, and this is what you should look for. If an organic mix is not pH balanced, the pH may be as acidic as 3.5 or lower. (Now that's acid!) In such a case, any nutrients you might apply would be locked up by the organic matter and probably never become available to the plant.

If you find a mix that is right for a particular plant, try to use the same brand and blend each time you pot up or transplant the plant.

Propagation

Starting seed indoors or outside is lots of fun and psychologically rewarding as well. To plant a seed, to moisten the soil, and to observe the first leaves that emerge spells success in anyone's book. When growing annuals and perennials from seed, there are tips in this guide for starting them indoors, or outside in the garden, but always remember to read the back of the seed packet before starting. The last frost date in your area is the key for starting many seeds indoors. Check with your local weather station for the last frost date in your specific area and, while you are at it, find out the first frost date of fall.

Many plants can be divided to increase their population and to have plants to share with a friend. Hosta and Daylilies are perfect models for division. Just dig up a clump, cut it into segments, replant, and water. Hardy Mums, Astilbe, and perennial Candytuft can also be divided.

Planting

Planting the right plant in the right environment means more than just knowing the amount of sun or shade it will receive; consider exposure to cold and wind. Find out the hardiness of a plant before purchasing it for your garden. Just because a friend in Trenton, New Jersey, grows beautiful red-flowering Hino Crimson Azaleas in his garden does not mean they will grow in your garden in Albany, New York. You must know the USDA Hardiness Zone for each species of plant. And the soil is part of the right environment, too. Check the drainage capability, its moisture-holding capacity, and, of course, its acidity or alkalinity.

Back in the late '60s, a new planting concept emerged, thanks to the late Jim Cross of Environmentals Nursery on Long Island. Jim coined the phrase, "Fall is for planting," and, sure enough, he proved that it was. The theory behind fall planting is rather simple. The air temperature is cooling while the soil remains warm. Roots continue to develop on most evergreens and deciduous plants until the soil temperature lowers to 40 degrees Fahrenheit, or below. The Ornamental Horticulture Department of Cornell University followed up with a study that proved Jim's theory to be correct. In the Tri-State area, "Fall is for planting" is now a recognized planting practice. Because there are always a few exceptions to every rule, check with your county cooperative extension educator for the list of trees and shrubs that are not recommended for planting in fall.

The latest recommendation for planting depth comes from urban and suburban horticulturists and foresters. They have learned that the planting hole should be no deeper than the depth of the rootball (or container root mass) but should be two to three times as wide to allow roots to spread. Do not add organic matter to the backfill. Backfill is the soil first removed and then used to fill the planting hole around the plant. If organic matter is needed for improving the soil in general, incorporate a well-rotted compost or milled sphagnum peat moss into the entire planting bed. This will create an improved area for root penetration.

Watering

In my opinion, water is the key to success or failure. No matter what plant you put in the ground—whether it's a colorful bed of Coleus, Climbing Roses with clusters of blossoms arching over a trellis, a ground cover of spreading Junipers to stop erosion on a sunny hillside, Flowering Dogwoods to line a driveway, or a Thornless Honeylocust to shade a patio—water the new plants immediately! And I mean immediately, not at the end of the day and not tomorrow. In fact, you'll find we often recommend not only watering immediately after planting, but coming back the following day with another big drink. In my opinion, it's the second drink that thoroughly soaks the rootball as well as the loosened backfill. After the two thorough drinks, adjust your watering practices to coincide with the weather conditions, type of plant, and soil type. Remember, for seeded and sodded lawns, the soil must be kept evenly moist, not wet, until the seeds germinate and grow and the sod knits into the parent soil. Never let seeds dry out after the original watering, or they will die.

For landscape plants, perennial beds, and patio container gardens, install drip irrigation. Drip irrigation saves as much as seventy percent of the amount of water you might use with sprinklers. You'll not only become a water-wise gardener, you'll save money too.

Fertilizing

We eat daily and so do our plants. I don't know how many friends I've given containers of plant food to, only to find out a few months later that the container is still full. Whether it be one for flowering plants like a 15-30-15 or 5-10-5, or a 10-6-4 or 5-1-1 for foliage plants, the only way a plant food is going to do any good is to take it out of the container and give it to the plant. Always read the label, of course, and follow the manufacturer's recommended rates and directions. There are only a few plants that do not appreciate extra nutrition, and this is mentioned in the description of how to grow the plant. Otherwise, feed your plants a balanced plant food.

Pruning

Pruning is the hardest gardening subject to address. My best advice is that if you don't know the name of the plant you are growing, leave your pruning shears in the toolshed until you see it bloom, or in the case of evergreens, observe one complete growing cycle. In general, for flowering trees and shrubs, plants that bloom in June or before (like Forsythia, Lilac, and Pussy Willow) are plants that bloom on last year's growth, so prune them right after bloom. And, in general, plants that bloom after June (like Rose of Sharon, Abelia, and Butterfly Bush) are plants that bloom on new growth, so they should be pruned in spring to push new flowering wood for summer. No matter what the season or time of year, however, if there is a dead or dying branch in a plant, prune it out immediately.

Deadheading is a form of pruning. It's the removal of spent flowers before seeds form. This practice is essential for keeping annuals in bloom from summer to the first killing frost of fall. Deadheading prolongs blooming of Lupines too. Be sure to deadhead Rhododendrons immediately after bloom. This reduces leggy growth and sets bigger and better flowerbuds for the following spring.

Mulching

Keeping down weeds and conserving moisture are reasons enough for using mulch. (Mulch is nothing more than a covering over the soil surface.) A decorative mulch, like pine bark mini-nuggets, bark chips, cocoa hulls, Jersey Shore washed beige gravel, or white marble, not only performs the above functions but also dresses up the environment. When selecting a mulch, keep in mind that a light-colored mulch used around a green plant encourages the plant to stand out as an individual. Dark-colored mulch spread around a green plant allows the plant to more easily blend into the environment.

Pest Control

The use of pest controls is the choice of the individual gardener. In fact, it may not always be necessary to use pesticides to control insects and other pests since they may not cause significant damage to individual plants. In certain cases, you should consider the use of organic pest controls. If you choose to use non-organic pest controls, it is recommended you consult your local cooperative extension educator, garden center or nursery professional for correct pest identification and control recommendations. Once you have decided to use a specific pest control product, you must read and follow label directions carefully.

Integrated Pest Management (IPM)

If you select the right plant and site it in the right place, you may need little or no pest control. From the outset, make an effort to select plants with resistance to diseases and insects, but remember: resistance means "resistance." It does not mean a pest *cannot* attack the plant. Integrated pest management is the sensible approach to pest suppression that is friendly to our environment. By knowing the plant you wish to grow and what its potential adversaries are, you will have already started to practice IPM.

How to Use This Book

Each entry in this guide provides you with information about a plant's particular characteristics, habits and its basic requirements for active growth as well as my personal experience and knowledge of the plant. I have tried to include the information you need to know about each plant to help you become a successful gardener. You will find such pertinent information as the plant's mature height and spread, bloom period and colors (if any), sun and soil preferences, water requirements, fertilizing needs, pruning and care, and pest information.

Preferred Zones

Cold-hardiness zone designations were developed by the United States Department of Agriculture (USDA) to indicate the minimum average temperature for an area. A zone assigned to an individual plant indicates the lowest temperature at which the plant can be expected to survive over the winter. The Tri-State area has a very wide range, from zone 3a to 7b. Though a plant may grow (and well) in zones other than its recommended cold-hardiness zone, it is a good indication of which plants to consider for your landscape. If you don't know the zone in which you live, take a look at the map on the facing page.

Sun Preferences

Icons represent the range of sunlight suitable for each plant:

Full Sun

Partial Sun/Shade

Full Shade

Additional Benefits

Many plants offer benefits that further enhance their appeal. The following icons indicate some of the more important additional benefits:

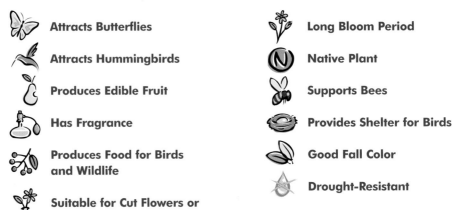

Attracts Butterflies

Attracts Hummingbirds

Produces Edible Fruit

Has Fragrance

Produces Food for Birds and Wildlife

Suitable for Cut Flowers or Arrangements

Long Bloom Period

Native Plant

Supports Bees

Provides Shelter for Birds

Good Fall Color

Drought-Resistant

My Personal Favorite

A "My Personal Favorite" box describes a specific cultivar or variety of the plant entry that I have found particularly noteworthy. In some cases, it is the species itself that I most highly recommend. In other cases, I do not have a specific Personal Favorite—perhaps you'll find your own.

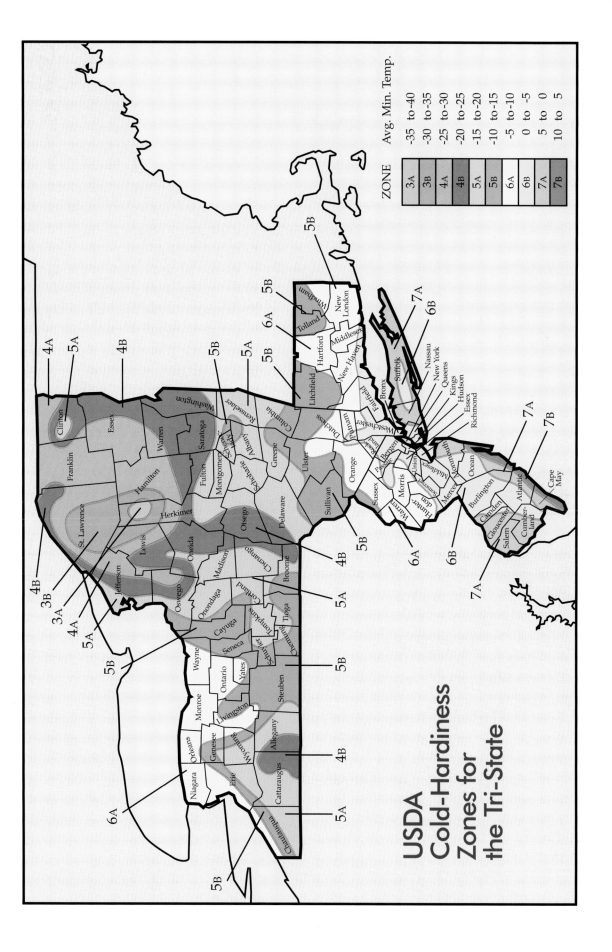

USDA
Cold-Hardiness
Zones for
the Tri-State

ZONE	Avg. Min. Temp.
3A	-35 to -40
3B	-30 to -35
4A	-25 to -30
4B	-20 to -25
5A	-15 to -20
5B	-10 to -15
6A	-5 to -10
6B	0 to -5
7A	5 to 0
7B	10 to 5

Annuals *for the Tri-State*

Color is your welcome mat for friends and neighbors. Have you ever thought of using color in the landscape as your calling card? This year you might put your best foot forward with different shades of red: splashes of bright-red blossoms peering out between evergreen shrubs, masses of cherry-red blossoms standing tall in containers on the deck or patio, and fiery red flowers cascading from windowboxes. Next year you might change the color theme to a palette of yellow. The following year you might choose a real smorgasbord of colors like red, white, blue, pink, yellow, orange, and bicolor. The way to change color in the landscape without digging up the perennial garden and flowering landscape plants, is simple: Plant annuals.

Provide Instant Color

An annual is a plant that completes its growing life in one year. You plant the seed and water it. The seed germinates, then sprouts into a seedling that produces leaves

and stems, and brings forth flowers. Many continue to flower from spring right up to the first killing frost of fall.

During spring in the Tri-State area, all of the garden centers, nurseries, mass-merchandisers, and even garden clubs have tons of colorful annuals for sale. They're available in cell-packs (four to six plants per pack), market-packs with multiple seedlings per unit, and as individual plants, often grown in peat pots.

How to Select Your Annuals

When you choose to grow annuals, it's recommended that you start with fresh, named varieties every spring. Select annuals by their growing requirements and habits—some annuals like sun and some like shade; some grow upright and some cascade.

It's human nature to gravitate to the budding transplants or the ones with flowers, but you're better off picking plants that have not started to bloom. This means you should select from plants that are properly labeled. There is nothing more frustrating than planting what you think are pink Snapdragons and finding out a few weeks later that they are really white Snapdragons. Experience has shown that only one pack in a flat of cell-packs may be labeled, and which one sells first? Of course it's the one with the label, and you may be left to guess the color of the remaining plants in the flat. Try to shop at outlets where you can select from properly labeled plants.

General Care for Annuals

Once an annual starts producing flowers, root development is greatly diminished. If you have purchased a Petunia with blossoms, pinch out the flowers when you plant it. Removing the flower encourages the plant to go vegetative for a short period (just a few days), and this allows the plant to develop a better root system. A well-developed root system serves to help a plant get through the hot days of summer.

Pot or plant annuals in soil that drains well but can remain damp, not wet. To reduce watering frequency for containers, blend a moisture-holding polymer such as Soil Moist® or Terra-Sorb® into a soilless mix. When using a moisture-holding polymer as an addition to a soilless mix, you *must* follow the label directions.

Provide water throughout the growing season, and supply nutrients. Whether chemical or organic, a water-soluble or liquid plant food formulated for flowering plants will keep Petunias, Marigolds, and Zinnias perking all season long.

Controlling Pests

Pests of annuals include those little green caterpillars that eat holes in Geranium buds and flowers; whiteflies, which develop like snow on Fuchsia and Lantana; spider mites, which spin their webbing on Marigolds and Verbena; and little green aphids that cause wilting of Petunias. Almost all of the critters on annuals can be suppressed with sanitation and organic pesticides. Rinse the plants with a gentle shower from a garden hose. Apply insecticidal soap or Hot Pepper Wax Spray® to suppress spider mites, whiteflies, and aphids, and use *B.t.*, *Bacillus thuringiensis*, the biological control for caterpillars. Read the label and follow the manufacturer's recommended rates and directions.

Ageratum

Ageratum houstonianum

Preferred Zones	Sun Preferences		Additional Benefits
NA	☀	◐	

If you are looking for clusters of small, powder-puff, buttonlike flowers in blue, pink, violet, or white to use as a ground cover among sun-loving Petunias or tall Snapdragons, I've got a plant for you: Dwarf Ageratum. These plants are only six to eight inches tall, and they thrive in our hot, dry summers. Bushy, compact, and uniform, they are easy to grow, and they bloom prolifically from early summer right up to first frost in the fall. They naturally grow in almost-perfect mounds. In addition to their excellence as large or small drifts of color in flower beds, and as edging along a landscape planting, they provide an excellent compact splash of color in a container garden. There will be butterflies aplenty if you plant Ageratum—and the taller varieties, including 'Blue Horizon' (to thirty inches tall) and 'Blue Mink' (to twelve inches tall), make excellent cut flowers.

Bloom Period and Color Blue, pink, violet, or white flowers bloom June to frost.

Mature Height × Spread 6 to 15 inches × 6 to 15 inches

When and How to Plant Start Ageratum seed indoors six to eight weeks before last frost date by sowing on the surface of a sterile seed-starting mix. Do not cover the seed with soil mix, as Ageratum seeds need direct light for the germination that takes five to ten days at 70 to 75 degrees Fahrenheit. Transplants, available as nursery-grown market- or cell-packs, should be set out after all danger of frost. Set 9 to 12 inches apart in a rich, well-drained garden soil or in a potting mix in containers, and keep well watered to prevent wilting. If in flower at planting time, pinch the growing tip of each stem to remove the first set of blooms. To enjoy Ageratum indoors in winter, take cuttings in September, root in slightly moist sand, and pot in 4- to 5-inch pots in a porous potting mix. Set on a sunny windowsill, keep soil evenly moist, and lengthen the day in winter with artificial light. The plants will bloom all winter.

Sun and Soil Preferences Locate in full sun to partial shade in a rich, well-drained garden soil.

Moisture Requirements Water thoroughly immediately after planting. After that, keep evenly moist.

Fertilizing Fertilize with a water-soluble 15-30-15 or equivalent according to label directions.

Pruning and Care Deadhead spent blossoms regularly to provide continuous bloom up to the first frost.

Pests and Diseases During excessive heat periods, watch for the webbing of spider mites. Apply insecticidal soap or another specific miticide.

Additional Species, Cultivars, or Varieties 'Blue Mink', 9 to 12 inches tall, has powder-blue flowers. 'Blue Lagoon', 8 inches tall × 10 inches wide, has nautical blue flowers. 'Hawaii' Hybrids are 8 inches tall; there is an improved blue, white improved, and royal deep lavender, each covered with magnificent blooms all summer long on compact plants. 'Pinkie' improved selection, 6 to 8 inches tall, is a dusty pink. 'Blue Horizon' Hybrid is a superb cut flower—it produces 3¼-inch clusters of mid-blue flowers on stems as tall as 2½ feet.

My Personal Favorite

NAME	SPECIAL CHARACTERISTICS
'Blue Danube' Hybrid	Spreading, 6-in.-tall plants / lavender-blue flowers

Celosia

Celosia argentea cristata

Preferred Zones	Sun Preferences		Additional Benefits
NA	☼	☽	🌷 🌼

When I was growing up in Mt. Vernon, Illinois, Mrs. Smith, our next-door neighbor, grew some of the most interesting bright-red "rooster tops" (as we called them) as a border around her sunny vegetable garden. I didn't know the name of the plants at the time but have since learned the name we gave them is not too far off. I've learned to grow crested Cockscomb (Cristata group) as well as plumed varieties (Plumosa group) for use as dried flowers in old-fashioned glass apothecary jars. Celosia retains much of its brilliant red color when preserved as a dried flower. I dry the Celosia by burying the flower head in silica gel, a commercially available flower-drying compound. It takes six weeks or more to preserve the "rooster's comb" and four to five weeks for the plumed varieties. Either kind of Celosia becomes a conversation piece when grown in containers and flower beds, and the distinctive characteristic of this plant is well loved by children of all ages, from 2 to 102. As a native of the tropics, Celosia is perfect for hot, sunny locations, including rooftop container gardens and city terraces.

Other Names Cockscomb / Woolflower

Bloom Period and Color Red, scarlet, rose, pink, orange, gold, yellow, cream, and even bicolor flowers bloom July to frost.

Mature Height × Spread 1 to 4 feet × 1 to 2 feet

When and How to Plant Since Celosia takes as long as 90 to 120 days to flower from planting, start seeds indoors five to six weeks before outdoor planting date (after frost) in order to have plants in bloom by midsummer right up to frost. Celosia takes up to two weeks for germination at 70 to 75 degrees Fahrenheit. Celosia transplants are available at garden centers and other plant shops during the spring planting season. Set transplants 6 to 18 inches apart, depending on the variety.

Sun and Soil Preferences To hold foliage and promote brilliant color in flower heads, plant in maximum sun, in well-drained average garden soil or well-drained artificial mix. Half-day sun or partial sun will produce beautiful flowers, but the color will not be as vivid.

Moisture Requirements Keep soil moist. A 1-inch layer of pine bark mini-nuggets, spread over the soil surface after planting, helps retain even moisture and reduces drying from the heat of summer.

Fertilizing Feed according to label directions with a water-soluble plant food for flowering plants.

Pruning and Care No pruning is required, but taller varieties may need staking to avoid stem breakage.

Pests and Diseases There are no particular pest or disease problems.

Additional Species, Cultivars, or Varieties 'Prestige Scarlet' (Cristata group), a 1997 AAS Winner, has a unique multibranched habit and resembles a Christmas tree loaded with scarlet ornaments. 'Gloria Mix' (Plumosa group) produces 2- to 4-inch plumes on dwarf 8- to 12-inch-tall plants; its colors are a brilliant rosy pink, warm yellow, and scarlet red, and it blooms 55 to 65 days after planting. 'Sparkle Mix' produces 7- to 8-inch, lush, feathered plumes on 18-inch-tall plants. 'Wine Sparkler', 30 inches tall, has brilliant wine-red plumes; it makes excellent cut flowers.

My Personal Favorite

NAME	SPECIAL CHARACTERISTICS
'Fireglow' (Cristata group)	6½-inch balls of blossoms to 20 inches tall / deep flaming red / makes excellent cut flowers and dried-flower specimens

Coleus

Solenostemon scutellarioides hybrids

Preferred Zones	Sun Preferences	Additional Benefits
NA	☼ ☼	🦋 🐦 🍃 ◈

It's hard to think of Coleus as an annual, but it is. I know of no other flowering annual with more colorful foliage. The closest is Caladium, which sprouts colorful foliage from a tuber, an underground root system. There are multitudes of varieties of Coleus that have some of the most interesting foliage color patterns. A favorite of mine is 'Rainbow Mix'. It has colors of green and white; green, purple, and pink; all pink; white and pink; and solid purple. You can plant single or mixed varieties to brighten a sunny windowsill or a filtered shade patio garden or, as I sometimes do, pot up a specimen Coleus as a single plant to offer as a gift for a shut-in. A couple of secrets of Coleus culture: Keep the soil evenly moist, and never let the plant flower. Pinch out a flower spike immediately as it forms.

Bloom Period and Color Treat Coleus as a foliage plant, not as a flowering plant.

Mature Height × Spread 12 to 24 inches × 12 to 18 inches

When and How to Plant Plant Coleus 10 to 18 inches apart in full sun or partial shade in a well-drained garden soil, or in prepared potting mix when growing in containers. Or start Coleus from seed indoors in a slightly moist, sterile seed-starting mix eight to nine weeks before the last frost date for planting outside. When starting Coleus from seed, read the back of the seed packet. It should tell you not to cover the seed with mix—the seed must have direct light for germination.

Sun and Soil Preferences Plant in full sun or partial shade. The root system of Coleus is very sensitive to cold soil; a soil thermometer should read at least 55 degrees Fahrenheit before planting.

Moisture Requirements Provide even moisture for Coleus, particularly when grown in direct sun. Never allow Coleus to wilt from lack of moisture, as the plant will drop its lower, colorful foliage, and it will produce a bare stem with a few colorful leaves at the top.

Fertilizing To encourage larger, more colorful foliage, apply a water-soluble plant food for foliage plants. The first number on the label of such a plant food is higher than the second—it is higher in nitrogen (N) than in phosphorus (P), as in 5-1-1 or 10-8-7. Be sure to follow label directions.

Pruning and Care Pinch frequently to create a bushy, leafy plant. Never allow a flower spike to develop. If it does, a Coleus plant will drop most of its older, colorful foliage and become a short telephone pole–like stalk with a few colorful leaves at the top. So pinch, pinch, and pinch again to maintain a Coleus with colorful foliage.

Pests and Diseases Aphids and whiteflies seem to come with Coleus. Apply insecticidal soap or hot pepper wax spray. During rainy weather, slugs may consume the colorful foliage. Apply a slug bait. Always follow the label directions.

Additional Species, Cultivars, or Varieties 'Brilliant Mix' shows bright colors in combinations of red, rose, pink, bronze, copper, ivory, and purple.

My Personal Favorite

NAME	SPECIAL CHARACTERISTICS
'Carefree Mix'	A self-branching 12-inch-tall plant / provides foliage hues of jade, gold, red, and pastels

Cosmos
Cosmos bipinnatus

Preferred Zones	Sun Preference		Additional Benefits
NA	☼		🦋 🌷 🌼

The flowers of Cosmos are daisylike and very ornamental. The name comes from the Greek word kosmos, meaning "ornament." A member of the Aster family and a native of Mexico, Cosmos is an attracter of butterflies and unbelievably easy to grow. All you need is sunshine, and soil that drains well. After the soil has warmed to at least 55 degrees Fahrenheit, loosen a section of the garden where no pre-emergent weed controls have been applied, scatter seeds directly, and cover with a thin layer of garden soil. Provide water and then step back and watch the plants grow. As they mature, the tall, slender stems, clothed with very fine threadlike foliage, make fantastic cut flowers; an attractive way to display them is to place them in a clear, cut-glass vase. The water and glass act as a magnifier, accenting the slender stems. Try planting Cosmos with other water-efficient xeriscape plants like Black-eyed Susan and Butterfly Weed. To preserve Cosmos stems and flowers for use in a dried-flower arrangement, harvest stems just as the flowers fully open, strip off the foliage, and hang loosely in small bunches in a warm, dark, dry place.

Other Name Mexican Aster

Bloom Period and Color Yellow, white, pink, and bicolor flowers bloom midsummer to frost.

Mature Height × Spread 3 to 5 feet tall (unlimited spread)

When and How to Plant Start seeds indoors five to seven weeks before planting outside, in a moist, sterile seed-starting mix at temperatures as high as 86 degrees Fahrenheit. After all danger of frost has passed, seeds can be sown directly outdoors. Cover the soil with a thin layer of mulch to retain moisture during the ten to twelve days required for germination. Cosmos transplants are also available at garden centers and plant shops during the spring planting season. Set transplants 9 to 24 inches apart depending on the variety.

Sun and Soil Preferences Plant in full sun. Cosmos loves well-drained, unamended, poor-to-average soil.

Moisture Requirements Do not water until the plant shows signs of wilting.

Fertilizing Feed with a water-soluble plant food for flowering plants according to the label directions.

Pruning and Care Remember that cutting helps production—the more you harvest, the more will grow. Tall varieties of Cosmos need staking, particularly if planted in a windy location. A gentle breeze provides an interesting swaying of the stems and blossoms, but a heavy wind will break them.

Pests and Diseases Cosmos is generally free of pest problems, including insects and diseases. During humid weather, watch for powdery mildew. Pinch out infected stems or apply a fungicide specifically recommended for powdery mildew. Read the label.

Additional Species, Cultivars, or Varieties 'Pied Piper Red' produces tubular petals of vivid crimson with a lighter reverse. *Cosmos atrosanguineus* is a perennial Cosmos. 'Chocolate', an 18- to 24-inch-tall plant, displays long-lasting burgundy blooms with a delicious chocolate fragrance.

My Personal Favorite

NAME	SPECIAL CHARACTERISTICS
'Versailles Mix'	A vigorous Japanese strain / 3- to 3½-foot-tall plants / comes in blush pink, carmine, pink, pink with deep eye, and white / an excellent cut flower

Fibrous-Rooted Begonia

Begonia semperflorens-cultorum hybrids

Preferred Zones	Sun Preferences	Additional Benefits
NA		

"I remember my mother growing slips of Begonias in small jelly jars on the windowsill just above the kitchen sink. When the plants rooted, which took only a week or so, she potted them in clay pots (there were no plastic pots back then). The soil was a homemade concoction, appropriately mixed to allow good drainage. Mother's Fibrous-rooted Begonias, with foliage colors of green, bronze, or mahogany, produced clusters of single or double flowers in shades of pink, red, or white. Since then, I've learned that Fibrous-rooted Begonias are one of the most versatile flowering annuals. At the Queens Botanical Garden, Flushing, New York, we used them to spell out "Q B G" in a flower bed by the front gate. You can plant Fibrous-rooted Begonias in hanging baskets, windowboxes, or deck or patio containers, or you can, as many do, grow them as flowering houseplants. Give them morning or afternoon sun and they'll bloom continuously."

Other Name Wax Begonia

Bloom Period and Color Bright-red, scarlet, pink, and white flowers offer continuous bloom.

Mature Height × Spread 5 to 12 inches × 8 to 12 inches

When and How to Plant For indoor use, start Fibrous-rooted Begonia at any time. For use outdoors, start seeds fourteen to sixteen weeks before the last frost date. Fibrous-rooted Begonia seed, which looks like "dust," should be scattered on the surface of a moist, sterile seed-starting mix. Do not cover the seeds, as they need light for germination. At 70 to 75 degrees Fahrenheit, the seeds germinate in fifteen to twenty days. Nursery-grown Fibrous-rooted Begonias are available at any time in containers and during spring planting season in market- and cell-packs. Set out after the last frost date.

Sun and Soil Preferences Plant Fibrous-rooted Begonias in full sun to partial shade in an organically rich soil that drains well.

Moisture Requirements Allow the soil to dry to the touch before watering. Fibrous-rooted Begonias do not like wet soil conditions.

Fertilizing Feed regularly with water-soluble food for flowering plants.

Pruning and Care Cuttings root easily at any time. Clip 2- to 3-inch-long cuttings from the tip portion of the stems. Pinch out any flowers or flower buds and slip the cuttings into a sterile, moist propagation mix. Fibrous-rooted cuttings root in ten to fifteen days. In late September, bring Fibrous-rooted Begonias indoors, place them in an east-facing window, and watch blooming continue. The almost iridescent, colorful blossoms will brighten any indoor environment during the drab days of winter.

Pests and Diseases Mildew may be suppressed by planting in areas with good air circulation and applying a mildew fungicide. Read the label.

Additional Species, Cultivars, or Varieties 'Brandy' has pink blossoms; 'Whiskey' has white blooms; 'Vodka' is scarlet; and 'Lotto' Hybrids come in red and pink.

My Personal Favorite

NAME	SPECIAL CHARACTERISTICS
'Paint Pink Splash'	The first variegated Fibrous-rooted Begonia to come true from seed / sports foliage of soft green splashed with creamy white / clusters of pale-pink blossoms

Geranium

Pelargonium × hortorum

Preferred Zones	Sun Preference		Additional Benefits
NA	☀		

Ask most gardeners if they know the name Pelargonium, *and chances are they will give you a blank stare. Ask about the Garden Geranium, however, and their eyes will brighten. For years the Garden Geranium has been the backbone of any garden that receives direct sunlight. From Atlantic City to New York City to Hartford and every spot in between, you'll see Geraniums growing in windowboxes, along sidewalk prome-nades, atop decks and patios. You might even spot a single potted plant on a terrace. The Geranium is the number-one flowering pot plant sold on Mother's Day. I like to wander the rural roads and villages where it is not unusual to see Geraniums displayed in discarded farm or seafaring equipment, such as a milk separator, a child's wagon, or in an old dinghy. Whatever will hold soil and plants together seems to make the ideal container. Sometimes it's like a history test as you try to guess what each container once was. Geraniums love sun, so plant with other sun-lovers like Marigolds, Salvia, and Petunias. P. species (Scented Geranium) is prized for its fragrant foliage and comes in a multitude of scents: apple, cinnamon, peach, mint, chocolate, and others.*

Other Names Garden Geranium / House Geranium / Zonal Geranium

Bloom Period and Color Red, pink, salmon, white, and "colors-in-between" flowers offer continuous bloom.

Mature Height × **Spread** 15 to 24 inches × 12 to 18 inches

When and How to Plant Seed-started Geraniums or rooted cutting transplants are available every spring in a profusion of varieties. Select stocky, heavy transplants, not plants that are leggy and thin. To sample fragrances of scented Geraniums, pinch the leaf with the index finger and thumb. Sniff the index finger. To test another variety, pinch with the thumb and middle finger, etc. Never sniff the thumb, as it will be a mixture of all of the scents. When grown from seed, Geranium plants must be started at least sixteen weeks before the last frost date in order to bloom by midsummer. Plant in spring after the last frost.

Sun and Soil Preferences Plant in full sun in well-drained soil.

Moisture Requirements Allow the soil to dry to the touch between waterings. Geraniums do not like wet feet.

Fertilizing Feed regularly according to the label directions with a water-soluble plant food for flowering plants.

Pruning and Care For container culture, allow a potted Geranium to become rootbound. As soon as a flower matures, gently tug on the peduncle (the long stem holding the flower to the main stem) to remove the wilting flower. To reduce leggy growth, clip back or pinch stems as needed. Leggy growth is often a result of insufficient direct sunlight and too much nutrition.

Pests and Diseases The green tobacco worm and canker worm (inchworm) eat holes in foliage and flower buds. Watch for the parent, a fluttering white moth, and apply *B.t. (Bacillus thuringiensis)*, the natural control for caterpillars. Botrytis fungus causes flowers and foliage to yellow and become moldy. Pinch off yellowing foliage and remove spent flowers immediately after petal drop. Apply a fungicide for botrytis if the disease persists.

Additional Species, Cultivars, or Varieties 'Orbit Mix' comes in colors of apple-blossom pink, deep salmon, scarlet, white, rose, and violet, and has the attractive, distinctive zonal foliage.

My Personal Favorite

NAME	SPECIAL CHARACTERISTICS
'Big Red'	Standard for red-flowering Geraniums / produces huge brilliant-red flowers

Impatiens

Impatiens walleriana

Preferred Zones	Sun Preferences		Additional Benefits
NA	☼ ☼ ☼		🐦 🌼

Because of their ability to produce hundreds, if not thousands, of blooms with no direct sunlight and very little effort, Impatiens are the number-one choice in America for flowering plants for shade or semishade. They are perfect for growing on a shady patio and for adding color to windowboxes on the north and east sides of a house. When grown indoors as a houseplant, they should be provided with at least a half-day of sun, preferably morning sun, which is the cooler sun of the day. You'll find that Impatiens grown indoors tend to bloom on the sunny side of the plant, so when friends come to dine, just turn the plant around to show off the blooms. For the shady perennial garden, add splashes of continuous summer color by planting Impatiens in the spaces among the early, midseason, and late-blooming perennials. For best show in deep shade, plant Garden Impatiens with white, light-pink, or light-salmon blossoms. Avoid red, purple, or dark-pink varieties, as dark colors are difficult to see in low light.

Other Names Garden Impatiens / Busy Lizzie / Patience Plant

Bloom Period and Color Flowers in all colors (except true blue) bloom June to frost.

Mature Height × Spread 8 to 30 inches × 8 to 20 inches

When and How to Plant Eight to ten weeks before the last frost date, start indoors in a sterile seed-starting mix. Press the seeds into the surface of the mix, leaving them uncovered, as light aids germination. Germination takes fourteen to twenty-one days at 70 to 75 degrees Fahrenheit. Set transplants 10 to 18 inches apart after the soil reaches at least 55 degrees Fahrenheit.

Sun and Soil Preferences Plant in morning sun to partial shade. Impatiens like a rich, fertile, well-drained soil and cannot stand cool soil.

Moisture Requirements To prevent damping-off (a deadly disease of Impatiens seedlings), supply moisture to the seed flat by watering from below. Set the seed flat, with drainage holes, in a shallow tray. Fill the tray with water often enough to keep the seed-starting mix only slightly moist. Water will be siphoned from the tray below into the seed-starting mix above through the drainage holes by the process of capillary action. For growing in containers, use a well-drained planter mix amended with a moisture-holding polymer.

Fertilizing Feed with a water-soluble plant food at half the recommended rate; too much nutrition produces magnificent foliage but fewer blooms.

Pruning and Care Little pinching or pruning is necessary with the newer varieties of Impatiens. If a plant should become leggy, pinch just above a node (the point where leaves are attached to the stem).

Pests and Diseases During hot, dry weather, watch for a fine webbing dusted with tiny grains of "moving sand" covering new buds, and a stippled, washed-out look of the foliage. These are symptoms of spider mites. Rinse infested plants with water, making sure to rinse undersides as well as new tip growth and apply the appropriate miticide. Read the label.

Additional Species, Cultivars, or Varieties New Guinea Impatiens (*I. hawkeri*) have extra-large blossoms and unusual foliage and are taller than standard Impatiens. They are sun-loving bloomers in almost every color.

My Personal Favorite

NAME	SPECIAL CHARACTERISTICS
'Accent' Hybrids	Lavender Blue, Burgundy, Pink, Salmon, White, Orange, Red, Violet, Rose, Pastel Mix, and Bicolor Mix / 2½-inch flowers

Marigold
Tagetes hybrids

Preferred Zones	Sun Preference		Additional Benefits
NA	☀		🦋 🐦 🧴 💐

The late Everett M. Dirksen, Senator and orator from the great State of Illinois, tried many times to have the Marigold named the official flower of the United States. I was sympathetic to this cause—in my garden, the Marigold is one of the most fantastic flowering annuals. I particularly enjoy the 'Inca' Series, so I always plant a large bed of yellow, orange, and gold Inca Marigolds as a focal point. Along a border of dark-green evergreen shrubs I usually plant the white Marigold, which can be ordered from Burpee Seed Company. In my cut-flower garden I plant blocks of Marigolds in mahogany and red colors. On my deck and patio I plant Marigolds in windowboxes and various wooden containers. The one growing requirement for all is sun, sun, and more sun! Butterflies and hummingbirds are a bonus in the Marigold garden.

Bloom Period and Color Yellow, orange, gold, white, mahogany, and red flowers bloom early summer to frost.

Mature Height × Spread 6 to 36 inches × 6 to 18 inches

When and How to Plant Start Marigold seeds indoors in a moist, sterile seed-starting mix, six to eight weeks prior to the last frost date. They germinate in just seven to ten days at 70 to 75 degrees Fahrenheit. Commercially produced plants are available in market- and cell-packs—select stocky plants with dark-green foliage, preferably without flowers. Plant after the last frost date and after the soil has warmed from winter's cold.

Sun and Soil Preferences Plant in full sun 6 to 18 inches apart, depending on variety, in average, well-drained soil.

Moisture Requirements Allow the soil to dry on the surface before watering, then provide a thorough soaking. Marigolds do not like continuous moisture.

Fertilizing Feed all Marigolds with a water-soluble plant food for flowering plants according to the label directions.

Pruning and Care Deadheading spent blossoms promotes continuous bloom right up to frost and reduces botrytis gray mold on the flowers.

Pests and Diseases During the heat of summer, watch for spider mites, indicated by a stippled, bleached look of the foliage and a fine webbing over the buds and flowers. Apply a miticide such as insecticidal soap according to label directions. Marigolds can actually fight pests that bother other plants. To suppress nematodes in the soil without using chemical pesticides, interplant *T. patula* 'Golden Guardian' with other plants. When densely planted among tomatoes and other vegetables, at the rate of 1/8 ounce of seed per 100 square feet, these Marigolds will kill 99 percent of root-feeding nematodes in just three months.

Additional Species, Cultivars, or Varieties *T. erecta* 'Jubilee' Golden, Orange, and Diamond (primrose yellow) have 4- to 5-inch double, spherical flowers. *T. patula* French Marigolds are single or fully double flowered—attractive in borders, varieties include 'Grand Prix Mix', 'Janie' Series, and 'Bonanza Bolero', a 1999 AAS Winner.

My Personal Favorite

NAME	SPECIAL CHARACTERISTICS
T. erecta American Marigold Hybrids	'Inca' Orange, Yellow, and Gold / blossoms are 4 to 5 inches across / great heat resistance

Pansy
Viola × wittrockiana

Preferred Zones	Sun Preferences		Additional Benefits
NA	☼ ◐		

The smiling faces of Viola × wittrockiana *are a joy to behold in spring and fall. They provide a complement of color to any spring-flowering bulb garden of Tulips, Daffodils, and Hyacinths. During fall and early winter, plant the smiling faces among late-blooming Mums. The "face" (flower) is made up of five petals . . . one that forms a "lower lip," two that point up, and two more that point out, one to the left and one to the right. It is not unusual in the Tri-State area to have Pansies peering up through a late dusting of snow in the spring, or through the first snow of winter. At the New York Botanical Garden in the Bronx, every spring and fall you may see blocks of giant smiling-face Pansies in raised planter beds near the entryway to the Enid Haupt Conservatory.* **Note:** *You can pick wide-open Pansy blossoms early in the morning, clean them by rinsing with cool water, and then freeze them in ice cubes for use in a tall glass of summer iced tea.*

Other Name Viola

Bloom Period and Color This cool-season flower blooms in multiple colors in spring and fall.

Mature Height × Spread 6 to 8 inches × 8 to 18 inches

When and How to Plant Ten to twelve weeks before the last spring frost date or sooner (started plants can tolerate frost), sow seeds of *V. × wittrockiana* indoors in a moist, sterile seed-starting mix. Cover the seeds with the mix, as they require darkness for germination. Expose the pots to refrigeration (the lettuce crisper drawer is ideal) for two weeks before germinating. After the cool treatment, germination takes two to three weeks at a warm 65 to 70 degrees Fahrenheit. Started transplants are available from nurseries and plant shops in market- and cell-packs in early spring for bloom during Daffodil time. They are available again in early fall, often providing color into early winter.

Sun and Soil Preferences Set transplants in moist, rich soil in full sun to partial shade. Pansies planted in containers need protection from the hot afternoon sun.

Moisture Requirements Pansies planted in containers must be kept evenly moist.

Fertilizing Apply a water-soluble plant food for flowering plants at half the recommended rate. Too much nutrition stimulates leaf growth in place of flowers.

Pruning and Care Deadhead spent blossoms to ensure continuous flowering. Mulch with a 1- to 2-inch layer of organic mulch, such as pine bark mini-nuggets, to keep the soil cool and damp.

Pests and Diseases During wet weather, watch for slug damage to the foliage (large missing sections of leaf tissue). Apply a slug bait according to label directions.

Additional Species, Cultivars, or Varieties Large Flowered Separates of *Viola × w.* are varieties that come in colors from blue to purple, yellow to orange, red and pink to white.

My Personal Favorite

NAME	SPECIAL CHARACTERISTICS
Large Flowered Mixtures	Giant Pansies with blooms as large as 3 to 3¾ inches across / blend of all the colors found in the Large Flowered Separates

Petunia

Petunia × hybrida

Preferred Zones	Sun Preference	Additional Benefits
NA	☀	🦋 🐦 🧴 🌼

Whether it be a Grandiflora with flowers to five inches across; a Floribunda with 3½-inch blooms; a Multiflora with 2½-inch-diameter flowers; a Milliflora "thousand-flowers" with one- to 1½-inch-diameter blossoms; or P. × hybrida, the Common Petunia—this flowering plant is the most popular for windowboxes in the city, patio containers in suburbia, hanging baskets in the country, and just about any sunny flower bed throughout the Tri-State area. 'Wave' Petunias in colors of pink, purple, rose, and misty lilac are recommended for hanging baskets and large planters, and as a ground cover in full-sun flower beds. There are many new varieties introduced each year, some winning recognition from the All-America Selections committee. You're bound to find a flower for your garden. Every year I grow white Petunias flanked by blue Ageratum at the perimeter of my water garden, just below the bright-red Crocosmia (better known in my garden as the "hummingbird flower"). The secret to keeping Petunias from becoming leggy is to pinch, pinch, and pinch again! Every time a flower fades, pinch it out.

Other Name Common Garden Petunia

Bloom Period and Color Red, rose, burgundy, plum, pink, coral, salmon, silver-blue, navy blue, blue, orange, white, and bicolor flowers bloom early summer to frost, with single or double blossoms.

Mature Height × **Spread** 6 to 24 inches × 3 to 4 feet (depending on variety)

When and How to Plant Start Petunia seeds indoors two weeks before last frost date, on the surface of a moist, sterile seed-starting mix at 70 to 75 degrees Fahrenheit. Germination will take ten to twelve days. Double and F1 Hybrids may require temperatures to 80 degrees. Do not cover the seeds. Once germinated, provide full sun, keep the soil slightly moist, and feed seedlings with a water-soluble plant food. Be patient. Petunia seedlings are very slow to establish in a growing container. Transplants are available from nursery growers in cell- and market-packs in time for spring planting.

Sun and Soil Preferences Petunias prefer full sun and a well-drained, organically rich soil with a pH range of 6.0 to 7.5.

Moisture Requirements Provide even moisture, particularly during the hot, dry days of summer.

Fertilizing Feed regularly with a water-soluble food for flowering plants.

Pruning and Care To encourage immediate branching from the main stem, pinch the leader (growing tip) of each plant when setting the plants into the ground at a spacing of 12 inches or more, depending on the variety. Continue pinching spent blossoms as they wilt.

Pests and Diseases Watch for pest problems such as aphids, spider mites, and tobacco worm. Each pest can be easily controlled with a nontoxic pesticide. Insecticidal soap controls aphids and spider mites, and *Bacillus thuringiensis (B.t.)* stops caterpillars.

Additional Species, Cultivars, or Varieties 'Purple Wave' spreads 5 feet or more across, growing as much as 2 inches per day; 'Pink Wave' spreads over 3 feet; 'Rose Wave' and 'Misty Lilac Wave' each have a 3- to 4-foot spread. *P. grandiflora* 'Prism Sunshine' Hybrid, a 1998 AAS Winner, is a light-yellow trumpet with a deeper yellow throat.

My Personal Favorite

NAME	SPECIAL CHARACTERISTICS
P. multiflora 'Lavender Angle'	8-inch-tall plants with a 15- to 20-inch spread / lavender blooms / four of five blossoms (80 percent) are doubles

Pinks

Dianthus chinensis

Preferred Zones	Sun Preference		Additional Benefits
NA	☼		🦋 🕊 🧴 🌼 🌿

When visiting a public garden or neighbor's garden, if you pick up the scent of a spicy, clover-like fragrance, you can bet that they are growing the Heddewiggi Group of Chinese Pinks, with their large, double, very fragrant flowers. You can grow them in your garden if you have full sun and gritty soil. If you plant Dianthus caryophyllus, the Wild Carnation with small clusters of fragrant flowers; D. barbatus Sweet William (modern cultivars have lost their fragrance, so pick the older standbys); or D. armeria 'Deptford Pink' (with showy, three- to six-inch-wide clusters of flowers), you can enjoy fragrance in your garden, too. One who plants Pinks in the garden is literally in the pink, so add a splash of Pinks along a pathway, clip stems of Pinks for cut-flower arrangements, and plant Pinks to attract butterflies. Other varieties of Chinese Pinks are scentless. Dianthus species did not get its common name from its color. The name Pinks came from the fringed edge of the flower petals, which look as if they have been clipped with a pair of pinking shears.

Other Names   Garden Pinks / Chinese Pinks

Bloom Period and Color   Flowers in shades of pink, red, maroon, and pure white bloom midsummer to fall. Many Pinks have blossoms in two or more shades.

Mature Height × **Spread**   6 to 12 inches (unlimited spread)

When and How to Plant   Start seed indoors six to eight weeks before the last frost date for planting outside. Germination takes one to three weeks in a moist, sterile seed-starting mix at 60 to 70 degrees Fahrenheit. Plant Pinks 6 to 12 inches apart. Market- and cell-pack transplants are available during the spring planting season at most garden centers and nurseries; plant them after the last frost date in your area.

Sun and Soil Preferences   Before setting transplants into garden soil, test the soil pH. Pinks prefer a slightly alkaline to neutral soil. An annual application of wood ashes stirred into the soil to a depth of 6 or more inches before planting will do the trick.

Moisture Requirements   Water transplants immediately after planting to reduce transplant shock. Do not mulch Pinks with organic mulches such as shredded bark or mini-nuggets, as both keep the soil too moist, which causes damping-off and root and stem rot. Allow the soil surface to dry before each watering.

Fertilizing   Provide nutrition for seedlings with a water-soluble plant food for flowering plants.

Pruning and Care   If the plant is in flower when transplanting into the garden, pinch out the bloom to encourage establishment of the fragile root system.

Pests and Diseases   During wet weather, watch for wilt disease, which means the literal collapse of individual plants. Pull out infected plants and discard immediately. There are few, if any, insect problems with Pinks.

My Personal Favorite

NAME	SPECIAL CHARACTERISTICS
'Melody Pink' Hybrid	2000 AAS Winner / 1-inch blossoms with delicate fringed petals atop the 1- to 2-foot-tall stems / soft-pink blooms / lace-like foliage in just twelve weeks from seed

Portulaca
Portulaca grandiflora

Preferred Zones	Sun Preference		Additional Benefits
NA	☼		🌸 💧

Years ago, when I was Executive Director of the Queens Botanical Garden in Flushing, New York, I fell in love with one of the brightest, almost-electric-in-color, showy, satiny flowers. Our horticulturist had planted a bed of Portulaca or Moss Rose right outside my office window. Much to my surprise, they came back year after year. I learned that Portulaca reseeds itself if left alone. The large bed became a sprawling carpet along the walkway that led into the office, and a smaller bed cascaded over the edge of a large planter next to the rear entrance. We even had Portulaca streaming over the sides of giant hanging baskets, and large planters at the entrance to the grass mall. The compact growth habit makes the P. g. F1 Hybrid 'Margarita Rosita' an ideal plant for rock gardens and container plantings. A reward that comes from growing Portulaca is that you don't have to look up to see if the sun is out—the flowers normally open only in sunny weather. **Note:** Did you know that a common weed found in most gardens, known as Purslane P. oleracea, is related to Portulaca? Purslane's iron-rich leaves are edible and often harvested for use in salads.

Other Names Moss Rose / Sun Plant

Bloom Period and Color Flowers in mixed colors and white, pink, red, lavender, and yellow bloom June to frost.

Mature Height × Spread 4 to 8 inches × 18 to 24 inches or more

When and How to Plant Start Portulaca indoors from seed in a slightly moist, sterile seed-starting mix, seven to eight weeks before the last frost date at 68 to 80 degrees Fahrenheit; germination will occur in ten to fifteen days. Do not cover the seeds, as they require light for germination. After sprouting, transplant seedlings into a sandy, well-drained growing medium, such as a cactus mix, for growing until it's time to plant into the garden. Carefully, to avoid transplant shock, set out nursery-grown transplants or home-grown seedlings after the last frost date and the soil has warmed.

Sun and Soil Preferences Transplant seedlings to a well-drained sandy soil in a full-sun location.

Moisture Requirements Little if any water is required, even during drought.

Fertilizing Portulaca loves poor soil, heat, and neglect, so back off on the plant food.

Pruning and Care No pruning is required; just let them grow.

Pests and Diseases Weeds are the only pest in a Portulaca patch. Avoid using pre-emergent weed controls in the Portulaca bed, as the previous year's plants self-sow for the coming season.

Additional Species, Cultivars, or Varieties F1 Hybrid 'Margarita Rosita', a 2001 AAS award winner, is a heat- and drought-tolerant plant that grows in a mounded habit (unlike others, that spread), and has large 1½-inch semi-double flowers. The 6-inch-tall plants in the Giant Radiance Series have semi-double blossoms that are 3 inches across. 'Swanlake', which grows to 4 to 6 inches tall, has large, white, double blossoms.

My Personal Favorite

NAME	SPECIAL CHARACTERISTICS
'Sundial' Hybrid	Grows to a height of 5 inches / fluffy, with double flowers 2 inches across / peach, fuchsia, peppermint (red and white stripes), white, mango, scarlet, and yellow colors

Salvia

Salvia splendens

Preferred Zones	Sun Preferences		Additional Benefits
NA			

Salvia splendens, *grown as an annual in the Tri-State area, can provide some of the most brilliant red color beginning in mid-June and going right up to the first killing frost of fall. This old-fashioned member of the Mint family, a tall-growing garden flower, was very popular back in the '50s and '60s but was available in only a few varieties, and most were shades of red. Nothing wrong with that, as Salvia was often planted as a backdrop to lower-growing annuals like white Petunias and blue Ageratum. For the patriotic, that's the red, white, and blue which can be in bloom by Flag Day in June. Salvia was also planted in perennial gardens to add color during the out-of-bloom times of other flowers. Today, however, plant breeders have introduced many varieties, tall and short and in different colors including scarlet-red, white, pink, salmon, burgundy, violet, and blue. Plant Salvia as a companion for the pink Butterfly Bush and the red Crocosmia. Hummingbirds and butterflies absolutely love Salvia, particularly the red varieties.*

Other Name Scarlet Sage

Bloom Period and Color Scarlet-red, white, pink, salmon, burgundy, violet, and blue flowers bloom mid-June to frost.

Mature Height × Spread 10 to 18 inches × 12 to 15 inches

When and How to Plant Purchase fresh *Salvia splendens* seeds and start them indoors in a moist, sterile seed-starting mix eight to ten weeks before the last frost date. Don't bother with last year's leftover seeds; *S. s.* seeds are not long-lived and should not be stored. Germination of fresh seeds takes twelve to fifteen days at 70 degrees Fahrenheit. Red-flowering Salvia requires light for germination, so don't cover these seeds. As soon as the seeds germinate and reach the first true two-leaf stage, transplant into individual containers for growing until it's time to plant outside, spacing 10 to 18 inches apart. With adequate sunlight and nutrition for flowering plants, Salvia should be in bloom shortly after planting outside. Set out transplants after all danger of frost has passed.

Sun and Soil Preferences Plant Salvia in full sun to partial shade in a well-drained, organically rich soil.

Moisture Requirements Mulch Salvia beds with a thin layer of pine bark mini-nuggets to conserve moisture and provide even moisture to the root systems. The soil surface can dry between waterings.

Fertilizing Apply a water-soluble plant food for flowering plants according to the label directions.

Pruning and Care To promote continuous bloom of taller varieties, pinch off faded flower spikes as soon as they mature to avoid seed formation. Dwarf Salvia requires no pinching or pruning.

Pests and Diseases There are no insect or disease problems.

Additional Species, Cultivars, or Varieties 'Flare', a remarkably heat-tolerant plant, grows 18 inches tall, with vivid scarlet spikes. *Salvia coccinea* 'Coral Nymph' grows to 24 inches and has bicolored blossoms in salmon-coral and white.

My Personal Favorite

NAME	SPECIAL CHARACTERISTICS
'Hotline'	Up to 12 inches tall and wide / blue streak, burgundy, salmon, white, red, or violet / starts flowering six to eight weeks after sowing

Snapdragon
Antirrhinum majus

Preferred Zones	Sun Preferences		Additional Benefits
NA	☀ ☀		

Snapdragons are another of the old-fashioned plants often found in cut-flower gardens. The Tri-State gardener often plants Gladiolus, Iris, Delphinium, Foxglove, and Cosmos, never leaving out Snapdragon, particularly the taller varieties. Some gardeners even go to the trouble of staking the individual Snapdragon stems with bamboo canes just so they will have erect, unbroken stems for flower arrangements. Snaps are quite cold hardy and will put up with the first and second light frosts leading into Indian Summer. They display some of the crispest colors along with their spicy scent, and they have a long bloom time, which is what makes them one of the finest cut flowers. They do perform best in spring and fall when the air temperatures are cool. Annuals recommended for planting with Snapdragons in the cut-flower garden include Marigolds, Coreopsis, Cosmos, Salvia, and Zinnia. A. pendula multiflora 'Chinese Lanterns', a trailing hybrid, comes true from seed as a cascading Snapdragon and blooms prolifically in hanging baskets, patio containers, and windowboxes.

Bloom Period and Color Pink, purple, purple-white bicolor, red, crimson, rose, white, yellow, lemon, golden, and bronze flowers bloom mid-June to frost.

Mature Height × Spread 8 to 36 inches × 10 to 12 inches

When and How to Plant Snapdragon transplants are available in market- and cell-packs at nurseries and garden centers for spring planting. Sow Snapdragon seed on the surface of a sterile seed-starting mix, eight to ten weeks before the last frost date, in cool temperatures of 55 to 60 degrees Fahrenheit. Germination takes two to three weeks. Do not cover the seeds, as they require light for germination. Once germinated, maintain seedlings in a cool 45 to 50 degrees at night to develop strong, sturdy stems.

Sun and Soil Preferences For best root development and production during the hot days of summer, plant Snapdragons in full sun to part shade in a well-drained sandy loam.

Moisture Requirements Provide moisture to the seed flat with bottom watering only, as newly germinated Snapdragon seeds are highly susceptible to damping-off. Place the seed flat with drainage holes in a shallow tray and fill the tray with water, allowing the moisture to be siphoned up into the starting mix by capillary action. After planting, water as needed.

Fertilizing Feed with a water-soluble plant food for flowering plants.

Pruning and Care Regardless of whether the plants are started indoors or are nursery-grown, pinch back the central leader (growing tip) to promote branching and development of multiple stems. Cut faded spikes after mid-summer to rejuvenate plants for repeated bloom well into fall.

Pests and Diseases To avoid rust disease (brown spots on the foliage), rotate the planting area and plant rust-resistant varieties.

Additional Species, Cultivars, or Varieties 'Bells Mix' Hybrids are Dwarf Snaps, 8 to 10 inches tall, in multiple colors. Intermediate Snaps include 'Black Prince', 16 to 20 inches tall, with elegant maroon foliage and deep-crimson flower spikes; and 'Lipstick Silver', 18 inches tall, with striking white flowers with bright red "lips." All make excellent cut flowers.

My Personal Favorite

NAME	SPECIAL CHARACTERISTICS
'Rocket' Hybrids	Tall Snaps / finest tall (30- to 36-inch) plants / long, fully packed spikes of bronze, pink, white, cherry, lemon, golden, or red flowers

Spider Flower

Cleome hassleriana

Preferred Zones	Sun Preference		Additional Benefits
NA	☀		🦋 🐦 💐 🔺

Cleome, better known in the Tri-State area as the "Spider Flower," is appropriately named. The individual flower, in clusters often six inches wide, looks like the friendly daddy-long-legs spider I remember as a child. It's the flower for the cut-flower connoisseur because it starts producing blooms on the top twenty-five percent of the stem when the stem is only twelve inches tall, and it continues bloom with its delicate spiderlike blossoms as the stately stem reaches three to four feet tall. The flower heads extend upward in a spiral growth pattern and are composed of continuously opening (every afternoon, every day) new Spider Flowers. They bloom from the bottom up and just keep growing. When planted in a sunny garden, Cleome Spider Flowers will become a Mecca for butterflies and hummingbirds. The plants are as prolific as their namesake. When they go to seed, expect lots of baby Spider Flowers the following spring. Plant the outstanding Queen Series—'Rose Queen' (cherry-rose), 'Pink Queen', 'Helen Campbell White', and 'Violet Queen'—and let the plants naturalize in the sunny garden.

Other Name Old-fashioned Spider Flower

Bloom Period and Color Cherry-rose, pinkish-purple, pink, lilac, violet, yellowish to greenish, and white flowers bloom early summer to frost.

Mature Height × Spread 3 to 4 feet × 12 inches

When and How to Plant Direct-sow seed into the garden soil or set out transplants after the last frost date of spring. To bring plants into bloom a few weeks earlier, start seeds indoors in a moist, sterile, seed-starting mix four to six weeks before the last frost date. Germination takes up to two weeks in a 70-degree-Fahrenheit medium. To reduce transplant shock, avoid setting out seedling transplants during the sunniest part of the day.

Sun and Soil Preferences Cleome like a sunny location with rich, well-drained soil.

Moisture Requirements Another addition to the xeriscape garden, drought-tolerant Cleome requires very little additional water once established.

Fertilizing To reduce transplant shock to the delicate seedlings or transplants when moving them to the sunny garden location or after trans-planting during drought periods, water them immediately with a dilute solution of a water-soluble plant food formulated for flowering plants.

Pruning and Care To ensure repeat generations year after year, avoid using a pre-emergent weed control in the area where Cleome is growing. Mature seedpods shatter, distributing seed for the following spring. Little care is necessary for Cleome if planted in full sun, in a warm, dry location. As it is native to the Caribbean, it withstands heat and drought.

Pests and Diseases Insects or diseases are seldom a problem with this beautiful flower.

My Personal Favorite

NAME	SPECIAL CHARACTERISTICS
Queen Series, 'Rose Queen'	Cherry-rose / hummingbirds love this variety

Sunflower
Helianthus annuus

Preferred Zones	Sun Preference	Additional Benefits
NA	☼	

Sunflowers, dwarf or giant, provide real growing fun for children (and adults). If you would like to grow the giant-blossomed Sunflowers (flowers up to twelve inches across on stems up to ten feet tall), be prepared to stake each plant by driving the stake into the ground before planting the seed. Plant tall varieties as a backdrop in any sunny garden or use them as a screen, hedge, or focal point. If you have a sunny patio or rooftop garden, plant 'Sunspot'. This is a unique ten-inch-diameter flower on a plant only two to 2½ feet tall. What a conversation piece! Sunflowers are valuable as seed for bird-feeding mixes, and hulled sunflower hearts and sunflower oils are used for cooking (I prefer sunflower oil for French-frying onion rings.) If driving through Nebraska in or around August, one might sight hundreds of acres of commercially grown Sunflowers. **Note:** Harvest Sunflower blossoms for seed just as they begin to mature. To determine the date, watch the birds. The day you see the birds circling the plant, pick immediately, or the birds will clean the flower of the mature seeds. You might say, "The early bird gets the seed."

Other Name Common Sunflower

Bloom Period and Color Yellow, lemon-yellow, gold, orange, crimson, white, and mahogany-red flowers, all with chocolate-brown centers (with the exception of the 'Teddy Bear' Series), bloom midsummer to frost, depending on the variety.

Mature Height × **Spread** 2 to 10 feet × 18 inches to 3 feet

When and How to Plant As Sunflowers must have warm soil for root development, direct-sow seeds after the last frost date and after the soil has reached at least 55 degrees Fahrenheit. Thin to 2 to 4 feet apart, depending on the variety and ultimate size of plant. Do not start Sunflower seeds in containers, as the roots of seedlings are extremely sensitive to transplant shock.

Sun and Soil Preferences Plant seeds directly in a sunny location in a well-drained, organically rich soil with a slightly acid to neutral pH.

Moisture Requirements Sunflowers are both heat- and drought-tolerant and require little maintenance. With the exception of providing moisture for germination in the first few weeks of growth, no extra watering is needed.

Fertilizing Incorporate a granular plant food such as 5-10-5 at planting time, at the rate of 3 to 5 pounds per 100 square feet; provide a water-soluble plant food at midseason for a nutritional boost.

Pruning and Care Staking is recommended in windy locations and with tall, large-flowered varieties (6 feet tall or taller).

Pests and Diseases Sunflowers have few if any pest problems except for the birds—they will tell you when the seeds are ripe and ready for picking!

Additional Species, Cultivars, or Varieties 'Dwarf Teddy Bear', a compact, 3-foot-tall plant, has fluffy, fuzzy flowers of brilliant golden yellow with no "centers." 'Giant Sungold', a full-sized version of 'Dwarf Teddy Bear', has 10-inch blossoms. 'Sunspot', which grows to 2 to 2½ feet tall, has 10-inch-diameter flowers with golden-yellow petals. *H. maximilianii* Prairie Sunflower, a 6- to 8-foot-tall perennial, has huge numbers of 3-inch yellow blossoms in late summer.

My Personal Favorite

NAME	SPECIAL CHARACTERISTICS
'Giganteus'	A competition winner / 12-inch blossoms / 10 feet tall (provide support)

Sweet Alyssum

Lobularia maritima

Preferred Zones	Sun Preference	Additional Benefits
NA	☼	🦋 ⚗ 🌼

Although many garden references recommend Sweet Alyssum (Lobularia maritima) for full sun to partial shade, I've taken the partial-shade recommendation out of this book because I have never had success in obtaining more than a few blossoms in partial shade. Growing in full sun is another story. Sweet Alyssum with its low growth and compact habit makes an absolutely ideal, colorful groundcover as fill between other annuals, perennials, and evergreens, or when grown alone in containers. In sunny windowboxes, Sweet Alyssum's trailing stems cascade with abandon, and pinching them back after the first bloom encourages an even bushier plant with more flowers. I've grown white-flowering Sweet Alyssum in shallow pockets of soil in the stone wall of my water garden. Such accenting is prominent during the day, and the whiteness of Sweet Alyssum is almost iridescent under night lighting around the pond. Do you have a cool (50 to 55 degrees Fahrenheit), full-sun windowsill in winter? Pot up a garden-grown Alyssum, keep it evenly moist, and enjoy blooms indoors all winter long.

Other Name Snowdrift

Bloom Period and Color Deep-rose, violet, lavender, and white flowers bloom early summer to frost.

Mature Height × Spread 4 inches × 8 to 10 inches

When and How to Plant Set out transplants, whether purchased or started indoors, only after the last frost date and after the soil has warmed. As Alyssum transplants are very fragile, plant them carefully, 5 to 8 inches apart. Start seeds indoors four to six weeks before the last frost date in a slightly moist, sterile seed-starting mix. Germination takes eight to twelve days at 65 to 70 degrees Fahrenheit. Do not cover the seeds, as light is necessary for germination. A windowsill greenhouse (seed-starting container with clear plastic top) is ideal for keeping the uncovered seeds moist during germination.

Sun and Soil Preferences Plant in full sun in a well-drained garden soil.

Moisture Requirements Although the soil surface may be allowed to dry, water thoroughly during dry weather and periods of excessive heat. Do not let the plants stress from lack of water, which will affect their blooming capabilities.

Fertilizing Alyssum is not a big eater. Apply a water-soluble plant food for flowering plants at half the recommended rate on the label.

Pruning and Care To encourage repeat bloom, give each plant a light clipping after each blooming cycle.

Pests and Diseases There are no particular pest or disease problems with this annual.

Additional Species, Cultivars, or Varieties The single plants of 'Easter Bonnet' have deep-rose, violet, and lavender flowers. 'Snow Crystal', a Fleuroselect Award Winner, has sweet-scented, pure-white blossoms. *Alyssum montanum* has flowers with Candytuft-like, yellow blossoms in late spring. The tiny yellow flowers of 'Basket of Gold' cover a 12-inch-tall plant.

My Personal Favorite

NAME	SPECIAL CHARACTERISTICS
'Carpet of Snow'	Fragrant white blossoms / 3- to 4-inch-tall plants / 15-inch spread

Zinnia

Zinnia elegans

Preferred Zones	Sun Preference	Additional Benefits
NA	☼	🦋 🕊 🌼 🌿

Zinnias, native to Mexico, are just about the easiest flowering plant to grow, if you select the newer varieties. Most are heat-tolerant and disease-resistant, important cultural attributes for the humid summers in our Tri-State area. The older varieties contracted mildew, rust, anthracnose, and botrytis, and I quit growing them for many years, but now they are back in my garden, primarily because of the new disease-resistant varieties. I enjoy them as a source of cut flowers and as attracters of butterflies and hummingbirds (particularly the red varieties). It seems that the more flowers I cut, the more I get. The blossom shapes are varied (resembling exhibition and pompon Mums and cactus Dahlias), and they come in an abundance of colors. They are most colorful in borders, along walkways or paths, and massed in windowboxes and planters. Blossom sizes vary from less than one inch in diameter to giants six inches across. You'll want to grow 'Profusion White' (the 2001 AAS Gold Medal Winner).

Bloom Period and Color Bright multicolored blossoms bloom from spring planting to frost in the fall.

Mature Height × **Spread** 6 to 36 inches × 6 to 24 inches (depending on variety)

When and How to Plant Start Zinnia seed indoors four weeks before the last frost date. In a slightly moist, sterile, seed-starting mix, germination takes five to seven days at a room temperature of 70 to 75 degrees Fahrenheit. Harden-off seedlings for five to seven days before setting them into the garden. Zinnia transplants are available at garden centers and nurseries in cell- and market-packs in the spring. Double-flowered Zinnias often revert to single types when experiencing transplant shock. Plant these types by direct-seeding after the last frost date.

Sun and Soil Preferences Plant in full sun and well-drained soil.

Moisture Requirements Water regularly, particularly during drought periods, to provide even moisture without getting it on the foliage.

Fertilizing For continuous colorful bloom, apply a water-soluble plant food for flowering plants according to the label directions.

Pruning and Care Zinnias grown as bedding plants should be pinched immediately after planting to encourage bushiness. The more you cut, the more they bloom—in fact, there is a variety called 'Cut and Come Again'.

Pests and Diseases Powdery mildew and alternaria blight are the bane of the Zinnia patch. Plant disease-resistant varieties and apply a fungicide for powdery mildew at the first sign of white blotches on the foliage.

Additional Species, Cultivars, or Varieties 'Thumbelina', 6 inches tall, has bright, multicolored, 1-inch-diameter blossoms. The Dwarf Zinnia 'Peter Pan' Hybrid is 12 inches tall and has 3-inch-diameter flowers in cream, plum, gold, pink, scarlet, and white. 'Ruffles' Hybrid offers compact, 2½-foot-tall plants and 3- to 3½-inch ball-shaped flowers with double ruffled blossoms in cherry, pink, yellow, and white. The 2001 AAS Gold Medal winner 'Profusion White', an 8- to 12-inch-tall plant, produces single, 2- to 2½-inch, daisy-like, pure-white flowers; it is disease-resistant. *Z. angustifolia*, 12 inches tall, is spreading, disease-resistant, and tolerant of heat and humidity. 'Starbright Mix' offers Star Gold, Star Orange, and Crystal White.

My Personal Favorite

NAME	SPECIAL CHARACTERISTICS
'Big Red' Hybrid	Blood-red flowers 5 to 6 inches in diameter / 3-foot-tall plants

Bulbs, Corms, Rhizomes

When the phrase "flowering bulb" comes up in a conversation, you probably think of spring-flowering bright red and yellow Tulips; giant trumpeted Daffodils; blue, red, pink, and white Hyacinths; and little yellow and purple Crocus popping up from the ground at the first sign of spring.

Well, there is much more in the bulb menu, including a whole host of summer-flowering bulbs. Technically these are not bulbs: they are tubers, corms, and rhizomes. They have one thing in common with bulbs, however, and that is that they produce a plant and beautiful flowers from something underground. Some are rather strange-looking things, such as the flat, pancake-like Caladium tuber, the Dahlia tuber with fingerlike toes, the knobby-looking Flowering Onion bulb, and the wrinkled root of a Tuberous Begonia.

Spring-Flowering Bulbs

The Netherlands FlowerBulb Information Center in Brooklyn, New York, refers to spring-flowering bulbs as Mother Nature's little miracles. A common question: "Why are spring-flowering bulbs planted in the fall?" The answer is that they need the cool or cold temperatures, generally 40 degrees Fahrenheit, to release the flowering mechanism that grows inside the bulb. The chilling process for a prolonged period converts the bulb into a blooming plant.

In the Tri-State area, as elsewhere, experience has taught us to select bulbs as soon as they arrive at the garden shop, because

& Tubers *for the Tri-State*

the early gardener gets the best bulbs. But experience has also taught that Tulips, Daffodils, Hyacinth, and Crocus planted too early (before the soil begins to cool) end up with unwanted foliage sprouting in the fall. Purchase the bulbs early, and then store them in a cool environment. If they're packaged in plastic bags, transfer them to paper sacks. And, of course, don't forget the label.

The one exception to late planting is Autumn Crocus bulbs. You will want to hurry home and get them in the ground because they may have already sprouted. In fact, it's best to have the bed prepared before you get home with these bulbs.

Summer-Flowering Bulbs

Summer-flowering bulbs are tender bulbs in that most are not winter hardy. They need to be dug in the fall before the first killing frost, cleaned, cured, and stored for winter.

Gladiolus corms, planted as the soil warms in spring, provide a spectacular show with their swordlike leaf blades and colorful blooms, but they must be dug before the frost, clipped back, dried, and stored dry over winter at 40 to 50 degrees Fahrenheit. Canna rhizomes need to be sprouted indoors in advance of planting time so you will be able to enjoy the magnificent bright red, orange, or yellow plumes of flowers by midsummer. Pot each rhizome in a shallow mum pot by mid-March to wake them, and then plant outside after the soil has warmed in late May to early June.

General Care

Before planting bulbs, whether they be spring, summer, or fall bloomers, check the soil's drainage by digging a hole six to eight inches deep and filling it with water. The soil must drain rapidly. These underground flowering miracles can't take wet feet. For nutrition, apply a bulb food as directed on the label.

Autumn Crocus

Colchicum spp. and hybrids

Preferred Zones	Sun Preferences		Additional Benefit
4 to 9	☀	◑	🐝

Colchicum *plants are not true Crocus plants. They look like them and they are called Autumn Crocus, but they are members of the Lily family. If in doubt as to whether a flower is a Crocus or a Colchicum, count the number of stamens: Colchicum has six stamens, while Crocus has only three. (Saffron Crocus, a true Crocus, not a Colchicum, is a fall-blooming bulb not known in the wild. It's believed to be from Asia and has long been used as a coloring for food and medicines.) Colchicum hybrid colors range from white to tones of lavender-pink, lilac-pink, and deeper purple. When planted in beds under Rhododendrons and Azaleas, as is done at the New York Botanical Garden in the Bronx, New York, Autumn Crocus doubles the blooming season. Azaleas and Rhododendrons bloom in spring while Autumn Crocus flowers in the fall. You may be aware of my recommendation to purchase spring-flowering bulbs early and to hold them until the ground cools before planting. Well, there is nearly always an exception to every rule, and Autumn Crocus provides this rule's exception. Prepare the soil in late summer, purchase the Colchicum bulbs, and hurry home to plant them immediately.*

Bloom Period and Color White to pink or purple flowers bloom September to October.

Mature Height Up to 12 inches

When and How to Plant Plant Autumn Crocus plants immediately after their arrival in late summer. No time should be lost getting them in the ground. Have the soil prepared, as the corms may have already extended their flowers and started to grow. Prepare the planting bed by working well-rotted compost, leaf mold, or even peat moss into the bed to a depth of 6 to 8 inches, making a rich, well-drained soil. Use a hand trowel and work in a random pattern to dig each planting hole no deeper than 3 inches, 6 to 9 inches apart. Carefully plant each corm so it is covered with no more than 2 to 3 inches of soil. To extend a garden's blooming season, plant Autumn Crocus under spring-blooming evergreens like Azaleas, Rhododendron, and Laurel.

Sun and Soil Preferences Plant in full sun to filtered shade in well-drained, organically rich soil.

Moisture Requirements Water the bed to settle the soil immediately after planting.

Fertilizing An occasional application of an organic bulb food and the spreading of a fine-textured organic mulch, like pine bark mini-nuggets, are all you'll need to do to enjoy a bed of *Colchicum* for years.

Pruning and Care Do not cut or remove the foliage that sprouts in spring until it matures.

Pests and Diseases Autumn Crocus has no insect or disease problems. Slugs, which may devour flower petals, can be suppressed with a slug bait. Read the label.

Additional Species, Cultivars, or Varieties The best and most reliable fall Autumn Crocus cultivars are *Colchicum hybridum* 'Lilac Wonder', 'Water Lily', and 'Giant'.

My Personal Favorite

NAME	SPECIAL CHARACTERISTICS
C. 'The Giant'	Deep mauve-pink with a pale throat / grows to 12 inches tall / has a fragrance like honey / one of the largest-flowered Autumn Crocus

Bearded Iris

Iris germanica

Preferred Zones	Sun Preference		Additional Benefit
3 to 10	☀		🌼

If you're into growing Iris, if you want to learn about growing Iris, or if you just want to see an absolute rainbow of color, take a trip to the Presby Memorial Iris Garden, Upper Montclair, New Jersey, in mid-May to late June. You can walk among thousands of Bearded Iris hybrids in bloom, as well as other species including Siberian Iris, Japanese Iris, and Yellow Flag Iris. I always feel it's a sight that's good for the soul. In my perennial garden, I've planted several species and varieties of Iris. I not only enjoy them as garden features, I love them as cut flowers too. The tiny I. pumila, in multiple colors and standing less than eight inches tall, looks delightful in a bud vase on the breakfast counter. The secret of success is to plant Bearded Iris in full sun, and to divide the rhizomes every four or five years.

Bloom Period and Color Many varieties in many colors bloom May to late June.

Mature Height Dwarf varieties, 8 to 12 inches; tall varieties, 2 to 3 feet

When and How to Plant Bearded Irises are best planted from freshly dug but cured divisions of rhizomes after flowering up to early fall. Plant three rhizomes 10 to 12 inches apart in each group: create a raised mound, dish out soil in the middle, press each rhizome division into the soil with the leaves pointing out from the center of the hole, and just barely cover them with soil. In the Tri-State urban area, the top side of the rhizome may be left exposed.

Sun and Soil Preferences The secret of bloom for most Irises is to plant them in a well-drained, organically rich, sandy soil with full-sun exposure.

Moisture Requirements Do not mulch, but water to settle the soil after planting.

Fertilizing Apply a slow-release 5-10-5 or equivalent at the rate of 3 to 5 pounds per 100 square feet in early spring when cleaning up the Iris bed.

Pruning and Care Clip out spent flower stems immediately after bloom to stop seed production, but leave the foliage until frost in order to continue growth. Standard Bearded Irises multiply rapidly and reach peak flower production during the third and fourth year after planting. After this time, dig, divide, and replant.

Pests and Diseases If iris borer attacks your plants, dig the infested plants, cut out damaged rhizomes, and destroy the white, fat, grublike borer. Inundate planted beds with beneficial nematodes after the soil warms to 55 degrees Fahrenheit; follow the directions that come with the nematodes. Indications of iris borer are yellow streaking of foliage and tunnelling in the rhizomes.

Additional Species, Cultivars, or Varieties *Iris siberica* 'Fourfold White', called Siberian Iris, is a pure white that may be planted in shade. 'Orville Fay', a bright navy blue, may also be planted in shade. *I. ensata* Japanese Iris 'Nikko', the palest purple-blue with dark centers, looks like an orchid; it is a great choice for a small-space, full-sun garden. *I. pseudacorus* Yellow Flag Iris is an unhybridized ("wild") species. It flowers from early to midsummer, is nearly indestructible, and flourishes with wet feet (plant in the bog garden next to your water garden).

My Personal Favorite

NAME	SPECIAL CHARACTERISTICS
'Hybrid Mix'	Plant this mix, and you will have every color of the rainbow.

Canna

Canna × generalis

Preferred Zones	Sun Preference	Additional Benefit
Tender	☀	🌼

If you live in the Tri-State area but yearn for that tropical look, either visit the Enid Haupt Conservatory Tropical House at the New York Botanical Garden, Bronx, New York, or grow Canna rhizomes in your garden. You can create an almost tropical look in a Northern garden by planting dwarf and standard Canna in borders, in mass plantings, or as features in foundation plantings, along walls, and in containers. The giant one- to two-foot-long green or variegated leaves on five- to six-foot-tall plants may remind you of the tropical Banana plant. In fact, during the summer months you can grow both Canna and Banana in your "tropical" garden, then take the Banana plant indoors for the winter. I get an early start by planting dwarf and standard Canna in shallow containers indoors so the rhizomes will sprout for earlier show. If you must plant a rhizome directly into garden soil without waking it first, take the temperature of the soil before planting: it must be 55 degrees Fahrenheit or warmer. Dwarf Canna are ideal flowering plants for containers on a sunny patio or a city rooftop. Canna should be chosen for their magnificent flower spikes as well as for their colorful foliage.

Bloom Period and Color Red, orange, yellow, pink, or bicolor flowers bloom midsummer to frost.

Mature Height Up to 6 feet (depending on variety); dwarf, to 3 feet

When and How to Plant Plant Canna rhizomes 18 to 36 inches apart, depending on variety, after the last frost date. To get a head start on the gardening season, start rhizomes indoors at least ten weeks before the last frost date and you will have flowers from early summer to frost. Canna may be started from seeds or by division of rhizomes, no later than mid-December. Start seeds indoors in a warm (75 degrees Fahrenheit), moist environment. In early March, divide the rhizomes into a minimum of two growing points each, pot in shallow mum pots in well-drained soil, keep slightly moist, feed with a 15-30-15 or equivalent, and grow indoors in direct sunlight until time to plant in the garden, after the last frost date. Mum pots are 8 to 12 inches in diameter and 6 inches deep.

Sun and Soil Preferences Plant Canna rhizomes in full sun in a well-drained soil (with neutral to slightly acidic pH) amended with well-rotted compost.

Moisture Requirements Provide even moisture.

Fertilizing Feed monthly with a balanced plant food for flowering plants.

Pruning and Care Since Cannas are not winter-hardy in the Tri-State area, cut back stems and foliage to 6 inches above the ground after a light frost. Dig clumps of rhizomes, leaving the soil attached, and store in a cool (40 to 50 degrees Fahrenheit), dry place.

Pests and Diseases Slugs and snails devour foliage during wet seasons. Set snail and slug traps at the base of a plant to trap these slimy critters.

Additional Species, Cultivars, or Varieties 'Pretoria', also called 'Bengal Tiger', offers 6-foot-tall plants with orange-yellow blossoms and yellow-striped leaves; it is an aggressive grower which multiplies as the season progresses. 'Red King Humbert' has bronze-purple leaves and red flowers.

My Personal Favorite

NAME	SPECIAL CHARACTERISTICS
Dwarf 'Tropical Rose'	AAS Award Winner of 1992 / 2 to 2½ feet tall / showy 3- to 4-inch blossoms in warm rose hues / ideal for container culture on the patio if placed in full sun

Crocosmia
Crocosmia spp. and hybrids

Preferred Zones	Sun Preference	Additional Benefits
To Zone 6	☀	🦋 🕊 🐝

In 1971, John Elsley of Wayside Gardens in Hodges, South Carolina, recommended that I plant what he called the "hummingbird flower" in my perennial garden. He warned me that Crocosmia may not be winter hardy in my area (I live and garden in zone 6), and that it might be necessary to dig the corms and store them in the refrigerator for the winter. Well, I planted twelve corms in early spring that year, and they have been in the ground ever since, multiplying into a massive bed. I have not made any effort to provide winter protection, but I must say that I do not rake the soil clean of leaves in the fall. Crocosmia, the favorite hummingbird flower talked about on my Garden Hotline® radio program, attracts families of hummingbirds when it's in bloom in July and August. I find it fascinating to sit by my pond and watch these tiny birds searching for nectar in the small, red, tubular blossoms. With your Crocosmia you can plant Salvia, Black-eyed Susan, Butterfly Bush, and Beebalm, which also attract butterflies, hummingbirds, and honeybees to your garden.

Bloom Period and Color Flame-red, yellow, apricot, and orange flowers bloom in July and August.

Mature Height 3 to 4 feet (spread 18 to 24 inches)

When and How to Plant Plant the corms 10 to 12 inches apart and 3 inches deep in any well-drained soil in late spring. After flowering ceases in August, gather seeds from the tips of the gracefully arching stems. After air-drying, store them in airtight containers (baby-food jars with lids that reseal work great). Hold the seeds until you're ready to chill them for germination. If grown from seed, Crocosmia requires two growing seasons to come into bloom. Prechill seeds in a moist, sterile seed-starting mix for two to three weeks at 35 to 40 degrees Fahrenheit. Allow to germinate at 70 to 75 degrees Fahrenheit, a process which may take as long as sixty days. Crocosmia transplants (started corms in pots) are available in spring, *but they do not transplant well.* Please start with dormant corms.

Sun and Soil Preferences Plant in full sun in well-drained, average soil with a neutral to slightly acidic pH.

Moisture Requirements Provide even moisture to start; then average rainfall will suffice.

Fertilizing During active growth, apply a water-soluble plant food for flowering plants according to label directions.

Pruning and Care To clean up the clump, cut the Crocosmia flower stems and foliage to the ground after frost. For protection from deep freezing during severe winters, apply a 3- to 4-inch layer of winter mulch over the soil surface at cleanup time in late fall. Rake away the mulch in early spring before new stems emerge.

Pests and Diseases During the heat of summer, watch for spider mites: the green foliage will have a stippled look. Apply insecticidal soap or hot pepper wax spray according to label directions.

Additional Species, Cultivars, or Varieties *C.* × *crocosmiiflora* is available in colors ranging from yellow to orange to red. *C. masoniorum* produces orange or orange-scarlet blooms.

My Personal Favorite

NAME	SPECIAL CHARACTERISTICS
C. 'Lucifer'	Produces flame-red flowers in July and August / 3- to 4-foot-tall, wiry stems / favorite of hummingbirds

Crocus

Crocus species

Preferred Zones	Sun Preferences	Additional Benefit
3 to 8	☼ ☼	🌷

Some of you may be familiar with the song lyric "the lonely little Petunia in the onion patch." Well, a single Crocus planted in the garden can be likened to that lonely little Petunia, and that is why I have always recommended planting Crocus in drifts of five or more (I prefer quantities of an odd number). Plant drifts of Crocus along a walkway, tuck them up to the base of a boulder in a rock garden, or scatter them throughout a bulb garden in the forest. To avoid the straight rows often created when planting bulbs, hold a handful of Crocus corms a foot or so above the ground and drop them to the surface. Plant them exactly where they land to create that random naturalized look. It's not unusual to have my Crocus emerge through a late-winter snow, declaring that spring is just around the corner. Spring-blooming species bloom February to April; fall-blooming species bloom September to November. Best bloom occurs after cold winters.
Note: *Other names to look for when purchasing Crocus bulbs are Dutch Crocus hybrids (Crocus × vernus), Snow Crocus (Crocus chrysanthus), Saffron Crocus (Crocus sativus) which is hardy only to zone 6, and Fall Crocus (Crocus speciosus).*

Bloom Period and Color White, purple, yellow, and bicolors bloom in spring or fall.

Mature Height 2 to 6 inches (spread 2 to 4 inches)

When and How to Plant Plant in the fall after the soil has cooled substantially, usually after mid-October. (Crocus corms planted while the soil is still warm will send up foliage that gets damaged by winter, although the flowers will not emerge). Plant spring-blooming Crocus corms 4 to 5 inches apart and 2 to 4 inches deep, depending on size. If you would like to force some Crocus, cover five or six spring-blooming corms with 1 inch of well-drained potting mix in a 5-inch pot. Cool the potted corms in the refrigerator for six weeks. Then move the pot to bright light with about 50-degree-Fahrenheit night temperatures. They'll bloom in just a week or so.

Sun and Soil Preferences Plant in full sun to light shade in a well-drained soil that has low fertility.

Moisture Requirements Mother Nature's rainfall is sufficient after the initial watering at planting time.

Fertilizing Don't fertilize forced Crocus. For naturalized areas in the garden, use bulb food, following label directions.

Pruning and Care No pruning is required; the foliage will disappear.

Pests and Diseases In some gardens, rodents are a problem. Squirrels and chipmunks love to dig up freshly planted corms. The first line of defense is a thorough watering to settle the soil—rodents will generally not bother corms if they have to work to find them. If the problem persists, lay old window screens over the freshly planted corms immediately after watering, but remember that the screens must be removed before sprouting in spring. One more step: apply an animal repellent according to label directions.

Additional Species, Cultivars, or Varieties 'Pickwick' has pale purple or lavender florets striped with dark-purple etchings; 'Peter Pan' has white petals; and 'Purpurea' has purple florets. 'Remembrance' has striking blue florets. Three fall-blooming Crocus that can be planted in August are C. *speciosus* (lilac color), C. s. 'Conqueror' (blue), and C. *sativus*, often called Saffron Crocus (purple).

My Personal Favorite

NAME	SPECIAL CHARACTERISTICS
'Yellow Mammoth'	Spring-blooming Crocus / crisp yellow petals

Crown Imperial

Fritillaria imperialis

Preferred Zones	Sun Preferences	Additional Benefits
10 to 11	☀ ☼	NA

This bulb has a long history, having been introduced into Europe from Persia (now known as Iran) in the 1500s. Known to many bulb connoisseurs as the Garden Aristocrat, Fritillaria imperialis is a unique flowering bulb. It is a real conversation piece, with its cap of green foliage perched atop drooping clusters of red, orange, or yellow flowers standing on stems that grow to two-and-a-half to four feet tall. (Its tuft of green foliage pointing upward above the blossoms reminds me of the Mohawk haircuts of the late 1960s.) Fritillaria has another characteristic that has inspired many organic gardeners to recommend it for warding off rodents, moles in particular, which have developed ever-increasing populations in the Tri-State area. The plant's bulb, stems, and flowers have a very pungent odor. Up close it smells like a sanitary landfill on a humid day!

Bloom Period and Color Red, yellow, or orange flowers bloom April to May. For the best flowering show and according to your desire, choose Crown Imperial by color: *Fritillaria imperialis* Red, *F. i.* Yellow, or *F. i.* Orange.

Mature Height Up to 4 feet

When and How to Plant As soon as the garden centers announce the arrival of spring-flowering bulbs, select and plant *Fritillaria* bulbs. Don't wait for the ground to cool as you do for Tulips and Crocus—plant *Fritillaria* as early as possible, as they lose their viability rather quickly. Even though Crown Imperial bulbs are the largest of the genus, don't plant them deeper than 3 to 4 inches.

Sun and Soil Preferences Plant in full sun to partial shade in porous, well-drained, sweet soil.

Moisture Requirements When the bulbs sprout in spring, water deeply to promote strong, active growth.

Fertilizing It is recommended that you add lime at the time of planting to sweeten acid soil. At fall planting, apply a topdressing of bulb food according to the label directions. Winter's rain and melting snow will carry the nutrients to the roots as they grow and develop over winter.

Pruning and Care Clip out stalks of mature (browned) foliage to keep the garden neat and clean.

Pests and Diseases Crown Imperial has no particular pest problems.

Additional Species, Cultivars, or Varieties *F. meleagris,* known as Guinea Hen Flower or Chequered Lily, is 12 inches tall and has single, nodding, checkered purple-and-white flowers. It needs partial shade in a woodsy location. *F. persica,* from Iran, has 3-foot-tall plants with violet-blue drooping blossoms.

My Personal Favorite

NAME	SPECIAL CHARACTERISTICS
'Rubra'	Fiery red flowers on 4-foot-tall stems

Daffodil

Narcissus hybrids

Preferred Zones	Sun Preferences		Additional Benefits
4 to 9	☀	◑	🜋 🌼

Have deer, woodchucks, or various four-legged rodents such as mice, squirrels, or chipmunks ever invaded your garden? If so, then you know the damage that can be done to spring-flowering bulbs like Crocus, Tulips, and Hyacinths. However, if you grow Narcissus (often referred to as Jonquils or Daffodils) in the same area of the garden, you will notice these flowers are never touched. I'm guessing deer just don't like them. In my garden, the deer journey through at about 6 a.m. each day and eat everything which grew overnight. At about 6 p.m. they saunter back, westbound, and eat everything I planted that day—except that they never touch a Daffodil. I've planted drifts of Daffodils in my perennial garden and pockets of Daffodils beside a winding stone wall, and have allowed Daffodils to naturalize along a woodland path. This is the one spring-flowering bulb that I can depend on, year after year. And remember: the bloom of the Daffodil always faces the sun!

Bloom Period and Color White, yellow, orange, pink, and bicolor flowers bloom early to late spring.

Mature Height 4 to 20 inches

When and How to Plant Select Daffodils as soon as they become available, but don't plant them until after the soil has begun to cool (generally after early October in the Tri-State area). To inhibit premature sprouting, soil temperature for Daffodils should cool to below 70 degrees Fahrenheit before planting. Use a soil thermometer to check. Plant Daffodil bulbs at a depth equal to three times their diameter. Incorporate trace elements by adding milled seaweed at planting time.

Sun and Soil Preferences Plant in well-drained soil that has an exposure of at least a half-day of sun.

Moisture Requirements Water newly planted Daffodils to settle the soil, then let Mother Nature take over—no additional watering should be needed in the Tri-State garden.

Fertilizing Do not add a chemical fertilizer at planting time, as it might burn the new roots. Feed Daffodil beds in late fall with a slow-release bulb food, which is low in nitrogen. Fall rain and winter snow will leach the nutrients into the soil for pickup by the roots.

Pruning and Care Immediately after bloom, pinch off spent flowers to prevent seedpod formation—stopping seedpod production in Daffodils will direct energy into next year's bloom. Lift and divide Daffodil bulbs every five to seven years. Bulbs originally planted 7 to 9 inches deep will often be found at 12 to 14 inches deep when they are lifted.

Pests and Diseases Daffodils have no pests, not even deer.

Additional Species, Cultivars, or Varieties 'Ice Follies' is an extra-large, out-facing, creamy-white flower with a big, bright-yellow, flat cup that matures to creamy white. 'Carlton' is a two-toned yellow flower with a delightful vanilla fragrance. 'Tete-a-Tete', the most popular dwarf Daffodil, stands only 5 to 6 inches tall. 'Dutch Master', a yellow trumpet Daffodil introduced before 1948, may be replacing the popular 'King Alfred'.

My Personal Favorite

NAME	SPECIAL CHARACTERISTICS
'King Alfred'	Introduced in 1899 / has been the most popular, best known, most magnificent yellow trumpet Daffodil for the last century

Dahlia

Dahlia hybrids

Preferred Zones	Sun Preferences	Additional Benefits
Tender		

A garden or patio container filled with flowering Dahlias becomes an artist's palette, with some of the purest colors in nature. Shades of clear crisp oranges, yellows, pinks, reds, purples, lavenders, and snow white are the gardener's delight. Whether it is the large decorative type, anemone-flowering, cactus type, border decorative (dwarf), pompon (dwarf), or spider type, a Dahlia's crispness appears almost artificial. One of the greatest joys I ever had in my garden was picking a dinner-plate-size Dahlia— fourteen inches across—from a plant that was seven feet tall. The only other flowers that are close in size to this Dahlia are the hardy Hibiscus with twelve-inch-diameter, bright-red, paper-thin blooms that last only one day, or the giant, ten-inch-diameter, yellow Sunflower that, when dried, can last forever. **Reminder:** *You'll need to stake giant Dahlias to support them against sudden strong winds.*

Bloom Period and Color Many colors and types bloom midsummer to frost.

Mature Height 15 inches to 6 feet

When and How to Plant Home-started tubers and nursery-started plants should not be planted outdoors until after the last frost date. Dahlia tubers that are planted directly in the garden after the soil temperature reaches at least 55 degrees Fahrenheit will bloom late summer or early fall. (To have Dahlias in bloom by midsummer, start the tuberous roots indoors in a shallow pot filled with a well-drained potting mix; cover the tubers with at least 2 inches of the mix. Keep evenly moist but not wet, and feed with a water-soluble plant food at half-strength according to label directions.) Stake tall-growing, large-flowered varieties at planting time.

Sun and Soil Preferences Plant in half-day to full sun in well-drained richly organic soil that has a neutral to slightly acidic pH.

Moisture Requirements Water regularly and thoroughly, but do not allow "wet feet."

Fertilizing Fertilize Dahlias regularly with a water-soluble plant food for flowering plants at half the recommended rate. Overfeeding produces a lush foliage plant with fewer blooms.

Pruning and Care To produce large blossoms, pinch off side buds as they sprout (this is known as *disbudding*). Disbudding directs the plant's energy into making bigger flowers. Although the Dahlia is often listed as a half-hardy perennial, in the Tri-State area it must be removed from the garden after the first light frost of fall. After frost has blackened the terminal foliage, dig the tuber from the ground, clean off the dirt, clip back the stem to 6 inches, air-dry the tuber, and store dry or in a box of sawdust at 60 degrees Fahrenheit. If stored in sawdust, sprinkle once a month with water to keep the medium from totally dehydrating the tuber.

Pests and Diseases Check with your county cooperative extension educator for controls for aphids, cutworms, slugs, and Japanese beetles.

Additional Species, Cultivars, and Varieties Patio gardeners will love *Dahlia pinnata* 'Magic Carpet Mix', a dwarf Dahlia, 18 inches tall, with masses of 2- to 3-inch blossoms.

My Personal Favorite

NAME	SPECIAL CHARACTERISTICS
D. pinnata 'Babylon Red'	Bright-red dinner-plate Dahlia / blooms grow 12 inches in diameter or larger

Fancy-Leaved Caladium

Caladium × hortulanum

Preferred Zones	Sun Preferences	Additional Benefits
Tender		

No more elegant leaf could arise from garden, windowbox, or flowerpot than the leaf that emerges from a Caladium tuber. The arrow-shaped leaves appear in striking color combinations of reds, pinks, greens, and whites, and are equaled only by the leaves of Coleus, the most colorful bedding plant annual. In the Tri-State area, the Caladium, a tender (non-hardy), pancake-shaped tuber with bumps on its upper side, must be removed from the garden before fall's first killing frost and stored indoors over winter. Inexperienced gardeners (and some experts) sometimes make the mistake of planting the tubers upside down. Apparently they think the bumps are where the roots develop—but the tubers should be planted with the bumps facing upward. I like to plant Caladium in terracotta mum or azalea pots, which are shallow and wide compared to standard clay pots. Later I can plant the Caladium, pot and all, directly into the garden, thus avoiding damage to the new shoots or the roots (do not transplant a growing Caladium from the original pot, as this will damage the roots and cause the plant to collapse). For container use on the patio, sink the growing pot into soil in a larger planter.

Bloom Period and Color Depending on variety, flowers bloom in many colors from May to frost but are insignificant and should be removed, as they delete strength from the leaves.

Mature Height 8 to 12 inches (spread 2 to 3 feet)

When and How to Plant Start Caladium tubers indoors during February or early March for planting outdoors when the soil has warmed after the last frost date. Start by placing the pancake-shaped tuber, bumpy side up, on a moist starting mix in a shallow clay container; cover the tubers with 2 inches of mix. To facilitate emergence of colorful foliage, supply bottom heat of 75 to 80 degrees Fahrenheit. Once a new plant has sprouted, keep it in filtered bright light or morning sun until it's time to plant outdoors. After night temperatures are consistently above 60 degrees Fahrenheit, leave the growing Caladium in the original clay container and plunge the pot, level to the rim, into well-drained garden soil. Set pots 10 to 12 inches apart.

Sun and Soil Preferences Plant in sun to partial shade, in well-drained, organically rich soil. The indoor gardener can grow a pot of Caladium in the morning sunlight of an east-facing window. You'll enjoy the colorful leaves for months on end.

Moisture Requirements Keep the soil moist but not wet.

Fertilizing Feed regularly with a water-soluble plant food at half the recommended strength.

Pruning and Care As leaves die, clip them off just above the soil line. In early fall, gradually withhold water until the leaves die, lift the containers from the garden, shuck off the potting mix, dry the tubers for several days in a well-ventilated, shady area, and store them in dry peat moss at 60 to 70 degrees until time to start the following spring. If not thoroughly dried, they will rot.

Pests and Diseases In damp environs, keep a watchful eye out for slugs and snails. Apply slug and snail bait according to label directions.

Additional Species, Cultivars, or Varieties *C. × h.* 'White Christmas' has broad snow-white leaves with green veining. 'Fancy-Leaved Mixed' comes in a gorgeous assortment of pink, red, green, and white colors.

My Personal Favorite

NAME	SPECIAL CHARACTERISTICS
Colocasia esculenta Elephant Ear Caladium	Huge 3- to 5-foot bright-green leaves / grows in shady, moist soil / gives the garden or patio a tropical look

Flowering Onion

Allium spp. and hybrids

Preferred Zones	Sun Preference		Additional Benefit
4 to 9	☼		🌼

Some of the more joyful and rewarding experiences I've had in my garden are the times that neighborhood kids come to visit. They love to see my water garden, to listen to the bullfrog, and to feed the koi and goldfish. During May and June, the kids get an extra treat. That's when my Alliums are in full bloom. I plant three or more Allium giganteum in a group, thus creating an "Allium forest." The globes of giant purple blooms (up to 6 inches in diameter) may be more than half the size of a child's head. And the flowers, perched on stalks as tall as four feet, may be more than the height of the little visitor. The flowers of Allium 'Globemaster' are globes that measure to ten inches in diameter on stems up to four feet tall. If left standing in the garden until dried, Flowering Onion varieties make outstanding specimens in dried-flower arrangements.

Bloom Period and Color Globes of white, blue, pink, or magenta bloom in early May to midsummer.

Mature Height Up to 4 feet (spread 12 inches)

When and How to Plant Plant in late fall. A healthy Flowering Onion bulb is knobby, 2 to 3 inches in diameter, and resembles a softball that should be retired: it is lopsided, dented, and scaly looking. Plant at a depth twice the diameter of the bulb (if a bulb is 3 inches in diameter, plant it to a depth of no more than 6 inches). Plant more than one for a show, 6 to 8 inches apart. After the second blooming season, carefully dig the bulbs. You will find two oddly shaped bulbs for each one you planted, because the original bulb will have split. Replant to increase your collection.

Sun and Soil Preferences Plant in full sun in a well-drained soil that has a neutral to slightly acidic pH.

Moisture Requirements Water well at planting. No extra water is required after that.

Fertilizing Stir in a slow-release bulb food at planting time because you will leave the bulb in place for two years.

Pruning and Care Little care is required. The leaves, six to nine in number and 5 to 8 inches wide, emerge from the soil as green straps in a rosette pattern; the thick, strong scape (stem) holding the lilac flowers emerges later. As the flower scape gets taller, the leaves lie on the ground. Let them remain there as long as they are green, for they are busy manufacturing food for next year's bloom.

Pests and Diseases Flowering Onion has no insect or disease problems.

Additional Species, Cultivars, or Varieties A. *giganteum* 'Mount Everest', the showiest Giant Onion, offers 3- to 4-inch-diameter white globes on 3-foot-tall stems. A. *rosenbachianum*, which grows up to 4 feet tall, has star-shaped, deep-lavender flowers.

My Personal Favorite

NAME	SPECIAL CHARACTERISTICS
Allium giganteum Traditional Giant Onion	3- to 4-foot-tall stems / small lilac-purple florets gathered into 6-inch or larger balls

Gladiolus

Gladiolus hybrids

Preferred Zones	Sun Preference	Additional Benefit
Tender	☀	🌼

There has never been a flower show held during summer or early fall in the Tri-State area that did not have Gladiolus as a class of entries. Tables filled with single-flowering stems standing in nondescript glass containers speak to the popularity of this flower. One of the "Glads" will likely earn "Best of Show." Of course all kinds of other flowering plants will be there too, including Begonias, Chrysanthemums, Marigolds, Snapdragons, Salvia, Sunflowers, and Dahlias, but the common Gladiolus, also known as Garden Gladiolus or Florist Gladiolus, is an outstanding cut flower that lasts for weeks. Cut three stems at different lengths, place them in a water-filled vase, and you will have your own flower show. The individual flowers start opening from the bottom of the stem to the tip, so harvest Glads with as many unopened flowers as possible. Of course you will want a few blossoms open for immediate enjoyment. As an individual flower wilts, pinch out the spent blossom. This flower's name comes from the Latin word gladius, meaning "sword," which describes the shape of the leaf, a long, flat blade.

Bloom Period and Color Flowers in multiple colors bloom 65 to 100 days after planting.

Mature Height Up to 5 feet (spread 6 to 8 inches)

When and How to Plant Plant after the danger of frost has passed; for a continuous supply of Gladiolus flowers, make successive plantings at two-week intervals. Plant the corms 4 to 6 inches apart; for extra support and stability of the long swords, plant 6 to 8 inches deep.

Sun and Soil Preferences Plant in full sun, in well-drained, slightly acidic, fertile soil.

Moisture Requirements Water thoroughly at planting time. Provide water during times of drought.

Fertilizing Apply a 5-10-5 or equivalent formula at planting time according to the label directions for flowering plants. As flower buds form, apply a water-soluble 15-30-15 or equivalent to boost flower production.

Pruning and Care To prevent breakage of stems from wind, staking may be necessary. Carefully push a bamboo cane 6 to 8 inches into the soil beside the corm, and tie the sword-like leaves loosely to the cane. Once the long blades of foliage yellow in late fall, dig the corms and allow them to cure in the sun for a few days. Clip off the dead foliage and stems, discard the spent corm attached to the bottom, and store the new corms dry at 40 to 50 degrees Fahrenheit until the next planting season.

Pests and Diseases Check with your county cooperative extension educator for recommended controls of gladiolus thrips and borers. Timing is critical.

Additional Species, Cultivars, or Varieties 'After Shock' is pink; 'My Love' is white with pink etchings; 'Break o' Dawn' is white with a subtle yellow throat; 'Priscilla' is white with pink edges and yellow spots in the center. Other popular Glads are 'White Friendship' (snow white), 'Nova Lux' (golden yellow), 'Mascagni' (rich red), and 'Rose Supreme' (light pink with creamy center). *G. nanus* 'Nymph' and 'Las Vegas' are two of the "Hardy Glads," which bloom in June and July and may remain in the ground year-round; plant them with 3- to 4-inch spacing in full sun in well-drained soil.

My Personal Favorite

NAME	SPECIAL CHARACTERISTICS
'Saphir'	Deep blue with white throat

Grape Hyacinth

Muscari armeniacum

Preferred Zones	Sun Preferences		Additional Benefits
3 to 8	☀ ◑		

For a splash of heavenly blue in a partially sunny rock garden, or for a sea of blue covering a sunny hillside, you'll never go wrong planting Grape Hyacinths, also known as Bluebells. I never cut the foliage from the tiny bulbs until it has had plenty of time to mature (unless it is to pick a few flowering stems and place them in a miniature bud vase). I consider the very pleasant fragrance a great treat at the breakfast table. A word of warning: Years ago I planted a small bag (perhaps fifty or so) of common blue Grape Hyacinth, just to the south side of my water garden. Now I have Grape Hyacinths popping up on the north side as well as to the east and west. I even have them blooming in the mulched areas under my apple trees. What I'm getting at is, nice as they are, Grape Hyacinths multiply and can get out of bounds if left unattended. Grape Hyacinths make reliable companions for early Tulips, Snowdrops, early Crocuses, and other early spring-flowering bulbs. When they bloom, you'll know spring is just around the corner.

Bloom Period and Color Blue, white, or pink flowers bloom in April and May.

Mature Height 6 to 12 inches (may spread over large area)

When and How to Plant Plant the tiny bulbs in late fall. The first step is crucial: with attention to proper spacing, lay all the bulbs 2 to 3 inches apart on the surface of the soil. Now you're ready to plant them 2 to 3 inches deep. Never plant bulbs by taking one out of the box, digging the hole, planting the bulb, and covering it. It's impossible to remember exactly where the last bulb was planted, and you'll end up with the strangest bunch of bulbs next spring, as one may be planted on top of another. Since Grape Hyacinths naturalize easily, choose their planting location with care—if left unattended, the bed will surely spread, sometimes more than you desire. It's not unusual for little blue blossoms to pop up in some of the strangest places, such as a crack in the driveway, between bluestone stepping-stones, or in the middle of a sunny, green lawn.

Sun and Soil Preferences Plant in full sun to partial shade, in well-drained, organically rich soil. To improve average garden soil in the Tri-State area, till or spade in 2 to 3 inches of well-rotted compost or leaf mold to a depth of 5 to 7 inches. Rake out the bed to remove debris.

Moisture Requirements Water at planting, then let Mother Nature take over. No additional watering is needed, even during times of drought.

Fertilizing A fall application of an organic plant food for bulbs will enhance next spring's bloom. Read the label.

Pruning and Care Clean up the beds in summer after foliage matures.

Pests and Diseases There are no pests and diseases.

Additional Species, Cultivars, or Varieties *M. botryoides* 'Album' has superb white flowers. *M. botryoides* 'Carneum' is a pink-flowering variety with an uncertain, washy hue.

My Personal Favorite

NAME	SPECIAL CHARACTERISTICS
'Heavenly Blue'	Bright-blue, fragrant blossoms/ spreads generously by offsets, making it a natural for large open slopes

Hyacinth

Hyacinthus orientalis

Preferred Zones	Sun Preference	Additional Benefits
4 to 8	☀	🧴 🌱

Select Hyacinth for its many brilliant colors. You don't need a garden to enjoy the fragrance of a Hyacinth, also known as Garden Hyacinth or Dutch Hyacinth. Purchase a Hyacinth waterglass and a single bulb. The waterglass, designed specifically to hold the bulb, looks like an old-fashioned soft-drink bottle, but with a wide-open top. Fill the glass with water and set the bulb in the glass with the point facing up. Place in the refrigerator at 35 to 40 degrees Fahrenheit for thirteen weeks (mark your calendar as a reminder to check the bulb). While in the refrigerated darkness, pure-white roots will grow down into the water and a small finger-like shoot will sprout from the top. Add water as needed. After the thirteen weeks pass, remove the waterglass with the rooted bulb to filtered bright light at room temperature for a few days while green (chlorophyll) forms in the shoot. Then move the bulb to a bright, sunny window for bloom in about three weeks. Oh, what a room refresher.

Bloom Period and Color Flowers bloom in many colors, by variety, from March to April.

Mature Height Up to 18 inches (spread 6 to 10 inches)

When and How to Plant Plant Hyacinth bulbs 6 inches deep in well-drained soil about 1 inch apart for best show. It takes just a few bulbs to satisfy a person's desire for the sweet fragrance. The second year's bloom will not be as spectacular as the first one. To have the best blooms, plant new Hyacinth bulbs each fall. **Note of Caution:** Some people are quite allergic to the papery wrapping of the bulb and severe dermatitis may result from handling it. If you know you are sensitive, wear gloves while planting the bulbs.

Sun and Soil Preferences Plant in full sun, in well-drained soil with a neutral to slightly acidic pH.

Moisture Requirements Water thoroughly at planting. No additional watering is needed.

Fertilizing Apply a bulb food in fall according to label directions.

Pruning and Care Clip off the spent flower stalk immediately after bloom and before the seedpods form, but allow the foliage to remain until completely mature. Recycle forced Hyacinth bulbs by letting them dry after bloom, shucking off the potting soil, and planting them in the garden in fall. They may not bloom as well the following year, but they should do well two years down the road.

Pests and Diseases There are none.

Additional Species, Cultivars, or Varieties 'Carnegie' is pure white; 'Blue Magic' is deep purple; 'City of Haarlem' is pale yellow; 'Blue Jacket' is lilac purple; 'Pink Supreme' is bright pink.

My Personal Favorite

NAME	SPECIAL CHARACTERISTICS
'Jan Bos'	Bright red

Lily
Lilium species

Preferred Zones	Sun Preferences		Additional Benefits
4 to 9			

Lilies looking up (Asiatic), Lilies looking down (Turk's Cap), and Lilies trumpeting their message of beauty straight out (Oriental)—with a little planning in a sunny garden, you can have Lilies in bloom from early summer often into early October. If you have space near the entrance of your perennial garden, do as I did some years back: plant three bulbs each of Asiatic, Turk's Cap, and Oriental Lilies as a welcome addition to the garden. The Turk's Cap Lily (Lilium lancifolium var. splendens), also known as Tiger Lily, can produce as many as twenty-five individual orange Turk's Caps per stem. Don't confuse the other common-named Turk's Cap, Lilium martagon, with Lilium lancifolium! Lilium martagon emits a rather rank scent from its purplish-pink blossoms and visitors will not be welcomed. In the perennial garden, Lilies make great companions for Cleome, Artemisia, Achillea, Rudbeckia, Digitalis, Coreopsis, and Canna, to name just a few. Lilies of all types make outstanding cut flowers, and some add fragrance to indoor arrangements.

Bloom Period and Color Flowers in many colors bloom summer to fall. Asiatic Lilies bloom from late spring to early summer. Oriental Lilies bloom from midsummer to early fall. The nodding, bright-orange American Turk's Cap Lilies, *L. superbum,* bloom from mid- to late summer.

Mature Height 2 to 8 feet (spread 18 inches)

When and How to Plant Plant either spring or fall. Virtually all Lily bulbs should be planted immediately after arrival from Holland (usually in fall). The planting depth, in general, should be three times the height of the bulb. Spacing is determined by the species and varies from as many as twelve bulbs per square foot to as few as one bulb per square foot.

Sun and Soil Preferences Plant in full sun to partial shade in well-drained soil that has a neutral to acidic pH.

Moisture Requirements Water thoroughly at planting time to settle the soil. No additional watering will be required.

Fertilizing Apply a bulb booster just as new shoots emerge in early spring, following label directions.

Pruning and Care Lilies open their flowers from the lowest bud on the stem to the upper tip. In many species, this flowering process takes several weeks to about two months. Once the flowering is complete, cut off the top portion where the flowers were attached, leaving the foliage and stem until mature. Once mature, cut the entire stem to the ground. Don't try to pull the stem, as damage to the bulb may result. **Caution:** Clip out the anthers (the yellow pollen-producers) before bringing open blossoms indoors, as the pollen may stain tablecloths and clothing.

Pests and Diseases Lilies are generally pest-free here, except that deer love them. Apply a deer-repellent as new sprouts emerge; reapply through bloom. Tiger Lilies, although popular in American gardens, can introduce a mosaic virus which infects other Lily species.

Additional Species, Cultivars, or Varieties 'Citronella', a nodding hybrid lily, is lemon yellow. The Oriental Lily *L. speciosum* 'Album' is pure white, blooms from late August into September, and is perfect for the evening garden. 'Alma Ata' is pure white; 'Black Beauty' is almost black; 'Rubrum' is reddish-pink; all three are outward-facing.

My Personal Favorite

NAME	SPECIAL CHARACTERISTICS
L. speciosum 'Uchida'	Bright raspberry with white edges / perfect candidate for the evening garden

Tulip

Tulipa spp. and hybrids

Preferred Zones	Sun Preference	Additional Benefits
3 to 7	☀	🌿🌼

In my garden, I treat most Tulips as annuals. I plant fresh bulbs each fall and discard them after bloom in spring. I did the same thing when I was Executive Director of the Queens Botanical Garden in Flushing, New York. We planted over 250,000 Tulip bulbs each fall for our springtime show, then we dug them up after bloom and added them to the compost pile. The reason? Tulips just don't bloom well the second year. I found I was getting lots of extra-wide straplike foliage the following spring, but few blooms— maybe one out of ten plants would bloom. With a little bit of planning (one of my mottoes: "Plan before you plant"), you can have a Tulip garden in bloom from early March well into June. To add interest to and fill out a bulb garden, plant Daffodils, Hyacinths, or other spring-flowering bulbs. Tulips, whether planted from hybrids or species, should be treated as annuals or short-lived perennials. Plant your bulb display with bloom time as the reference (see Additional Species, Cultivars, or Varieties on the facing page).

Bloom Period and Color Tulips bloom early spring to early May, depending on the species and variety. They come in red, white, pink, yellow, orange, purple, and bicolor, and there is even a "black" Tulip (actually a deep, deep purple).

Mature Height 12 to 30 inches

When and How to Plant For a spectacular show the following spring, plant new bulbs each fall after the soil cools in October or early November. In the Tri-State area, late planting prevents premature sprouting of foliage. Plant the bulbs 4 to 6 inches apart. *Planting depth equals 2 to 2¹/2 times the diameter of the bulb.*

Sun and Soil Preferences Plant in full sun in well-drained, fertile soil of neutral to slightly acidic pH.

Moisture Requirements Water the bed after planting.

Fertilizing Apply a bulb-booster-type fertilizer just as the foliage emerges.

Pruning and Care Do not mulch a Tulip bed until the ground begins to freeze in winter. To avoid seed production, remove spent flowers just as petals drop. *Do not* remove foliage until it is yellowed or brown.

Pests and Diseases To reduce damage from squirrels, water newly planted beds to settle the soil. To deter deer from dining on Tulips, apply turfgrass fertilizer Milorganite™ (processed Milwaukee sewage) at the recommended rate for turf as the bulb foliage emerges in late winter or early spring. The slight fragrance of the processed sewage repels deer when they bend down to browse in the Tulip garden.

Additional Species, Cultivars, or Varieties *T. tarta*, a white flower with a yellow eye, blooms on stalks 6 to 8 inches tall in March. Low-growing red or yellow Emperor blooms in early April. Double 'Peach Blossom' blooms in early May. Lily-flowered 'Red Shine' blooms mid-May. The Darwin hybrids 'Apeldoorn' and 'Golden Parade' and the Parrot Tulips 'Blue Parrot' and 'Red Fantasy' bloom early to mid-May. Greigii hybrid 'Oriental Splendor', heavily mottled and striped with purple foliage, flowers early to mid-May. Follow with the late-May-blooming Darwin Tulips 'Golden Age' and 'Pink Supreme'.

My Personal Favorite

NAME	SPECIAL CHARACTERISTICS
'Red Emperor'	Scarlet red / grows to 18 inches / strong stem holds flowers erect

City & Small-Space

A gardener of the 21st Century who wishes to grow plants in a small-space garden has it made when compared to the person who tried to grow plants in tight quarters earlier in the 20th Century. For every full-size plant of yesteryear, there are compact or dwarf varieties today.

Plants for Small Places

The nursery industry has been working hard to breed plants that have the same characteristics as their parents but will flourish in small places. Examples are Laceleaf Japanese Maple 'Dissectum', an umbrella-shaped dwarf tree with colorful foliage; 'Emerald Green' Arborvitae, a wall of dark-green foliage with a three- to four-foot spread; Dwarf Alberta Spruce, a dwarf evergreen the shape of a giant Christmas tree; and Zuni Crape Myrtle, a compact shrub with dark-lavender flowers all summer long. You can also have your own personal shade tree in a small-space garden by planting a Fastigiate European Hornbeam, a Young's Weeping Birch, or a 'Skyrocket' English Oak.

Improved Containers

Containers have also been improved. In place of heavy concrete planters that cracked because of the freezing and thawing of the soil in winter, and clay pots that shattered all too often, there are now almost indestructible containers made of fiberglass, plastic, and rigid rubber. Manufacturers have even learned how to build attractive, durable, wooden containers that can endure winter without falling apart. Lightweight plastics—a result of the space age—and soilless mixes have opened opportunities for growing all kinds of plants in containers.

Japanese Wisteria, dripping with blue, white, or pink blooms, can be seen in rooftop gardens and on balconies in the five boroughs of New York, as well as apartments and townhouses throughout the Tri-State region. When you are in Albany or Buffalo, New York, look closely at the container culture and you may see the hardy

Gardens *for the Tri-State*

Swiss Stone Pine, one of the slowest growing needled evergreens. Check the terrace planters in Stanford and New Haven, Connecticut, and you might spot the Dwarf White Pines `Nana' and 'Pygmaea'. In Newark and Atlantic City, New Jersey, look for a wall of Silver Lace Vine with fragrant greenish-white flowers, growing from containers in various small-space gardens.

Fertilizing Container Plants

Most soilless mixes are made of a blend of milled sphagnum peat moss, perlite, and vermiculite, and are pH adjusted. Adjustment of the soil pH facilitates the process of nutrient uptake by the roots of the plant. You must feed during the growing season.

Containers in Winter

If possible, move plants out of direct wind and sun in winter. The soil temperature in an exposed container in winter can get as cold as the air temperature around it. Daily freezing and thawing and bitter cold nights will damage the roots more than the shoots. When a containerized plant expires in winter, it is often because the roots froze. The larger the container, the better the root system is insulated from cold.

Containerized plants may also need water during winter. On a warm winter day, carry buckets of water to moisten the soil.

Applying an antidesiccant to the foliage of needled and broadleaf evergreens will help reduce winterburn.

Do Your Homework

Before you start a garden on the rooftop or balcony, check with the building department or superintendent to get approval. There are local building codes and weight limits. Containers filled with soil and plants and water can add hundreds of pounds of dead weight that could overload a structure.

Whether you want to feature a deciduous flowering tree, an evergreen flowering shrub, or an evergreen wall, check with your local garden center professional in the Tri-State area for plants that will fill the bill. This is just making sure that you plant the right plant in the right place.

Bird's Nest Spruce

Picea abies 'Nidiformis'

Preferred Zones	Sun Preferences	Additional Benefit
3 to 7	☼ ◑	🐝

If you would like to create a dwarf conifer garden, the Bird's Nest Spruce could very well be its centerpiece. Its name is derived from a growth habit that makes it look like a bird's nest—there is a depression in the center where you might imagine a bird has nested. If you are planting either the deep-green Norway Spruce variety or a dwarf Colorado Blue Spruce cultivar, leave room for growth. Both are slow growers but within fifteen years will reach five feet in width. For container culture, whether at ground level or on the twenty-fourth floor, winter protection is a must. Move the containerized Bird's Nest Spruce to a protected area (for that you'll need wheels), or pack layers of straw or styrofoam around the container to reduce the constant freezing and thawing. In general, it is not the upper part of the plant that dies—the roots die first. Complementary plants in a dwarf conifer garden might include Dwarf Globe Blue Spruce, Dwarf Scotch Pine, many of the cultivars of Creeping Junipers, and Compact or Dwarf Mugo Pine. Large mature specimens are available from nurseries and garden centers as balled-and-burlapped plants in spring, summer, and fall.

Bloom Period and Color Flowers are not showy.

Mature Size 2 feet tall × 5 feet

When and How to Plant Plant any time of the year. Plant a balled-and-burlapped or container-grown plant in a hole no deeper than the rootball, with a width two to three times the width of the rootball. Use unamended soil as the backfill. To help remove the rootball from a container, first thoroughly moisten the soil. Water acts as a lubricant, making it much easier to slip the rootball from the container.

Sun and Soil Preferences Although the best site is in full sun, Bird's Nest Spruce will grow in half-day sun in well-drained, acidic soil, pH 5.5 to 6.5.

Moisture Requirements Just ensure that the rootball gets a thorough soaking at planting time and that the plant receives adequate moisture during extreme drought periods. Immediately after planting the dwarf conifer garden, spread a 2- to 3-inch layer of organic mulch, like pine bark nuggets or shredded hardwood bark, over the planting area, and maintain the mulch year-round.

Fertilizing Feed with an organic or slow-release plant food for evergreens annually, in early spring.

Pruning and Care Prune only in early spring as the new buds begin to elongate into needled stems; clip only the new-growth tips.

Pests and Diseases During hot, dry weather, keep a watchful eye out for spider mite infestations. Infested plants will have needles with a bleached-out look. To test for mites, hold a piece of pure-white paper under a section of the needles, tap the needles vigorously, and then gaze at the "dust" which falls to the paper. If the "dust" moves, the tree has mites. Rinse the entire plant with hose-pressure water to wash off much of the infestation, then apply a miticide such as insecticidal soap: read the label!

Additional Species, Cultivars, or Varieties 'Repens' is shorter and more spreading than 'Nidiformis'. 'Pendula', the Weeping Norway Spruce, grows 3 to 5 feet tall.

My Personal Favorite

NAME	SPECIAL CHARACTERISTICS
'Pumila'	Dwarf Norway Spruce grows 3 to 8 feet tall / better for cold climates / buds break later in spring, so they are protected from late killing frosts

Boston Ivy
Parthenocissus tricuspidata

Preferred Zones	Sun Preferences	Additional Benefits
3 to 8		

 *You might not notice Boston Ivy as it grows on a large brick wall in a city in summer, but go back in late September into October to see the show when the five- to eight-inch green leaves with three-lobed margins will have turned bright red. Boston Ivy is a tough, low-maintenance, fast-growing deciduous vine for the urban as well as the suburban environment. On a patio, deck, or rooftop garden, plant Boston Ivy in wooden containers set at the base of a trellis and you will have a wall of green for summer, turning to a colorful wall of red in fall. When I was Director of the Queens Botanical Garden in Flushing, New York, we planted Boston Ivy in the narrow strip of soil (about twelve inches wide) along the foundation of the administration building. To help the tendrils grasp the stone we attached threads of fishing filament to the wall. Boston Ivy may be used as ground cover or as a vine for walls, fences, pergolas, and trellises. It is particularly valuable when planted in locations with limited soil space where a large wall of green is desired.*

Other Name Japanese Creeper

Bloom Period and Color Inconspicuous greenish-white flowers bloom in summer; the real show is the bright-red to crimson foliage in fall.

Mature Size To 50 feet long

When and How to Plant You'll find 3- to 5-inch pots at garden centers in early spring, when they may be planted; or purchase bare-root cuttings by mail order and plant in early spring for a quick cover. Set plants 10 to 12 inches apart for in-ground plantings. For a terrace garden, plant five or more plants in a container as large as a whiskey half-barrel.

Sun and Soil Preferences Plant in sun or shade. For in-ground plantings, soils should be improved with well-rotted compost or milled sphagnum peat moss . . . but Boston Ivy will grow in just about any soil except water-logged soil.

Moisture Requirements Boston Ivy is an excellent plant for water-efficient gardening, as it is drought tolerant.

Fertilizing Feed annually with a slow-release or organic plant food for foliage plants like trees and shrubs.

Pruning and Care If you need to prune Boston Ivy to reduce its spread, clip the vine just above a node. New shoots will emerge from the older nodes on the stems and increase the density of the green wall. With careful pruning, Boston Ivy can be grown on a relatively confined trellis.

Pests and Diseases Working in a confined area, apply a fungicide for foliage infections of powdery mildew. Apply insecticidal soap if soft-shell scale appears on the stems.

Additional Species, Cultivars, or Varieties The foliage of 'Green Showers' becomes a burgundy color in fall. The bright-green, maple-like leaves of 'Veitchii' turn orange to scarlet in fall. Virginia Creeper *Parthenocissus quinquefolia*, a climbing, vigorous species that grows 70 feet high, has leaves consisting of three or five serrated leaflets that turn crimson in fall.

My Personal Favorite

NAME	SPECIAL CHARACTERISTICS
'Purpurea'	Displays unique red-purple foliage throughout the growing season

Climbing Hydrangea
Hydrangea petiolaris

Preferred Zones	Sun Preferences	Additional Benefits
4 to 7	☀ ☽	🦋 🧴 🌼 🐝

A trip to Mohonk Mountain House in New Paltz, New York, is a treat in itself, but go in late June to mid-July if you wish to see an example of a Climbing Hydrangea as it should be cared for and used—in bloom, dripping with pure-white flowers. This specimen is growing on the eastern side of the rustic stone inn where plant and foliage seem to go on without end. It has been trained as an espalier, rambling in all directions on the wall, covering three or more stories in height. The rich, green leaves emerge in spring and remain on the plant until frost in the fall. During winter, the exfoliating bark stands out. The people at Mohonk have been taking care of their Climbing Hydrangea organically ever since it was planted in the early 1920s. Visit the Skylands Botanical Gardens in Ringwood, New Jersey, to see another specimen of this deciduous vine, Skylands Giant, at the main entrance of the manor house. This one blooms about two weeks earlier than its sister at Mohonk.

Bloom Period and Color White flat-topped flowers up to 8 inches in width bloom in later June to mid-July.

Mature Size 75 feet long

When and How to Plant Climbing Hydrangea is best planted from container-grown stock in early spring before new buds expand on the stems to allow maximum time for rooting into the parent soil. This deciduous climbing vine produces aerial roots from the nodes along the stems that cling to rough surfaces. To train the vine for its climbing experience on a trellis or wall, it may be necessary to help the stems attach themselves by securing them with a "sticky" adhesive tape or twist-ties.

Sun and Soil Preferences Plant balled-and-burlapped or container-grown transplants during spring or fall in full sun to partial shade in a well-drained, organically rich, fertile soil that retains moisture and has a pH of 5.5 to 7.0.

Moisture Requirements Water thoroughly at planting time to completely wet the backfill and rootball. Provide even moisture throughout the first year, as it is slow to root into the parent soil.

Fertilizing Feed in early spring with a plant food for flowering plants like 5-10-5 or an equivalent. If a Climbing Hydrangea refuses to produce its white flowers, check the amount of light the plant receives. It may grow well as a vine, but it may refuse to bloom in deep shade.

Pruning and Care Climbing Hydrangea is a duel-use plant. With pruning to encourage branching and to keep it confined, it makes an attractive ground cover in partial shade to full sun.

Pests and Diseases Once established, Climbing Hydrangea has few, if any, pest or disease problems.

My Personal Favorite

NAME	SPECIAL CHARACTERISTICS
Climbing Hydrangea	*H. petiolaris*, the species / rich green leaves remain until frost

Crape Myrtle

Lagerstroemia indica

Preferred Zones	Sun Preferences	Additional Benefits
6 to 9		

Crape Myrtle, often referred to as the "Southern Lilac," is particularly adaptable to the urban environments of the Tri-State area, as it loves the protection and warmth of nearby buildings during winter. I know it is marginally hardy in our area because my own Crape Myrtle, which produces lavender-blue flowers, dies back to the ground one out of three years, particularly if there is no snow cover. If you garden in zone 6 or warmer, you have a chance for success and it's worth every effort to see it bloom. Plant well-rooted container-grown specimens into a protected environment. The Queens Botanical Garden, Flushing, New York has a collection that receives morning sun and has a solid wall to the west that stops cold westerly winds. Newer cultivars developed by the United States National Arboretum are disease-resistant, flower well, and have highly ornamental bark. Spring planting is recommended—otherwise, there may be winter damage. The extra few months will allow for more root growth into the parent soil. In colder regions, marginally hardy varieties of Crape Myrtle can be sustained by planting in a southeast exposure, with winter wind protection on the northwest side.

Other Names Southern Belle / Southern Lilac

Bloom Period and Color White, pink, red, and lavender flowers bloom midsummer.

Mature Size 15 to 20 feet tall × 10 to 15 feet

When and How to Plant Plant in spring. When planting balled-and-burlapped or container-grown stock, set the rootball no deeper than the depth of the rootball, backfill with unamended soil, and mulch the planting area.

Sun and Soil Preferences Plant Crape Myrtle in full sun to partial shade, in well-drained acidic (pH 5.0 to 6.5) soil.

Moisture Requirements Provide sustained moisture during droughts.

Fertilizing Apply a slow-release or organic plant food for flowering shrubs as the soil warms in the spring.

Pruning and Care To produce multiple blooming stems and increase the density of the shiny, dark-green Crape Myrtle foliage, prune every stem by as much as 1 foot in early spring, just as new growth begins. All new growth has bloom potential for the summer. To develop a tree form, remove lower branches and basal suckers as soon as they appear. Crape Myrtles that appear to have been killed by winter's ravages often come back from sprouts emerging at ground level. These new shoots have bloom potential, so be patient and wait until mid-June before giving up.

Pests and Diseases You may discover aphids on tender new growth in early summer. Apply insecticidal soap or hot pepper wax spray according to label directions.

Additional Species, Cultivars, or Varieties 'Zuni' (Zuni Crape Myrtle) has dark-lavender blooms summer to fall and small rounded leaves with foliage colors of red, orange, and purple in fall; it can be maintained in a multiple-stemmed shrub form or pruned into a single-stem tree shape.

My Personal Favorite

NAME	SPECIAL CHARACTERISTICS
'Chickasaw'	Known as Chickasaw Crape Myrtle / the result of more than thirty years of breeding by the United States National Arboretum / heavily flowered / dwarf (20 inches tall × 26 inches wide) / mildew-tolerant / first in a planned series of miniature hybrids of *L. indica* × *L. fauriei*

Dwarf Alberta Spruce
Picea glauca 'Conica'

Preferred Zones	Sun Preferences	Additional Benefit
3 to 8	☼ ☽	△

One of the most popular miniature evergreen shrubs used for landscaping in the Tri-State area is the Dwarf Alberta Spruce, Picea glauca 'Conica'. It is actually an evergreen tree with a single stem. After years of observation, I can say without a doubt that it's the most popular evergreen for container gardens on decks, patios, and rooftops. You'll find this little guy sitting in front of every plant shop in New York City, sold as a potted shrub. It comes in sizes as short as six inches to as tall as a mature plant of four feet, and the taller it is, the more expensive it is. A local garden center just outside of New York City stocks a whole section of Dwarf Alberta Spruce just to take care of weekend shoppers from the city. In addition to being available in its natural conical shape, you'll find pruned specimens of spiral or poodle cut.

Other Name Dwarf White Spruce

Bloom Period and Color It does not bloom.

Mature Size 4 feet tall × 2 to 3 feet

When and How to Plant Plant any time the soil is workable. A Dwarf Alberta Spruce grown on a sunny deck or a sunny front stoop must be planted or double-potted in a light-colored container. A dark-colored container will absorb the light energy and heat that might dry and cook the roots. Added insurance for keeping the roots cool includes placing the growing container on spacers about 1 inch high, raising the pot from the hot deck, and improving air circulation. If you are making an in-ground planting, set the specimen in a hole no deeper than the depth of the rootball.

Sun and Soil Preferences Site in full sun to partial shade in well-drained loam to sandy soil.

Moisture Requirements Although Dwarf Alberta Spruce grows best in moist loam, it is drought-tolerant in the Tri-State area. During severe or extended drought, a thorough soaking will benefit the plant.

Fertilizing Feed with organic or slow-release plant food for evergreens according to label directions.

Pruning and Care Dwarf Alberta Spruce grown in the spiral or poodle cut won't stay that way on its own. Someone, likely yourself, will need to clip the tips several times throughout the growing season to maintain the shape.

Pests and Diseases Watch for spider mites, particularly if the tree is planted next to a light-colored wall such as that often found at the foundation of a house or a front stoop. The added light reflection and heat encourage spider mites, particularly during mid- to late summer. A thorough prophylactic spray of insecticidal soap is in order by the end of June, with a repeat in late July.

Additional Species, Cultivars, or Varieties For an unusual form, plant 'Sander's Blue'; this blue form of Dwarf Alberta Spruce often reverts to the green form.

My Personal Favorite

NAME	SPECIAL CHARACTERISTICS
'Conica'	Popular miniature evergreen shrub / believed to be a hybrid of *P. glauca* and *P. engelmannii*

Dwarf White Pine

Pinus strobus 'Nana'

Preferred Zones	Sun Preferences		Additional Benefits
3 to 8			

Compact and dwarf Pine varieties make ideal container plants for small-space gardens, whether on a patio, rooftop, or in a tiny backyard anywhere in the Tri-State area. Select named cultivars like Pinus strobus 'Nana' and 'Pygmaea' for small spaces and containers. With a little clipping, these needled evergreens will remain "dwarf" for decades. 'Nana' is kind of a catch-all name for Dwarf White Pine, so shop with care. The most dwarf cultivar I have ever seen is 'Sea Urchin', an extremely small form with bluish needles and a high price tag. Other species which are considerably less expensive yet are quite suitable for small-space gardens and containers are P. densiflora 'Soft Green'; Mugo Pine P. mugo 'Compacta'; Dwarf Scotch Pine P. sylvestris 'Albyns'; and P. cembra Swiss Stone Pine. To retain moisture in containers and insulate the soil from drying sun and heat of summer, grow these needled evergreens in containers that are light-colored, not black or dark brown. Dark colors absorb light and generate heat that will damage sensitive roots. The larger the growing container, the better it will retain moisture and insulate the roots during winter.

Bloom Period and Color Yellow "pollen-producers" bloom in spring.

Mature Size 5 feet × 5 feet

When and How to Plant Plant in spring, summer, fall, or any time the soil is workable. Plant a balled-and burlapped or container-grown specimen no deeper than the depth of the rootball. Use unamended backfill.

Sun and Soil Preferences Site in full sun to partial shade. Dwarf White Pine grows best in fertile, moist, well-drained soil, but will also grow in dry, sandy soil to wet peat bogs.

Moisture Requirements Apply a 2- to 3-inch layer of a decorative mulch like pine bark mini-nuggets or bark chips to the soil surface, and set the growing container on spacers at least 1 inch off the patio surface. Remember: container-grown evergreens need water throughout winter. During the warm days of the January thaw, give each container-grown Pine a thorough watering.

Fertilizing Feed annually with a balanced plant food formulated for needled and broadleaf evergreens. A slow-release fertilizer is fine.

Pruning and Care To retain compactness and density of foliage, pinch or prune the growing tips of each new candle before developing needles emerge in early spring. **Caution:** *Do not* pinch or prune the leader candle of an upright-growing Pine, or multiple crooked stems will develop.

Pests and Diseases White pine weevil may infest the terminal shoots, killing the new terminal growth. Apply an insecticide sold specifically for this pest. Timing is crucial, so check with your county cooperative extension educator to learn about the latest recommended pesticide and the time for application.

Additional Species, Cultivars, or Varieties *Pinus densiflora* 'Soft Green', a form of Japanese Red Pine with bright-green needles, is a dwarf that grows up to 6 feet tall. *Pinus mugo* 'Compacta' Mugo Pine, 4 feet tall and 5 feet wide, can be sheared to retain compactness. *P. sylvestris* 'Albyns', Dwarf Scotch Pine, grows to 2 feet tall and 6 feet wide and has gray-green needles that are 1 to 2 inches long. *P. cembra* Swiss Stone Pine is an extremely slow-growing evergreen with dense, dark-green needles and an upright growing habit, to 35 feet tall.

My Personal Favorite

NAME	SPECIAL CHARACTERISTICS
Dwarf White Pine 'Nana'	A real dwarf / compact, green mound of soft white pine needles

English Ivy

Hedera helix

Preferred Zones	Sun Preference	Additional Benefits
5 to 9	☀☽	NA

English Ivy and its varieties can provide a year-round blanket of evergreen foliage as a ground cover or can be a dressing on an arbor, trellis, or wall. It clings with adventitious rootlets produced from its stems. For ground cover use, all that is needed is a pair of pruning shears to clip back the vines that grow out of bounds. Hanging baskets filled with one of the many varieties of English Ivy can be grown outdoors during summer and enjoyed indoors during winter. I know the issue is debatable, but I come down on the side that does not recommend letting English Ivy grow up a tree. The density of the Ivy foliage provides a home for many insect pests. When allowed to grow up the side of the house, Ivy will grow under shingles or siding, lifting and destroying their integrity. If you have a trellis or stone wall, I say, okay, let it grow. Two particularly hardy forms of Hedera helix are '238th Street' and 'Baltic'. Under city conditions, the '238th Street' variety is even resistant to winterburn.

Bloom Period and Color Flowers are insignificant.

Mature Size Unlimited, depending on support

When and How to Plant Set transplants at any time the soil is workable. There will be less winter damage in windy areas if the English Ivy is planted in spring for rooting into the parent soil. Plant rooted cuttings or transplants 12 inches apart.

Sun and Soil Preferences Plant in partial shade. It does best in well-drained, rich, organic soil with an acid or alkaline pH, but it can even be planted in ordinary garden soil.

Moisture Requirements Water during extremely dry periods.

Fertilizing Feed English Ivy with an organic fertilizer as the soil warms in spring. Avoid feeding in late summer or early fall, as feeding at this time will stimulate new growth that is often damaged by winter winds.

Pruning and Care English Ivy allowed to climb or cling to structures should be watched with care. The vines have been know to grow into cracks at the base of windows or under lapped siding, and rootlets have grown into mortar between bricks and stonework. Prune vines as needed during spring or early summer. Selective pruning of escaping vines may be done at any time of year. In fall, it may be necessary to rake fallen leaves from Ivy beds, as an accumulation of leaves may smother the Ivy.

Pests and Diseases During excessively warm, dry weather, watch for spider mites. Apply a miticide according to label directions if needed.

Additional Species, Cultivars, or Varieties 'Baltic', like '238th Street', is a particularly hardy form. 'Glacier' has pale foliage, splotched with white and gray, that takes on a pinkish cast during winter. *H. colchica* 'Sulphur Heart' Persian Ivy has large (to 10 inches long) heart-shaped leaves with large yellow centers; to grow perfect foliage, plant only in a wind-free location.

My Personal Favorite

NAME	SPECIAL CHARACTERISTICS
'238th Street'	A particularly hardy form of *Hedera helix* / resistant to winterburn under city conditions

English Oak

Quercus robur

Preferred Zones	Sun Preference		Additional Benefits
4 to 8	☀		

Are you looking for a real conversation piece? If you live in tight quarters in Brooklyn, Queens, the Bronx, Manhattan, Staten Island, or any other city with limited space, but have a space where you can plant a tree, consider 'Skyrocket' English Oak. This is an unusually narrow upright Oak that grows up to forty-five feet tall and has only a fifteen-foot spread. The spread can be contained to an even smaller space with a little pruning in early spring. If the fifteen feet of 'Skyrocket' is too wide, try the cultivar Q. r. 'Fastigiata'—it's as narrow as eight feet (maximum spread is fifteen feet) and grows up to fifty or sixty feet tall. And by the way . . . if you have no access to the backyard except through the living quarters, measure the maximum size that will go through the door before you buy a tree for your backyard. It will be frustrating if it doesn't fit.

Other Name Upright English Oak

Bloom Period and Color Blossoms are not showy.

Mature Size 40 to 60 feet tall × 15 feet

When and How to Plant Plant a balled-and-burlapped specimen anytime during spring through fall, in holes prepared no deeper than the rootball. This plant is generally not available as a container-grown tree.

Sun and Soil Preferences Plant in full sun in well-drained, acid to slightly alkaline soil.

Moisture Requirements Immediately after planting, water the rootball and backfill thoroughly, and do so again the following day.

Fertilizing Feed in spring with a plant food formulated for trees and shrubs. Follow the label directions.

Pruning and Care To conserve moisture and reduce weed competition, apply a 2- to 3-inch layer of organic mulch such as wood chips or pine bark nuggets to the planting area.

Pests and Diseases Powdery mildew may appear on foliage where air circulation is poor; it may be suppressed with a mildew fungicide. Follow the label directions.

Additional Species, Cultivars, or Varieties *Quercus palustrus* Pin Oak is an ideal street tree because it has a taproot instead of a spreading root system that may damage curbs and sidewalks; it has a strong pyramidal growth habit, growing to 70 feet tall and 40 feet wide. *Q. p.* 'Green Pillar' has a spread to only 30 feet and is recommended for even more confined city gardens because of its narrower, upright growth habit. *Q. r.* 'Fastigiata' grows to 60 feet tall and only 8 to 15 feet wide. It is slow-growing, making it resistant to breakage. The branches grow upright.

My Personal Favorite

NAME	SPECIAL CHARACTERISTICS
'Skyrocket'	Grows to 45 feet tall / narrow form with dark-green leaves turning yellow to brown in the fall

Evergreen Southern Magnolia

Magnolia grandiflora

Preferred Zones	Sun Preferences		Additional Benefits
6 to 9	☼	◑	

Magnolia grandiflora, *the famous Magnolia of the South, with its leathery evergreen foliage and huge lemon-scented white flowers, is marginally hardy in zone 6 but well worth the effort if you want to try to grow it. One variety in particular, M. 'Edith Bogue', is hardy in zone 6 and possibly to zone 5 (in a protected site). It passed the test of ice, snow, and cold at the Morris Arboretum in Philadelphia, Pennsylvania. It is slow to flower, but is definitely worth the wait. It grows to thirty-five feet tall by fifteen feet wide with lustrous dark-green, narrow leaves, making it an ideal small- or medium-space garden tree. In a protected urban environment, the warmth of the city reduces the potential of winter damage to Southern Magnolia. If our area is into global warming, will Magnolias be far behind? A trip to Planting Fields Arboretum in Oyster Bay, Long Island, New York, is a must during the bloom time of deciduous Magnolias in early to mid-April. The magnificent estate turns into a springtime floral jubilee with its Magnolias and other flowering trees ablaze.*

Other Names Evergreen Magnolia / Bull Bay

Bloom Period and Color White 6- to 10-inch flowers bloom in spring to early summer.

Mature Size Species size is 80 to 100 feet tall × 40 to 60 feet

When and How to Plant Plant a container-grown or balled-and-burlapped specimen in late winter or spring, in a hole no deeper than the depth of the rootball and two to three times its width. This plant is an exception to the frequent "unamended backfill" suggestion: I recommend you mix well-rotted compost or milled sphagnum peat moss with the soil taken from the hole to use as backfill. More organic matter increases the moisture-holding capacity of the soil. To further reduce moisture loss, apply a 2- to 3-inch layer of organic mulch like pine needles or pine bark nuggets over the root zone.

Sun and Soil Preferences Site in full sun to partial shade. Plant in organically rich, acidic soil (5.0 to 6.5 pH). When planting in an average soil, whether it be a clay type or sandy, first blend 3 to 5 inches of well-rotted compost or milled sphagnum peat moss into the planting area to a depth no deeper than the rootball.

Moisture Requirements In well-drained soils, water to a depth of 10 or more inches with drip irrigation, particularly during summer and early fall.

Fertilizing Avoid feeding in midsummer to late fall, as nutrition at that time could initiate new growth which may be easily killed by the first frost of fall.

Pruning and Care Leaves drop daily from Southern Magnolia. Don't panic, just pick them up and add them to the compost pile. Although the mature size can be 100 feet tall × 60 feet wide, M. g. can be pruned after bloom to create a dwarf, compact specimen.

Pests and Diseases Southern Magnolia is essentially pest-free.

Additional Species, Cultivar, or Varieties 'Saint Mary' grows 20 feet tall and has large, fragrant flowers. It is marginally hardy, and is recommended for the protected urban environment.

My Personal Favorite

NAME	SPECIAL CHARACTERISTICS
'Edith Bogue'	Gold Medal winner from 1992 / compact variety / blooms in June and July / marginally hardy in the Tri-State urban area, but worth the effort

Fastigiate European Hornbeam

Carpinus betulus 'Fastigiata'

Preferred Zones	Sun Preferences	Additional Benefits
4 to 7		

Columnar, oval, pyramidal, upright, dense, perfectly symmetrical, usually fine-textured: all these words describe the 'Fastigiata' European Hornbeam, an ideal deciduous hardwood tree for the urban small-space garden. This tree is a candidate for planting as a bonsai, as a specimen in a container or aboveground planter, as an espalier, as a hedge, along a sidewalk, or as a street tree. Other advantages are its drought tolerance and the facts that it's not troubled by urban pollution and it grows in full sun to partial shade. All of these are important cultural characteristics when growing in today's urban environment. For centuries, this species of European Hornbeam has been planted in landscapes and used as screening. Its dark-green summer foliage is capped off with yellow to red in the fall. An alternate to C. b. 'Fastigiata' is 'Columnaris', which has a narrow, spire-like shape. Another "fastigiate" (which means it has upright, almost parallel branches tapering toward the top) plant for small-space gardens is the Upright English Oak, Quercus robur 'Fastigiata'. Grafted specimens are rigidly upright, making them ideal trees for confined corners.

Bloom Period and Color There are white flowers in spring, but they are not showy.

Mature Size 30 to 40 feet tall × 20 to 30 feet

When and How to Plant Balled-and-burlapped specimens are best planted in early spring, while container-grown specimens can be planted in spring or fall. Coiled roots often result in girdling roots as the tree becomes established. If you have purchased a rootbound container-grown plant, the coil of roots that has developed in the bottom of the container must be pulled like a bedspring-like coil and cut off. The fibrous roots on the outside of the rootball should be butterflied in order to spread them out into the backfill. Balled-and-burlapped and container-grown plants should be set no deeper than the depth of the root mass.

Sun and Soil Preferences Plant in full sun to partial shade in well-drained acid to alkaline soil. The roots will survive in almost any soil conditions, from dry and gravelly to wet.

Moisture Requirements Water thoroughly immediately after planting, and follow up the next day with an equally large drink of water; the second watering will make sure the rootball is thoroughly moistened. In confined areas, provide supplemental water during periods of drought, for the roots are unable to spread as they do in an open landscape.

Fertilizing Apply an organic or slow-release plant food for trees and shrubs annually, in spring as the soil warms.

Pruning and Care Pruning is seldom required; the tree is considered low-maintenance.

Pests and Diseases With the exception of Japanese beetle adults chewing on its foliage, the 'Fastigiate' European Hornbeam is usually pest-free.

Additional Species, Cultivars, or Varieties 'Columnaris', a slow-growing tree, is densely branched with a narrow upright growth habit; 'Pendula' grows with a weeping habit.

My Personal Favorite

NAME	SPECIAL CHARACTERISTICS
'Fastigiata'	Oval-vase shape / dark-green foliage changing to yellow in the fall

Flowering Callery Pear

Pyrus calleryana

Preferred Zones	Sun Preference	Additional Benefits
5 to 9		

You are probably familiar with the saying, "Don't put all your eggs in one basket." Well, this is particularly true when it comes to growing plants. Do we remember the death of the Elm trees that shaded every community's main street? Perhaps not, for in the Tri-State area during April and early May, all you see are streets lined with the magnificent white blossoms of the Pyrus calleryana Flowering Callery Pear. It's no wonder that the Callery Pear, a deciduous shade tree, has become the love of the community planner and shade-tree commissions. It's pest- and pollution-resistant, drought- and wet soil–tolerant, and compact. It is beautiful—but still, let's not plant too many of this one variety. We should try to remember the lesson of the Elms.

Bloom Period and Color White flowers bloom in late April to mid-May.

Mature Size 40 feet tall × 10 to 30 feet (by variety)

When and How to Plant Container-grown specimens must have their roots spread out into the backfill. Callery Pear and its many cultivars, available balled-and-burlapped, can be planted in early spring before budbreak or during late fall after leaf drop. It can be planted while dormant in late winter to early spring. Bare-root whips to 3 to 4 feet tall are available from mail-order suppliers.

Sun and Soil Preferences Site in full sun in almost any type of soil, from sand to clay. It tolerates a wide range of soil pH as long as the soil is well drained.

Moisture Requirements Newly planted Callery Pear trees need water for the first season after planting. In an urban street environment where little care is available, a 2- to 3-inch layer of organic mulch (such as pine bark mini-nuggets or bark chips) helps conserve precious moisture, particularly after the initial watering at planting time. With adequate moisture, the glossy-green foliage will turn to bright crimson at maturity in fall.

Fertilizing Apply a slow-release or organic plant food for flowering trees and shrubs each spring.

Pruning and Care Prune during late winter or early spring if needed.

Pests and Diseases Callery Pear is basically pest-free.

Additional Species, Cultivars, or Varieties The United States Plant Introduction Station introduced 'Capital', which has white flowers and a compact, narrow, upright crown; it is suitable for a small-space garden or narrow city street. Urban-tolerant 'Aristocrat', with its showy white blossoms and more open growth habit, is recommended for sidewalk cutouts, parking lot islands, containers, and aboveground planters.

My Personal Favorite

NAME	SPECIAL CHARACTERISTICS
'Redspire'	Pyramidal-shaped variety / grows to 30 to 35 feet / developed by Princeton Nursery, Princeton, New Jersey / blooms with even larger white flowers in larger clusters than those of *P. c.* 'Bradford'

Golden Biota
Platycladus orientalis 'Aurea'

Preferred Zones	Sun Preferences		Additional Benefit
5 to 9	☀	☽	🐝

" *Aurea, or "gilded," describes the golden tips of each branch and the overall appearance of this densely foliaged, evergreen landscape shrub. A Golden Biota that receives at least a half-day's sun, whether planted in front of a brownstone in Brooklyn, New York, or at the corner of a woodframe home in Hoboken, New Jersey, becomes a focal point or feature in the landscape. In a smaller-space garden, plant 'Aurea Nana', the dwarf which can be easily maintained at three feet or less with just a little pruning in early spring. After clipping, the new growth regenerates its golden tips. One can plant dwarf varieties in containers on a terrace or rooftop garden; just make sure there is good drainage. I once saw a row of oaken whiskey half-barrels planted with 'Aurea Nana' and used as a screen on a terrace garden in Manhattan. For colder zones (3a to 4b), a different species, Thuja occidentalis 'Emerald' Arborvitae with dark-green foliage, thrives in dappled shade. **Note**: If you have trouble finding Platycladus orientalis aurea, look for either Biota orientalis aurea or Thuja orientalis aurea, which are the older botanical names for the same plant.* "

Other Name Golden Oriental Arborvitae

Bloom Period and Color Flowers are not significant.

Mature Size To 5 feet tall × 4 feet

When and How to Plant Plant balled-and-burlapped or container-grown Biota in spring, summer, or fall, in a hole that is absolutely no deeper than the rootball and two to three times its width. Use unamended backfill. If in active growth, take care not to crack the soil rootball when handling the plant.

Sun and Soil Preferences Site in full sun to partial shade. Plant in moist but well-drained soil with an acidity range of 5.5 to 7.5 pH.

Moisture Requirements The key to growing success is watering-in for the first season. A decorative mulch of pine bark mini-nuggets, spread 2 to 3 inches deep, keeps the soil evenly moist and reduces drying. Deep-root watering is recommended in late fall or early winter, following periods of summer and fall drought.

Fertilizing Apply an organic plant food for evergreens during early spring, following the label directions.

Pruning and Care Pruning to shape Arborvitae should be performed in early spring before new growth starts. If drastic pruning is necessary, it must be completed before the end of March in the Tri-State area.

Pests and Diseases Watch for bagworms and spider mites. Apply *Bacillus thuringiensis (B.t.)* for bagworms and insecticidal soap for spider mites. Read the labels, as timing is crucial. In suburbia, Arborvitae can be a delicacy for hungry deer, particularly during late fall through spring. Apply a deer-repellent spray that works through both taste and aroma before the deer start to browse.

Additional Species, Cultivars, or Varieties 'Elegantissima', Gold-tipped Biota (Arborvitae), grows 25 feet tall and sports hardy green foliage tipped with gold in summer. *Thuja occidentalis* 'Nigra', Dark American Arborvitae, is one of the best of the taller Arborvitae; growing to 30 feet tall, it has dark-green, compact growth and shears well.

My Personal Favorite

NAME	SPECIAL CHARACTERISTICS
'Baker'	Bright green foliage / broad conical shape / grows to 8 feet tall / requires little or no shearing / ideal specimen plant for a small-space city garden or for hot, dry environments

Japanese Aucuba

Aucuba japonica

Preferred Zones	Sun Preference	Additional Benefits
6 to 10	☀	NA

To give a shady city or small-space garden an almost tropical look, plant Aucuba, with its three- to seven-inch-long and one and one-half- to three-inch-wide glossy, dark-green or variegated (green-and-white) leaves. This evergreen shrub is easy to grow, with just a little care. And when I say shady, I mean it. Aucuba detests direct sun. In Brooklyn, in a brownstone backyard that had full-sun exposure, I examined a three-foot-tall Aucuba with totally blackened leaves. It looked as if someone had put a torch to the foliage, and although it wasn't dead, it was badly burned. The owner had thought the taller buildings nearby would provide enough shade and protection for his backyard, but they didn't. Because the stems were still alive (bright green), we pinched off all the blackened leaves and transplanted the Aucuba to the shade of a little toolshed. Soon after, the owner called to let me know that the almost dead plant had been resurrected. It was alive once again with lush dark-green foliage

Other Name Green Aucuba

Bloom Period and Color In late spring, the male plant exhibits purple, upright, terminal, 2- to 4½-inch panicles; the female has purple blossoms in the axils of the leaves.

Mature Size 4 to 6 feet tall × 4 to 5 feet

When and How to Plant Plant in late spring to early summer. Four- to 5-inch-long cuttings may be taken for propagating more plants from the terminal shoots right after the new growth stops growing. Scratch the lower 2 inches of the stem to create a slight wound. Dip the wounded portion of the cutting in rooting hormone and place it in a container filled with slightly moist, sterile propagation mix. To create a greenhouse environment and speed the rooting process, set the container with the cutting into a clear plastic bag. Seal the bag, be patient, and you will have a new rooted Japanese Aucuba in just about thirty days. To produce the luxuriant large red berries on Japanese Aucuba, you must plant both male and female plants.

Sun and Soil Preferences Never expose the plant to prolonged direct sun, as the leaves will shrivel and blacken almost immediately. Plant container-grown or balled-and-burlapped stock in well-drained, moist soil, in the shade.

Moisture Requirements Provide even moisture all season long.

Fertilizing To stimulate foliage growth, feed with an organic plant food for foliage plants like 5-1-1 (fish emulsion) or an equivalent.

Pruning and Care Japanese Aucuba, a marginally hardy plant in the Tri-State area, benefits from pampering and a little protection, particularly in winter. Once a month, check for adequate soil moisture and put up a windscreen of burlap to reduce drying winter winds. Upon the arrival of spring, clip the tips of each stem to promote new growth from within the shrub.

Pests and Diseases There are generally no serious pest problems. Stem dieback should be pruned out immediately when observed.

Additional Species, Cultivars, or Varieties 'Variegata', the Gold-dust Tree, grows 6 feet tall by 6 feet wide.

My Personal Favorite

NAME	SPECIAL CHARACTERISTICS
Japanese Aucuba	A. *japonica*, the species / 3 to 8 inches long / leathery, lustrous, dark-green leaves

Japanese Maple

Acer palmatum

Preferred Zones	Sun Preference		Additional Benefits
5 to 9			

Every time I get into a conversation about Maples, my mind's eye automatically pictures a small, upright, outwardly-branching and layered look, or an umbrella-shaped tree with red leaves. This means I'm thinking of the Japanese Maple, Acer palmatum. The reason I think of this species is that I truly love this deciduous tree. Whether it be 'Bloodgood' (with spring foliage of bright red, changing to dark green by fall), 'Burgundy Lace' (with spring and fall red foliage changing to green during summer), or 'Dissectum' (the umbrella-shaped laceleaf), the Japanese Maple has a soft spot in my heart because it is essential in the small-space garden. Color and character are the two reasons for growing a Japanese Maple in the city or small-space garden. The green or red foliage and muscular look of the trunk and branches of the many cultivars make for a beautiful focal point when grown in a container or above-ground planter, near a deck or patio, or as a bonsai. The trees make ideal companions for gold-tipped Junipers and Biota, and a bed of green-and-white-leaved Hosta planted underneath the Maple enhances its character.

Bloom Period and Color Blooms are insignificant.

Mature Size 20 feet tall × 20 feet

When and How to Plant Balled-and-burlapped or container-grown trees are best planted in early spring, in a somewhat protected environment where there are no drying winds. When removing the rootball from a container, take care not to damage the roots: wet the soil before trying to slip the plant out of the pot, and the water will act as a lubricant. Never plant Japanese Maple any deeper than the depth of the rootball.

Sun and Soil Preferences The foliage of Japanese Maples often scorches during the summer from direct sun, so although it loves direct morning sunlight, position the plant in partial, afternoon shade. Plant in a well-prepared, organic, slightly acid soil.

Moisture Requirements Japanese Maples are one group of plants that cannot stand "wet feet" and should not be within the stream of an automatic sprinkler. Maintain a thin layer, 1 to 2 inches deep, of organic mulch over the root system to protect the shallow roots from cultivation.

Fertilizing Feed lightly in early spring with a slow-release or organic plant food for trees and shrubs.

Pruning and Care To continue the shape of a well-formed Japanese Maple canopy, prune to develop strong, well-structured branches with wide angles of attachment to the main trunk.

Pests and Diseases Japanese Maple has surprisingly few pest problems. Once in a while, spring canker worms will munch on the foliage, and adult Japanese beetles may eat a leaf or two.

Additional Species, Cultivars, or Varieties If there's room in your small-space garden, create a Maple collection. In addition to A. *palmatum*, plant A. *griseum* (Paperbark Maple), which grows to 30 feet tall and 25 feet wide and has maturing bark that becomes darkened and cinnamon-colored and peeling; and A. *japonicum* (Fullmoon Maple), a very dense, symmetrical tree that grows to 15 feet tall by 10 feet wide and has soft-green foliage that changes to bright red in fall.

My Personal Favorite

NAME	SPECIAL CHARACTERISTICS
'Bloodgood'	Spring foliage is bright red / foliage changes to dark green by fall

Japanese Wisteria

Wisteria floribunda

Preferred Zones	Sun Preferences	Additional Benefits
5 to 9		

Wisteria, with its dense, pendulous racemes of white, pink, or violet-blue flowers, which grow to 18 inches long depending on the species or cultivar, is a plant with no equal. It's not unusual to find this deciduous climbing vine cascading over an arbor shading a patio, trained to a trellis or front door entryway, or as a feature in the landscape growing as a free-standing "tree." I've seen many Wisteria, some as old as 75 years, with twining trunks eight to ten inches in diameter. One vine seems to wrap around the next, and the next, and so on, all in a clockwise direction. When we purchased our home we inherited a Wisteria that had been planted years earlier near a giant Oak and had become quite aggressive over the years. The Wisteria had used the tree as its trellis, climbing ever upward, until it was blooming high in the branches overhead. After seeing the Wisteria bloom in spring, we cut out the vine, including its roots. The weight of the vine had caused some tree branches to break, and the vine had started to choke several large limbs on the Oak.

Bloom Period and Color White, pink, and violet to violet-blue blossoms appear in spring.

Mature Size Unlimited if left unpruned

When and How to Plant Japanese Wisteria is planted from cuttings to ensure bloom at an early age. Seed-propagated Japanese Wisteria may take thirty or more years to flower! Plant dormant bare-root cuttings in early spring. When grown in containers, Japanese Wisteria develops a root mass of tangled, girdling roots very quickly. Container-grown plants may be planted in spring or fall but must have their roots spread out into the backfill.

Sun and Soil Preferences Plant in full sun to partial shade, in a moist but well-drained soil. Japanese Wisteria grows in a wide range of soil types and is not particular about soil pH.

Moisture Requirements Keep evenly moist, particularly as the roots are becoming established.

Fertilizing Japanese Wisteria does not appreciate extra nutrition.

Pruning and Care This tough drought-tolerant climber insists on being pruned right after flowering and again in late winter. If left unpruned, you might find your Japanese Wisteria clinging from the neighbor's trees. To grow Japanese Wisteria in "tree" form, attach the trunk to a 5- to 6-foot heavy cedar stake, trim away all but the topmost branches, and clip back the top branches as needed to keep the plant bushy and in bounds. When pruning in late winter, always leave six to eight nodes of last year's growth on each branch, as these nodes contain the flowering mechanisms for the coming spring.

Pests and Diseases Japanese Wisteria may have assorted pests, from mealybugs and vine weevil to powdery mildew and stem canker. Contact your county cooperative extension educator for control of these pests.

Additional Species, Cultivars, or Varieties 'Rosea' produces fragrant 15- to 18-inch-long rose-pink racemes of blossoms. 'Royal Purple' flowers in bright violet-purple racemes. 'Plena' produces fragrant, double, blue racemes of flowers with no seedpods. *W. sinensis* Chinese Wisteria, the most popular form, produces bluish-violet flowers on 1-foot-long racemes before the foliage emerges in spring; it twines in the counterclockwise direction.

My Personal Favorite

NAME	SPECIAL CHARACTERISTICS
'Alba'	Produces magnificent, pure-white, 18-inch-long racemes of densely packed flowers

London Plane

Platanus × acerifolia

Preferred Zones	Sun Preference	Additional Benefits
5 to 9	☀	

A relative of London Plane, Platanus occidentalis, *our native Sycamore, was planted for decades as a street tree in the Tri-State area. The strong-structured canopy and resistance to limb breakage made the ideal shade tree. You can still find them—they are the giants growing along Riverside Drive in Manhattan—but there has been a problem: heavy infections of anthracnose disease, particularly during wet, cool springs. Anthracnose results in complete defoliation (leaf drop) by early summer, causing the tree to resemble autumn in June. By mid-June the giant leaves have shriveled up like crumpled crepe paper, littering the sidewalks and streets wherever Sycamores grow. Luckily,* Platanus × acerifolia *London Plane Tree is resistant to anthracnose. It is a recommended replacement for the Sycamore, with cultivars like 'Bloodgood', 'Columbia', and 'Liberty'. Don't forget to notice this deciduous shade tree's bark in winter: cream, olive, and light brown weathering to gray.* Platanus *is an ancient plant, as fossils indicate the tree has been around as part of Earth's flora for at least 100,000,000 years.*

Other Name London Plane Tree

Bloom Period and Color Blooms are not showy.

Mature Size 50 to 60 feet tall × 50 feet

When and How to Plant Plant in spring, summer, or fall as long as water is available to water the tree throughout the first growing season. Plant a balled-and-burlapped London Plane Tree in an extra-wide planting hole (three to four times the width of the rootball) that has been prepared to a depth only as deep as the rootball. The extra width allows for better root development for the shallow root system. Use unamended backfill.

Sun and Soil Preferences Plant in full sun. London Plane will grow in almost any soil, tolerating a wide pH range.

Moisture Requirements Water thoroughly at planting time and continue watering throughout the first year.

Fertilizing Apply an organic or slow-release plant food for trees annually, following label directions.

Pruning and Care London Plane Tree requires little pruning, but if it's needed, prune when dormant to avoid bleeding.

Pests and Diseases Although the tree is resistant to anthracnose, powdery mildew may show on the foliage. Check with your cooperative extension educator for a recommended fungicide for control.

Additional Species, Cultivars, or Varieties *P.* × *acerifolia*, a result of a cross between *P. orientalis* × *P. occidentalis*, is sometimes listed only as *Hybrida*—London Plane. The cultivars should be chosen with care. 'Bloodgood' is resistant to anthracnose but highly susceptible to mildew; 'Yarwood' is resistant to mildew but susceptible to anthracnose. 'Columbia' and 'Liberty' are most resistant to powdery mildew and eastern strains of anthracnose.

My Personal Favorite

NAME	SPECIAL CHARACTERISTICS
'Columbia'	Resistant to powdery mildew and Eastern strains of anthracnose

Mimosa

Albizia julibrissin

Preferred Zones	Sun Preferences	Additional Benefit
6 to 9	☀ ◑	△

Many new homes in Tri-State suburbia that were built during the 1950s and '60s were blessed with a Mimosa as a first deciduous flowering tree. The fragrant silky flowers, two-inch powder puffs of pink, bloom from late April to July. Many folks planted Mimosa by the patio because they loved the fragrance, the filtered shade, and the fact that Mimosa has very small, thumbnail-sized leaves. These leaves, not much larger than 1/2 inch, made fall cleanup a breeze. The leaves seemed to disappear or they just blew away. Other new homeowners planted Mimosa as a feature in the front yard. Although it is slow to leaf out in spring, often as late as early June, it's definitely worth the wait. The species Albizia julibrissin is susceptible to fusarium wilt, a vascular disease that kills the tree. Don't despair . . . new wilt-resistant varieties are now available, such as A. julibrissin 'Charlotte', 'Tyron', and 'Union'.

Bloom Period and Color Light- to dark-pink flowers bloom in May, June, July, and August.

Mature Size 20 feet tall × 35 feet

When and How to Plant In the Tri-State area, plant Mimosa only in early spring. If possible, select a location that is somewhat protected from northern cold winter winds. Start with a small plant, as the root system tends to branch out from the base of the tree with only three or four large, fleshy roots. For speedy establishment, incorporate well-rotted compost or leaf mold into the soil around the planting hole. The new roots will find the loosened soil an ideal environment for growth. Set the plant at the same level it was in the container, no deeper.

Sun and Soil Preferences Site in full sun to dappled shade. Plant in average garden soil, which may even be high in pH or salinity.

Moisture Requirements Provide even moisture for establishing a newly planted specimen. Once established, Mimosa withstands drought.

Fertilizing Apply a plant food for flowering trees and shrubs according to the label directions.

Pruning and Care The large, fleshy roots can become a problem as they spread out if they are allowed to grow under a sidewalk or patio surface. Their size and strength make it possible for them to lift a concrete slab. Root-pruning will help, but it needs to be repeated frequently. In turf or landscape areas, the surface roots can be camouflaged by planting over with Pachysandra or Vinca as a ground cover. Pruning to encourage upright growth increases strength in the trunk and lateral branches; storm and ice damage may occur on poorly branched trees. Fall cleanup from this tree is no problem—the thumbnail-sized leaves seem to blow away with the first breeze.

Pests and Diseases Mimosa is susceptible to fusarium wilt disease. Plant resistant varieties.

Additional Species, Cultivars, or Varieties 'Charlotte', 'Tyron', and 'Union' are reportedly wilt-resistant varieties; they are difficult to find, but definitely worth the effort.

My Personal Favorite

NAME	SPECIAL CHARACTERISTICS
Mimosa	A. *julibrissin*, the species / take a chance on the "wilt" and plant—the bloom is worth the risk

Silver Lace Vine

Polygonum aubertii

Preferred Zones	Sun Preferences	Additional Benefit
4 to 9	☼ ☼	

Silver Lace Vine is experienced by city gardeners as a vine with rampant growth. With a little support, Silver Lace Vine can cover a twenty-foot area in one season. The fragrance of the white panicles of lace-like blooms is a real treat from midsummer to early fall. The root system produces underground stems (rhizomes) that can sprout in some of the darndest places. I saw Silver Lace Vine in a backyard in Manhattan—planted on the western side of a slate patio set in sand, it came up in the middle of the patio between the slates and, shortly thereafter, on the eastern side. Silver Lace Vine drops its foliage after the first hard frost, but don't cut down the vines. They will leaf out the following spring. This deciduous vine will succeed where many other vines have failed.
Note: *Silver Lace Vine has a pesky relative which grows annually in most gardens, Prostrate Knotweed P. aviculare. It thrives in compact, infertile soils along dirt paths and in driveway cracks, and is often found near the batter's box on a Little League baseball field.*

Other Name Fleece Vine

Bloom Period and Color Greenish-white, infrequently pinkish, fragrant panicles bloom midsummer to early fall.

Mature Size Unlimited if left unpruned

When and How to Plant Plant bare-root rhizomes, which are available from mail-order nurseries, in spring. Container-grown plants in active growth can be planted at any time as long as water is available to water-in the plants. In both cases, the soil should be prepared with generous amounts of well-rotted compost or milled sphagnum peat moss—the addition of the organic matter makes for an ideal bed for underground root and rhizome growth. The plants will multiply underground by rhizomes; if you have a neighbor who grows Silver Lace Vine, ask him or her to lift a start for you in early spring.

Sun and Soil Preferences Grow this vine in sun or partial shade. As the fastest growing vine, it is plantable in almost any type of soil once the soil has warmed.

Moisture Requirements Provide plenty of water, particularly during dry periods. Especially in containers—you must remember to water.

Fertilizing Feed according to label directions with a balanced plant food for flowering plants.

Pruning and Care Prune aggressively-growing Silver Lace Vines at any time to encourage branching so they may be trained onto a trellis, fence, arbor, or other non-solid surface. As spring arrives, prune back the winter-killed vine to resurrect the plant.

Pests and Diseases If you have Japanese beetles, inoculate the soil with milky spore disease according to the label directions.

My Personal Favorite

NAME	SPECIAL CHARACTERISTICS
Silver Lace Vine	*P. aubertii*, the species / blooms from midsummer to early fall

Yew

Taxus × media

Preferred Zones	Sun Preferences	Additional Benefits
4 to 7		

Other than the ubiquitous Juniper, the number-one plant species in the Tri-State landscape is Taxus, commonly called Taxus Yew. It comes in species that grow prostrate, upright, and spreading. Taxus × media and its many cultivars provide the city or small-space gardener with an unlimited supply of plants. This shrub is popular because it has species that will grow in sun or shade and will also put up with air pollution. It is rated as the highest-quality needled evergreen in the landscape—characteristics include good rate of growth, resistance to disease and some insects, excellent year-round color, compact-to-loose growth habit, winter hardiness, and ease of planting. This is real quality. The only planting restriction is that you must check the drainage. Yews absolutely cannot have wet feet: prepare a soil that drains well.

Other Name Anglojapanese Yew

Bloom Period and Color Flowers are insignificant; there are red fruits (berries) in fall. **Caution:** Seeds and foliage are poisonous.

Mature Size 2 to 20 feet tall × 3 to 20 feet

When and How to Plant Plant any time of the year except when the ground is frozen. For rooftop and patio gardens, position the container so the plant is out of winter's wind. The planting soil for container culture should be a mixture of sand, potting soil, and well-rotted compost or milled sphagnum peat moss, in a 1:1:1 ratio.

Sun and Soil Preferences Plant container-grown or balled-and-burlapped Taxus in any soil but a wet soil, in full sun to shade. The plants adjust well to container culture if planted in a well-drained potting mix in a large container with a drainage hole.

Moisture Requirements Water as needed—approximately 1 inch per week including rain will do.

Fertilizing Feed annually with a slow-release plant food formulated for evergreens, following the label directions.

Pruning and Care To even up a scraggly plant, clip the growing tips of each stem as new grow begins. Taxus can be sheared into almost any shape, including poodle cut, twisted cone, a flat wall of green, and pyramid. If you have an overgrown Taxus, don't pull it out. Try drastic pruning instead. Drastic pruning is performed only in March in the Tri-State area.

Pests and Diseases To control the taxus weevil, whose damage is manifested by chewed leaflets (notched around the edges), apply beneficial nematodes to the soil according to label directions.

Additional Species, Cultivars, or Varieties Anglojapanese Yew is a hybrid of *T. baccata* and *T. cuspidata*; it has rather tight, intermediate growth and many varieties, including 'Everlow', a male clone with no fruits that grows wide and low; and 'Hatfield', which has a broadly upright to pyramidal habit, growing 10 feet or more.

My Personal Favorite

NAME	SPECIAL CHARACTERISTICS
'Hicksii'	An upright female selection that becomes broad with age / originated in Hicks Nurseries, Westbury, Long Island, New York

Young's Weeping Birch

Betula pendula 'Youngii'

Preferred Zones	Sun Preference		Additional Benefits
3 to 8	☀		🐝 🪺 🦋

"*A true weeper with slender, very pendulous branches, 'Youngii' is a classic in the small-space garden. I've seen many Weeping Birches in large wooden containers on rooftop patios, all growing with great success. Yes, it is likely the tree will eventually become too large for its home, but until that happens, just root-prune it in late winter to keep it more easily confined. Root-pruning at this time will diminish spring growth by diminishing stored food in the roots from last year's growth—this reduction in food supply will ensure dwarfed growth. The Weeping Birch's dark-green summer foliage turns a showy yellow in fall, quite lovely when backdropped by a brick wall or evergreen hedge. In winter, the white bark and weeping character become outstanding features. If you lack room for the weeper, consider B. p. 'Fastigiata', which is an upright grower . . . although its bark is not as attractive in winter as is the bark of 'Youngii'.*"

Bloom Period and Color Brown catkins, 1 to 3 inches long, in spring.

Mature Size 30 to 45 feet tall × 20 to 35 feet

When and How to Plant Bare-root transplants are available for planting only in early spring. Container or balled-and-burlapped plants may be planted at any time during the growing season, but for best results (for maximum rooting time for the first growing season) they should be planted in spring. The planting hole should drain well and be no deeper than the rootball. Use unamended backfill.

Sun and Soil Preferences Plant in full sun. Soil preparation goes a long way in making Young's Weeping Birch happy in a small-space garden. Adding well-rotted compost or milled sphagnum peat moss is not recommended, but spade organic matter into the adjacent soil outside the planting hole.

Moisture Requirements Organic matter spaded into adjacent soil will retain moisture and loosen the soil, allowing easier spreading of the shallow roots. To ensure success, it must be planted and watered-in before budbreak. Maintain organic-type mulch over the spreading roots, and expand the mulched area each year to eliminate weeds and grass from under the graceful canopy. The shallow, spreading root system must be protected from cultivation damage. Water total should equal 1 inch per week including rain. Provide supplemental irrigation during the growing season.

Fertilizing Feed with a slow-release or organic plant food for trees and shrubs each spring as the soil warms.

Pruning and Care To avoid excessive bleeding of sap, do not prune from February through July.

Pests and Diseases B. pendula and its cultivars, including 'Youngii', are susceptible to serious damage from the bronze birch borer; consequently, they are often short-lived. For the latest in controls, contact your county cooperative extension educator, a Master Gardener, or a professional arborist.

Additional Species, Cultivars, or Varieties Other considerations are 'Tristis', with a single leader weeping habit looking like a mop; 'Dalecarlica', with deeply lobed, lacy leaves on pendulous branches; and 'Fastigiata', with its upright growth habit. B. populifolia, Grey Birch, grows to 30 feet and thrives in a seaside location. B. platyphylla japonica 'Whitespire', Whitespire Birch, is one of the most pest-resistant of all Birches and grows to 50 feet tall.

My Personal Favorite

NAME	SPECIAL CHARACTERISTICS
Young's Weeping Birch	Slender and perfectly pendulous branches

Ground Covers *for the Tri-State*

Are you tired of planting grass under the Maple tree, only to have it germinate and die soon after sprouting? Have you had a hard time mowing the grass on the slope near the street? Are you disappointed with the brown mulch along the walkway? The solution to some of the most difficult planting conditions is to establish a living ground cover and then let it be. There are evergreen, deciduous, and herbaceous ground covers, some with flowers, for sun, for shade, and for wet or dry.

A Wealth of Ground Covers

Imagine a bed of pink, red, or white flowers springing up from a lush green mat creeping along the base of the stone wall where it's impossible to mow. Creeping Phlox will do the job.

Under the Maple tree, where not even weeds seem to grow, plant an evergreen ground cover. Pachysandra or Vinca make an attractive green bed within just two years of planting. Once the plants become established, there is little maintenance to worry about, other than raking off fallen leaves.

For that sunny sand dune that seems to shift with the winter winds, plant a ground cover that spreads and stays low to the ground. Shore Juniper is the answer. It loves the sun and dry soil, and it tolerates salt spray.

In that damp, shady patch next to the water garden, plant Ajuga. The evergreen, purple foliage and white, blue, or rose-pink flowers do not mind the dampness.

To create that natural look along a woodland path, or for something on the shady side of the house, plant a bed of Lady Fern.

Avoid Common Ground Cover Mistakes

The ground covers in this chapter are selected for ease of growing and maintaining. The biggest mistake made when planting a ground cover is the tendency to spread plants too far apart in an effort to save money. Don't be penny-wise and pound-foolish. If the suggested spacing is the span-of-a-hand (which is the recommended spacing when planting a bed of Pachysandra), it does not mean twelve inches apart. Stretching the spacing between the plants

increases the time (which could be measured in years) for growing into a solid bed. This additional spacing and time for filling in leads to another problem, and that is weeds. Most ground covers, if planted properly, will form a solid mat that can compete with weeds.

The other mistake in planting a ground cover is allowing weeds to become established. Make every effort to start with a weed-free bed for planting. Either strip away all vegetation, or kill off all existing grasses and broadleaf weeds with a herbicide. BurnOut® (made of lemon juice and vinegar) or Safer's Superfast® weed- and grass-killer (a formula based on a potassium fatty acid) are two organic post-emergent weed- and grass-killers that are safe for the environment as long as the label directions are followed. For established ground cover beds, either handpull weeds as they emerge, or apply a chemical pre-emergent weed control such as eptam, sold under the trade name Preen for Ground Covers®. Read and follow label directions, as this product must be applied before weed seeds germinate and it must be watered into the soil. Set up a sprinkler and water until the total volume of water needed is delivered. A rain gauge, set in the sprinkler pattern, is a handy tool for determining delivery of the required water to the ground cover bed. Do not depend on Mother Nature to water-in a pre-emergent, chemical weed control. It may rain, but not enough to dissolve the chemical and carry it into the soil where the weed seeds are lurking.

Blue Fescue
Festuca ovina

Preferred Zones	Sun Preferences	Additional Benefits
4 to 8	☀ ☽	NA

*One of the neatest plants I've ever grown is the Blue Fescue, a rounded mound, almost derby hat–like, in a blue-gray color. This is an evergreen ornamental grass that doubles as a ground cover, and it thrives in the Tri-State area. I planted a bed three plants wide on a staggered basis, eighteen inches apart, along the eastern edge of my water garden. In two years I had a solid bed of rolling mounds that reminded me of puffy cumulus clouds. As a specimen plant next to a large boulder in a rock garden, the wispiness of the foliage of Blue Fescue is quite an eye-catcher. This grassy-looking ground cover has a soft, airy, almost iridescent look when highlighted at night with low-voltage garden path lights. (In fact, night lighting does wonders for a great many plants, particularly those with blue-gray colors like Blue Rug Juniper and the Italian Blue Pine.) **Note:** The word glauca, from the Latin, when found in a plant name description refers to a color combination formed by shades of blue and green.*

Other Names *F. glauca* / *F. cinerea* / *F. arvernensis* / *F. caesia* / Blue Sheep's Fescue / Gray Fescue

Bloom Period and Color Beige or tan spikes are present from late June through early fall; foliage color is blue-gray to blue-green from mid-May to frost in fall.

Mature Height × Spread 16 inches × 8 to 10 inches

When and How to Plant Nursery-grown container plants may be planted at any time as long as water is available. Plant clumps, or divisions, of Blue Fescue 12 to 15 inches apart and no deeper than the soil mass on the roots. For consistency in color and growth habit, propagate by division in early spring or fall.

Sun and Soil Preference Site in full sun to partial shade; the soil should be well-drained. In sandy soil, spading in a 2- to 3-inch layer of compost or milled sphagnum peat moss to a depth of 10 to 12 inches will ensure adequate moisture even during drought conditions.

Moisture Requirements Once established, Blue Fescue is generally drought-tolerant.

Fertilizing To promote slow, even growth, feed each spring with slow-release organic plant food according to the label directions.

Pruning and Care In early spring, clip back all Blue Fescue to 3 inches high with a hedge clipper. After two to three years, it may be necessary to divide and transplant each clump by removing the dead or dying center plant and replacing it with the newer plants from the perimeter.

Pests and Diseases Blue Fescue has no significant pest problems.

Additional Species, Cultivars, or Varieties There are many varieties of Blue Fescue, for the most part differing only in height and shade of blue. 'Tom Thumb', 4 to 5 inches tall, turns green during the heat of summer and should be spaced 6 to 8 inches. 'Azure Blue' grows 12 to 16 inches. 'Blue Finch', with a soft-blue, fine-textured foliage, grows 8 to 10 inches tall.

My Personal Favorite

NAME	SPECIAL CHARACTERISTICS
'Elijah's Blue'	8 to 10 inches tall

Bugleweed

Ajuga reptans

Preferred Zones	Sun Preference		Additional Benefit
4 to 9	☀		🐝

With all of the new home construction in the Tri-State area comes one question, particularly now that builders have learned that trees, large ones in particular, add value to a home. The question: What is a fast-growing ground cover that will put up with shade? The answer: Bugleweed Ajuga reptans and its many cultivars. I often recommend the semi-evergreen species, which has dark-green leaves and blue flower spikes in spring. This is a particularly attractive plant when planted en masse at a woodland edge where morning sunshine reaches the ground, or under a Flowering Dogwood or a Weeping Flowering Cherry. Bugleweed is herbaceous to semi-evergreen. During springtime bloom, the bed may be abuzz with the hum of bumblebees. The only downside to growing this plant is its tendency to become aggressive, creeping out into the lawn. For gardens or landscape plantings where spreading is undesirable, you may instead plant Ajuga genevensis, a non-stoloniferous species that is easier to contain than A. r. **Note:** Herbalists have recommended and used the foliage from A. reptans for all sorts of ailments. It is said to produce a mild narcotic effect; check with your herbalist for its many uses.

Other Names Ajuga / Bugleflower / Creeping Carpet Bugle

Bloom Period and Color Blue, white, or rose-pink flower spikes appear mid-spring.

Mature Height × Spread 6 inches (unlimited spread)

When and How to Plant Bugleweed is available from early spring to late fall as rooted plantlets in nursery flats (as many as 25 to 30 plantlets per flat) or as individual plants in 2½- to 3-inch peat pots. Set plants a "span-of-the-hand" apart. If you are new to that term, stretch out your hand and plant one transplant at the tip of your little finger and one at the tip of your thumb. To transplant from an existing Bugleweed bed, lift individual plants in spring or early fall.

Sun and Soil Preference Bugleweed prefers partial shade and a well-drained, organically rich but well-aerated soil with an acidic pH. I know some gardeners recommend Bugleweed for full-sun environments, but I have found that it burns up, particularly during droughts with excessive heat.

Moisture Requirements Water the bed immediately after planting.

Fertilizing Bugleweed does not need excessive nutrition. Apply an organic fertilizer to provide a slow-release source of nutrients, once, in early spring.

Pruning and Care Bugleweed requires little care if planted in well-prepared soil. To alleviate conditions that cause fungus, make sure the soil is well aerated and organically rich, and divide the plants every four to five years in early spring just as new growth starts.

Pests and Diseases In poor, overly wet soil, crown rot, which is caused by a devastatingly fast-growing fungus, can wipe out a Bugleweed bed in just a few days. Improve air circulation by thinning overgrown beds.

Additional Species, Cultivars, or Varieties 'Alba' produces green foliage with white blossoms; 'Atropurpurea' has bronze-purple foliage; 'Giant Green' has large, metallic-bronze foliage; 'Variegata' has foliage of gray-green edged with splashes of cream.

My Personal Favorite

NAME	SPECIAL CHARACTERISTICS
Common Bugleweed	A. reptans, the species / 3- to 4-inch-long, medium glossy semi-evergreen leaves that form a rosette / 4- to 6-inch-tall flower spikes / masses of long-lasting bluish-violet flowers

Common Periwinkle
Vinca minor

Preferred Zones	Sun Preferences	Additional Benefits
4 to 9	◐ ☀	NA

" I have a question for you: What has pink, white, or blue flowers and shiny dark-green leaves, and thrives in shade under a Maple tree, Flowering Dogwood, or Weeping Cherry? It's the evergreen, carpetlike Vinca minor, a ground cover that curtains the roots of the aforementioned trees so you don't trip over those roots when you mow the grass. In fact, if you plant Vinca minor (Common Periwinkle), you won't have to mow under the trees ever again. Common Periwinkle, also called Vinca, grows into a solid bed of dark-green leaves with enough density to keep out the weeds. I've planted it on a shady slope near my fern collection and underneath tall, white-flowering Rhododendrons. The only drawback to Common Periwinkle is that it can't take foot traffic; if you must traverse an established bed, inlay slate steppingstones. The slate will look classy against the dark green of the Common Periwinkle. "

Other Name Myrtle

Bloom Period and Color Lilac-blue flowers, and other colors depending on variety, bloom April to early May.

Mature Height × Spread 6 to 8 inches (unlimited spread)

When and How to Plant *Vinca minor,* one of the easiest ground covers to establish, is available most economically by mail order in spring as tied or banded (ten to twenty stems each) bare-root cuttings. It is available from nurseries and garden centers in flats of twenty-five to fifty rooted clumps per flat. Rake the bed to remove debris, including rocks. Put on kneepads, kneel down, and plant Common Periwinkle clumps 8 inches on center on a staggered basis. The individual clumps in a flat are separated for planting—do not pull apart an individual clump in an attempt to make the Common Periwinkle go further. To cover 100 square feet (a 10x10-foot area) with a solid bed, you will require 196 clumps and two growing seasons.

Sun and Soil Preference Plant in partial to full shade. Common Periwinkle prefers a moist but well-drained, slightly acid soil. Incorporate 2 to 3 inches of well-rotted compost and an organic fertilizer in the soil as deeply as possible. You'll probably hit many roots, but don't worry about that.

Moisture Requirements Water immediately after planting, and then water as needed to keep the bed slightly moist but not wet. Drought-stressed Common Periwinkle appreciates an occasional watering.

Fertilizing Apply a slow-release fertilizer in early spring at the rate recommended for perennials.

Pruning and Care The nemesis of any ground cover bed is weeds. Apply a pre-emergent weed control for ground covers according to label directions after weeds have been eliminated. Once Common Periwinkle has become a solid bed, little or no care is required other than raking off fallen leaves.

Pests and Diseases Common Periwinkle has no appreciable insect or disease problems.

Additional Species, Cultivars, or Varieties Select from 'Alba', pure white flowers; 'Atropurpurea', deep-purple flowers; and 'Jekyll's White', white flowers. *Vinca major* Big Periwinkle has 1½- to 2-inch, light-blue flowers that bloom in early spring in a bed of evergreen foliage.

My Personal Favorite

NAME	SPECIAL CHARACTERISTICS
'Bowles'	Lavender-blue flowers

Creeping Juniper
Juniperus horizontalis

Preferred Zones	Sun Preference	Additional Benefit
3 to 9	☀	✦

" *Visit any garden center or nursery in the Tri-State area, from Atlantic City, New Jersey; to Buffalo, New York; to Torrington, Connecticut, at any time of the year that plants are sold, and you will find rows of nursery cans (from one-quart to five-gallon) filled with evergreen Creeping Junipers. The varieties are almost limitless, as Junipers are among the most cold-hardy plants and will grow almost anywhere. As they grow, the branches creep across the soil surface, creating a mat of green, blue, steel-blue, purple, or variegated color, green-and-white or -gold. When I say they grow almost anywhere, I mean in the heat, in full sun, in dry, sandy soil, and even along the shore where there is salty spray. Plant Creeping Junipers along a sunny walkway, let them cascade over a sunny rock retaining wall, or plant them instead of turfgrass to cover a large sunny slope. The only condition they don't like is shade. There are multitudes of cultivars available, in colors like blue-green, bright green, grayish-green, and silver-green. Some Creeping Junipers remain the same color through winter, and some turn plum-purple to purplish-green, complementing almost any landscape planting.* "

Other Name Groundcover Juniper

Bloom Period and Color There are no blooms.

Mature Height × **Spread** 4 to 6 inches × 3 to 5 feet (or more, depending on age)

When and How to Plant Container-grown plants are available early spring to late fall. Their roots may be a solid mass of fibrous material. To establish, butterfly the roots by slicing the mass on three or four sides from top to bottom. Pull on the cut roots and spread them into the backfill as the hole is filled. Larger specimens are available balled and burlapped. Plant spacing varies from 3 to 4 feet on center, depending on the cultivar.

Sun and Soil Preference The one absolute requirement for successfully growing Creeping Juniper is full sunlight. All cultivars adapt very well to a wide range of soils with acid or alkaline pH.

Moisture Requirements Water immediately after planting. This plant is recommended for the xeriscape garden.

Fertilizing Apply a slow-release organic plant food annually in early spring.

Pruning and Care To foil weeds, install a barrier of landscape fabric before the weeds invade, and cover it with a pine-bark or wood-chip mulch. Other than that, there is little maintenance required. Pruning is needed only if Creeping Juniper begins to grow in an undesirable direction.

Pests and Diseases When planted in full sunlight, Creeping Juniper is far less susceptible to tip blight. Signs of tip blight include browning and dieback of tips. Watch for spider mites during excessively hot days in summer.

Additional Species, Cultivars, or Varieties 'Plumosa Compacta' Andorra Compact Juniper, is 18 to 24 inches high and has plum-purple foliage during winter. 'Wiltoni' Blue Rug Juniper is 4 to 6 inches high. 'Prince of Wales', 6 inches high, displays a uniform, starburst pattern. *Juniperus conferta* 'Blue Pacific' Shore Juniper, 9 to 12 inches high, has ocean blue–green foliage. *J. procumbens* 'Nana' Japanese Garden Juniper creates a mound of soft green 18 to 24 inches high as it spreads. **Note:** The word *procumbens* refers to the procumbent, horizontal-spreading growth habit.

My Personal Favorite

NAME	SPECIAL CHARACTERISTICS
'Bar Harbor'	Excellent landscape qualities / to 10 inches tall with spread of 6 feet or more / steel blue, turning purplish blue in fall

Creeping Phlox
Phlox subulata

Preferred Zones	Sun Preference		Additional Benefit
3 to 9	☼		Ⓝ

Just down the street from where I live, a resident with large rock outcrops (actually giant boulders) has installed Creeping Phlox as a ground cover instead of the traditional grass lawn. Every April into May, this ground cover is a solid mat of bright-pink flowers. When out of bloom, it looks like a bed of moss with upward-pointing foliage. The reason this homeowner planted Creeping Phlox in place of Kentucky Bluegrass is that there is a scarcity of soil between the giant boulders—where there's a lack of soil, Creeping Phlox will survive much better than a grass. Other uses for Creeping Phlox: Plant it along stone walkways, or make it a feature along a fieldstone wall. One plant can stand alone as a feature in a rock garden or several plants can be grouped to provide a complete evergreen cover. To enjoy a splash of early springtime cascading color in large containers on the patio or from a windowbox, dig clumps of Creeping Phlox from the garden as soon as the soil is workable, enjoy the bloom, then transplant them back into the garden after bloom.

Other Names Moss Pink / Thrift

Bloom Period and Color Blue, pink, red, reddish-purple, bicolor, or white flowers bloom early to mid-spring.

Mature Height × Spread 3 to 6 inches × 2 or more feet

When and How to Plant Creeping Phlox, available at most garden centers in spring and early summer, can be successfully planted up to mid-summer, even when in bloom. If you are setting out transplants purchased from perennial growers, be sure to remove the "plantable" pot—the pressed-paper or pressed-peat plantable pots will not decay fast enough to allow the roots to spread into the soil. Plant clumps of Creeping Phlox 12 to 15 inches apart in well-drained soil.

Sun and Soil Preference Plant in direct, full sun in well-drained soil. This early-spring-blooming ground cover thrives in hot, dry locations, making it an attractive candidate for the sandy beach property.

Moisture Requirements Water well after planting, and provide water during extreme drought.

Fertilizing Don't feed.

Pruning and Care Immediately after flowering, use hedge shears to clip back the stems by half to encourage compact growth for the next year's spring bloom. Clippings taken at pruning time can be propagated in moist, coarse sand, and in just a few weeks you'll have tons of plants to give to friends. After three to five years, divide clumps after flowering to produce strong, new plants.

Pests and Diseases Creeping Phlox is virtually bug- and disease-free.

Additional Species, Cultivars, or Varieties For springtime color in your garden, select from 'Alexander's Pink' (pink), 'Blue Emerald' (blue), 'Red Wings' (crimson-red flowers with dark-red centers), or 'Scarlet Flame' (bright-scarlet flowers). *P. s.* var. *atropurpurea* creates a carpet with purple flowers.

My Personal Favorite

NAME	SPECIAL CHARACTERISTICS
'Alba'	White flowers

Creeping Wintergreen

Gaultheria procumbens

Preferred Zones	Sun Preferences	Additional Benefits
3 to 7	☼ ☀	

> *Possibly pollinated by ants, Creeping Wintergreen's pinkish-white, nodding, urn-shaped flowers appear early to mid-spring. Bright, edible, scarlet-red fruits to one-and-a-half inches in diameter nestled among leathery, dark-green, elliptical, two-inch-long leaves on a ground cover standing no more than five inches tall—this is the picture of Creeping Wintergreen from midsummer through winter. The shiny dark-green leaves take on attractive tones of purple in fall. Native to the eastern forests of the Tri-State region, Creeping Wintergreen loves the richness of the soil of the forest floor. Not more than twenty-five feet from my back door is a bed of Creeping Wintergreen combined with Prince's Pine. Together they create the look of a beautiful evergreen woodland carpet, which has spread no more than five feet in twenty years. **Note:** Wintergreen, harvested in the fall at the time the leaves and fruits are highest in oils containing methyl salicylate (a compound found in aspirin) is prized medicinally for rubbing on sore muscles. Oh, how good it feels (and smells) after returning from a busy day in the garden.*

Other Names Teaberry / Mountain Tea

Bloom Period and Color Spring blooms grow in white blushed with pale pink.

Mature Height × **Spread** 6 inches (unlimited spread)

When and How to Plant Container plants are often available in spring from perennial plant growers and specialty nurseries. Set no farther apart than 12 inches. Creeping Wintergreen is one of the slowest ground covers to establish—it takes about two growing seasons for it to fill in. Divisions or clumps up to 6 by 6 inches by 4 inches deep (a flat nursery spade with a 6-inch blade makes the ideal tool for digging) can be dug from well-established beds in early spring and used as transplants. Seed sown in fall will germinate the following spring.

Sun and Soil Preference Plant in a rich, organic, acidic, moist soil in slight to total shade.

Moisture Requirements If there is continuous moisture, Creeping Wintergreen can even be planted in morning sun or a sandy soil. Avoid the hot afternoon sun.

Fertilizing Topdress bed with an organically rich compost every year in spring just as new growth starts.

Pruning and Care Once established, Creeping Wintergreen is a ground cover that takes care of itself. All it requires is a light fluff-raking in early spring to remove accumulated fallen leaves.

Pests and Diseases There are no appreciable pest or disease problems.

Additional Species, Cultivars, or Varieties The cultivar 'Macrocarpa' is even more compact than the species. *G. hispidula* Creeping Pearl Berry is a slow-growing evergreen carpet or mat with shiny white berries. Creeping Wintergreen is a natural for planting alongside and under its Ericaceous cousins (Rhododendrons, Mountain Laurels, Japanese Andromeda, and Azaleas). Don't ever add lime to the soil—Ericaceous plants detest it!

My Personal Favorite

NAME	SPECIAL CHARACTERISTICS
Creeping Wintergreen	*G. procumbens*, the species / spring growth / light green with a touch of wine tinge, turning into tough, leathery, shiny dark-green foliage

Deer Fern

Blechnum spicant

Preferred Zones	Sun Preference	Additional Benefits
5 to 8	☀	Ⓝ 🍃

Deer Fern, known by all fern lovers as the ultra-hardy evergreen fern, has glossy, rich, dark-green fronds that resemble those of a small Christmas Fern. With its attractive evergreen foliage, this North American native is ideal for naturalizing in our woodland gardens because it loves the Tri-State area's acid soils. I've planted pockets of Deer Fern in rich forest-floor soil, tucking them in to accent a red rock outcrop along with several varieties of Rhododendron. The Rhodies bloom from early spring right up to July. Use the Deer Fern as the foundation of your fern garden, complemented with the Royal Fern. For a shady patio garden, plant clumps of Deer Fern six inches apart in redwood planters filled with a blend of fifty percent well-rotted compost or leaf mold and fifty percent sand. As they grow, they take on the look of a year-round Boston Fern.

Other Names   Hard Fern / Ladder Fern

Bloom Period and Color   There are no blooms (glossy, rich, dark-green fronds appear spring to frost).

Mature Height × **Spread**   6 to 8 inches × 6 to 8 inches

When and How to Plant   Plant in early spring only. Till or spade organic matter into the soil to a depth of 8 to 10 inches. Plant clumps or divisions, available from specialty perennial growers, only as deep as the root mass and 12 to 14 inches apart.

Sun and Soil Preference   Soil preparation and location are the key to success when growing Deer Fern. The planting bed must be in full shade, with organically rich soil that has a neutral to slightly acid pH. It wants no direct sun but will grow in filtered shade and does best in full shade. For average clay-type soil in the Tri-State area, spread 3 to 4 inches of well-rotted compost or leaf mold over the planting bed.

Moisture Requirements   Water immediately after planting to settle the soil around the roots; thereafter, continue watering to keep the soil slightly moist. This fern requires moisture but not wet feet. Be patient. It often takes several weeks to two months for new fronds to emerge. Provide water during extreme drought.

Fertilizing   Topdress the fern bed with an organically rich compost in early spring before new growth emerges. Once a year, spread a 2-inch layer of organic mulch, such as well-rotted compost or leaf mold, over the fern bed to continue soil richness.

Pruning and Care   Clip out broken and maturing fronds as needed throughout the growing season.

Pests and Diseases   There are no appreciable pest or disease problems.

Additional Species, Cultivars, or Varieties   For the full-sun-to-partial-shade environment, consider *Osmunda regalis*, commonly called Royal Fern. It will thrive in zones 4 to 9 and grows to 4 feet tall and wide, so give it plenty of room when planting. The Royal Fern produces bright-green fronds composed of triangular leaflets, topped with fertile tassel-like tips.

My Personal Favorite

NAME	SPECIAL CHARACTERISTICS
Deer Fern	*B. spicant*, the species / one of the hardiest evergreen ferns

Lady Fern

Athyrium filix-femina

Preferred Zones	Sun Preferences		Additional Benefits
3 to 8	◐	☀	

If you're planning to naturalize a landscape, particularly if it has a moist, shady gentle slope, Lady Fern should be one of its main features. Reaching a height of up to thirty-six inches, its soft-green, gracefully arching, long, pointed leaves will make it stand out as a specimen when planted singly. In a group planting of ten to fifteen inches on center, Lady Fern will grow into a bed that takes on the attributes of a naturalized planting. This deciduous Fern dies back to the ground for winter, but come spring, brand-new fronds emerge from the ground with dependability. Add contrast to the Lady Fern patch by planting a small drift of Athyrium × 'Branford Beauty', a cross between A. f-f and A. nipponicum 'Pictum'. The red-stalked, gray-flecked leaves emerge from an extremely vigorous plant that reaches two feet tall and two-and-a-half feet wide. The only downside to a fern garden is that you must be patient. From practical experience, I have learned it often takes three to five years for fern transplants to become established.

Bloom Period and Color There are no blooms (light-green foliage appears spring to frost).

Mature Height × Spread 16 to 36 inches (unlimited spread)

When and How to Plant Plant in spring or fall. Stock is available in quart or ½-gallon containers from specialty growers throughout much of the growing season. Plant clumps or divisions by setting the Lady Fern crown just below the soil surface. If necessary to increase moisture retention, add well-rotted compost to the backfill of each planting hole.

Sun and Soil Preference Plant in full to partial shade in a highly organic, acidic, well-drained soil with ample moisture.

Moisture Requirements Immediately after planting, water thoroughly. Spring plantings require watering until late fall, and fall plantings should be watered until the killing freeze. After establishment, Lady Fern is fairly drought-tolerant. During extended drought, a soaker hose twined through the fern bed and turned on to a slow trickle when needed is an efficient way to water.

Fertilizing Topdress the Lady Fern bed with a well-rotted compost before fronds emerge in spring.

Pruning and Care If a Lady Fern leaf should break or become damaged, cut it to the ground. New stems will emerge throughout the growing season.

Pests and Diseases If the Lady Fern is planted in a naturalistic setting, slugs, a common pest, will need to be controlled. Contact your county cooperative extension educator or Master Gardener for the latest recommendations for slug and snail control. If a pesticide is recommended, be sure to read and follow the label directions.

Additional Species, Cultivars, or Varieties A companion fern, the Japanese Painted Fern (*A. niponicum* 'Pictum'), grows to 18 inches tall and has silver-green fronds; the fronds' midribs are flushed maroon-purple. *A. f-f.* 'Cristatum', Crested Lady Fern, has sculptured fronds reaching to 24 inches high; plant it in consistently moist, highly organic, slightly acid soil.

My Personal Favorite

NAME	SPECIAL CHARACTERISTICS
A. f-f. var. *angustum* Northern Lady Fern	Most popular / native from Virginia to Newfoundland

Pachysandra

Pachysandra terminalis

Preferred Zones	Sun Preferences	Additional Benefits
4 to 8	☽ ☀	NA

Have you ever tried to grow grass under a Maple tree or a spreading Flowering Dogwood? I'll bet the seed germinated, and maybe a few wispy blades emerged for a very short time, but eventually it folded over and died—right? How about trying to grow grass on a steep shady slope where every time you had to mow you worried if you might slip under the mower or down the hill? Well, in the Tri-State area, the solution to both these problems is a bed of evergreen ground cover called Japanese Spurge, or Pachysandra. It is truly the Cadillac of ground covers in places where it is impossible or impractical to maintain grass. I've planted beds of Pachysandra under many trees, with 100 percent success. Over time as a tree grows and spreads, the Pachysandra bed will follow the shade and spread as well. If you need a path through a bed of Japanese Spurge, inlay bluestone steps or spread a path of pine-bark chips.

Other Name Japanese Spurge

Bloom Period and Color White flowers bloom in early spring.

Mature Height × Spread 8 to 10 inches (indefinite spread)

When and How to Plant Pachysandra is available spring and fall in flats of 50 to 100 rooted cuttings per flat. Planting under a spreading tree with shallow roots is no easy task—the shallow roots make it almost impossible to prepare the soil: you can't till or spade. Put on your kneepads and dig out pockets of soil no more than a "span-of-the-hand" apart (that's the distance from the tip of the little finger to the tip of the thumb with the hand spread out).

Sun and Soil Preference Site in partial to full shade. Pachysandra prefers a well-drained, slightly acidic soil but will grow quite well in almost any soil in the Tri-State area as long as it is not wet.

Moisture Requirements Immediately after planting, water thoroughly to settle the soil around each cutting, and continue light watering throughout the season. Remember: During the growing season, both the Pachysandra and a tree-root system will benefit from supplemental watering.

Fertilizing Apply a slow-release plant food according to label directions after planting, and before long the bed will become a feature of the garden. Feed annually in early spring.

Pruning and Care Rake leaves from the top of the bed to reduce smothering from fallen leaves.

Pests and Diseases Two summer problems are two-spotted spider mites which leave stippled leaves and *Volutella*, a leaf and stem disease that exhibits tell-tale signs of browning leaf tips. To suppress two-spotted spider mites, thoroughly spray the Pachysandra bed with insecticidal soap according to the label directions. Check with your county cooperative extension educator or Master Gardener for recommended controls of *Volutella*.

Additional Species, Cultivars, or Varieties 'Variegata' has a green leaf with white margins. *P. procumbens* Allegheny Pachysandra, a coarse-textured ground cover for shaded areas, spreads by underground stems.

My Personal Favorite

NAME	SPECIAL CHARACTERISTICS
'Green Carpet'	Makes an evergreen carpet under the Maple tree / has wider, dark-green foliage

Wintercreeper

Euonymus fortunei

Preferred Zones	Sun Preferences		Additional Benefits
4 to 8	☀ ☽ ☀		

Wintercreeper is a popular colorful ground cover for full sun to full shade. It has shiny, rich, dark-green leaves, one to two inches long, that turn purplish-red in fall and remain that color throughout winter and well into spring. You will delight in the sight of the purplish-red leaves sticking up through freshly fallen, pure-white snow. What a show! You can plant Wintercreeper on the top side of a stone retaining wall and let it trail over the edge. The little rootlets growing from nodes on the stems permit the stems to climb a trellis or tree trunk. For impossible-to-mow sunny slopes, plant Wintercreeper en masse. In a very short time you'll have an evergreen, or should I say a half-green and half-purple, ground cover.

Bloom Period and Color There are no blooms.

Mature Height × Spread 8 to 12 inches (unlimited spread)

When and How to Plant Wintercreeper planted in early spring has adequate time to establish a strong root system before winter. Larger plants, in containers or balled-and-burlapped specimens, may be planted throughout the year as long as the ground is workable. Plant bare-root cuttings 8 to 10 inches apart. Container-grown transplants, usually commercially available in quart containers, should be planted 24 inches apart. You can also root your own. Take cuttings 8 to 10 inches long from the tips of the stems; they will root easily in moist, coarse builder's sand in just six to eight weeks.

Sun and Soil Preference Plant in full sun to full shade. A versatile plant when it comes to soil, plant in clay, sand, or organically rich soil.

Moisture Requirements Water-in the plants thoroughly after planting.

Fertilizing Apply a slow-release plant food for evergreens during cleanup in spring.

Pruning and Care Prune stem tips during early spring to encourage compact growth and to keep plants in bounds.

Pests and Diseases To keep out weeds, apply a pre-emergent weed control containing treflan or eptam in early spring, according to label directions. During May and June, and again in August and September, examine stems for scale insects, which appear as tiny, elongated white scales that coat the stems and leaves. Read the label and apply an appropriate scalicide according to directions.

Additional Species, Cultivars, or Varieties 'Emerald 'n' Gold', 2 to 3 feet high, has foliage of dark green with yellow margins; 'Emerald Gaiety', also 2 to 3 feet high, has dark-green foliage with irregular white margins. 'Kewensis', a dwarf plant to 3 inches tall, has tiny, dark-green foliage. Other available species are *Euonymus japonica* 'Gold Spot', 'Silver King', and 'Silver Queen', which grow 10 to 15 feet, and *Euonymus kiatschovica* 'Manhattan' and 'Sieboldiana' (Spreading Euonymus); the latter two grow 6 feet, have extra-dark-green glossy foliage, and are real favorites for flower arrangements.

My Personal Favorite

NAME	SPECIAL CHARACTERISTICS
'Coloratus'	Dark-green foliage / purplish fall and winter color / as the stems spread, they root to the ground and provide excellent erosion control

Lawns *for the Tri-State*

A lawn can be the grassy strip that functions as a walkway, winding its way through colorful flowerbeds. It can be an island of turf next to the driveway where you get out of your car. It might be that somewhat disheveled grass patch where the kids' sandbox and playset are located. Or the lawn may be that prized expanse of green carpet stretching from curbside to the treeline in back.

Good for the Environment

Whatever its purpose, turfgrass is an environmental asset. According to the Professional Lawn Care Association of America, the benefits of turf include the following:

- Six hundred and twenty-five square feet of lawn provides enough oxygen for one person for an entire day.
- On a block of eight average homes, the front lawns collectively have the cooling effect of seventy tons of air-conditioning.
- Turf absorbs gaseous pollutants such as carbon dioxide and sulfur dioxide.
- Turf traps an estimated twelve million tons of dust and dirt released annually into the atmosphere.
- A buffer zone of grass around buildings retards the spread of fire.
- Turf prevents soil erosion, filters contaminants from rainwater, and reduces runoff.

Select the Right Turfgrass

The philosophy of planting the right plant in the right place is of prime importance when selecting turfgrass varieties. Review the site and environment before purchasing seed. There are grass seed varieties for full sun, for partial shade, and for deeper shade. There are grasses for sandy soils and for clay-type soils, and every soil type in between. Some grass varieties flourish in damp soil and some thrive in dry.

A visit to your local garden center, nursery, or mass merchandiser can be quite intimidating with all of the different varieties and mixes for planting turf. Take time to read the package. Some blends are utility mixes that will accept foot traffic, and some are premium mixes for the finest lawn in the neighborhood. As new turf varieties are introduced every year, check with your county cooperative extension educator for a particular variety or mix recommended for the soil and environmental conditions in your area.

Prepare for Planting

No matter which species or variety you wish to establish, spend time preparing the seedbed before planting. Prepare soil samples for analyzing soil pH, the test for soil acidity or alkalinity. A soil pH ranging from 6.2 to 7.2 is generally acceptable for most turf varieties in the Tri-State area. Lime can be applied to raise the soil pH, and sulfur, well-rotted compost, leaf mold, and milled sphagnum peat moss can be used to lower the pH. Record the test results and the products applied for correcting the soil pH in your garden records.

While you are waiting for the soil sample to be tested, strip away or kill off all existing vegetation such as weeds and perennial grasses. When applied to actively growing vegetation according to label directions, a post-emergent chemical herbicide like Kleenup® or Roundup® will kill weeds and grasses.

After the weeds and grasses have died, spread lime if needed, and two to three inches of weed-free organic matter over the soil surface. Till the ingredients into the soil to a depth of eight to ten inches, the deeper the better. Rake out debris and stones, level the seedbed, and then spread the seed at the pounds-per-1000-square-feet rate prescribed by the label directions for that particular mix. Apply a starter turf fertilizer, also according to label directions. To calculate the number of pounds of fertilizer to apply to your lawn to get the equivalent of 1 pound nitrogen/1000 square feet, divide 100 by the percentage of nitrogen in the bag (represented by the first number on the label). Example: A 10-6-4 fertilizer contains 10 percent nitrogen (the first number), so divide 100 by 10:

$$100 \div 10 = 10 \text{ pounds of fertilizer}$$

In this case, you will apply 10 pounds of fertilizer per 1000 square feet. Rake the seed and fertilizer lightly into the soil. Roll the seedbed to ensure contact between the soil and seed. Cover the seedbed with a thin layer of salt hay or the new, recycled paper mulch made exclusively for seeding. Apply water to keep the seedbed evenly moist, not wet. Then step back and watch it grow. (Well, almost.)

The Instant Lawn

For an instant sod lawn, follow all the above steps right up to the seeding process. Lay the sod according to the procedure recommended by the sod supplier, roll to ensure contact of the sod with the parent soil, and water. Never allow sod to dry before the roots penetrate the soil below, anchoring the grass. A gentle tug on the sod will tell you when it is rooted in.

After the grass knits into a solid turf, one inch of water per week (collectively between rain and irrigation) should do. This one-inch recommendation varies according to weather conditions. If it's hot, sunny, and windy, it may take more water. If it's cloudy, cool, and calm, the turf may require considerably less water. It might pay to invest in a rain gauge.

The Importance of Mowing

Mowing at the proper height and frequency is essential for top-quality turf. The latest recommendation for Bluegrass, Ryegrass, and Fescue is to set the mower at its maximum cutting height of three inches or more, cutting off no more than one-third of the grass blade at one time. Leave the cutting height at three inches throughout the growing season.

Zoysia and Bentgrass are exceptions to the three-inch mowing height rule. They must be mowed at their specific, recommended height. For newly seeded grass and sod lawns, it is necessary to let the soil dry a little before mowing. Use a walk-behind mower, not a riding mower, until the grass is well established.

Feeding the Turf

There is no need to pick up grass clippings if you use a mulching blade to chop up and recycle the clippings. As they decompose, they release nutrients back into the soil.

Plan a feeding program and then follow it. Three applications are recommended for most turf varieties with the exception of Zoysia. Apply a slow-release chemical or organic turf food according to the label directions during the Memorial Day weekend, the Labor Day weekend, and the Thanksgiving weekend. A slow-release fertilizer will not burn while it gradually feeds the grass plants. If quick greening is a must in spring, apply a fourth feeding in March. The spring feeding can make grass more susceptible to disease.

Controlling Lawn Pests

For weed control, start with that pesky crabgrass. Select a pre-emergent control and apply it according to the label directions. (An old rule of thumb is to do it before the blossoms drop from the Forsythia.) Read the label and follow the recommended rates and directions because the chemical must be watered properly to dissolve the ingredients, getting them into the soil. Please don't depend on rain! If a pre-emergent crabgrass control is used in conjunction with new seedings, the bag must say "for use with new seedings." Otherwise, you can select one of the many formulas for crabgrass control.

For broadleaf weeds such as dandelions, chickweed, and plantain, apply a post-emergent broadleaf weed control according to the label directions. The timing and rate of application determine success. If there are just a few weeds invading the turf, consider getting down on your knees and pulling them out by hand. For dandelions, use the long-blade dandelion knife to ensure that you get enough of the taproot. Otherwise, two new dandelions will emerge at each spot where you cut one out. It is not always necessary to use a weedkiller.

Critter and disease suppression in turf is as varied as the number of varieties being planted. In the Tri-State lawn, grass varieties containing endophytes may suppress above-ground feeding insects such as chinch bugs and sod webworms. Below-ground pests, such as grubs and weevils, may be controlled with beneficial nematodes. Diseases such as leaf spot, brown patch, snow mold, dollar spot, stripped smut, and mildew may require a fungicide.

Plan an IPM (Integrated Pest Management) program for both insect and disease suppression. Your county cooperative extension educator or local garden center professional can help you set up an IPM program, and they can help you identify any invaders before applying a control.

Moles thrive on grubs. Inoculate the soil with milky spore or beneficial nematodes to suppress the grubs, and the moles will pack up and go somewhere else for food.

Time to Start a Lawn

In the Tri-State area, the best time to start a new lawn or to overseed is in early fall when the soil is still warm, the annual weeds have begun to die, and the air temperatures have begun to cool. The second-best time is in early spring, before the weeds emerge. The downside to spring seeding is crabgrass. You will need a pre-emergent crabgrass control for use with seeding. Read the label.

Creeping Bentgrass
Agrostis palustris

Preferred Zones	Sun Preference	Additional Benefits
3 to 10	☀	NA

*The softness and texture of Creeping Bentgrass make it an ideal picture frame or well-manicured turf for the lawn area around any high-class perennial garden. If you're a golfer in the Tri-State area, you've probably putted that little white ball on Creeping Bentgrass, most likely the variety Penncross. If you're a member of an exclusive country club, you not only putted on Bentgrass but you probably drove the ball off a tee seeded with Creeping Bentgrass, and if you landed in the fairway, you chipped the ball off a closely mown Colonial Bentgrass to the green. My hat is off to the golf course superintendents of Connecticut, New Jersey, and New York, because they not only put up with persnickety golfers, they must grow grass during our oppressive humidity and summer heat. And that's not all—they are growing a crop that requires water, and lots of it. Dealing with water conservation will be their next challenge. **Note:** Creeping Bentgrass seed is the finest-sized seed used for turf, containing 6,500,000 seeds per pound. Kentucky Bluegrass is next in line with 2,200,000 seeds per pound. (Perennial Ryegrass has only 230,000 per pound).*

Type and Color A cool-season grass, Creeping Bentgrass is medium green.

Mowing Height 3/16 to 5/16 inch (reel-type mower only)

When and How to Plant Creeping Bentgrass can be established from seed at virtually any time the soil is workable, from early spring through September in the Tri-State area. Before taking on the monumental task of establishing Creeping Bentgrass as your turf, it is highly recommended that you consult with a local golf course superintendent to discuss its maintenance requirements, including mowing schedules, insect and disease control, watering requirements, and so on. He or she may convince you to use a different species of grass. Prepare the bed by adding great quantities of coarse sand to a depth of at least 10 inches. Rake and level the bed. Seed at the rate of 1 to 2 pounds per 1000 square feet. Rake lightly to cover the tiny seeds with no more than 1/4 inch of soil.

Sun and Soil Preferences Creeping Bentgrass performs best in full sun in a sandy soil. It tolerates a wide range of soil pH, as high as 8.0. When planted in clay-type soil, drainage must be improved.

Moisture Requirements Water lightly several times a day, keeping the soil moist but not wet, until germination (seven to fifteen days), and then until seedlings are well established, usually within thirty days.

Fertilizing Apply 1 to 2 pounds of actual nitrogen, in a slow-release turf fertilizer, per 1000 square feet, per growing year. See Lawn introduction on p. 153 for calculation procedure.

Mowing and Care You'll need a special greens mower to maintain the low cutting height, and you'll need to mow the turf at least every other day.

Pests and Diseases Be prepared to apply fungicides for specific diseases of cool weather and hot, humid weather. Apply insecticides for grubs and weevils as needed. Check with your county cooperative extension educator for diseases and pests affecting Creeping Bentgrass in your area and for their least-toxic controls.

Additional Species, Cultivars, or Varieties Seed of established cultivars include Seaside, Penncross, Emerald, Pennlinks, Penneagle, Prominent, Providence, South Shore, SR1020, and L93. **Caution:** Endophytic varieties are not recommended for grazing or pasture use.

Creeping Red Fescue

Festuca rubra

Preferred Zones	Sun Preferences	Additional Benefit
3 to 9		

Creeping Red Fescue, often simply referred to as Red Fescue, is a cool-season turfgrass with fine, narrow, deep-green blades. It does best in spring and fall in the Tri-State lawn. If planted in the shade of tall trees, the carpet of green appears as a soft bed after mowing. If you have not raised the lawnmower to its highest setting, do so now, and notice the difference in appearance of the Creeping Red Fescue lawn. If left unmown at the perimeter of the lawn and garden, the blades can become an attractive dark-green transition between woodland plantings and a more formal garden. All of the Fescues have three growing characteristics in common: they are shade tolerant, they stay green all year in the Tri-State area, and they show very good resistance to drought. One of the biggest steps forward in Creeping Red Fescue varieties is the introduction of endophytes (symbiotic fungi) to the grass plant and seed. Endophytes have improved the drought-resistance of the turf as well as its resistance to aboveground invasions from chinch bugs and sod webworm, and there is now resistance to some diseases.

Type and Color This cool-season grass is dark green.

Mowing Height 2½ to 3 inches or higher

When and How to Plant Fall is the best time to establish Creeping Red Fescue from seed; sod can be laid at any time the soil is workable, up to one month prior to the time the ground freezes in the fall. Preparation of the seedbed is more difficult in the shady environment, due to competing roots from trees. In semi- or dappled shade, let Mother Nature determine which will do best by planting a Bluegrass blend that contains Creeping Red Fescue.

Sun and Soil Preferences This grass loves partial to full shade and a cool, moist, acidic soil.

Moisture Requirements Provide even moisture during germination and establishment. In a shady environment, water much less than for grass grown in the sun. Keep sod moist, not wet, until roots penetrate the parent soil; a tug on the sod will tell you when it is rooted in.

Fertilizing Apply a seed-starter turf fertilizer at planting time. Apply fertilizer at a rate of 2 pounds or less actual nitrogen per 1000 square feet per year. See Lawn introduction on p. 153 for calculation procedure.

Mowing and Care When mown at the recommended 2½ to 3 inches or higher, Creeping Red Fescue planted in moderate shade and well-drained soil will produce some of the finest turf imaginable. Maintain a sharp blade on the mower throughout the season, as the wiry, narrow grass blades can be tough to cut during dry weather.

Pests and Diseases Plant endophyte-enhanced varieties resistant to aboveground insect pests and diseases. For grubs, apply the biological control milky spore disease, or contact your county cooperative extension educator for the latest recommended natural, organic, or chemical pesticide.

Additional Species, Cultivars, or Varieties Improved cultivars include strong Creeping Red Fescue types Boreal, Ensylva, and Shademaster; and the slender Creeping Red Fescues Dawson and Seabreeze. The inclusion of *Neotyphodium typhinum* and *Epichloe typhina* endophytes in Creeping Red Fescue cultivars has resulted in improved drought tolerance, resistance to some diseases, and tolerance of some aboveground insects. **Caution:** Endophytic varieties are not recommended for grazing or pasture use.

Hard Fescue

Festuca longifolia

Preferred Zones	Sun Preferences	Additional Benefits
4 to 9	☼ ☀	NA

Without a doubt, Hard Fescue is one of the hardiest of all turfgrasses in the Tri-State area. It is the only Fescue that is salt-tolerant, so you will find it growing along a sunny or shady sand dune, often backdropped by stands of Black Pine, Shore Rose, or Russian Olive. It's not unusual to find patches of this species of Festuca growing in the deepest shade of the forest, along reclamation plantings, or as part of a soil-erosion program. When left unmown, Hard Fescue naturalizes into an attractive, low-growing, stiff-bladed mat of grass. As with Creeping Red Fescue, the introduction of endophytes (symbiotic fungi) in Hard Fescue varieties has resulted in improved insect tolerance, drought resistance, and resistance to some diseases. I wouldn't call Hard Fescue the grass for the lazy gardener, but this noncreeping, bunch-type grass can be allowed to grow with infrequent mowing and will survive with little or no extra nutrition.

Type and Color Hard Fescue, a cool-season grass, is blue-green.

Mowing Height 3 inches or higher (removing no more than 1/3 of the leaf at any mowing)

When and How to Plant If irrigation is available, plant Hard Fescue seed at any time the soil is workable, from spring to late fall. As a new planting, or to fill in the areas between grass clumps, plant Hard Fescue seed during the cooler months of spring or late fall. Check with your county cooperative extension educator or Master Gardener for varieties recommended for your area.

Sun and Soil Preferences Plant in full sun to partial shade in well-drained soil with a slightly acid pH.

Moisture Requirements When the Hard Fescue is a conservation planting, or in areas where water is not available, the spring and fall rains generally provide adequate moisture for establishment.

Fertilizing An early-spring application of a slow-release turf fertilizer will benefit the grass but is not absolutely necessary.

Mowing and Care As Hard Fescue is primarily used for soil stabilization, it is not necessary to mow unless it's being grown in a more formal setting. If mowing seems necessary, cut at a height of 3 or more inches. Did the grass get ahead of you while you were on vacation? No matter how long it grew, never cut off more than 1/3 of the grass blade in a single mowing. Mow at the highest setting on the mower, then lower the setting and mow again in a few days.

Pests and Diseases Plant endophyte-enhanced varieties of Hard Fescue for resistance to diseases and aboveground insects like sod webworm and chinch bugs. Control Japanese beetle grubs naturally with one application of milky spore disease. Read the label.

Additional Species, Cultivars, or Varieties Biljart, Reliant, Scaldis, and Silvana are cultivars with improved heat, drought, and disease tolerance. The inclusion of *Neotyphodium typhinum* and *Epichloe typhina* endophytes in Hard Fescue varieties have shown improved insect tolerance, drought resistance, and resistance to some diseases. Other recommended varieties are Discovery, Warwick, and Spartan. Check with your county cooperative extension educator or Master Gardener for varieties recommended for your area. **Caution:** Endophytic varieties are not recommended for grazing or pasture use.

Kentucky Bluegrass

Poa pratensis

Preferred Zones	Sun Preferences	Additional Benefits
3 to 9	☀ ☀	NA

The cool-season grass Poa pratensis *and its many cultivars range in color from bright green to deep bluish green. I write about Kentucky Bluegrass because it is the most popular genus grown in Tri-State lawns. Everywhere you look, you see varieties of this grass. We have learned not to plant only one Bluegrass variety. Remember the Merion Kentucky Bluegrass? It came down with smut disease and everyone's (and I mean everyone's) pure stand of Merion died almost overnight. There has been recent debate on the value of even having a lawn, because lawns require water, mowing, and nutrition. Let me make just one statement: "Kentucky Bluegrass and other lawngrasses are environmental assets." The mat formed by grass plants and their roots filters pollutants from the soil, cools the air, and supplies oxygen to the atmosphere. If you recycle the clippings, the lawn can almost feed itself. Kentucky Bluegrass spreads by underground rhizomes, is rather slow at establishment, puts up with foot traffic, and has very good cold tolerance in the Tri-State area.*

Type and Color The cool-season Kentucky Bluegrass is bright green to deep bluish green.

Mowing Height At 3 inches (removing no more than 1/3 of the leaf at any mowing)

When and How to Plant Seed is best established during the cool days of fall when there is less competition from weeds. Germination takes ten to thirty days once water is applied. Lay sod at any time of the growing season up to four weeks before the ground freezes in the fall. Kill off existing turf and weeds, and apply lime if needed, as Kentucky Bluegrass prefers a pH range of 6.2 to 7.2. Spread organic matter in the form of well-rotted compost or milled sphagnum peat moss over the soil surface, and till in all ingredients to a depth of 8 to 10 inches. Rake. Level. Seed. Finally, roll the area.

Sun and Soil Preferences Plant in well-drained, slightly acidic soil, in full sun to partial shade. Whether establishing from seed or sod, test the soil pH.

Moisture Requirements Once established, Kentucky Bluegrass requires a total of 1 inch of water from rain or sprinkler per week. As soon as sod is laid, water must be applied with regularity to keep the sod moist until it roots into the soil beneath.

Fertilizing Depending on the variety, apply 1 to 6 pounds of actual nitrogen per 1000 square feet per year. See Lawn introduction on p. 153 for calculation procedure. Schedule the application of a slow-release, high-nitrogen lawn fertilizer according to label directions, during the three holiday periods of Memorial Day, Labor Day, and Thanksgiving.

Mowing and Care Recent research has proven that the mowing height should be maintained at 3 inches or higher for the entire growing season. This encourages deeper rooting for sustained growth in warm weather and allows greater competition with weeds. Even when watered in summer, Kentucky Bluegrass is affected by heat and drought. Stressed grass goes into a dormant state (turns brown), and recovery will occur during the cooler, damper weather of fall.

Pests and Diseases When selecting varieties of Kentucky Bluegrass, consider resistance to leaf spot, striped smut, and patch disease. Apply a biological control for grubs. Consult your county cooperative extension educator for the newest varieties and recommended pest controls.

Additional Species, Cultivars, or Varieties There are more than 200 species of Bluegrass and hundreds of cultivars. The four species commonly referred to in turf management are Kentucky Bluegrass, Canada Bluegrass, Rough Stalk Bluegrass, and Annual Bluegrass.

Perennial Ryegrass
Lolium perenne

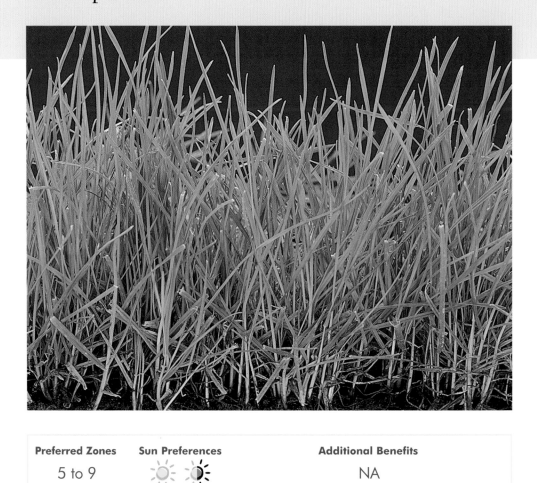

Preferred Zones	Sun Preferences	Additional Benefits
5 to 9	☀ ☀	NA

*Perennial Ryegrass is the workhorse of the turf industry. You'll find it installed on athletic fields as well as in home lawns throughout the Tri-State area. With the high disease- and insect-resistant qualities of the newer Turf-type Perennial Ryegrass, often called Turf-type Rye, it has become one of the toughest and most wearable turf covers. The reason for Perennial Ryegrass's popularity is its ease of establishment—but if you'll spend the time to properly prepare the soil, a Perennial Ryegrass lawn can be as attractive as your neighbor's Kentucky Bluegrass lawn. Some folks just throw down the seed and it grows. I don't recommend that as a planting procedure, but if it works for you, I guess that is okay, too. **Caution:** Some of the newer varieties of Turf-type Perennial Ryegrass contain endophytes and are not suitable for pasture use. If you have cattle or horses, goats or sheep, and so on, graze them elsewhere.*

Type and Color Perennial Ryegrass, a cool-season grass, is a shiny bright green.

Mowing Height 3 inches (remove no more than 1/3 of the leaf blade with any one mowing)

When and How to Plant Turf-type Ryegrass is best established from seed in early fall when the soil is still warm and the air temperature has begun to cool. Sod may be laid at any time up to one month before the ground freezes. Follow standard planting procedures: Test the soil pH, add lime and organic matter if needed (tilled 8 to 10 inches deep), and rake and level the soil. Seed at the label rate per 1000 square feet, and roll. Lay sod after following the same preparation steps.

Sun and Soil Preferences Plant in full sun to partial shade, in well-drained soil with a neutral to slightly acid pH. Germination takes only three to seven days in warm soil with even moisture.

Moisture Requirements Remember, once a seed has been moistened, it must have adequate moisture to complete germination and to become established. For established Turf-type Ryegrass, provide water during drought.

Fertilizing For seed or sod, apply a starter turf fertilizer according to the label directions, and then provide water. Always follow the recommended rates on the fertilizer label. To green up Turf-type Ryegrass in early spring, apply 1 pound of actual nitrogen per 1000 square feet. See Lawn introduction on p. 153 for calculation procedure. For the entire growing season, apply no more than 4 to 5 pounds of actual nitrogen per 1000 square feet per year.

Mowing and Care Maintain a mowing height of 3 or more inches throughout the growing season. To patch thin turf, rake vigorously to remove debris and scratch the soil surface. Seed at the recommended rate on the seed label; rake again to ensure contact of the seed with the soil; and then water.

Pests and Diseases Plant endophyte-enhanced varieties to minimize disease infection and infestations of aboveground insects. Apply grub controls as recommended by your county cooperative extension educator.

Additional Species, Cultivars, or Varieties The inclusion of *Neotyphodium lolii* endophyte in Perennial Ryegrass has resulted in resistance to some diseases, improved drought tolerance, and tolerance of some aboveground insects. Improved Turf-type Ryegrass cultivars include Citation, Derby, Diplomat, Manhattan II, Pennant, Pennfine, and Repell.

Tall Fescue

Festuca arundinacea

Preferred Zones

5 to 10

Sun Preferences

Additional Benefit

If you played football or soccer, or marched in the school band, you probably did so on a turf of Tall Fescue. Newer Turf-type Tall Fescue is finer in texture and performs better in the summer heat of the Tri-State area. Once established, it's even drought-tolerant. If you ever planted a "playground" seed mix in the backyard, you probably used a Tall Fescue, in particular Kentucky-31 Tall Fescue, which has been the standby for lawns where lots of foot traffic is anticipated, from playgrounds to athletic fields. The shiny, rather coarse, broadleaf blades are almost indestructible. Of course there are exceptions: If ten thousand people congregate at a rock concert, or if the whole football team is gathered on the fifty-yard line, such uncommon wear will certainly destroy some grass.

Type and Color Tall Fescue, a cool-season grass, is a glossy medium green.

Mowing Height 3 inches (remove no more than 1/3 of the blade in any mowing)

When and How to Plant Overseeding of thinned turf, or planting of a new Tall Fescue lawn, is best done in fall. Although it will be a little more expensive, plant only the newer, improved Turf-type Tall Fescue. For a new lawn, kill off all weeds and existing turf with a post-emergent, glyphosate-type weed- and grass-killer, following the label directions. Till or spade the soil to a depth of 8 to 10 inches. Rake and level the seedbed, and seed at the rate of 6 to 10 pounds per 1000 square feet. Rake lightly to cover the seed with 1/4 inch of soil, then roll the seedbed to ensure contact of the seed with soil.

Sun and Soil Preferences Plant in full sun to partial shade. Test the soil for acidity (Tall Fescue prefers a slightly acid to neutral soil pH), and apply lime if needed.

Moisture Requirements Water as needed to keep the soil moist but not wet during germination (seven to twelve days). Continue watering until the new turf has been mown at least four times.

Fertilizing Feed with a balanced slow-release turf fertilizer as recommended on the label.

Mowing and Care Mow Tall Fescue at 3 inches or higher to maintain a thick turf. As the bunch-type grass becomes clumpy, overseed to fill in the spaces between the plants.

Pests and Diseases Plant endophyte-enhanced varieties that are resistant to disease and tolerant of aboveground insects. Apply a biological control such as milky spore disease for grubs.

Additional Species, Cultivars, or Varieties With the introduction of *Neotyphodium coenophialum* endophytes to Tall Fescue, many cultivars have shown resistance to some diseases, improved drought resistance, and tolerance of some aboveground insects. Rebel, Jaguar, and Bonsai are a few of the latest introductions. Alta and Kentucky-31 have been the most popular cultivars. *Festuca elatior*, Meadow Fescue, is similar to Tall Fescue in general appearance and growth habit but is less persistent under drought and heat stress. **Caution:** Endophytic varieties are not recommended for grazing or pasture use.

Zoysia Grass

Zoysia japonica

Preferred Zones	Sun Preferences		Additional Benefit
5 to 10	☼	☀	◈

During early spring, late fall, or any time in winter, a drive through any Tri-State suburban community which was built in the 1960s or '70s will reveal lawns with large "dead" spots, and some lawns will appear totally "dead." These "dead" spots and lawns are more than likely made up of resting Zoysia Grass. From the onset of 50- to 55-degree-Fahrenheit soil temperatures in late September, clear through to late May the following spring, Zoysia assumes dormancy, and except for a few weeds in early spring, your grass will be brown. For this reason I do not advocate Zoysia lawns in the Tri-State area. It is true that once the seeds have germinated and the grass becomes established (or the plugs have grown together into a solid mat), Zoysia is a solid, durable, bright-green turf from June through mid-September—and this is one reason people often ignore my advice to avoid planting Zoysia! Keep in mind that once it's established, it is almost impossible to eradicate. Zoysia is not compatible with any other grass, as it will dominate the turf. Know where you want it to grow before planting.

Type and Color A warm-season grass, Zoysia is medium green.

Mowing Height $1/2$ to 1 inch

When and How to Plant If you don't mind having a dead-looking, totally-brown lawn (except for a few weeds like wild onions or nutgrass poking their heads through in spring) from the onset of 50- to 55-degree temperatures in late September until late May the following spring, plug or seed your lawn with Zoysia. Start any Zoysia lawn by eliminating all weeds and grasses. Apply a complete weed- and grass-killer according to the label directions, or cover the entire area to be planted with a sheet of black plastic for three to four weeks (weed and grass plants covered with the black plastic do not receive light, so they will die). Plant actively growing Zoysia plugs in early summer; plant Zoysia seed at the same time (the active growing season for Zoysia in your area). Zoysia planted from seed can become a solid turf in just five months of growing time.

Sun and Soil Preferences Plant in full sun to partial shade. Zoysia Grass plugs may be planted in sandy soils along the coast of the Tri-State area—it is drought-resistant and tolerant of salt.

Moisture Requirements Irrigate only to sustain color and growth during drought periods.

Fertilizing Fertilize with no more than $1 1/2$ to 3 pounds of actual nitrogen per 1000 square feet per year. See Lawn introduction on p. 153 for calculation procedure.

Mowing and Care To retain a uniform surface, mow with a reel-type mower, not a rotary mower.

Pests and Diseases Chinch bugs, sod webworms, and grubs will need to be controlled. Contact your local cooperative extension educator for the latest recommended controls.

Additional Species, Cultivars, or Varieties Meyer Z-52, selected by the United States Department of Agriculture as "superior," is the most popular Zoysia in the Tri-State area. Zenith is one of the newest hybrids of Zoysia available.

Perennials *for the Tri-State*

Planning a perennial garden is like conducting an orchestra: as the oboe finishes, you motion to the violins and let them take over. Close your eyes and think of your garden as that orchestra. Imagine Bleeding Heart dripping with pink blossoms followed by Candytuft's white clusters of bloom. As the music continues, Bearded Iris in multiple colors and giant red Peonies open their flowers. For summer bloom you have white Daisies and yellow Sunflowers. For the finish of the masterpiece are fall Chrysanthemums in gold, red, white, or purple. If there is a gap in the blooming cycle, you can beef up the orchestra by planting colorful annuals in between.

Plan Before You Plant

Now down to serious business. Since perennials come back year after year, spend some time planning before you plant. Make a list of "seats" you want to fill in your blooming orchestra. Each seat, a one-by-one-inch square of paper, will be labeled with a plant's name, its bloom time, its size, the space it requires, and the bloom color. You'll find it is much easier to move a plant by picking up a piece of paper than it is to physically dig a hole in the garden, put in the plant, and then find that it is in the wrong place.

You don't have to be a landscape architect or artist to be successful in designing your garden. Take a piece of plain white paper and draw each area you want to plant, using a scale of 1-inch-equals-2-feet (could be larger or smaller). Now take the pieces of paper with their written descriptions (you could even do this in color with crayons), and lay them out to make your orchestra bloom from left to right, front to back, and so on. Try not to cram too many plants in too small a place. In other words, don't put too many oboes (Coral Bells, Pansies, or Phlox) in one seat.

Prepare the Soil Properly

Since perennials come back year after year, the soil must be prepared properly before planting—once the plants are in the ground, there is little you can do to make substantial improvements. Start by eliminating all weeds or grasses because they, too,

are perennial, and will compete with your orchestra of flowers.

Analyze the soil: test the soil pH and nutrient content. Dig a hole and fill it with water to check the drainage. Next, add lots of organic matter in the form of well-rotted compost, leaf mold, or milled sphagnum peat moss. The more organic matter, the better.

If you're starting a completely new garden, spread lime over the entire area (if test results dictate the need, of course). Put down fertilizer for flowering plants at the rate recommended on the label, then spread one to two inches of organic matter over the garden surface. Spade or till all the ingredients into the soil to a depth of eight to ten inches or more. Rake out the soil to level the planting bed, removing debris as it's raked.

Now you're ready to plant. You may want to take a day off to shop for your "orchestra members," your new perennials, and allow your back to rest for the day.

Time to Plant the Perennials . . .

Lay out the entire "orchestra," plant by plant, adjusting the spacing as needed. Put on a pair of kneepads, get out the hand trowel, and put in the plants. If a container-grown plant is in a "plantable" pot, it's really best to take it out before planting—the pressed paper pots are too slow at breaking down and during the hot, dry summers here in the Tri-State area, the roots may never leave the pot.

Set a bucket of water next to you and give each plant a drink immediately after planting. After putting the last plant in the ground, give the entire perennial garden an additional watering. If you like (and I recommend it), set up a drip irrigation system before you start the last step in planting your perennials.

The last step is the application of a decorative mulch to dress up "the pit," keep down the weeds, and conserve moisture throughout the season. The drip system can be covered with the decorative mulch. Pine bark mini-nuggets, cocoa hulls, or shredded hardwood bark will do just fine.

Then sit back and watch the music (your perennials) play.

Astilbe

Astilbe × arendsii

Preferred Zones	Sun Preferences	Additional Benefit
3 to 8	☀ ☀	🌼

"There's a rule I follow when gardening in shade: I plant flowers that are white, shocking pink, light pink, pale peach, light salmon, light blue, and all shades of yellow, but never flowers of red, purple, or dark blue. Why, you ask? Because red, purple, and dark blue are not visible colors in shade. They need direct sunlight to excite the colors . . . which leads me to my next recommendation. One of the most versatile perennial flowers for the shade garden or woodland landscape—and it reemerges year after year—is Astilbe. A shady environment will come to life with these flowers of shocking pink, pure white, and pale peach. If the plumes are left on the plant over winter, they will add character to a snow-covered garden. So let me repeat—for best exhibition and enjoyment, plant Astilbe with white or pink blossoms in the shadiest locations. Red Astilbe wins room in the sunny section near my water garden."

Other Name False Spirea

Bloom Period and Color White, red, pink, peach, salmon-red, ruby-red, rose-pink, and lilac flowers bloom June till August.

Mature Height × Spread 2 feet × 18 inches

When and How to Plant Plant dormant bare-root transplants of Astilbe in early spring before new growth starts. Plant nursery-grown container stock throughout the growing season as long as water can be supplied. Transplant or divide Astilbe every three to four years to retain maximum vigor in early spring just as new growth emerges, or in fall as growth finishes. The mother plant will have become weakened, so add her to the compost pile. Divide and transplant juniors to fill in the garden.

Sun and Soil Preferences Plant in partial shade to full shade. A slightly acidic, well-drained soil rich in organic matter makes an ideal growing environment.

Moisture Requirements Water as needed and provide a 2- to 3-inch layer of organic mulch to keep the soil slightly moist at all times. Mulch is particularly important during dry periods of summer or when rainfall is scarce.

Fertilizing Apply a 5-10-5 or equivalent slow-release plant food during spring cleanup time, following the label directions.

Pruning and Care Clip out spent flower spikes as the florets wither.

Pests and Diseases There are no particular pest problems. A 2- to 3-inch layer of pine bark mini-nuggets used as a mulch will reduce weeds and conserve moisture.

Additional Species, Cultivars, or Varieties 'Red Sentinel' has bright-red flower spikes; 'Rheinland' has clear-pink flower plumes; 'Fanal' has red flowers; and 'Peach Blossom', pale-pink florets. *Astilbe simplicifloia* 'Sprite' is a dwarf form, 1 foot tall, that produces shocking-pink blooms in midsummer; it was voted by the Perennial Plant Association as the Plant of the Year in 1994. *A. chinensis ×* 'Visions' produces 24- to 30-inch-tall raspberry-colored plumes as a late-blooming variety; it is one of the most drought-tolerant Astilbe.

My Personal Favorite

NAME	SPECIAL CHARACTERISTICS
'Snowdrift'	A sport of A. 'Irrlicht' / selected by the Bloom Family of Bressingham Gardens in England / one of the whitest Astilbe to date

Beebalm
Monarda didyma

Preferred Zones	Sun Preferences	Additional Benefits
4 to 10	☼ ☼	🦋 🐦 🌷 🌼 Ⓝ 🐝 ◇

Beebalm, another addition to the butterfly, hummingbird, and bee garden, belongs to the mint family, Labiatae. A bed of Beebalm planted as companions to Crocosmia, Salvia, Rudbeckia, and Butterfly Bush will likely be host to not only its namesake, but to many winged friends, who will appear every day from mid-morning after the dew dries right up to sunset. In my garden, Beebalm comes alive with bees by 10 a.m. The butterflies arrive by 11 a.m. and the hummingbirds fly in by 1 p.m. It's a real joy to sit under the shade of the native Eastern Dogwood only a few feet away and watch the hummingbirds dart from Beebalm to Crocosmia and then to the Red Salvia. Once the Butterfly Bush comes into bloom, it's hard to keep track of all the flying creatures (I often wonder why they don't collide). At the end of the day, I pinch off a few fresh leaves from Beebalm to steep a fine cup of tea.

Other Names Oswego Tea / Bergamot

Bloom Period and Color Bright-red, pink, rose-pink, violet, lavender, and cream-white flowers bloom summer to early fall.

Mature Height × Spread 30 to 36 inches × 18 to 24 inches

When and How to Plant Start *Monarda didyma* seed indoors at least ten weeks before the last frost date in a moist, sterile seed-starting mix. A windowsill greenhouse with a clear plastic top provides a warm, humid environment for germination. Germination takes fifteen to twenty days at 70 degrees Fahrenheit, and the seedlings are relatively slow growers. Set out nursery-grown or home-grown transplants 12 to 18 inches apart at the level they were growing in their containers. Seed can be sown outdoors, spring through summer, until two months before the first frost date. A late seeding will likely be damaged by the first killing frost.

Sun and Soil Preferences Plant in full sun to partial shade in average, unimproved garden soil.

Moisture Requirements Beebalm requires even moisture while becoming established, then is relatively drought-tolerant.

Fertilizing In mid-season, boost flower production with a water-soluble plant food for flowering plants.

Pruning and Care Groom Beebalm by removing fading flower clusters after the sun goes down (so you will avoid contact with the bees). To maintain a healthy strong-stemmed plant, cut back hard in late fall, and divide three- to four-year-old beds during early spring as new growth emerges.

Pests and Diseases Beebalm has no real pests and diseases—just lots of bees, butterflies, and hummingbirds. Planting in an airy location will reduce mildew.

Additional Species, Cultivars, or Varieties There are many improved varieties for the Beebalm garden. Choose from 'Croftway Pink', sporting rose flowers in July; 'Snow White', with white flowers in July; and 'Petite Delight', with light-pink flowers perched on a compact dwarf plant that grows only 12 to 15 inches tall. *M. fistula* 'Violet Queen' is a troublefree perennial with intense violet-purple flowers and foliage that is resistant to mildew.

My Personal Favorite

NAME	SPECIAL CHARACTERISTICS
'Cambridge Scarlet'	Another improved variety / red flowers bloom July and August

Black-Eyed Susan

Rudbeckia species

Preferred Zones	Sun Preferences	Additional Benefits
3 to 10		

Rudbeckia and its varieties are among the easiest groups of flowers to grow. When planted as a background to gently swaying wispy plumes of ornamental grasses, Daylilies ('Stella d'Oro' with golden yellow trumpets), and Sedum ('Autumn Joy' with domes of pink flowers turning to copper in fall), the Black-eyed Susan species, Rudbeckia fulgida, makes quite a show. (This description is actually a snapshot of part of my perennial garden that grows on the south side of my water garden—the species is taller than the others and is recommended for background planting.) The dark-centered, golden-yellow flowers, more than three inches across, are exhibited on long rigid stems. Their stem characteristics make them great candidates for use in cut-flower arrangements. R. fulgida 'Goldsturm', an eighteen- to thirty-six-inch-tall orange-yellow bloomer from summer to fall, is easy to grow in large containers on the patio.

Other Name Coneflower

Bloom Period and Color *Rudbeckia* flowers in shades of golden yellow, with dark centers, blooming midsummer into autumn.

Mature Height × Spread 18 inches to 7 feet (spread depends on variety)

When and How to Plant Plant or divide Black-eyed Susan in early spring in the Tri-State area. Container plants may be set at any time up to late fall, planting no deeper than the soil line in the pot. Set transplants 12 to 18 inches apart, giving them room for good air circulation, a requirement for controlling powdery mildew on the foliage. For wildflower plantings, watch the weather reports: if snow is at hand, bundle up, and go out and scatter the seeds of *R. hirta* Black-eyed Susan. Then step back and watch them grow in the spring.

Sun and Soil Preferences Plant in full sun to light partial shade in any well-drained soil.

Moisture Requirements Once established, *Rudbeckia* is both heat- and drought-tolerant. In fact, you'll find this species listed on xeriscape plant lists.

Fertilizing Apply a plant food for flowering plants in early spring according to the label directions.

Pruning and Care Remove spent blossoms immediately after bloom to prolong the flowering season.

Pests and Diseases Apply 2 to 3 inches of organic mulch to keep down the weeds. Aphids may appear in spring and early summer. Apply insecticidal soap. Read the label. Check with your county cooperative extension educator for the latest control for powdery mildew.

Additional Species, Cultivars, or Varieties Rudbeckia and its varieties are among the easiest perennials to grow. The species *R. fulgida* grows very tall and is recommended for planting as a backdrop to the perennial garden. *R. fulgida* 'Goldsturm', an 18- to 36-inch-tall orange-yellow bloomer from summer to fall, loves full sun to partial shade. *R. hirta*, referred to as an annual, biennial, or a short-lived perennial, can be started from seed indoors seven to eight weeks before the last frost date.

My Personal Favorite

NAME	SPECIAL CHARACTERISTICS
R. hirta 'Indian Summer'	Largest-flowered Black-eyed Susan / 6- to 9-inch, golden-yellow blossoms on 3-foot-tall plants / a 1995 AAS Award Winner

Bleeding Heart
Dicentra species

Preferred Zones	Sun Preferences			Additional Benefits
3 to 8				

Depending on the species of Bleeding Heart you grow, you can have pink, cherry-pink, and/or white heart-shaped flowers dripping from gracefully cascading stems all the way from mid-spring right up to the first killing frost of fall. For spring bloom, I plant Dicentra spectabilis *Old-fashioned Bleeding Heart*, as it produces delicate, pink, heart-shaped flowers on twenty-four- to thirty-inch-tall plants. In May through June, D. s. 'Alba' showcases white blossoms on twenty-four- to thirty-inch-tall petioles. The only drawback with Old-fashioned Bleeding Heart and 'Alba' is that when they finish blooming, the plants wither and disappear. After spring-blooming Bleeding Heart disappears from the scene for the summer, plant a shallow-rooted colorful annual like Impatiens to fill in the space. In my zone 6 garden, Dicentra formosa 'Luxuriant', the Ever-blooming Bleeding Heart, exhibits cherry-pink heart-shaped flowers above twelve- to fifteen-inch, blue-green, fernlike foliage from early April to frost in the fall. This ever-bloomer is located under a Dogwood tree where it receives direct morning sun but is protected from the hot afternoon sun. It's splendiferous!

Other Names Valentine Flower / Lady's Locket / Old-Fashioned Bleeding Heart / Fringed Bleeding Heart

Bloom Period and Color Pink, cherry-pink, and white flowers bloom from mid-spring to fall frost, depending on the species.

Mature Height × Spread 12 to 30 inches × 18 to 24 inches

When and How to Plant Plant dormant bare-root divisions in early spring at a depth that permits the tip of the bare-root crown to barely show at the soil surface. Plant nursery-grown container plants in spring to early summer at the same soil level they were in their containers.

Sun and Soil Preferences Bleeding Heart tolerates direct sun to partial or deep shade. The key to success is soil preparation; it loves rich, humusy forest soil. Improve your soil by incorporating generous quantities of well-rotted compost or milled sphagnum peat moss to a depth of at least 12 inches. *Dicentra* loves a soil that is moist but not wet.

Moisture Requirements Ever-blooming Bleeding Heart must be watered during prolonged drought periods to ensure continuous bloom.

Fertilizing Feed Bleeding Heart with a slow-release granular plant food for flowering plants in early spring.

Pruning and Care Little care is needed for spring-blooming Bleeding Heart. Just spend a few moments each week snipping out yellowed foliage.

Pests and Diseases There are none.

Additional Species, Cultivars, or Varieties D. s. 'Alba' showcases white blossoms on 24- to 30-inch-tall petioles, flowering in May through June. *Dicentra formosa* 'Luxuriant' Ever-blooming Bleeding Heart exhibits cherry-pink heart-shaped flowers above 12- to 15-inch blue-green, fernlike foliage from early spring to frost in the fall. D. f. tolerates full sun to partial shade, but light shade in midafternoon prolongs bloom; deadhead spent flower spikes immediately upon maturing for best, continuous bloom. D. eximia Fringed Bleeding Heart or Wild Bleeding Heart exhibits pink hearts on a neat mound of finely dissected foliage. D. e. 'Snowdrift' produces pure-white Bleeding Hearts on the same style of plant.

My Personal Favorite

NAME	SPECIAL CHARACTERISTICS
Dicentra spectabilis Old-fashioned Bleeding Heart	Produces delicate, pink, heart-shaped flowers on 24- to 30-inch-tall plants in early spring

Butterfly Weed

Asclepias tuberosa

Preferred Zones	Sun Preference		Additional Benefits
3 to 9	☼		🦋 🔆

This irresistible-to-butterflies plant is appropriately named. When in full bloom with its almost artificial-looking yellow, orange, or red flowers (depending on the cultivar), Butterfly Weed is likely to be covered with butterflies, monarchs in particular. Because it emerges late in the season, it needs protection from springtime cultivation. I know this from experience. A few years back I was working in my Rhododendron collection when I noticed a large swarm of monarch butterflies darting in and out of several plants. Curious, I walked over to see what was attracting them. Much to my surprise, I discovered that a lush, well-branched Butterfly Bush had sprouted in between two of my favorite Rhododendrons. It was in full flower, and yes, it was pulsating with monarch butterflies. Now that I know the plant is there, I mark the ground to avoid any possible damage during springtime cleanup.

Bloom Period and Color Bright orange, fiery red, and yellow flowers bloom late June to August.

Mature Height × Spread 2 feet × 2 to 3 feet

When and How to Plant Collect seeds from mature Butterfly Weed flowers in late summer before the seedpods shatter, and scatter them to the wind. Or scatter the featherlike, prechilled (three to six weeks) seeds on the surface of a prepared seedbed as the soil warms in spring. Small potted nursery-grown transplants are available from perennial growers and specialty plant catalogs for spring planting; they are best started in the same location in which they are to be enjoyed. Since Butterfly Weed is slow at sprouting in late spring, it is imperative that you mark the locations of last year's plants. Don't cultivate the soil, as you will probably destroy the crown and roots of an up-and-coming plant. Once the plants are established, leave well enough alone—don't dig up a well-established plant, as fatal shock is inevitable. Small seedlings no more than 1 to 2 inches in size, often found at the base of the mother Butterfly Weed, may be transplanted if this is done right away, as they sprout in spring and before a taproot develops. Take a core of soil (4 to 5 inches deep) with each transplant in an effort to protect the developing taproot.

Sun and Soil Preferences Plant in full sun in average, unimproved garden soil.

Moisture Requirements Provide even moisture while starting seed. Once established, the plants are drought-tolerant.

Fertilizing No fertilizing is needed.

Pruning and Care To enjoy Butterfly Weed as a long-lasting cut flower, sear the base of the cut stem with a flame immediately upon harvesting. Take the flame to the garden; don't wait even five minutes.

Pests and Diseases There are none. Any caterpillars are probably from monarch butterflies and should be left alone.

Additional Species, Cultivars, or Varieties *A. incarnata* 'Ice Ballet' produces large clusters of showy white flower heads on 3-foot-tall, 2-foot-wide plants.

My Personal Favorite

NAME	SPECIAL CHARACTERISTICS
'Gay Butterflies Mix'	Exhibits blossoms with hues in pale to rich golden-yellow, bright orange, and shades of red

Columbine

Aquilegia hybrids

Preferred Zones	Sun Preferences	Additional Benefit
3 to 9	☀ ◑	🦋

Let your imagination run. Dream of a cross between a doctor bird (hummingbird) and a Cattleya Orchid. The prodigy could very well be a delicate, colorful blossom called Columbine! When planted where exposed to a gentle breeze, Columbine blossoms dance on thin stalks for hours on end. For the past six years I have been growing Columbine in a whiskey half-barrel placed next to the love seat on a brick patio next to my water garden. As the blossoms mature, I make sure the seeds are well distributed in the soil in the container. Over the years I have noticed a change in colors, the likes of which would excite any artist who works in watercolors or pastels; allowing Columbine to go to seed allows self-hybridizing to many different colors. Ideal companion plants for a Columbine garden are Siberian Iris and Lupine.
Note: *Columba of Columbine refers to the stylized likeness of the flower spurs to a clutch of pigeons, and aquila is Latin for "eagle".*

Other Name Granny's Bonnet

Bloom Period and Color Virtually every color and shade in the rainbow can appear in late spring to early summer.

Mature Height × **Spread** 10 inches to 3 feet × 12 to 15 inches

When and How to Plant After chilling in the refrigerator for three weeks, start Columbine seed indoors on a well-drained, sterile seed-starting mix at 70 to 75 degrees Fahrenheit (start the seeds indoors six to eight weeks before the last frost date to have transplants ready for spring planting). Do not cover seeds with soil. Sprouting takes three to four weeks. Allow a few seedpods to fall to the ground to ensure reseeding and replenishment of Columbine for years to come. Outdoor sowing may be done anytime from early spring through summer.

Sun and Soil Preferences Columbine grows in full sun to partial shade. For best exhibition, thin direct-seeded plants or set container-grown transplants 1 to 2 feet apart in well-drained soil in light shade.

Moisture Requirements Keep Columbine well watered.

Fertilizing Feed monthly with a water-soluble plant food formulated for flowering plants.

Pruning and Care Do not use pre-emergent weed controls in perennial gardens where Columbine seeds are to be started.

Pests and Diseases There are no particular pest problems.

Additional Species, Cultivars, or Varieties 'McKana Giants Mix', growing to 3 feet tall, produces a mixture of colorful Columbine flowers on strong stems that make excellent cut flowers. Rocky Mountain Columbine *A. caerulea*, the state flower of Colorado, is sky blue with a white corolla, 2 to 3 inches across, and stands to 2 feet tall; it is hardy from zones 2 to 7. *A. flabellata* 'Ministar', a dwarf Columbine with blue-and-white flowers, standing only 6 to 8 inches tall, produces flowers from late spring to early summer. The native species is *A. canadensis* Wild Columbine.

My Personal Favorite

NAME	SPECIAL CHARACTERISTICS
'McKana Hybrids'	Comes back year after year / 2 feet tall / produces a mixture of colorful Columbine flowers on strong stems, making excellent cut flowers

Coral Bells

Heuchera spp. and hybrids

Preferred Zones	Sun Preferences	Additional Benefit
3 to 9	☼ ☀	🌼

As an edging along a walkway . . . in a rock garden . . . next to a water garden . . . or as a ground cover . . . Coral Bells in many varieties produces small bell-shaped flowers in colors of white to deep crimson to pale pink, all dangling from twenty-four-inch-tall panicles perched above mounds of evergreen, heart-shaped, bronze-colored foliage. Sounds attractive, doesn't it? If planted in partial shade and watered during drought, Coral Bells will flower every year from early summer into early fall. When finished blooming, they will continue to add color to the garden with their attractive heart-shaped foliage as a ground cover. In my garden, I have varieties of Coral Bells that double as foliage plants. Their leaves are chocolate-bronze, deep purple, deep red with silver variegation, or solid green. Because of our acid-soil conditions, I add dolomitic limestone before planting to sweeten the soil. Plant Heuchera not only for its summer color but also for its winter interest. The bronze-to-purple-red foliage seems to stand out even more during the first snowfall of winter.

Bloom Period and Color White, red, crimson, and pale-pink flowers bloom early summer to early fall.

Mature Height × **Spread** 12 to 24 inches × 18 to 24 inches

When and How to Plant To start seeds indoors, plant in a well-drained, sterile seed-starting mix and maintain the soil at 55 degrees Fahrenheit during germination. Germination takes up to three weeks in a damp (not wet) seed-starting mix. For seedling emergence in late spring to early summer, sow Coral Bells seed outdoors, after the soil cools to 55 degrees Fahrenheit in late fall, or while the soil is still cool in early spring. Plant container-grown plants after the last frost date in spring. Set nursery-grown transplants or thin direct-seeded plants to 9 to 15 inches apart.

Sun and Soil Preferences Plant in partial shade to full sun in a rich soil with excellent drainage.

Moisture Requirements Keep Coral Bells well watered during dry seasons.

Fertilizing Apply a granular 5-10-5 or equivalent plant food in spring. Topdressing in early spring with organic compost rich in nutrients provides a slow-release source of nutrition from late spring to early fall bloom.

Pruning and Care Pinch out spent flower spikes to force continuous bloom later into summer. Divide mature clumps (3 to 4 years old) as new growth emerges in spring.

Pests and Diseases There are no particular pest problems.

Additional Species, Cultivars, or Varieties *H. sanguinea* 'Bressingham Hybrids' offers sprays of carmine, white, and pink blooms on panicles 12 to 18 inches tall; this Coral Bells is a semi-evergreen, suitable for shade. *H.* 'Pewter Moon' produces delicate pink flowers on 18-inch-tall maroon stems above a bed of marbled leaves that are pewter in color on top and maroon on the undersides.

My Personal Favorite

NAME	SPECIAL CHARACTERISTICS
Heuchera 'Palace Purple'	Outstanding show, whether as a single specimen or planted as a ground cover / sprays of white flowers above bronze-to-purple-red foliage

Daylily

Hemerocallis hybrids

Preferred Zones	Sun Preferences		Additional Benefit
3 to 9	☀	☽	🌼

*I've heard it said, "If you can't grow anything in that part of the garden, plant Daylilies," and I believe that's true. Daylilies, literally thousands of varieties, grow best in a sunny garden, but they certainly will survive in the shade. I have Daylilies growing along a stone wall where they get morning sun, and they bloom. I have Daylilies growing in a corner where the greenhouse attaches to my house; they get afternoon sun, and they bloom. I have Daylilies growing on an impossible-to-mow slope (for erosion control), and they bloom. I have Daylilies growing in the shade of Butterfly Bushes near the water garden, and they bloom. Get the picture? Hemerocallis is the magic plant in most gardens. Some are classified as evergreen, some as semi-evergreen, and some as dormant. Others are classified by height and flower size. **Note:** Did you know Daylilies have long been known for their culinary properties? Chop freshly picked tight buds and open flowers; sauté them in a virgin olive oil . . . Oh, what a nutty taste.*

Bloom Period and Color Orange, pink, purple, red, maroon, white, yellow, and bicolor flowers bloom summer to fall.

Mature Height × Spread 1 to 4 feet (spread also depends on variety)

When and How to Plant Daylilies can be planted just as they sprout in early spring, or in fall after they have gone into dormancy for the winter. Plant bare-root transplants or container-grown Daylilies at a depth that allows the crown of the plant to rest just below the soil surface. Spacing depends on the variety.

Sun and Soil Preferences Plant in full sun or partial shade. Although they will adapt to differing soil conditions, from sand to clay, they'll do best in well-drained, deeply worked, organic soil.

Moisture Requirements Daylilies require little watering after planting, as long as water is available to help them get established. Mulch with shredded pine or hardwood bark, and water during drought periods in the Tri-State area.

Fertilizing Give Daylilies a light feeding in early spring with a complete plant food for flowering plants.

Pruning and Care Established beds need to be divided after three to five years, in spring just as new growth emerges, or in fall after foliage dies down.

Pests and Diseases There are no appreciable pest problems. A bed of Daylilies will need an occasional weed removed.

Additional Species, Cultivars, or Varieties 'Buffy's Doll' and 'Eenie Weenie' are dwarfs at just 6 inches tall. 'Texas Sunlight' exhibits large yellow flowers that grow to 2 feet tall when spaced 2 feet apart. 'Rocket City' has bright-orange blossoms on 2-foot-tall stems. 'Red Rum' blooms with red trumpets on 1- to 1½-foot-tall stems with a long flowering period of June, July, and August.

My Personal Favorite

NAME	SPECIAL CHARACTERISTICS
'Stella d'Oro'	The most popular in Tri-State gardens / 1 to 2 feet tall / yellow flowers / blooms May through September / clip out spent blossoms immediately after flower wilts to direct energy into the next bloom

Evening Primrose

Oenothera missourensis

Preferred Zones	Sun Preference	Additional Benefits
3 to 9	☀	

What a joy to take a tall glass of summer iced tea to the garden, pinch a sprig of peppermint for its flavoring, then sit down next to the water garden and drink in the pleasing fragrance from a bed of Evening Primrose in bloom. Exclusively a New World genus, Oenothera missourensis with its four- to six-inch yellow blossoms opens late in the day and closes the next morning. (O. fruticosa, or Common Sundrop, is the daytime version of Primrose, opening its blossoms early in the day.) When I was Executive Director of the Queens Botanical Garden in Flushing, New York, our floriculturist planted fragrant lemon-yellow Evening Primrose in beds next to the benches where visitors rested. There was just one problem: when it became closing time we had a hard time convincing the visitors that it was time to leave. They would inevitably ask to stay "just a few more minutes." I couldn't blame them. With water conservation of prime importance in the Tri-State area, Evening Primrose and its family members have become candidates for the xeriscape garden, as they are very drought-resistant.

Other Names Ozark Sundrop / Missouri Primrose

Bloom Period and Color Yellow flowers bloom May to September.

Mature Height × **Spread** 10 inches (spread depends on variety)

When and How to Plant Plant from May to July. Before sowing Evening Primrose seeds directly into the garden, prepare the soil by incorporating well-rotted compost to a depth of 12 inches or more. As the plant becomes established it will develop a large taproot, making it an excellent flowering plant for dry summer conditions. In early spring, start seeds indoors in a moist, sterile seed-starting mix at 70 to 75 degrees Fahrenheit for germination in fifteen to twenty days. Keep the mix evenly moist (not wet) during this time. Transplant individual seedlings into separate containers for growing until transplanting outside. Set out transplants, homegrown or nursery-grown, at the same level they were in their containers, 18 to 24 inches apart. If you have a moist soil, plant in a raised mound or bed and do not mulch.

Sun and Soil Preferences Plant in full sun. Although it will establish in just about any soil of somewhat neutral pH, Evening Primrose, native to the Great Plains, will do much better in deeply prepared soil.

Moisture Requirements After establishment, Evening Primrose requires little if any additional watering.

Fertilizing Feed with a water-soluble plant food formulated for flowering plants at half the rate called for on the label. Read the label!

Pruning and Care If you would like to use them in dried-flower arrangements, collect the seed capsules, which are tan, egg-sized, light, and papery, with four thin wings, in the fall.

Pests and Diseases Slugs and snails may be a problem. Apply a slug and snail bait according to the label directions.

Additional Species, Cultivars, or Varieties *O. speciosa*, also fragrant and an evening bloomer, produces soft-pink to white flowers on a mounded plant only 12 inches tall; the mother plant spreads by underground rhizomes and profusely reseeds itself. *O. berlandier* 'Siskiyou' has 2-inch-wide, fragrant, light-pink flowers all summer long; this species makes a great ground cover.

My Personal Favorite

NAME	SPECIAL CHARACTERISTICS
Evening Primrose	*O. missourensis*, the species / 12 inches tall / 4- to 6-inch yellow blooms open each evening throughout summer

Fernleaf Yarrow
Achillea filipendulina

Preferred Zones	Sun Preference	Additional Benefits
3 to 8	☀	🦋 💐 🌼 🔺

If you enjoy growing flowers for dried-flower arrangements, Fernleaf Yarrow should be in your garden. It's easy to grow and twice as easy to dry. Simply cut the twelve- to eighteen-inch stems when their flowers are at their brightest color, strip off some of the leaves, and tie three or four stems in a bunch. Hang the bunches upside down in a cool, dark, well-ventilated area and they will dry in six to eight weeks. They make virtually everlasting dried flowers. You'll want to grow several species so you can use not only the traditional golden colors but also have bright pink and white. I grow both species of Yarrow, A. filipendulina 'Cloth of Gold' (bright mustard-yellow blooms) and 'Coronation Gold' (bright-gold flower heads); and A. millefolium Common Yarrow, 'Pastel Mix' and 'Red Beauty'. The secret to retaining color is to dry them in the dark. To liven up the sunny summer garden, combine the golden-yellow, silver-foliaged Yarrow with bright-red Salvia, blue Delphinium, and tall pink Phlox.

Other Name Milfoil

Bloom Period and Color White, gold, and red-violet flowers bloom in June and repeat in September.

Mature Height × **Spread** 4 to 6 feet (spread is variety-dependent)

When and How to Plant Yarrow is easy to propagate from seed, by division, or from terminal cutting. Plant in spring or summer, up to two months before the first frost in the Tri-State area. Start seeds indoors by scattering them over a moist, sterile seed-starting mix, or scatter them over a prepared seedbed outside. Do not cover the seeds, as they must have light for germination. Germination takes about ten days indoors at 70 degrees Fahrenheit and up to twenty-one days when directly seeded into the garden. Space container-grown seedlings or nursery-grown transplants 1 to 2 feet apart.

Sun and Soil Preferences Plant in full sun in an average-to-poor soil.

Moisture Requirements Water new transplants immediately to settle the soil. A plant recommended for xeriscaping (water-efficient gardening), Yarrow needs little water once established.

Fertilizing Feed in spring with a 5-10-5 or equivalent at the label rate.

Pruning and Care After the late-spring to early-summer bloom, prune back the plant to just above the crown of foliage at the base. New stems will emerge with more flowers.

Pests and Diseases There are none of significance.

Additional Species, Cultivars, or Varieties 'Coronation Gold' has bright-yellow flowers on 3-foot-tall plants; space them 2 to 3 feet apart. *A. tomentosa* 'Aurea' has a fernlike foliage, creating a silvery, creeping mat topped with golden-yellow blossoms to 6 inches high. *A. millefolium* Common Yarrow 'Pastel Mix' and 'Red Beauty' grow 18 to 24 inches tall and bloom June through August. *A. m.* 'Cerise Queen' Hybrid grows to 2 feet tall with shell-pink to cherry-red flowers.

My Personal Favorite

NAME	SPECIAL CHARACTERISTICS
'Cloth of Gold'	Five feet tall / space at 2 feet / flowers with bright, mustard-yellow blooms

Foxglove

Digitalis purpurea

Preferred Zones	Sun Preferences	Additional Benefit
4 to 10	☀ ☀	🌼

Foxglove, a biennial or short-lived perennial with white, pink, yellow, and purple spikes of glovelike blooms, is unique. Just as you think it has disappeared from the garden, up comes a new seedling and another new bloom. I've planted Foxglove along the sunny path by my water garden and had it return each year. My Digitalis purpurea 'Excelsior' has become one of the most dependable flowering spikes in my garden. Like clockwork, this biennial produces huge flower spikes with florets all around the five-foot stems. I always leave a few early-flowering stalks so seedpods will form and drop to the ground for fall germination and flowering the next year. I avoid using pre-emergent weed controls in this part of the garden, as such controls would spell the end of the Foxglove. **Caution:** *Tell garden visitors, particularly children, that all types of Foxglove are toxic if eaten.*

Bloom Period and Color Assorted colors bloom in early summer.

Mature Height × **Spread** 30 inches (spread depends on variety)

When and How to Plant If you want plants to bloom the following year, sow Foxglove seeds outside in prepared soil by midsummer (up to two months before first frost). Keep the seed bed moist by sprinkling with a gentle mist of water. A thin layer of straw mulch over the seed bed will reduce drying and aid germination. Seeds sown indoors in a moist, sterile seed-starting mix will take up to twenty days to germinate at 70 degrees Fahrenheit. Keep the mix slightly moist, not wet. Set transplants no deeper than they were in the growing container, two or more feet apart.

Sun and Soil Preferences Plant in full sun in loose, organically rich, well-drained soil. Spring-started plants may be grown in partial shade over summer and then transplanted into full sun, their final home, in the fall.

Moisture Requirements Provide even moisture throughout the growing season.

Fertilizing In early spring, provide a general application of 5-10-5 or equivalent in that part of the garden where Foxglove is growing.

Pruning and Care To produce additional spikes for continuous bloom, cut spent flower spikes to just above the crown as soon as the last blossoms drop. A little winter protection with evergreen boughs or salt hay is desirable in the coldest gardens of the Tri-State area. The mulch, if placed gently on the plants, will not crush the crown. Do not use pre-emergent weed controls where *Digitalis* is expected to reseed.

Pests and Diseases There are none in particular.

Additional Species, Cultivars, or Varieties 'Excelsior' strain has flowers all the way around the stem. 'Foxy', only 30 inches tall, blooms the first year when seeded. 'Apricot' is appropriately named, with soft, apricot-colored gloves on spikes to 42 inches tall.

My Personal Favorite

NAME	SPECIAL CHARACTERISTICS
Common Foxglove	Biennial / flowers are usually purple-pink spotted with purple, but there are strains of white, pink, lavender, rose, and apricot

Garden Chrysanthemum

Dendranthema × grandiflora

Preferred Zones	Sun Preference		Additional Benefits
5 to 9	☀		🦋 🌷 🌼

Garden Mums are the backbone of the late-summer and fall flower garden. Because Mums are available in the trade by the thousands, these plants are a quick way to add color to garden or patio. The American Chrysanthemum Society has listed fifteen official flower types, with over 3000 different varieties, and more are being registered each year. Mum types include one- to six-inch flower heads with daisylike, cushion, button, spoon, spider, giant pompon, "football," and many more types of blooms. For gardeners in the Tri-State area, the major question may be: are they winter hardy? Some are and some are not. Mums set buds in response to day length. They may be considered in three groups that can be divided according to their response to day length: early bloomers bloom late July through August; others bloom August through September; and later bloomers bloom October through November (some into December, depending on where you live). To ensure they come back year after year, I plant Hardy Mums in late spring so they will have a chance to root into the soil.

Other Names Garden Mum / Hardy Mum

Bloom Period and Color Myriad colors bloom summer to late autumn.

Mature Height × **Spread** 4 feet (spread is variable to 3 feet)

When and How to Plant Plant by midsummer, not fall—tens of thousands, if not millions, of fall-planted "Hardy" Garden Mums are pronounced dead each spring. To establish a collection of Garden Mums, set transplants or rooted cuttings in a part of the garden where no night lighting like that of yard lights or porch lights can reach them: if the light is turned on during the night for as short a period as one minute each night during flowerbud induction, the Mums will not set bud.

Sun and Soil Preferences Plant in a well-drained soil with full-sun exposure.

Moisture Requirements Mums appreciate regular watering during their entire growing cycle.

Fertilizing Mums are big eaters, so feed regularly with a water-soluble plant food for flowering plants, following label directions.

Pruning and Care Pinch Mums to keep them from becoming a floppy flowering mess. During mid-May, established Hardy Mums must be pinched back by one-half. By mid-June, pinch again by one-half, pinching all the new shoots that emerged from the mid-May pinch. If the variety is an early bloomer, pinch again by July 1. If it is a late bloomer, wait until mid-July to perform the final pinch. Remember: no light at night.

Pests and Diseases Spittle bug, aphids, Japanese beetles, and slugs may be problems. Consult your county cooperative extension educator for the latest recommended controls.

Additional Species, Cultivars, or Varieties *Dendranthemum pacificum* is recommended for seashore planting. **Note:** *Tanecetum cinerariaefolium* and *T. roseum* are the source of pyrethrum, an organic insecticide. It is made by grinding dried flower heads into powder or, as a liquid extract, from soaking the flowers.

My Personal Favorite

NAME	SPECIAL CHARACTERISTICS
Garden Chrysanthemum	*D.* × *grandiflora*, the species / many for you to choose from

Garden Phlox
Phlox paniculata

Preferred Zones	Sun Preference	Additional Benefits
4 to 8	☀	🧴 🌷 Ⓝ

If you've ever seen a Garden Phlox left unattended during mid- to late summer in an open field or abandoned garden, at a distance it was probably quite beautiful. Up close, though, it may have lost its beautiful pink or purple color and taken on a muddy magenta look. Since the flower heads in the unattended garden were probably not removed, the seeds produced by nature likely reverted back to the wild form of Phlox paniculata whose colors are duller than those of the garden cultivars. A small patch of the old-fashioned Phlox next to my woodpile has reverted to a brownish magenta. The plants have been coming up for over thirty years and I kind of like having them around, so I just make sure no one mows that "patch of weeds." The modern Garden Phlox, with its many cultivars with single blossoms large enough to make bouquets by themselves, have largely replaced the old-fashioned Summer-blooming Phlox. **Note:** Phlox is a native of North America. The genus name of these brilliantly colored flowers comes from the Greek word Phlox, which means "flame."

Other Names Border Phlox / Summer-Blooming Phlox

Bloom Period and Color Blossoms in assorted colors—white, pink, red, cherry red—bloom July through September.

Mature Height × Spread 30 to 40 inches (spread depends on variety)

When and How to Plant Set transplants in early spring or late fall. Plant container-grown Garden Phlox 2 to 3 feet apart, no deeper than the soil level in the container, allowing plenty of space for air circulation.

Sun and Soil Preferences Garden Phlox is a somewhat demanding plant. It requires direct sunshine and a soil that is extremely well prepared. The soil must be porous, fertile, and enriched with great quantities of well-rotted compost or leaf mold to a depth of 12 or more inches.

Moisture Requirements Water deeply at root level during dry periods. If overhead sprinklers must be used in the garden, water in the early morning so the foliage has adequate time to dry before dark.

Fertilizing Apply a 5-10-5 or equivalent during spring according to the label directions for flowering plants.

Pruning and Care To maintain healthy Garden Phlox, divide plants every two to three years in early fall, replanting only strong, small, outer divisions. Throw mother out.

Pests and Diseases Phlox is highly susceptible to powdery mildew. If this disease is prevalent in your garden area, apply a fungicide recommended for powdery mildew, following the label directions. Check with your county cooperative extension educator or Master Gardener for the latest recommended fungicide. Make every effort to select mildew-resistant types.

Additional Species, Cultivars, or Varieties Outstanding varieties of Garden Phlox available in today's market include 'Bright Eyes', a blush-pink with a crimson eye, and 'Mt. Fuji', a pure white. 'David', said to be the best white variety, is mildew-resistant and stands to 40 inches tall; 'Eva Cullum', featuring clear-pink blossoms with dark-red eyes, growing to 3 feet tall, is also mildew-resistant; and 'Starfire' is the best red variety.

My Personal Favorite

NAME	SPECIAL CHARACTERISTICS
'Bright Eyes'	Blush-pink flower with a crimson eye

Goldenrod

Solidago spp. and hybrids

Preferred Zones	Sun Preference	Additional Benefits
3 to 9	☀	

Certain drives in midsummer and well into fall—from Bear Mountain down the Palisades Parkway into New York, down the Garden State Parkway to Atlantic City, up I-95 into Connecticut to Boston—are enhanced by the beauty of one of the most maligned flowers. Goldenrod has been blamed for triggering sneezing attacks, producing runny noses, and causing watery eyes, even though the real bad guy and the one to blame is Ragweed. You'll find Goldenrod everywhere in the Tri-State area. The perennial Solidago canadensis is the handsome native wildflower with yellow plumes; vast numbers of flower heads make up the exhibition of showy inflorescence. When used as dried flowers, stems of Goldenrod hold their color and florets for months. In Europe, Goldenrod is prized both as a garden plant and as a cut flower. In addition to S. canadensis are several other species grown in formal and wildflower gardens: S. altissima, S. graminifolia, S. rigida, S. rugosa, and S. sempervirens.

Bloom Period and Color   Bright yellow or gold flowers bloom August to September.

Mature Height × **Spread**   24 to 36 inches × 18 to 24 inches

When and How to Plant   Goldenrod is available from many perennial growers for springtime planting and is easily established from young, small transplants. Set out transplants 12 to 18 inches apart no deeper than the soil line in the growing containers after the last frost date so the plants will become established for summer bloom. Start Goldenrod seed indoors early in March, in a sterile seed-starting mix under warm, humid conditions. A windowsill greenhouse kit with a clear plastic top makes an ideal germination chamber.

Sun and Soil Preferences   Plant in full sun in average garden soil.

Moisture Requirements   Provide supplemental water only during the driest of summers. Avoid overhead irrigation.

Fertilizing   No fertilizing is necessary, as this is a native plant that grows in nature without fertilizer.

Pruning and Care   Other than pruning out broken stems caused from summer storms, no pruning is needed. During garden cleanup in late fall, prune dead stems to just above the ground.

Pests and Diseases   There are no general pest problems. The best control for rust, the bronze pustules found on the stems and undersides of the leaves, is to plant in the proper location: with good air circulation, full sun, and a well-drained soil, this fungal disease can be suppressed.

Additional Species, Cultivars, or Varieties   'Crown of Rays' is a 2- to 3-foot-tall plant with bright-yellow plumes. 'Golden Thumb', also known as 'Tom Thumb' and 'Queenie', grows to about 1 foot high with yellow flowers and yellowish-green leaves; this plant is a candidate for a sunny rock garden. *S. rigida*, a native Goldenrod, grows to 5 feet tall and is perfect for a wild-flower garden.

My Personal Favorite

NAME	SPECIAL CHARACTERISTICS
Solidago 'Cloth of Gold'	Dwarf but vigorous plant / 18 to 24 inches tall / deep-yellow flowers

Hosta

Hosta spp. and hybrids

Preferred Zones	Sun Preferences	Additional Benefits
3 to 9	☼ ☼ ☼	

A year does not pass without the introduction of new varieties of the herbaceous ground cover Hosta, also known in the Tri-State area as Funkia. Look around and you will discover dwarf varieties only six inches tall, giants to three or more feet tall, and many in between. You can rightly say that Hosta has become the number-one shade perennial throughout the United States as well as in the Tri-State area. In shady gardens, you may find the entire area planted in Hosta. A single plant specimen will become symmetrical in shape as it grows and spreads. Some species have fragrant white, powder-blue, or pale-violet flowers. The foliage colors— solid green, green-and-white, white-and-green, cream-and-green, or blue—are complemented by flower spikes reminiscent of the taller-growing Lilies; some have seersucker, or wrinkled, foliage. There is one downside to a Hosta garden, and that is, when winter arrives in the Tri-State area, the Hostas disappear. But never fear, they'll be back the following spring.

Other Names Funkia / Plantain Lily

Bloom Period and Color White, pale-lilac, or violet flowers, depending on variety, bloom in summer.

Mature Height × **Spread** 1 to 3 feet × 1 to 3 feet

When and How to Plant Bare-root transplants are best planted in spring. Plant container-grown plants no deeper than they were in their containers, at any time as long as water is available. Spacing depends on species and variety.

Sun and Soil Preferences Depending on the variety, Hosta are plantable in full sun to deep shade, in a well-drained, richly organic soil.

Moisture Requirements Provide even soil moisture throughout the growing season.

Fertilizing Feed with a 5-10-5 or equivalent plant food in early spring just as new growth starts.

Pruning and Care Remove spent flower spikes as seedpods form. Remove all dead foliage at the end of gardening season. Dig and divide overgrown Hostas, replanting the divisions at the same depth.

Pests and Diseases The bane of the Hosta collection is the slug, a snail without a shell. Clean up overwintering debris. In early spring, set out shallow containers filled with beer (any brand will do). Slugs are attracted to the beer and seem to die quite happily in it. Browsing deer are the other menace in suburbia: apply a commercially prepared deer-repellent according to the label directions, or use Milorganite™, a turf fertilizer made from processed tankage waste. As new leaves emerge, and continuing through fall, spread the Milorganite™ throughout the Hosta bed, following the label directions for turf. When deer bend down to browse, they get a whiff of the fragrance of the waste, and they usually pack up and go to your neighbors.

Additional Species, Cultivars, or Varieties Fragrant Hostas include but are not limited to 'So Sweet', which has glossy dark-green leaves with white flowers, and 'Grandiflora', which has green deeply ribbed leaves with huge white flowers. Look in any catalog and you'll find names and pictures for 'Frances Williams', 'Gold Standard', 'June', 'Elegens', and the list goes on and on. There are over 800 named varieties.

My Personal Favorite

NAME	SPECIAL CHARACTERISTICS
'Fragrant Bouquet'	Chartreuse leaves / pale-lavender flowers / fragrant

Lamb's Ear

Stachys byzantina

Preferred Zones	Sun Preferences	Additional Benefits
3 to 9	☼ ◐	NA

"Soft as felt." "As cuddly as lamb's wool." "Softer than a ball of cotton." All statements probably heard from a child (or adult) describing the sensation derived from touching a leaf of Lamb's Ear. Lamb's Ear produces twelve- to fifteen-inch-tall flower spikes with tiny lavender flowers. To keep the plant in tiptop shape, pinch out the flower spikes, directing energy into making more fuzzy Lamb's Ear leaves. The mound of silver-gray foliage, densely covered with soft pubescence (hair), is ideal as an edging plant for borders or where it can cascade over the edge of a retaining wall. I planted several Lamb's Ears in partial shade under a variegated Dogwood and pinched them several times until they grew into a soft, fuzzy mat of foliage, a perfect bed for Dude, my cat! For a season-long show, combine Achillea, Columbine, and Solidago with ground-hugging Stachys byzantina 'Silver Carpet'. Grow Lamb's Ear in a decorative pot and set it in a sunny spot next to the front door. I defy anyone not to touch it as they pass by.

Bloom Period and Color Small lavender-pink blossoms bloom late spring to early summer.

Mature Height × Spread 6 to 8 inches (flower spikes to 12 inches tall) × 12 to 18 inches

When and How to Plant Plant container-grown plants or freshly dug divisions 12 to 18 inches apart in spring or early fall. New plants may be started from seed planted in early spring, but they will not flower until the following year.

Sun and Soil Preferences Plant in full sun to partial shade in a very well-drained soil.

Moisture Requirements Be sure to avoid any overhead irrigation, particularly where the foliage might remain wet overnight. A wet plant going into a warm, humid night is sure to collapse into a mushy mess.

Fertilizing Apply a 5-10-5 or equivalent in spring as new growth starts.

Pruning and Care Repeat blooming may be achieved until frost if spent flowers are removed immediately after the blooms begin to fade.

Pests and Diseases There are generally no pest problems.

Additional Species, Cultivars, or Varieties 'Silver Carpet', a sterile cultivar, does not produce flowering stems so must be propagated vegetatively by divisions. *S. officinalis* 'Alba' has white flowers, and 'Rosea' has clear-pink flowers. *S. officinalis* is a bushy clump that grows to 18 inches tall and has a spread of 12 to 18 inches; it has round-toothed, wrinkled, oblong 1- to 4-inch foliage and is often hairy, but nothing like Lamb's Ear.

My Personal Favorite

NAME	SPECIAL CHARACTERISTICS
'Helen von Stein'	Also called 'Big Ears' / resistant to summer melting-out caused by heat and humidity / largest ears on a low, spreading plant

Lenten Rose

Helleborus hybridus

Preferred Zones

4 to 9

Sun Preferences

Additional Benefits

Years ago, in late winter, I fell in love with Lenten Rose after visiting a friend's garden in Greenwood, South Carolina. He had planted the Lenten Rose, in virtually every variety and color, underneath his tall Oak trees, along with compact evergreen Azaleas and Rhododendrons which, at that time, were budded up for bloom. I went right home and planted Lenten Rose, although mine still haven't equaled his. A real perennial, Helleborus comes back year after year, forming a dense ground cover even under trees with shallow roots. The evergreen foliage, standing twelve to sixteen inches high, produces long-lasting two- to two-and-a-half-inch flowers from winter through late spring. A bonus: Helleborus is deer-resistant! That's particularly important in my garden because I have a whole herd of deer that march through the garden every day. Don't be afraid to cut a few flowers for indoor enjoyment. As cut flowers, Lenten Rose blossoms last for weeks.

Bloom Period and Color Pure-white, rose, or maroon flowers bloom late winter to early spring.

Mature Height × **Spread** 1 to 1½ feet × 1½ to 2 feet

When and How to Plant You may direct-sow in a shady garden in late fall, or, to start from seed indoors, freeze *Helleborus* seed to break dormancy, then start them in a sterile seed-starting mix. Plant container-grown plants throughout spring or fall. When setting homegrown or nursery-grown plants, plant no deeper than the soil line in the growing container and allow 2 feet or more between the plants.

Sun and Soil Preferences Lenten Rose is a shade-lover and greatly appreciates a rich organic soil.

Moisture Requirements Plant container-grown plants in well-drained soil with moderate moisture. To ensure a rich soil and to help keep even moisture around Lenten Rose, sprinkle a thin layer, 1 to 2 inches, of well-rotted compost or pine bark mini-nuggets over the soil surface between the plants every year in late spring. Do not cover the crown of the plant with mulch.

Fertilizing Lenten Rose will spread on its own with a little help from a fertilizer. Apply a water-soluble 15-30-15 or equivalent in midseason to boost growth.

Pruning and Care As seedlings emerge from the mother plants, dig them as transplants to expand the garden or to share with a friend.

Pests and Diseases There are none.

Additional Species, Cultivars, or Varieties 'White Magic' produces white flowers fading to pale pink. *H. foetidus*, commonly known as "Stinky Helleborus", produces apple-green blossoms. Christmas Rose, *Helleborus niger*, is the winter bloomer with pure-white flowers that age to rose as they mature.

My Personal Favorite

NAME	SPECIAL CHARACTERISTICS
Lenten Rose	*Helleborus hybridus*, the species / the earliest of bloomers / flower colors range from cream to dusky rose / blooms from late winter to early spring

Lilyturf
Liriope muscari

Preferred Zones	Sun Preferences	Additional Benefits
5 to 10	☼ ☀	

Lilyturf is fast becoming one of the most popular ground covers in the Tri-State area, primarily because of its tolerance of drought and its adaptability to sun or shade. The dry summers of the late 20th century left landscapers and homeowners scrambling for water-efficient plants, and Lilyturf happens to be one of them. Professional landscapers are planting it as a ground cover in front of commercial buildings, along sidewalks, and in parking lot islands where irrigation is limited or nonexistent. Homeowners have learned quickly that this is a low-maintenance garden plant that is hardy year-round. All we have to do is give it a haircut, either with a rotary lawn mower set at its maximum height or with a pair of hedge shears, in early spring before new growth starts. Best if grown in partial shade, the solid-green grassy-foliage Lilyturf or the variegated green-and-white form will produce a solid mass of ground cover in just one season. For a year-round grassy look on the 24th-floor terrace, on the rooftop garden, or on the patio of a brownstone, plant containers of Lilyturf. You'll need only a pair of snips, not a lawn mower, to keep them in bounds.

Other Name Liriope

Bloom Period and Color Depending on the cultivar, lilac, lavender, purple, or white flowers, useful in flower arrangements, bloom in August and September.

Mature Height × **Spread** 1 to 1½ feet × 1 to 1½ feet

When and How to Plant Lilyturf is easily established by planting container-grown stock or field-grown clumps or divisions at any time during spring or fall; or set bare-root transplants in early spring. Set plants about 12 inches apart, and plant no deeper than the soil line on bare-root transplants or in the pot.

Sun and Soil Preferences Plant in full sun to partial shade in almost any soil condition.

Moisture Requirements Just provide a thorough watering immediately after planting.

Fertilizing Spring-feed with a granular 5-10-5 or equivalent, following label directions.

Pruning and Care Cut off last year's foliage in early spring to encourage new growth and a fresh look for the grasslike blades.

Pests and Diseases At the first sign of spring, start slug and snail controls, using a commercially prepared slug bait according to the label directions.

Additional Species, Cultivars, or Varieties 'Monroe White', 8 to 10 inches high, has white flower spikes from August through September. 'Variegata', 10 to 12 inches, blossoms with lavender flower spikes August through September. *L. spicata* 'Creeping Lilyturf', with lavender flower spikes August through September, grows with mounds of narrow grassy leaves supporting 3-inch-tall flower clusters on 12- to 15-inch-tall spikes of pale lavender or almost white, and is hardy to zone 4; it grows in partial shade in almost any soil. *L. spicata* 'Silver Dragon', 10 inches tall, produces strikingly attractive silver-white variegated leaves from August through September.

My Personal Favorite

NAME	SPECIAL CHARACTERISTICS
'Big Blue'	Grows 12 to 18 inches tall / produces lavender-blue flower spikes from August through September

Lupine

Lupinus hybrids

Preferred Zones	Sun Preferences	Additional Benefit
4 to 6	☼ ☼	❀

For a Lupine show, visit Mohonk Mountain House in New Paltz, New York. Stroll through their perennial garden when the Lupine bloom in late June through July. Mohonk's Lupine 'Russell Hybrid Mix', which produces virtually every color in the rainbow and offers plants started from their own collected seed, blooms later than mine, as they are in a colder zone. You may find some of the hybridized two-tone combinations, pink-and-white or blue-and-yellow. Take your camera and lots of film. Since Lupine seldom comes true from seed (one hundred seeds taken from one plant may produce one hundred different varieties), plant it from named transplants, or start with hybrid seed and then let it be. Once the taproot develops on the mother plant, transplanting can spell disaster if that taproot is cut.

Bloom Period and Color Almost every color in the rainbow, bicolors, and pastels bloom June through July.

Mature Height × **Spread** 3 feet × 1¹/₂ to 2 feet

When and How to Plant Set out container-grown Lupine no deeper than the soil line in the pot, in early spring or mid-fall. For starting "new" varieties of Lupine, allow a few flower spikes to remain on the plant to maturity. Collect seed in a nylon stocking slipped down over a spent flower spike before the seeds mature. Tie the stocking to the stem so the seeds do not fall out or fly away. Lupine seedpods explode as they mature, scattering seeds to the wind. To facilitate seed germination, scratch the Lupine seed coat (scarify), or soak seed in slightly warm water overnight before planting.

Sun and Soil Preferences Plant in full sun to partial shade (direct morning sun with protection in the hottest afternoon), in well-drained average soil with an acid to neutral soil pH.

Moisture Requirements A winter mulch of Oak leaves or straw will provide protection from winter desiccation in exposed locations. Remove the mulch as soon as new sprouts appear in spring.

Fertilizing Feed with a balanced plant food for flowering plants as new growth emerges in spring. Additional feeding as the first flowering subsides will produce a stronger second bloom.

Pruning and Care Immediately after the initial flowering, and before seedpods form, prune back spent flower spikes to the basal leaves. New flower spikes will likely emerge with additional blooms.

Pests and Diseases Watch for aphids, plant lice that can pierce and suck the life from the flower spikes. Apply an aphicide, such as insecticidal soap, according to the label directions.

Additional Species, Cultivars, or Varieties Other outstanding Lupines include 'My Castle' with brick red flowers on 2- to 3-foot-stems, and 'The Chatelaine', with pink-and-white bicolor flowers. *Lupinus perennis*, a native species with 24-inch-tall spikes of blue flowers, is hardy in zones 3 to 7.

My Personal Favorite

NAME	SPECIAL CHARACTERISTICS
Lupinus hybrids 'Russell Hybrid Mix' and 'Gallery Mix'	Standby for any Lupine garden / 15 to 18 inches tall / dwarf series in blue, pink, red, and white

Michaelmas Daisy

Aster novi-belgii

Preferred Zones	Sun Preferences		Additional Benefits
4 to 9			

A drive up the New York State Thruway, along the Garden State Parkway of New Jersey, or the Connecticut Turnpike any time from midsummer through to the killing frost of fall, will show you the most prolifically blooming plants of the Tri-State area. You'll see millions, if not billions, of the violet-blue blossoms of Hardy Asters, the New York Aster, and New England Aster. These are relatives of the Asters many of us enjoy in our gardens and as cut flowers. I myself tried Hardy Asters in my garden, but what with Bambi and all her relatives munching through every day, the attempt was a dismal failure. I neglected to apply a deer-repellent immediately after planting, and only plant stubs were visible the next day. Despite my experience, I highly recommend planting Michaelmas Daisy (the Hardy New York Aster) or any of its cultivars—but only if you don't have browsing deer.

Other Name Hardy New York Aster

Bloom Period and Color Flowers in brilliant to sky blue, white, pink, purple, deep purple, or lavender with gold centers bloom August to frost.

Mature Height × Spread 6 inches to 4 feet (spread depends on variety)

When and How to Plant Hardy hybrids must be propagated vegetatively to retain the variety. Plant Michaelmas Daisies with divisions taken from healthy outer portions of the mother plant. In spring, set divisions or container-grown plants no deeper than the soil level in the growing container or the soil line on the division at any time when the soil is workable. When planting *en masse*, allow 18 or more inches between plants.

Sun and Soil Preferences Plant in full sun to partial shade in well-drained, moist, fertile soil.

Moisture Requirements Provide moisture during establishment and during drought.

Fertilizing Fertilize sparingly with a plant food for flowering plants.

Pruning and Care To keep plants compact and bushy, pinch new spring growth when it reaches 6 inches in height, and once again by mid-June. Do not pinch after mid-June or bloom will be delayed into late fall. Divide Michaelmas Daisies every two or three years to maintain vigor.

Pests and Diseases These Daisies are extremely susceptible to mildew, so plant only with excellent air circulation, and if necessary, apply a fungicide labeled for mildew as directed on the label. Apply a deer-repellent according to the label directions starting after the first pinch of spring, or immediately after planting, and continue through fall.

Additional Species, Cultivars, or Varieties In addition to the species, cultivars include 'Alert', with deep-crimson blooms, 12- to 15-inch stems; 'Boningdale White', with semi-double to double clean white flowers on 4-foot-tall plants; and 'Rose Serenade', with masses of cherry rose-colored flowers.

My Personal Favorite

NAME	SPECIAL CHARACTERISTICS
Aster × frikartii 'Monch'	Also called 'Monk' / one of the top six garden flowers ever / blooms twice as long as others, from early summer until frost / masses of clear-blue flowers on upright 30-inch plants

Oriental Poppy

Papaver orientale

Preferred Zones	Sun Preference		Additional Benefits
2 to 7			

In the Tri-State area, water conservation and water-efficient gardening have become dominant and commanding topics, and I often receive calls to my Garden Hotline® radio program requesting recommendations of plants for dry soils. One of my first responses is often Oriental Poppy. These drought-tolerant Poppies make notably colorful additions to xeriscape gardens. (By the way, xeriscape gardening means water-efficient gardening—it doesn't mean you turn off the water.) I planted Oriental Poppy in my garden long before water conservation became the "in" thing. What a joy to see those solitary, four- to six-inch, globe-shaped flowers with crepe-paper-thin petals in red, pink, orange, and white standing in the garden during late June and July. Since the foliage of Oriental Poppy dies down during midsummer, use other water-efficient plants like Rudbedkia, Salvia, Coreopsis, and Butterfly Weed to fill in the gap created by the "missing" Poppy. If you want to add Oriental Poppies to your garden, plant two or three groups of different colors, with three plants of each variety, accompanied by Asters. The Aster fills in the hole left by the dormant Poppy during late summer and fall.

Bloom Period and Color White, red, pink, and orange flowers bloom
June to early July.

Mature Height × **Spread** 2 to 4 feet tall (spread is variety-dependent)

When and How to Plant Since Oriental Poppies do not transplant well,
direct-sow seeds in late fall or early spring. Unlike the seeds of other species
of Poppy, the seeds of Oriental Poppy should not be covered. They need light
for germination. To settle the seeds, which appear as larger specks of dust,
sprinkle them with a heavy mist of water. After germination, thin the seedlings
to 12 to 18 inches apart. If you want to start seeds indoors, start them in a
moist, sterile seed-starting mix maintained at a cool 55 degrees Fahrenheit.
A windowsill greenhouse with a clear plastic cover is an ideal germination
chamber for seeds without soil cover. Germination takes ten to fifteen days.

Sun and Soil Preferences Plant in full sun into rich, well-drained garden
soil in the exact place where they are to grow.

Moisture Requirements No extra watering is needed even in the driest of
summers in the Tri-State area.

Fertilizing No fertilizing is required.

Pruning and Care To maintain vigorous, healthy, blooming plants, divide
Oriental Poppies while dormant every four to five years by lifting the roots
and cutting them into 3- to 4-inch sections. The time for division is right after
bloom, just as the leaves disappear. Plant the root sections 3 inches deep and
upright in well-drained sandy soil. Oriental Poppy foliage reappears in early
fall. To prolong Poppies as cut flowers, harvest the blossoms when they are at
their maximum moisture content in the early morning. Singe the base of the
hollow stem with a flame to seal in water.

Pests and Diseases There are none.

Additional Species, Cultivars, or Varieties Popular cultivars include
'Lavender Glory' with lavender flowers; 'Salmon Glow' with double flowers of
salmon-orange; 'Harvest Moon' with large double golden-yellow flowers;
'Julianna' with brilliant pink flowers; 'Marcus Perry' with brilliant scarlet-red
flowers; 'Snow Queen' with large white flowers with black basal spots; and
'Springtime' with white flowers with pink margins.

My Personal Favorite

NAME	**SPECIAL CHARACTERISTICS**
'Bonfire'	Fire-red flowers

Peony

Paeonia lactiflora

Preferred Zones	Sun Preference		Additional Benefits
3 to 10	☼		🧪 🌼 Ⓝ

Read almost any article about Peonies and you'll find them referred to as the "Queen of Flowers." Grow them in your garden and you'll understand why they've been given that name. My collection of Peonies (P. lactiflora Common Garden Peony) has been well established for more than twenty years, and when the plants bloom in May and early June, they are much admired by friends and neighbors. Every five to seven years I divide the plants, as the roots tend to become overcrowded, causing diminished bloom. Of course those same friends and neighbors become the recipients of many of the divisions. One overgrown Peony root system, cut up into three or more eyes per division, gives me ten to fifteen divisions. In the Tri-State garden, Peonies thrive in full sun and are unbelievably hardy, once established. With thousands of registered varieties, I'm sure you can find a Peony you'll enjoy.

Bloom Period and Color Red, pink, white, lavender-pink, crimson, burgundy-red, apple-blossom pink, and light yellow flowers bloom May to June.

Mature Height × Spread 18 to 40 inches × 24 to 30 inches

When and How to Plant Container-grown Peonies may be set spring or fall. Plant divisions of dormant Peony roots (available from garden centers and mail-order nurseries) in October. Each division should have at least three to five eyes, the little pink buds perched on the top side of the roots. The divisions should be planted at a depth that allows the eyes to be no deeper or shallower than 1 to 1½ inches, or there will be no flowers. As pink shoots emerge, position a Peony ring over the plant. The Peony ring, with 3-foot-tall wire legs, is a wire hoop with a gridwork of crosswires attached to the hoop. The new stems grow up through the hoop for support, particularly important if it rains just as the huge blooms open. Spacing depends on variety.

Sun and Soil Preferences Plant in full sun in well-drained, organically rich garden soil.

Moisture Requirements Provide even moisture, particularly during flower-bud set and blooming.

Fertilizing A late-fall feeding with a balanced plant food formulated for flowering plants will benefit next year's bloom.

Pruning and Care Pinch off infected buds (those that turn black and fail to open). After frost, trim stems and foliage to the ground; remove debris. When using as cut flowers, harvest Peonies just as the blossoms show color. Crush the stem end with a wooden mallet and place that stem base in tepid water.

Pests and Diseases *Botrytis cinerea* (gray mold) is the bane of the Peony patch. You'll recognize this when the flowerbuds turn black and fail to open. The suppression of this disease starts with garden cleanup in the spring. As pink shoots emerge, apply a fungicide recommended for botrytis. Repeat applications as needed through bloom. If ants are present, just rinse them off with water; they are harmless.

Additional Species, Cultivars, or Varieties 'Cytherea' is a midseason peony, faintly scented with deep-cherry blossoms fading to pale peach. 'Sarah Bernhardt' has large, apple-blossom-pink, double flowers late in the season.

My Personal Favorite

NAME	SPECIAL CHARACTERISTICS
'Monsieur Jules Elie'	Huge, fragrant, early double flowers of silvery rose pink / ideal for cutting

Siberian Iris

Iris sibirica

Preferred Zones	Sun Preferences	Additional Benefits
4 to 10	☼ ☼	🌼 △

After Iris germanica, *the Bearded Iris, has finished in your Iris garden, continue the bloom by adding its grassy-looking cousin* Iris siberica, *the Siberian Iris. Siberian Iris plants make great companions in a Peony collection, a Yarrow patch, or a grouping of Oriental Poppies. The original popular species, found everywhere in the Tri-State area, has shiny, wispy, grasslike foliage, capped off by bluish-purple blooms. Hybridizers have developed a host of improved cultivars and colors, including shades of blue, purple, white, bicolor, and even yellow. Over the years I've given away more starts from my Siberian Iris beds than from the beds of any other plants I grow. To share transplants in late summer when their roots are in active growth, I use a flat, heavy-bladed nursery spade to dig out eight-by-eight-inch, six-inch-deep clumps. That's a square plug that can be planted as is, at the same planting depth. I've even dug clumps using my back-hoe (those beds were well rooted!). Nothing ventured, nothing gained. It worked.*

Bloom Period and Color Deep-purple, blue, pink, or white flowers bloom late May through June.

Mature Height × **Spread** 2 to 3 feet (unlimited spreading)

When and How to Plant Container plants may be planted at any time the soil is workable. Bare-root Siberian Irises are available from mail-order sources for planting in early spring. Dig holes 6 to 8 inches deep and 15 to 18 inches apart. Spread out the roots, cover, water, and then step back and watch them grow. That's it, except for patience: newly planted Siberian Iris require two to three years to produce high-quality blooms.

Sun and Soil Preferences Siberian Irises are quite versatile. Plant in full sun to light shade, in wet or dry areas, in clay-type or sandy soil.

Moisture Requirements The plants require even moisture for establishment, then their thick roots grow deeply into the soil, making them drought-resistant.

Fertilizing Apply 5-10-5 or equivalent as new foliage emerges in spring, at the label-recommended rate.

Pruning and Care After bloom, cut out the spent flower stems. Save the stems of the dried brown seedpods, as they are prized in dried-flower arrangements. Garden cleanup includes cutting back the grassy foliage to about 4 inches after a hard freeze. Overgrown or crowded clumps of Siberian Iris can be dug during late summer, divided, and replanted immediately.

Pests and Diseases There are none.

Additional Species, Cultivars, or Varieties Hybridizers have graced the Siberian Iris collector with greatly improved varieties in shades of blue, purple, white, bicolors, and even yellow. Cultivars include 'Dreaming Spires', with huge, rich-blue blossoms waving freely on 28-inch-tall plants; 'Blue King', a 30- to 36-inch-tall plant with bright-blue flowers; and 'Caesar's Brother', a 36-inch-tall plant that produces very rich deep-violet flowers. 'King of Kings', 34 inches tall, is an outstanding pure-white flower. The backbone of the Iris rainbow of color is *Iris* × *germanica* Tall Bearded Iris.

My Personal Favorite

NAME	SPECIAL CHARACTERISTICS
'Butter and Sugar'	Award winner from 1981 and 1986 / blossoms with white standards (upright petals) and unique yellow falls (lower petals)

Solomon's Seal

Polygonatum commutatum

Preferred Zones	Sun Preferences	Additional Benefits
4 to 9		

"Gracefully arching stems of green foliage at the shady base of a meandering fieldstone wall . . . Elegant green foliage bowing outward with white bell-like blossoms hanging from below, growing along a woodland path . . . Soft, sweet, fragrances riding the breezes outward from a bed of foliage near a sitting area in the woods . . . What do these portraits have in common? They all describe plantings of Solomon's Seal or one of its relatives. In fall, the pendulous flowers turn into round, dark-blue fruits. If you plant Solomon's Seal, be sure to plan ahead and give it plenty of room. For companion plantings, tuck Solomon's Seal in a bed of Lily-of-the-Valley, interplanted with Ever-blooming Bleeding Heart. I've planted it along a wood-chip-covered pathway in my woodland garden where Mountain Laurel and Rhododendron maximum *grow as natives. At first unaware of its tendency to spread, I now feel the need to confine its growth. Perhaps I will move the path and let the Solomon's Seal remain where it is!"*

Other Name Great Solomon's Seal

Bloom Period and Color White flowers bloom late spring to early summer.

Mature Height × Spread 5 feet (unlimited spread)

When and How to Plant Plant divisions of Solomon's Seal in the shady garden in spring or fall. Plant bare-root transplants or container plants just below the soil surface. Space 3 or more feet apart. Direct-sow seed in fall. Mulch Solomon's Seal with shredded hardwood bark to maintain acid soils, to retain moisture in the soil, and to keep down the weeds.

Sun and Soil Preferences Plant in partial to full shade in well-drained, humusy, continuously moist soil.

Moisture Requirements The soil should remain moist throughout the growing season without becoming waterlogged. To improve the moisture-holding capacity of sandy soils, add well-rotted compost to a depth of at least 10 inches.

Fertilizing For maximum growth, apply a fertilizer for flowering plants in early spring and provide water, particularly during drought in the Tri-State area.

Pruning and Care After the first killing frost, clip the browning stems to the ground (do not pull). To divide the bed, dig chunks of root after fall frost.

Pests and Diseases There are none.

Additional Species, Cultivars, or Varieties *P. odoratum* 'Variegatum' produces foliage with bright-green leaves with clean white edges and flowers with a soft, sweet fragrance. *P. humile*, Dwarf Japanese Solomon's Seal, grows to only 10 inches tall, making it ideal for a small-space shade garden. *Smilacina racemosa*, False Solomon's Seal, is often confused with true Solomon's Seal. The primary difference is in one flowering characteristic: False Solomon's Seal's long stems are tipped with a plume of fragrant, star-like, creamy-white flowers.

My Personal Favorite

NAME	SPECIAL CHARACTERISTICS
Great Solomon's Seal	*P. commutatum*, the species / American native / gracefully large, arching stems up to 5 feet tall / drips with 1-inch yellowish-green-to-white flowers from the underside of each stem / fruits are dark, navy blue in color / spreads with vigor, so provide plenty of room

Speedwell

Veronica species

Preferred Zones	Sun Preferences	Additional Benefit
4 to 9	☀ ◑	✿

For late spring and summer color, the erect flower spikes of Speedwell, its species and improved cultivars, provide a rather interesting candelabra-like look in a perennial garden when planted according to height and habit of growth. A Speedwell collection of varieties such as 'Minuet' (with erect pink flower spikes only twelve to eighteen inches tall) planted in front, backed by 'Blue Peter' (a deep blue with flower spikes up to thirty-six inches tall) and 'Alba' white or 'Giant Blue' (both up to four feet tall), reminds me of the columnar pipes of an organ standing ready to play. The species prostrata 'Heavenly Blue', a sapphire blue color, can be positioned in front of 'Minuet', as it reaches only eight inches tall. Veronica is remarkably hardy in the cold winters of northern New York and the heat and humidity of summers in southern New Jersey. As cut flowers, the spike-like blossoms of the taller varieties of Speedwell mix well with other summer bloomers like Rudbeckia, Coreopsis, Lupine, Phlox, and Yarrow.

Other Names Veronica / Veronica Speedwell

Bloom Period and Color White, blue, pink, or red flowers, depending on species and variety, appear late spring to frost.

Mature Height × Spread 4 feet × 2 feet

When and How to Plant For best establishment of *Veronica* and its species in a full-sun-to-partial-shade perennial garden, start directly in the garden by planting seeds in spring or summer, up to two months before frost. In the Tri-State area, you can start indoors in a moist, sterile, seed-starting mix by mid-March. Keep the medium at 70 degrees Fahrenheit for germination in fifteen to twenty days. A windowsill greenhouse with a clear plastic top makes an excellent seed-starting chamber. Set container-grown nursery plants and home-started transplants 12 to 15 inches apart and no deeper than the soil line in the container in the garden.

Sun and Soil Preferences Plant in full sun to partial shade. The garden soil should drain well and be average in texture. Organic matter improves the moisture- and nutrient-holding capacity of sandy soils and improves drainage and aeration of clay soils: spade in well-rotted compost or leaf mold to a depth of 10 to 12 inches.

Moisture Requirements Mulch the flowerbed to conserve soil moisture during dry periods. Water during drought.

Fertilizing Apply an organic or slow-release plant food for flowering plants to stimulate a greener plant with more flower spikes. Too much nutrition results in a plant with stem strength that is inadequate to hold up flower spikes.

Pruning and Care Divide Speedwell every three years, just as new shoots emerge in spring.

Pests and Diseases There are none.

Additional Species, Cultivars, or Varieties *Veronica longifolia* cultivars include 'Alba', white; 'Blue Giant', 4 feet tall, with dark-blue spikes; and 'Romiley Purple', a deep purple only 18 inches high. V. 'Goodness Grows', a hybrid, is a unique dwarf which produces violet-blue flowers from April to frost. 'Icicle' grows 18 to 24 inches tall and flowers with white flowers from July through August. 'Minuet' sports spikes of pink flowers in June and July.

My Personal Favorite

NAME	SPECIAL CHARACTERISTICS
Veronica 'Sunny Border Blue'	Produces 18-to 20-inch-tall violet-blue flower spikes from June through August

Stonecrop
Sedum spectabile

Preferred Zones	Sun Preferences		Additional Benefits
4 to 10	☀	◐	🌸 ✦

For a spectacular show of powder-puff-like flowers alongside a water garden or in a perennial flower border, rock garden, or containers on a sunny to lightly shaded patio, plant Sedum 'Autumn Joy', the most popular of the Sedum cultivars. In mid- to late summer, it produces large clusters of flowerbuds that gradually turn bright pink, then mature to a warm rosy-pink, then a rusty red, and finally to a rich brown. That's what I see each year when I watch the patch of Sedum planted on the uphill side of my water garden. For a long-lasting display next to the patio, allow the rich-brown seedheads of Sedum spectabile to remain uncut through winter. I allow stems with dried flower clusters to remain in the garden over winter, and this provides for an additionally interesting landscape when covered with a light snow. Sometimes they remind me of little snow-capped soldiers. Gather stems in full color for long-lasting cut flowers, or dry them for winter flower arrangements.

Bloom Period and Color Rosy-pink, glowing-pink, and dusty-pink flowers bloom midsummer to late frost.

Mature Height × **Spread** 2 to 3 feet (spread is variety-dependent)

When and How to Plant Plant container-grown transplants at any time from early spring to midsummer. Bare-root transplants or divisions should be set out in the spring before new growth starts. Set the eyes, or buds, just below the soil surface. Space nursery-grown container plants or divisions 18 to 24 inches apart, no deeper than the soil line in the container.

Sun and Soil Preferences Plant in full sun to partial shade in well-drained soil.

Moisture Requirements Water to establish transplants or divisions; otherwise, Stonecrop is quite drought-resistant, making it an ideal plant for the xeriscape garden.

Fertilizing In early spring, apply 5-10-5 or equivalent according to the label directions.

Pruning and Care Little care is needed other than garden cleanup of dried stems in late winter, after the snow. To prevent weak and floppy growth, divide large clumps in early spring every three to four years.

Pests and Diseases There are none. Occasionally during hot rainy weather, a few leaves may become blighted. Just pinch the blighted leaves off the stems.

Additional Species, Cultivars, or Varieties 'Brilliant' is raspberry red; 'Meteor' is rose; 'Stardust' is white; 'Matrona' has dark pinkish-red flowers. *S. spurium* 'Dragon's Blood' provides a 3- to 4-inch-tall carpet of star-shaped crimson flowers from June to September. *S. s.* 'John Creech', just 2 inches tall with pink flowers, is rated as the best ground cover Sedum for sun to partial shade. *S. kamtschaticum* 'Weihenstephaner Gold' makes an attractive 6- to 12-inch-tall carpet of yellow flowers from late spring to late summer.

My Personal Favorite

NAME	SPECIAL CHARACTERISTICS
Sedum 'Autumn Joy'	Rosy-pink flowers / most popular cultivar of Sedum

Threadleaf Coreopsis

Coreopsis verticillata

Preferred Zones	Sun Preference		Additional Benefits
3 to 9	☼		🌷 🌿 ◇

" When planted in a sunny, slightly breezy location in the perennial garden, a clump of Threadleaf Coreopsis swings and sways, looking a little like a hula dancer's grass skirt. In early summer, right at the corner of a raised bed I planted a container-grown Coreopsis that was well under way with growth and yellow flowers. From the time I watered it in after planting, I knew it was in the right place. A gentle breeze was in the air, and the hula dance began. It is shimmering to this day. Of course it dies back in winter, but every season thereafter it has reemerged. I continue to enjoy my dreams of Hawaii. Another important characteristic of Threadleaf Coreopsis: this plant is drought-tolerant. Once established in the xeriscape (water-efficient) garden, further watering is not a consideration. "

Other Name Tickseed

Bloom Period and Color Yellow to gold flowers bloom June to October.

Mature Height × Spread 2 to 3 feet × 2 feet

When and How to Plant Plant in spring or fall. Plant containerized nursery-grown plants (or clumps of divided Coreopsis obtained from a neighbor) in unamended soil. In sandy soil, the underground stems of Coreopsis self-propagate quite easily, and may indeed become quite invasive.

Sun and Soil Preferences Plant Coreopsis in direct sun, in well-drained, unamended soil.

Moisture Requirements A real bonus of Coreopsis is its drought-tolerance. Once established, it needs little additional water to survive and shimmer in the garden.

Fertilizing General applications of 5-10-5 or equivalent in spring will be adequate for Coreopsis.

Pruning and Care Divide this long-lived perennial every two to three years in spring or autumn to encourage a vigorous growing clump. Left unattended, the normal bloom time is in early and midsummer, with sparse bloom in autumn. To encourage vigorous rebloom in September and October, shear or deadhead immediately after the midsummer bloom. A hedge shear or mechanical string-trimmer can be used to clip. Pick up prunings, as unwanted reseeding is a concern. Since deadheading prevents reseeding, it might be desirable to allow a few stems of dried flowers to remain to produce seeds for new plants. Leaving the deadheads of the second bloom will provide an interesting plant for winter.

Pests and Diseases There will be aphids on new tender shoots. Apply insecticidal soap according to the label directions.

Additional Species, Cultivars, or Varieties 'Zagreb' grows to only 12 inches high so definitely needs no support. This variety is very drought-tolerant and recommended for xeriscape landscaping.

My Personal Favorite

NAME	SPECIAL CHARACTERISTICS
'Golden Showers'	Grows up to 3 feet / may need staking in breezy locations to keep the plant upright

Thyme

Thymus vulgaris

Preferred Zones	Sun Preference	Additional Benefits
5 to 9	☀	

You've heard the lyrics "Tip-toe through the tulips." You'll be thinking up lyrics about walking or winding through the Thyme if you plant Thymus (particularly, Mother of Thyme) around random steppingstones. Thyme thrives in a sandy soil, like that used to fill the cracks of a slate patio or walk. Another cultural advantage of the sandy soil is that it offers few nutrients, and Thymus detests extra nutrition! A friend on Long Island couldn't wait for Mother of Thyme to grow and fill in the cracks of her walkway, so she planted almost-mature specimens, each with a six- to eight-inch spread. What a job! She root-pruned each plant severely and removed most of the root soil. She was rewarded with instant success. (Reminds me of another friend: too impatient to wait for his lawn to grow, he ordered sod.) Thymus vulgaris planted as a companion to Broccoli, Brussels Sprouts, and Cabbage is said to control flea beetles, cabbage white butterflies (adult of the imported cabbage worm), and other cabbage pests.

Other Name Common Thyme

Bloom Period and Color White, pink, and rose blossoms bloom early to late summer.

Mature Height × Spread Both are dependent on species and variety.

When and How to Plant Plant spring, summer, or fall. Rooted cuttings or small potted transplants of *T. praecox arcticus* Mother of Thyme, which grows only 2 inches tall and forms a mat ¼ inch thick, can be planted 12 inches apart in the cracks between bluestone steps, along rocky paths, or as cascading (creeping) mats growing over a stone wall.

Sun and Soil Preferences The soil for Common Thyme *Thymus vulgaris* and all of its hundreds of species and thousands of cultivars must be porous and lean in nutrient content. Plant Thyme in full sun, in well-drained unimproved soil. Clay soil can be amended with coarse builder's sand to improve drainage. In damp soils, plant Thyme in a raised bed to keep the roots out of moisture.

Moisture Requirements Give Thyme a small drink of water to settle the soil; it is quite drought-tolerant after establishment. Water only in dry periods.

Fertilizing This herb, like many others, is from the wild where no one but Mother Nature was there to feed them. Too much nutrition stimulates lush disease-prone plants with more susceptibility to winterkill. Remember: no extra feeding.

Pruning and Care Cut back winter-damaged plants in early spring. Every time you harvest, take the pinch from the stem tip. Pinching creates bushiness.

Pests and Diseases There are none.

Additional Species, Cultivars, or Varieties Common Thyme, a shrubby plant 6 to 8 inches tall, has cultivars 'Argentus' with white-variegated foliage, 'Aureus' with leaves variegated with yellow, and 'Roseus' with pink flowers. A cross between *T. v.* and *T. pulegioides* named *T. citriodorus* is called Lemon Thyme, a 12-inch-tall shrubby plant with pink flowers in May and June. *T. pseudolanguinosus* Woolly Thyme grows to 2 to 3 inches high with rose-pink flowers in June and July.

My Personal Favorite

NAME	SPECIAL CHARACTERISTICS
T. praecox 'Coccineus' Creeping Thyme	Only 2 to 6 inches high / bright-pink flowers in June and July

Yucca

Yucca filamentosa

Preferred Zones	Sun Preference	Additional Benefits
4 to 9	☀	🦋 🐦 🌸 ⚜

*Want to give your garden a desertlike tone without moving to Florida, Arizona, or the Sahara desert? Plant Adam's Needle Yucca filamentosa. The needle-sharp, one- to one-and-a-half-inch-wide evergreen leaves with threadlike filaments at their margins grow in rosette form from the center of the plant. The real treat is the flower stalk that sprouts to eight feet tall (in nature, it can reach fifteen feet). When the flowerbuds open, waxy, creamy-white, fragrant bells droop in full sun and then reach for the sky after dark. At night, moths visit to pollinate the fragrant open flowers, which are also a treat for tiny hummingbirds. The roots of this plant travel: my neighbor planted Yucca in his perennial garden sometime back, and much to his surprise, a Yucca plant emerged next door. By the way, this is another plant for that xeriscape (water-efficient) garden. **Caution:** Because of its extra-sharp, pointed, needlelike leaves, avoid planting Yucca where children are present or where there will be human traffic.*

Other Name Adam's Needle Yucca

Bloom Period and Color White, very showy, 2- to 2½-inch blossoms on 4- to 6-foot-tall panicles bloom late spring to midsummer.

Mature Height × Spread 3 feet × 3 feet

When and How to Plant Set divisions in early spring and container-grown plants at any time when the soil is workable no deeper than the soil line on the stem of the division or no deeper than the soil level in the container. Being sure to wear gloves, dig out offshoots from the existing mother plants for transplanting. Space transplants 2 to 3 feet apart. The planting depth is important, too: plant so the top of the crown is at or slightly above ground level. Don't guess—lay a straightedge across the planting pit and check the level before pulling in the backfill.

Sun and Soil Preferences Yucca thrives in full sun in loose, well-drained soil. A sandy soil is great and needs no amendments, but if planting in a clay-type soil, incorporate coarse builder's sand to a depth of at least 10 inches. The sand will improve drainage and aeration.

Moisture Requirements Yucca cannot stand wet soil, making it a candidate for the xeriscape or water-efficient garden.

Fertilizing No feeding is necessary. The roots will spread and take in all the nutrition necessary to produce the flower spike and blossoms.

Pruning and Care After the flowers brown and die, prune to remove the flower spike, and clip out weathered-looking leaves. Again, use gloves.

Pests and Diseases There are none.

Additional Species, Cultivars, or Varieties *Y. filifera* Floppy Yucca or Weakleaf Yucca, with 1½- to 2-foot-long, pale-green leaves with pointed tips, grows from a whorl from the center.

My Personal Favorite

NAME	SPECIAL CHARACTERISTICS
'Ivory Tower'	A stately plant / appropriately named, with ivory-white blossoms on 3-foot-high spikes

Roses *for the Tri-State*

You won't find a group of plants with more fragrance, stateliness, stature, and grace than the family called *Rosa*. This family offers compact plants that produce flowers from late spring well into fall. It's not unusual to have roses in bloom right up to Christmas in Atlantic City gardens, up to Thanksgiving in New York City and New London, Connecticut, and up to Halloween in Syracuse, Watertown, or Niagara Falls, New York.

Selecting Your Roses

When selecting roses for your patio or garden, review the latest varieties recommended from the All-America Rose Selections Committee. Such roses have been grown in more than thirty-four test gardens throughout America, and they ought to do well here. Whether they are Hybrid Teas, Climbers, Shrub Roses, or Miniature Roses, look for those varieties that are resistant to blackspot and mildew.

Not all roses are hardy in all planting zones, so check every variety for hardiness before planting in your garden.

Provide Plenty of Sunlight

The most important rule for planting roses in the Tri-State area is to position them so they receive plenty of sunshine—six hours or more. Due to the humidity and oppressive heat of July, August, and September, roses need all the help they can get to ward off disease. Early-morning direct sun followed by midafternoon sun is best. With direct sunlight on the foliage at morning's early light, the overnight dew deposited on the foliage dries from the leaf surface without having time to incubate blackspot and mildew diseases.

If you live in the cold country of Glens Falls and Watertown, New York (or on a

terrace in New York City), plant roses in containers that have wheels. Such a container can be moved to maximum light all day long, and when time for winter arrives, it can be rolled indoors or into the garage for protection from winter's bitter ravages. When moved into a sunny garden room, roses will bloom all winter if kept evenly moist, fed with a 15-30-15 or equivalent, and rinsed regularly with water to suppress spider mite invasions.

The Five-Dollar Hole

Planting is the second most important consideration for a rose. The new planting procedure for trees and shrubs does not apply to roses, as a rose tends to develop a taproot when it becomes established. Dig an extra-deep hole. The hole for a Climber, Floribunda, Grandiflora, Hybrid Tea, or Shrub Rose can be dug down to three feet deep; it's a matter of planting a "50-cent plant in a 5-dollar hole." If you do this, you'll have a "5-dollar plant" shortly.

Mix as much as thirty percent by volume of well-rotted compost, leaf mold, or milled sphagnum peat moss into the soil taken from the deep hole, whether it be clay-type or sandy in structure. Organic matter increases the moisture-holding capacity of the soil, which is crucial for roses during those hot, dry days of summer. As organic matter decomposes, the end product (humic acid) holds clay-type soil particles open for better drainage and improves sandy soil by holding the particles together to hold more moisture. Literally pack the prepared mix back into the hole to the proper planting depth for your area. As the taproot grows, it will penetrate the prepared planting soil in the bottom of the hole. For everblooming varieties, this extra moisture is especially important for continual bloom.

Caring for Your Roses

Roses need plenty of good air circulation. They don't have to be in the wind, but if planted where there is stagnant air, blackspot and mildew will be a problem. Blossoms with poor air circulation are also susceptible to gray mold, *Botrytis*. Climbers should be trained so the stems do not cross or become entwined. Hybrid Teas should be pruned so new growth extends out and up, never into the middle. Shrub Roses, Grandifloras, and Floribundas can be pruned to thin out a few of the oldest stems. All of these pruning practices increase airflow through the plants and definitely reduce diseases.

Feed roses with a prepared plant food formulated for roses. Electra®, Plantone®, or fish emulsion provides a slow-release form of all the nutrients essential for bloom.

Water, Water, Water!

Install a drip irrigation system so each plant has its own personal emitter or dripper. Attach the system to your garden hose, and water as needed. It's much better to water long and deep, not short and shallow. And never water roses with a sprinkler during the afternoon, early evening, or early night. If foliage goes into the dark of night in a wet condition, you're guaranteed to have disease, even on some of the disease-resistant varieties.

Winter Protection

Roses in the north of New York and along the northern border of Connecticut will need winter protection; if they are grafted varieties, plant the graft two to three inches below the soil surface so the soil will insulate the graft from constant freezing and thawing. Just make sure that water does not puddle around the stem. For additional protection, pull up more soil around the stems to a depth of eight inches before the soil freezes. Push the extra soil away as spring arrives. In southern New Jersey and Long Island, the grafted rose can be planted with the graft at, or slightly above, the soil line.

233

Climbing Rose
Rosa

Preferred Zones	Sun Preference	Additional Benefits
4 to 9	☀	🦋 🧴 🌷 🌼 🐝

I often hear the question, "Do Climbing Roses really climb?" The answer is simple: "No!" If left unattended, a Climbing Rose, sometimes called a Rambling Rose, would be nothing more than a pile or mound of long canes, as it doesn't have tendrils for clinging to a trellis. To get Climbers to climb, you must tie the canes to a support. With a little help, new canes can be encouraged to twine their way through a trellis, thus securing their own support. There are two classic Climbers I recommend highly for new gardeners: 'Blaze' is a bright-red, slightly fragrant, two-and-a-half- to three-inch-diameter flower that repeats bloom throughout the season, right up to the hard killing freeze of winter (in my garden in zone 6, it's not uncommon to find 'Blaze' in bloom right up to Christmas); 'New Dawn' is a pearl-blush, delightfully fragrant, three- to four-inch flower that was introduced in 1930 as the world's first patented rose.

Bloom Period and Color Spring-, summer-, and fall-blooming flowers display colors that vary with variety.

Mature Height × Spread 20 feet × 4 to 5 feet

When and How to Plant Bare-root roses must be planted in early spring before new growth emerges. Container-grown plants are best planted in spring but may be planted throughout the growing season as long as they are watered thoroughly immediately after planting. In the coldest areas of zones 4 and 5, plant grafted, bare-root, or container-grown Climbing Roses with the graft at or slightly below ground level. Otherwise, plant at or slightly above the ground level.

Sun and Soil Preferences Plant in full sun in a well-drained, slightly acid soil. Climbing Roses must have soil with improved moisture-holding capacity: add well-rotted compost or milled sphagnum peat moss.

Moisture Requirements Water regularly, especially during hot, dry weather.

Fertilizing Feed with a balanced rose food according to the label directions.

Pruning and Care Since most Climbers bloom on last year's growth, prune out only the oldest canes (two years old or older) in early spring, making sure you leave last year's canes. The previous year's new growth is easy to identify: the shiny green canes, not the brown, woody, two-year-old canes. Climbing Roses do not have tendrils for clinging, so tie the canes loosely to the support. For winter protection in exposed or windy gardens, untie the canes from the climbing support and gently bend them to the ground; anchor with wire "hairpins" made from the shoulders of wire coat hangers. This procedure protects buds for the following season's bloom.

Pests and Diseases Aphids, Japanese beetles, blackspot, and mildew may present problems. Contact your county cooperative extension educator for the latest controls.

Additional Species, Cultivars, or Varieties 'Golden Showers' produces crisp golden-yellow, fragrant, 5- to 5½-inch blossoms from spring to late fall. 'Iceberg', a classic Floribunda climber, produces snow-white blossoms on old wood only, which means it increases in productivity as it ages.

My Personal Favorite

NAME	SPECIAL CHARACTERISTICS
'New Dawn'	Climbs 10 to 12 feet high / 3- to 4-inch pearl-blush flowers / sweetly fragrant / a classic introduced in 1930 / quite disease-resistant

Floribunda Rose

Rosa

Preferred Zones	Sun Preference	Additional Benefits
5 to 10	☀	🦋 🧴 🌷 🌼 🐝

Early in the 20th century, an effort to bring larger flowers and repeat bloom to winter-hardy roses by crossing Polyantha roses with Hybrid Teas resulted in the Floribunda rose. It is a bushy plant with more disease resistance and hardiness than the Hybrid Teas, making most Floribundas excellent candidates for the Tri-State rose garden. Another strength is their ability to bloom profusely over a long period of time. Their bushiness, topped off with large clusters of flowers, makes them ideal specimen plants for mixed borders. The taller varieties are recommended for hedges. You won't go wrong with Floribundas which have won All-America Rose Selections awards, such as 'Betty Boop', ivory-yellow with red edge, 1999; 'First Edition', coral-orange, 1977; 'Pleasure', coral-pink, 1990; and 'Class Act', a pure white, 1989. The pristine, white-flowered Floribunda 'Iceberg', my favorite, was the Royal National Rose Society Gold Medal winner in 1959. In zone 5 or below, provide winter protection for Dream™ Roses, or grow them in large containers on the sunny deck or patio. Move them indoors in winter.

Bloom Period and Color Flowers in a wide range of colors bloom May through October.

Mature Height × **Spread** 3 to 7 feet × up to 4 feet

When and How to Plant Plant bare-root stock before new growth starts, or plant container-grown Floribundas at any time. To improve root establishment, plant as early in the season as possible, at the same level as the plants were in containers. Plant the graft union below soil level in cold climates, zones 4 and 5, and slightly above soil level in the warmest regions.

Sun and Soil Preferences Floribundas require at least six or more hours of direct sunlight beginning with the first light of morning. Plant in well-drained soil with extra moisture-holding capacity. For container culture, blend a moisture-holding polymer with the planter mix before potting.

Moisture Requirements Keep soil moist but not wet at all times. Drip irrigation delivers water only where it is needed. A soaker hose is also a convenient watering system in a rose garden. Avoid wetting the foliage.

Fertilizing Feed with a rose plant food according to the label directions. To avoid stimulating new growth which would be damaged by the first killing frost of fall, do not feed from mid-August through September.

Pruning and Care Since most Floribundas bloom on last year's wood, avoid pruning the shiny stems from last season's growth. Two-year-old stems may be pruned as needed. Place the containers on casters for mobility.

Pests and Diseases Select disease-resistant varieties to reduce blackspot and mildew, and apply a fungicide if needed. Contact your county cooperative extension educator for aphid and Japanese beetle controls.

Additional Species, Cultivars, or Varieties A Floribunda destined to become a classic in time is 'Betty Boop', a 1999 AARS winner, hybridized from R. 'Playboy' × R. 'Picasso'—this cross produced fragrant, 4-inch, semi-double flowers with petals of ivory-yellow with a red edge. Two Dream™ Rose varieties, hybridized by Jerry Twomey, are strong, compact bushes with quick-repeat-blooming flowers: Dream Red is one of the richest velvety reds ever, and Dream Orange is a vibrant iridescent orange.

My Personal Favorite

NAME	SPECIAL CHARACTERISTICS
'Iceberg'	Known in France as 'Fee des Neiges' / known in the Tri-State area as a classic, long-lasting, profusely blooming, white-flowered rose with pink centers / fragrant

Grandiflora Rose

Rosa

Preferred Zones	Sun Preference	Additional Benefits
4 to 9	☼	🦋 🧴 💐 🌼 🐝

Queen Elizabeth II granted hybridizer Dr. Walter E. Lammerts the right to use her name, British lawmakers confirmed the decree with an act of Parliament, and Grandiflora roses (a result of crossing Floribundas with the classic Hybrid Tea) were introduced in 1954. The very first specimen, a lovely soft-pink rose, was presented to Her Majesty and was, of course, given the name 'Queen Elizabeth'. Grandifloras combine the long stems of Hybrid Tea roses with the clustered flowers of Floribundas. Because of the Grandiflora's height (from the Hybrid Tea parent), the plants are well suited for planting as hedges. The parent Floribunda provides the multiple flowers on long stems, making them candidates for cut flowers. All-America Rose Selections award winners include 'Aquarius', medium pink, 1971; 'Camelot', coral, 1964; 'Love', red with white reverse, 1980; 'Pink Parfait', light to medium pink, 1961; and 'Tournament of Roses', shades of coral pink, 1989.

Bloom Period and Color The flowers bloom spring to fall, colors depending on variety.

Mature Height × Spread 3 to 7 feet × 3 to 4 feet

When and How to Plant Grandifloras establish best if planted in early spring, as bare-root roses before new growth starts. As long as water is available, container-grown roses may be planted throughout the growing season from spring through fall. Plant the graft union below soil level in cold climates.

Sun and Soil Preferences Plant in full sun in well-drained soil that retains moisture without becoming soggy. To improve sandy or clay-type soils, add well-rotted compost or milled sphagnum peat moss to the planting mix to a depth of at least that of the root mass.

Moisture Requirements Always improve moisture-holding capacity of soils for roses, and water during dry, hot weather.

Fertilizing Feed with a standard rose food according to label directions.

Pruning and Care Grandiflora roses are somewhat hardier than Hybrid Teas, but you prune them the same way. Cut back a cluster of spent flowers by pruning the stem to just above the first five-leaflet set. Failure to prune allows the shoot closest to the top of the plant to sprout; this is a blind shoot containing no flowering potential. To extend the life of cut-flower roses, start with a clean vase—the bacteria in a dirty vase will put the flowers to sleep. Harvest the roses in early morning. Fill the vase with tepid water, and pull off foliage that would be below the water line. Make a fresh cut underwater before placing the stem in the vase, and add floral food.

Pests and Diseases Select disease-resistant varieties to reduce blackspot and mildew. Check with your county cooperative extension educator for the latest controls for aphids and Japanese beetles.

Additional Species, Cultivars, or Varieties 'Sonia', with perfectly delicate, classic, Hybrid Tea–shaped pink blossoms, is excellent as a cut flower. 'Gold Medal', an extra-hardy Grandiflora with 3½- to 4-inch blossoms, deep gold with a touch of orange-red, is uniform in color even in hot weather.

My Personal Favorite

NAME	SPECIAL CHARACTERISTICS
'Lasting Peace'	Descendant of the Hybrid Tea 'Peace' / produces cuplike blooms / persimmon-orange buds / deep marigold-orange flowers

Hybrid Tea Rose

Rosa

Preferred Zones	Sun Preference	Additional Benefits
5 to 9	☀	🦋 💐 🌷 🌼 🐝

When you mention the word "rose" to most people, their response is "Hybrid Tea," even though older Hybrid Teas were grown for the florist trade on plants that were not particularly attractive, were not particularly fragrant, were disease prone, and lacked good-quality foliage. But the beautiful blossoms of the Hybrid Tea are still the most popular roses in the garden, whether formal or casual, and there have been great improvements in disease resistance, fragrance, and cane strength. Hybrid Tea roses became a class as a result of crossing two Old Garden roses, Hybrid Perpetuals and Teas. The first Hybrid Tea was introduced in 1867 under the name of 'La France'. It was a silver pink with bright-pink reverse flowers four to four-and-a-half inches wide. Modern Hybrid Tea roses include names like 'Tiffany', 'Midas Touch' (my favorite), 'Sterling Silver', 'Peace', 'Mr. Lincoln' (accredited by many rose experts as the best red ever), 'Ingrid Bergman', and 'Elizabeth Taylor'. A single Hybrid Tea rose cut just as the bud begins to open is a classic in a bud vase.

Bloom Period and Color Hybrid Teas bloom late April to Thanksgiving or later. Colors vary widely.

Mature Height × **Spread** 7 feet × 4 feet

When and How to Plant Plant bare-root roses before they sprout in early spring. Container-grown roses may be planted throughout the growing season if watered immediately after planting. Plant the graft union of Hybrid Teas below the soil level in colder climates, zones 4 and 5; and slightly above the soil level in the warmest regions.

Sun and Soil Preferences Plant Hybrid Tea roses, either bare-root or container-grown, in an area that receives a minimum of six hours direct sun, starting with morning sun. Clay-type soils should have well-rotted compost added along with coarse sand. The decaying organic matter, humic acid, improves soil structure by holding soil particles together as well as apart. Improve the moisture-holding capacity of sandy soils by adding great quantities, as much as 50 percent by volume, of well-rotted compost or milled sphagnum peat moss.

Moisture Requirements Water during dry, hot weather.

Fertilizing Feed with an all-purpose rose food according to label directions.

Pruning and Care In early spring, cut back the canes to 6 to 12 inches above the graft union to force new canes with bloom potential for May and June. After May/June bloom, cut back spent blossoms and stems to just above the first five-leaflet set. To improve air circulation, prune the roses so they grow out and up, not toward the center.

Pests and Diseases Foliage that remains wet overnight leads to blackspot and powdery mildew, dreaded diseases of many Hybrid Teas. Plant disease-resistant varieties. Foil cane-borer invasions by capping each freshly cut stem with softened canning wax, coating the cut with fingernail polish, or inserting a large upholstery tack in the end of each cut cane.

Additional Species, Cultivars, or Varieties 'Peace' Hybrid Tea, known as the "Rose of the Century," has a history as unique as its flower. In 1935, Francis Meilland discovered this rose in seedling form and managed to send it to the United States on the last plane to leave France for America before war broke out. The day that Berlin fell, it was given its name: 'Peace'.

My Personal Favorite

NAME	SPECIAL CHARACTERISTICS
'Midas Touch'	Most brilliant yellow blossom of all Hybrid Teas / sports a pleasing, fruity fragrance

Miniature Rose

Rosa

Preferred Zones	Sun Preference	Additional Benefits
5 to 9	☀	🦋 🧴 🌼 🌿 🐝

Miniature Roses, in their multitudes of colors, are quite adaptable to rock gardens, borders, patio containers, and hanging baskets, as long as the little plants and dainty flowers get plenty of direct sunlight and water. Today's city dwellers not only grow them in windowsill planters on the south side of the building, but they also grow them indoors under artificial light. Some years back, before we built a greenhouse, I grew mini-roses easily in clay pots indoors in a south-facing window greenhouse. I kept the soil evenly moist, temperature cool at night and warm during the day, and practiced integrated pest management (long before it was know as IPM). I rinsed the plants with running water once every two weeks: hence, no mites and no aphids. I provided a water-soluble 15-30-15 according to the label directions. The result: roses in bloom every month during winter. Attend a flower show anywhere in the Tri-State area and you'll be sure to find a class of Miniature Rose. Likely displays are the yellow beauty 'Rise 'N' Shine', the dark red 'Red Beauty', red-and-white-striped 'Stars 'N' Stripes', and 'Little Jackie', a fragrant blossom of orange blended with pink and yellow.

Bloom Period and Color Flowers in various colors bloom June through late fall; some are repeat bloomers.

Mature Height × Spread 6 to 18 inches × 10 inches to 2 feet

When and How to Plant Plant Miniature Roses, particularly those grown on their own rootstock, at any time during the growing season. Grafted varieties are best planted in early spring. Bare-root stock must be planted while dormant in early spring. Container-grown plants should be potted into containers with excellent drainage capacity.

Sun and Soil Preferences Grow in full sun. To survive growing in a container, the roots of Miniature Roses must have a constant balance of moisture and free oxygen in the soil; use a potting mix blended with a moisture-holding polymer. Miniature Roses can be planted directly into garden soil as long as they receive full sun and the soil holds adequate moisture.

Moisture Requirements Water, water, and more water . . . whether indoors or outdoors or container-grown on the patio or a sunny windowsill, the soil of Miniature Roses needs to be kept evenly moist. When watering, avoid wetting the foliage. If you have a large collection of plants, consider installing a drip irrigation system, putting the system on a timer.

Fertilizing Feed actively growing Miniature Roses with a balanced water-soluble plant food, following the label directions.

Pruning and Care To encourage continuous bloom, prune back the stems of spent blossoms to just above the first five-leaflet set.

Pests and Diseases Watch for spider mites and diseases like blackspot and mildew. Even in the cleanest of growing environs, roses will succumb to spider mites. To control spider mites, rinse the plants weekly with running water, making sure to rinse the bottom sides of the foliage as well as the top. If necessary, apply a miticide according to label directions. To control blackspot and mildew, provide air circulation and pinch off infected leaves immediately. If necessary, apply a fungicide recommended for blackspot and mildew.

Additional Species, Cultivars, or Varieties 'Black Jade' has flowers of Hybrid Tea form opening from almost-black buds to midnight-red fragrant blooms. 'Rise 'N' Shine' is the best yellow mini-rose.

My Personal Favorite

NAME	SPECIAL CHARACTERISTICS
'Loving Touch'	A rich apricot, mildly fragrant bloom opening from a brandy-hued bud / 5- to 18-inch-tall shrub

Shrub Rose

Rosa

Preferred Zones	Sun Preference	Additional Benefits
4 to 9	☼	

Shrub Roses are an ever-expanding category. They can include the Old Shrub Roses, such as Bourbon Rose, Damask Rose, Alba Rose, Moss Rose, and Hybrid Musk Rose, the Modern Shrub Rose, and the fantastic Meidiland group of hardy Landscape roses. Without recognition of any specific species or variety, the Wild Rose was named the New York state flower in 1955. The two common growing requirements for all roses are direct sunlight and plenty of water. In late April of 1995 I planted fifty bare-root 'Flower Carpet Pink' roses (a low-growing Shrub Rose) in the lower section of my terraced garden. Believe it or not, in early May I had to go into the garden to have a talk with my new roses. I advised them that they had better be in bloom for July 23 because that was the day my daughter was going to be married. They must have been listening. On the wedding day there were at least five-thousand pink roses in full bloom. (Don't tell how this happened.) Shrub Roses are good for perennial gardens, rock gardens, foundation plantings, and patio planters as long as there is full sun.

Bloom Period and Color Flowers in variable colors, depending on variety, bloom late spring to frost in fall.

Mature Height × Spread 18 inches to 4 feet × 2 to 5 feet

When and How to Plant Plant bare-root Shrub Roses before they sprout in early spring; plant container-grown plants any time throughout the season as long as water is available. With the oppressive heat and humidity potential in our area, select heat- and disease-resistant roses. "Resistance" does not mean a rose will never succumb to a problem, but a resistant rose has better chances. Shrub-type roses can be grown in the Tri-State landscape as long as they receive at least six hours of direct sunlight, the proper plant food, and plenty of water. Dig the planting hole three to four times the width and twice the depth of the rootball or root mass. Set plants at the same depth they were growing in their containers. Spacing depends on variety.

Sun and Soil Preferences Grow in full sun. Incorporate well-rotted compost and coarse sand into the backfill for all soil types, including soil that drains poorly. The finished product must hold moisture without remaining "wet."

Moisture Requirements Provide plenty of water.

Fertilizing Provide proper nutrition with an organic or water-soluble plant food according to the label directions.

Pruning and Care It is not absolutely necessary to deadhead spent flowers, but pruning pays off. Prune back spent flowers to a five-leaflet node to encourage repeat bloom.

Pests and Diseases Many Shrub Roses are disease-resistant, and you should select such roses. Insect pests like aphids, Japanese beetles, and rose chaffers may be controlled organically. Check with your county cooperative extension educator.

Additional Species, Cultivars, or Varieties 'The Fairy', a hybrid, produces clusters of dainty pink rosette flowers that blossom profusely. 'Red Fairy', with small cherry-red flowers, bred by Ralph Moore, blooms nonstop from late spring to fall on a plant reaching 2½ by 3½ feet.

My Personal Favorite

NAME	SPECIAL CHARACTERISTICS
Flower Carpet Series™	Includes 'Flower Carpet Pink', 'Flower Carpet White', 'Flower Carpet Red', and 'Flower Carpet Appleblossom' / resists blackspot and mildew / repeat bloomer

Seaside Favorites

It's estimated there are over five hundred miles of coastline from the southern tip of New Jersey up to New York, out to the tip of Long Island and back to the westernmost point of Connecticut, and back east to the boundary of Rhode Island. The question is: Is that mileage estimated at high tide, or at low tide? Who knows? We just know it's a lot of coastline . . .

With all that coastline comes the need for a type of plant life that will survive the ocean winds of summer and winter, the summer sun and heat, the salt spray, and the occasional hurricane. This chapter gives the coastline gardener a choice of twenty-three landscape plants and their many cultivars, from grasses to ground covers, from evergreen trees to flowering shrubs, including favorites like Shore Rose and Russian Olive. You'll also find out how to grow the Montauk Daisy and be the envy of many gardeners.

Seashore Planting Times and Procedures

With little organic matter content, the moisture-holding capacity in most of the coastline sand dunes is nil, making it necessary for the seaside gardener to pay particular attention to planting times and procedures. For trees, shrubs, ground covers, or perennials, planting during dormancy generally spells success. The ideal cycle for pushing spring growth is to have the plant begin root development in the sandy soil before there is need for water. (If there is adequate water available from irrigation, planting can be carried out throughout the entire growing year.)

To help plants become established, incorporate organic matter into the sandy soil adjacent to the planting hole in the form of well-rotted compost, leaf mold, milled sphagnum peat moss, or decomposed seaweed. Roots will spread out into the moisture-holding organic matter, as well as into the sandy soil.

To improve the sandy soil in a ground cover bed or flower garden, incorporate organic matter throughout the entire bed before planting.

The addition of nutrients is not absolutely necessary, because most of the plants recommended for seashore land-scaping are native plants already adapted to sandy, low-nutrient

soil—but a slow-release organic or chemical plant food applied in late winter or early spring will benefit summer and autumn growth. American Beachgrass and Little Bluestem will develop much better root systems if provided extra nutrition just before they wake up in early spring.

Sunburn Protection

One other tip for successful seashore planting: Select the right plant and put it in the right place. The blistering heat on a sunny day, plus reflection from sand, can cause sunburn in just a few hours. A ground cover bed of Bearberry planted under a tall evergreen such as Black Pine, or under a shrub such as Bigleaf Hydrangea, can provide substantial cooling of the soil below. This shading will be most helpful during the heat of a sunny day.

Just think of yourself as the plant. If you have ever sunbathed on the beach around 2 p.m. on a sunny, breezy summer day, you know how easy it is to sunburn. Let the ground cover be the sunblock and the Black Pine the umbrella.

American Beachgrass

Ammophila breviligulata

Preferred Zones	Sun Preference	Additional Benefits
4 to 7	☀	🌿 Ⓝ 🍃

" Maritime beach communities are found all along the coastlines of the Tri-State area of New Jersey, from Cape May to Sandy Hook, from New York's Coney Island to Montauk and back to Port Chester, and up the Long Island Sound north shore to Avondale, Connecticut. In every one of these communities you'll find American Beachgrass growing on oceanside dunes, along bays and harbors, and at the base of bluffs beside the Long Island Sound. A unique characteristic of American Beachgrass is its ability to grow even as nature buries it with sand. The grass captures sand that blows across it, creating dunes. The grass responds to being buried by sending up a new rhizome (underground stem), and a new shoot emerges from the rhizome. American Beachgrass does produce seed, but seedlings have a tough time getting established in a hot, dry environment, so it is generally the rhizomes that help the plant spread. 'Cape' is a superior strain of American Beachgrass discovered on Cape Cod, Massachusetts, in 1965, and it is now available from commercial growers along the coast of the Tri-State area. "

Bloom Period and Color Spike-like panicles of pale yellow to straw in color are present summer to fall.

Mature Height × **Spread** 2 to 3 feet (underground rhizomes spread up to 10 feet annually)

When and How to Plant American Beachgrass can be planted from October 15 to March 31 in the Mid-Atlantic, as long as the sand is not frozen. The United States Department of Agriculture Natural Resources Conservation Service offers this planting advice: Plant strips of Beachgrass parallel to the coastline. It is easily done by hand. The row closest to the ocean should be at least 100 feet above the mean high-tide line. Plant a 40- to 50-foot-wide strip along the ocean if space permits, but at least be sure it is no less than 20 feet wide and 10 rows deep. This permits the planting to trap blowing sand and to build a dune. On most sites the recommended plant spacing within the rows is 18 inches. Where erosion is severe, decrease the spacing to 12 inches. Plant two 18- to 24-inch stems in a hole approximately 7 to 9 inches deep. Stagger the rows. An 18-inch spacing requires 38,000 culms (stems) per acre, or 889 culms per 1000 square feet. Compact the sand firmly around the plants.

Sun and Soil Preferences Plant in full sun in sandy, well-drained soil.

Moisture Requirements Plants and roots must be kept moist before and during planting. Try using wet burlap.

Fertilizing Broadcast turfgrass fertilizer over the planting at a rate equivalent to 1.4 pounds of actual nitrogen per 1000 square feet (see p. 153 for the calculation procedure). Fertilizer should be applied thirty days after the planting date, but not before April 1.

Pruning and Care Protect your new plantings from foot and vehicle traffic by placing snow fencing around it.

Pests and Diseases There are no serious pest problems.

Additional Species, Cultivars, or Varieties 'Cape' and improved varieties are recommended by the United States Department of Agriculture Natural Resources Conservation Service (some groups believe it is better to plant Beachgrass that is collected and propagated from the local area in which it is to be planted).

Artemisia

Artemisia spp. and hybrids

Preferred Zones	Sun Preference	Additional Benefits
3 to 8	☀	

Aromatic foliage, deer resistance, drought tolerance, low maintenance requirements, and no need for fertilizing make this sun-lover and its species ideal for that sandy beachfront landscape. Artemisia plants do well in inland soil as long as it is average to poor in quality and has excellent drainage. During late summer and early fall, flower spikes with small yellow flowers develop. Pinch or clip off the flower spikes before seeds form, and that energy will be directed into making better leaves. If seed production is allowed, I find the inner, lower foliage will drop. Depending on the species, the fuzzy silver or gray-green foliage can be used to accent other flowering plants. The mounds of foliage are very attractive when planted among plants with shiny, dark-green leaves. Artemisia stelleriana, called Beach Wormwood, Old Woman, or Dusty Miller, grows only six inches high and makes an ideal ground cover for beachfront property, producing sixteen-inch-tall yellow flower spikes in late summer. To put a silver edge on a perennial garden or along the path to your home, plant perennial Dusty Miller on twelve- to eighteen-inch centers and let the plants grow together.

Bloom Period and Color Summer blooms are somewhat insignificant, yellow 1/4-inch flower heads in slender, dense panicles (Artemisia is grown for its felted, fuzzy, gray-green foliage).

Mature Height × Spread 12 to 24 inches (unlimited spread)

When and How to Plant Divisions of Artemisia can be planted in early spring or fall, and nursery-grown stock can be planted at any time in almost any type of soil as long as there is excellent drainage.

Sun and Soil Preferences Plant in full sun. Plant only in soil that drains very well—Artemisia makes an ideal plant for the sandy coastal garden. To improve drainage in clay-type soils, incorporate coarse sand and well-rotted compost to a depth of 12 inches or more, well below the root zone.

Moisture Requirements There is only one rule to remember: Artemisia cannot stand roots that are constantly wet. Continuous dampness and heavy mulch promote stem rot. Water new transplants until they become established, and then turn off the water. Plant where overhead sprinklers are nonexistent. If using decorative mulch in the garden where Artemisia is growing, take care to use only a thin layer of the mulch near the plant's stems.

Fertilizing Avoid feeding, as extra nutrition stimulates weak, spindly growth.

Pruning and Care Artemisia tends to become a floppy mess with a dead-looking center if it is left unattended. To ensure compactness, shear back the mound to about half its height by late June, using a hedge clipper. Pinch or clip the tips of new transplants to encourage branching and compactness.

Pests and Diseases There are no particular pest problems, except root rot in wet soils.

Additional Species, Cultivars, or Varieties Artemisia arborescens 'Powis Castle', 2 feet tall, has soft, fine, textured, almost ostrich feather–like foliage; it withstands the humidity of the seashore and is very hardy and long-lived.

My Personal Favorite

NAME	SPECIAL CHARACTERISTICS
Artemisia stelleriana 'Silver Mound'	Soft, silky-white, gray-green foliage / loves the seashore environment / grows to 24 inches high / requires drastic pruning during early summer (shear it back almost to the ground)

Bayberry

Myrica pensylvanica

Preferred Zones	Sun Preference	Additional Benefits
2 to 7	☀	🍒 🐝 Ⓝ 🍃

" *The species Myrica pensylvanica, which is Common Bayberry, thrives along the coast of New Jersey, Long Island, and Connecticut, and has even been found growing all the way to Newfoundland. Now that's hardy! Bayberry is a plant that flourishes in a salty, sandy environment. In fact, it can be used in many poor-soil sites. Look for Bayberry plantings along highway dividers where salt spray is prevalent. This mound of semi-evergreen aromatic foliage, each leaf one-and-a-half to four inches long and one-half to one-and-a-half inches wide, can reach to nine feet high and even wider; along the shoreline it tends to become sculpted by wind and spray, making it somewhat shorter. You'll see Common Bayberry used as foundation plants around some of the estates along Dune Road on Long Island, only a few hundred yards from the shoreline. Group plantings of Bayberry on the leeward side of a sand dune to make a fantastic naturalized landscape.* "

Bloom Period and Color Spring flowers are white, followed by waxy-gray glabrous fruit in fall. (The waxy-gray berries are harvested in fall and used to make the Bayberry candles found in most candle shops for the holidays. If you want to purchase a Bayberry candle, act fast—the supply diminishes quickly.)

Mature Height × Spread To 9 feet × 9 or more feet

When and How to Plant Container-grown or balled-and-burlapped specimens establish easily if planted in spring just as new growth begins, or in early fall; plant in unamended soil. Plant both sexes if you want fruit.

Sun and Soil Preferences Plant in full sun. Bayberry is a shrub that loves poor, sandy, nonfertile soil.

Moisture Requirements Even when planted in sand, water-in the new transplants well.

Fertilizing No extra nutrition is desired by Bayberry.

Pruning and Care If Bayberry becomes a bit scraggly, pruning may be done in late winter or early spring. If you like, take a few of the longer berried branches for indoor decoration during the holidays. Otherwise, not much maintenance is required.

Pests and Diseases There are no serious pests or diseases.

Additional Species, Cultivars, or Varieties 'Northern Bayberry' is an improved variety with decorative gray berries and glossy green foliage.

My Personal Favorite

NAME	SPECIAL CHARACTERISTICS
Bayberry	M. pensylvanica, the species / mound of semi-evergreen aromatic foliage / available from nurseries along the shore

Bearberry

Arctostaphylos uva-ursi

Preferred Zones	Sun Preference	Additional Benefits
3 to 7	☀ ☀	

Bearberry provides a year-long show. The lustrous, dark-green, leathery evergreen foliage, each leaf one inch long, turns bronzy or reddish in winter and then green in spring, when the white-to-pinkish quarter-inch-long flowers show off at the ends of the stems. The berrylike fruits are shiny, up to one-half inch in diameter, starting out green in summer and turning bright red for fall. Plant A. u. 'Radiant' (standing to eighteen inches tall), as it is well suited to coastal exposure and has bright-red berries that persist well into winter. I've see many plantings along the south shore of Long Island where improved cultivars have actually colonized (grouped together). Whichever Arctostaphylos uva-uris or improved cultivar you choose, you can plant it as an evergreen ground cover under a Beach Plum, between clumps of American Beachgrass, or as a naturalized area of erosion control. Sandy environments with no nutrition or low fertility seem to be an ideal home for Bearberry. **Note:** *The scientific name* Arctostaphylos *comes from the Greek word* arctos, *"a bear," and* staphyle, *"a bunch of grapes."*

Other Names Kinnikinick / Hog Cranberry / Sandberry / Bear's Grape

Bloom Period and Color White-to-pinkish flowers in mid-spring are followed by bright-red fruits.

Mature Height × Spread 4 inches (unlimited spread)

When and How to Plant Planting time is spring. Set nursery-grown transplants from 3-inch pots 12 inches apart, and gallon-sized transplants 24 inches apart.

Sun and Soil Preferences Plant in sun to light shade, in a sandy or clay-type soil. Incorporate well-rotted compost or leaf mold to improve drainage of clay soils and to improve moisture-holding qualities of sandy soils.

Moisture Requirements Provide water until the plants have become established.

Fertilizing Don't fertilize.

Pruning and Care Virtually no maintenance is required for a bed of Bearberry, with the exception of lifting (removing) plants when they crawl out of bounds; give those plants to a neighbor or gardening friend.

Pests and Diseases Leaf gall, black mildew, or rust may cause problems. Plant resistant cultivars.

Additional Species, Cultivars, or Varieties Horticultural selections are many in number and have added versatility to the plant. 'Wood's Compacta' is 4 inches tall. 'Radiant', 18 inches tall, is well suited to coastal exposure.

My Personal Favorite

NAME	SPECIAL CHARACTERISTICS
'Emerald Carpet'	Eighteen inches high / more shade-tolerant than other cultivars

Bigleaf Hydrangea
Hydrangea macrophylla

Preferred Zones

7 to 9

Sun Preferences

Additional Benefits

" *The colorful red, pink, or blue Bigleaf Hydrangea is a deciduous flowering shrub that is traditionally forced into flower for the Easter holiday. If you garden in zone 6 or 7, particularly along the coastal Tri-State area, you can purchase one in bloom and plant it into the garden, but don't set it out until after the last frost date in your area. (If you garden in zone 5, provide extra protection, particularly from cold west and north winds.) Even though the plant is hardy to cold, the newest, tender growth that has been forced in a greenhouse environment will not have been hardened-off, which is particularly true if the Easter holiday falls in March instead of late April. Many years ago I planted an Easter Hydrangea on the protected eastern slope of my perennial garden, out of winter's winds, and it still provides giant clusters of pink or blue flowers year after year. I adjust the soil pH to intensify the color. If you would like to celebrate the red, white, and blue of our American flag in your landscape or garden, plant a collection of Hydrangea cultivars that bloom reliably each year in bright red, pure white, and deep blue.* "

Other Name Florist's Hydrangea

Bloom Period and Color Red, white, pink, or blue flowers bloom in summer.

Mature Height × **Spread** 3 to 5 feet × 5 to 6 feet

When and How to Plant Bigleaf Hydrangea may be planted outside after the danger of frost has passed. In the northern half of the Tri-State area, it must be planted with protection from winter's bitter winds. Prepare the soil by adding well-rotted compost to a depth of 10 inches or more. Divide overgrown multiple-stemmed Hydrangea before new growth begins in early spring. Container-grown or balled-and-burlapped plants should be set no deeper than the depth of the root mass.

Sun and Soil Preferences Site in morning sun with afternoon partial shade. To maintain the blue color, lower the soil pH to 5.0 to 5.5 with the application of aluminum sulfate. Raise the soil to an alkaline pH with lime to achieve pink or red flowers.

Moisture Requirements Added organic matter will help retain moisture during the heat of the day, as Hydrangea need a continual source of water. During drought, you must supply extra water.

Fertilizing Apply a 5-10-5 plant food yearly according to the label directions.

Pruning and Care Prune back last year's stems by no more than half their height. Two-year-old canes can be cut to the ground. During garden cleanup in the spring, check the tips of last year's shiny green canes. If they are winter-damaged, prune dried tissue, but do not cut stems down by more than half or you will have nothing but *big* leaves and *no* flowers. New growth sprouts from pairs of buds on last year's stems. It's tempting to break out the dried, bare canes after the leaves drop, but you'd be removing next year's blooms.

Pests and Diseases There are no serious pests and diseases.

Additional Species, Cultivars, or Varieties 'Blue Billow' and 'Blue Wave' blossom with blue flowers. In addition to its blue lacecap, 'Mariesii Variegata' has stunning dark-green foliage with silver-white edges; it is hardy to zone 5. 'Pink Lacecap' has bright-pink blossoms. 'White Wave' has pure-white flowers.

My Personal Favorite

NAME	SPECIAL CHARACTERISTICS
'Nikko Blue'	Most reliable of the blue Hydrangeas / produces some of the most colorful deep-blue flowers when planted in acid-soil conditions / hardy to zone 5

Black Gum

Nyssa sylvatica

Preferred Zones	Sun Preferences	Additional Benefits
4 to 10		

Black Gum has two distinguishing features. The first and most impressive is its fall foliage: brilliant red, yellow, deep-apricot, hot-orange, and purple. The other outstanding but less desirable characteristic is the "litter" splashed on cars, sidewalks, and patio furniture as the birds and other wildlife are attracted to the olive-shaped blue-black fruit in fall. Nyssa sylvatica is native to the woodlands of the Tri-State area. It may grow to seventy-five feet or more in height when in full sun, and to fifty feet when in partial shade. It does very well at the edge of freshwater ponds and streams, either in full sun or partial shade. Though Black Gum is recommended as a street tree on several street-planting lists, I can't believe the citizenry would appreciate it along their town or village streets. The foliage colors would be beautiful, but the bird litter would probably lead to angry residents.

Other Names Sour Gum / Black Tupelo

Bloom Period and Color White flowers that are not showy bloom in spring.

Mature Height × Spread 50 to 75 feet × 20 to 30 feet

When and How to Plant Attempt planting only before new growth starts in early spring. I say "attempt" because the success of transplanting is greatly reduced if the plant has developed a taproot. Start with a young, small, balled-and-burlapped or container-grown Black Gum—the younger, the better. Newly planted Black Gum is often slow to become established. Get the tree established before it develops its strong taproot. To encourage spreading of the roots, spade well-rotted compost into the soil around the planting hole. Once the tree takes root it should not be moved, so spend some time picking the location of its final home. It is best to plant it in a protected environment, sheltered from excessive wind.

Sun and Soil Preferences Plant in full sun to partial shade in well-drained, moist, loamy soil. Black Gum tolerates a wide range of soil pH.

Moisture Requirements Water immediately after planting, and continue to provide moisture during the entire first growing season. An inch of water per week should do.

Fertilizing Apply a balanced fertilizer for trees and shrubs in early spring, and keep the soil moist throughout the root zone.

Pruning and Care Although little pruning is needed to maintain its pyramidal growth habit, it is best to do corrective pruning in the fall when there is little movement of sap.

Pests and Diseases Leaf spot, rust, or scale may pose problems, but they are not serious in the Tri-State area.

Additional Species, Cultivars, or Varieties 'Sheffield Park' offers the bonus of changing to fall color about two weeks earlier than other cultivars.

My Personal Favorite

NAME	SPECIAL CHARACTERISTICS
'Jermyns Flame'	Larger leaves than those of the species / shades of yellow, orange, and crimson during fall

Candytuft

Iberis sempervirens

Preferred Zones	Sun Preferences		Additional Benefit
3 to 9	☼	☀	✿

" *Candytuft, in any of the recommended varieties, is a slow-growing evergreen mound or mat of dark green foliage that produces white blooms from early spring into midsummer. Sempervirens, the species name for Candytuft, means "always green" or "evergreen." It can be planted to tie together taller plants in a perennial garden, or as a mat-like ground cover cascading over walls. When in summer bloom with its mass of white flowers, Candytuft looks like a snowdrift, an appearance that seems out of place when the plantings surround or include a sand dune. Candytuft is quite tolerant of salt spray, and it dearly loves three of the growing conditions found at the seashore: heat, lots of sun, and dry sand or soil that drains well. If you have an inland garden, you might plant it as a border around an Iris bed, or, as I have done on the shady side of my water garden, plant it with evergreen shrubs, Bleeding Hearts, and Hosta.* "

Bloom Period and Color White flowers bloom in spring to midsummer.

Mature Height × **Spread** 1 foot × 2 feet

When and How to Plant Plant in spring or fall in soil with excellent drainage—an absolute for success. Container-grown plants may be planted at any time the soil is workable. The more you divide Candytuft, the happier it will be. Prepare the soil by spading well-rotted compost or milled sphagnum peat moss into the entire planting bed before planting, and then set the plants 12 inches apart.

Sun and Soil Preferences Plant container-grown transplants, or divisions dug from existing plants, into well-drained soil in full sun to partial shade.

Moisture Requirements Water thoroughly to settle the soil after planting, and provide an occasional deep watering during drought and hot weather.

Fertilizing One feeding in early spring, with a 5-10-5 fertilizer or equivalent, is quite adequate. Candytuft prefers low nutrition but greatly appreciates a little lime added annually to sweeten the soil.

Pruning and Care To maintain compact plants, a light shearing of no more than 3 inches will induce branching of perennial Candytuft if done immediately after the midsummer bloom. The shearing can be rooted in moist sand and used to expand the Candytuft bed.

Pests and Diseases There are no serious pests and diseases.

Additional Species, Cultivars, or Varieties 'October Glory', 8 to 12 inches tall, produces white flowers in April and September. 'Snowmantel', 8 inches high, produces white flowers from April to May. 'Little Gem', a petite 6 inches tall, produces white flowers from April to May.

My Personal Favorite

NAME	SPECIAL CHARACTERISTICS
'Alexander's White'	9 to 12 inches tall and 18 to 30 inches wide / white blossoms appear a little earlier than most in the Tri-State area, during April, after shearing, and again during September

Clematis
Clematis hybrids

Preferred Zones	Sun Preference	Additional Benefits
4 to 9	☀	NA

How do you pronounce Clematis? You hear it pronounced cle-MAT-is and CLEM-a-tis. According to my dictionary it's CLEM-a-tis, but for today's gardener, it's become acceptable to pronounce it either way. Patience is a virtue when growing the "Queen of the Climbers," as it is not unusual for Clematis to take two or three growing seasons to reach its full magnificence. Depending on the species and variety, it has blossoms as large as nine inches across, in almost every color of the rainbow, and often blooms for months at a time. The first time I planted Clematis, I started with what I thought was a misfit. It was a packaged plant from the garden center with only one thin stem and two sets of leaves sticking up from the potting mix. The package directions stated "plantable pot." So I dug the hole, added peat moss to the backfill, and carefully set in the plant. When pulling in the backfill, I broke off the upper portion of the stem. Disaster, I thought! But it finally sprouted two months later, and it bloomed in its third year.

Bloom Period and Color White, blue, purple, red, or pink flowers bloom spring to fall, depending on variety.

Mature Height × Spread Unlimited if left unpruned

When and How to Plant Plant in early spring just as the plant begins to sprout. Prepare an extra-wide planting hole to allow the roots to spread with little resistance. Incorporate well-rotted compost. Set container-grown transplants about 4 inches deeper than they were in the container to encourage a larger crown to develop below the soil. This leads to more stems and roots and insurance against breaking brittle stems which are easily replaced from below.

Sun and Soil Preferences Plant in a rich, loose, well-drained soil, in a location where the tops will be in full sun and the roots shaded.

Moisture Requirements Provide even moisture during hot, dry weather.

Fertilizing Feed Clematis in early spring and summer with a water-soluble plant food for flowering plants. Do not feed from August through October, as new growth might be initiated, and this growth would not harden-off before the first killing frost in the Tri-State area.

Pruning and Care For pruning maintenance, Clematis can be divided into three groups. Prune *early spring–flowering* Clematis right after flowering to encourage vigorous stems for the following spring's bloom. In March, prune back *early summer–flowering* varieties 6 to 8 inches to a pair of strong buds. *Summer and fall bloomers* should be pruned back severely in early spring, as far back as 12 inches above the ground.

Pests and Diseases Botrytis fungi and spider mites may present problems. Check with your county cooperative extension educator for the latest recommended controls. Follow the label directions.

Additional Species, Cultivars, or Varieties C. p. 'Nelly Moser' has huge 7- to 9-inch flowers with pale-pink petals set off with central bars of red; it blooms in early summer and again in early fall. 'Ville de Lyon' has flowers in shades of deep crimson with golden stamens; it blooms from June to September. 'Mrs. N. Thompson' offers violet-purple blossoms with pronounced red stripes down the center, and blooms in May and June. 'William Kennett', the earliest large-flowered Clematis to bloom, has lavender-blue flowers.

My Personal Favorite

NAME	SPECIAL CHARACTERISTICS
C. p. 'Jackmanii'	Deep-purple blossoms from June to September / traditional Clematis in any garden

Eastern Redcedar

Juniperus virginiana

Preferred Zones	Sun Preferences	Additional Benefits
3 to 10	☼ ☼	

> "You can grow your own oval, columnar, or pyramidal bird feeder if you plant the Eastern Redcedar, whose fruits are berrylike, blue-gray cones that persist until eaten by the birds. Cardinals and blue jays seem to be particularly attracted to this upright-growing evergreen. Imagine the visual charm of a beautiful red bird, perched on the snowladen branches of an evergreen, pecking away at the blue-gray fruits. As an ornamental, the Eastern Redcedar may be used as an accent plant in your landscape, or line up several to create a wall of soft green. Plant named cultivars, as they offer plant specimens with fuller, denser foliage and more color and character than the native conifer species, Juniperus virginiana. At an estate on Long Island I saw the Eastern Redcedar growing as a winter barrier on the western side of a winding driveway, starting at the entrance off the road and continuing right up to the house on the beach. These trees created a dense screen and windbreak which was certainly much more aesthetically pleasing than snow fencing."

Bloom Period and Color Flowers are not showy.

Mature Height × Spread 20 to 50 feet (variable spread)

When and How to Plant Container-grown named varieties should be planted in early spring. Plant balled-and-burlapped and container-grown plants no deeper than the depth of the root mass.

Sun and Soil Preferences Plant in full sun to light shade. Eastern Redcedar thrives in sand along the coast, or inland in clay soil, and does quite well in a wide range of soil pH.

Moisture Requirements The trees should be watered well for the first growing year. Apply mulch in the root zone area to help retain precious moisture during hot dry periods. You'll find them growing natively in open abandoned fields; the only condition they don't like is being continuously wet.

Fertilizing As this is a native plant in many soil types, no extra nutrition is required.

Pruning and Care The native species of Eastern Redcedar often needs spring pruning to encourage a compact plant. Check with your county cooperative extension educator or Master Gardener for any local restrictions on planting near Apple orchards, as Eastern Redcedar is the alternate host for cedar apple rust.

Pests and Diseases Cedar apple rust (which is deformed, grotesque, brownish apple-shaped growths on the stems), and bagworms (which are caterpillars that form "bags" of cedar needles) may present problems. Another disease to watch for is juniper twig blight, which is dieback of the branch tips. Consult with your county cooperative extension educator on the latest controls.

Additional Species, Cultivars, or Varieties In addition to the species of *Juniperus virginiana*, which grows with much variation, recommended cultivars include 'Grey Owl', a spreading shrub with a bright, silver-gray color; 'Hillspire', with emerald green foliage that is particularly attractive in winter; and 'Pendula', a large upright shrub with a weeping habit.

My Personal Favorite

NAME	SPECIAL CHARACTERISTICS
'Emerald Sentinel'	Tall columnar habit / excellent blue-green winter color

Firethorn

Pyracantha coccinea

Preferred Zones	Sun Preferences		Additional Benefit
5 to 9	☼	◐	🫐

> In almost any community in the Tri-State area you'll find one or more specimens of the deciduous to semi-evergreen Firethorn grown as espalier, either following the brick chimney up the side of a house or stretching out against a fieldstone wall. (It should be planted on the sunniest side, because Firethorn needs sun.) You might even find this thorny plant with its clusters of bright-red fruits trained on a splitrail fence. When planted as a hedge, the thorns of Pyracantha assure privacy, for no one will try to push through. In our growing environment of summer heat and high humidity I only plant cultivars that are resistant to scab and fireblight. 'Rutgers' Firethorn, a low-growing moundlike hybrid ideal for the sunny rock garden, is proving to be completely free of both diseases. 'Mohave' is also disease-free. For a holiday treat, cut berryladen branches for use in holiday decorations and floral displays—pruning a few branches won't harm the mother plant.

Other Name Scarlet Firethorn

Bloom Period and Color White, very showy, somewhat fragrant flowers bloom in late spring.

Mature Height × Spread To 8 × 8 feet

When and How to Plant The best time to plant Firethorn is in early spring, just before the plant starts to open its buds. But container-grown specimens may be planted successfully at any time the ground is workable, from spring to fall, as long as water is available. A container-grown plant will likely be quite rootbound, so take care to untangle its roots and spread them out into the backfill. If you want to plant along the foundation of a home where construction debris may be present, either replace the soil or amend it with well-rotted compost or milled sphagnum peat moss.

Sun and Soil Preferences Plant in full sun to partial shade. Firethorn will grow in almost any soil and tolerates a wide range of pH.

Moisture Requirements Apply a 2- to 3-inch layer of organic mulch as soon as the planting is finished and the first thorough watering has been completed. Follow the next day with another thorough watering. It is this drink that will finally moisten the rootball as well as the backfill. During periods of drought, water as needed to keep the soil slightly moist, not wet.

Fertilizing To encourage flowering, feed annually with a plant food formulated for flowering trees and shrubs. Read the label.

Pruning and Care Prune with care, as the thorns are very sharp. Leave the short leafless stems, as they are the fruiting spurs for the next flowering season.

Pests and Diseases Fireblight, scab, twig blight, aphids, lace bug, and scale are sometimes problems. Select disease-resistant cultivars and consult your county cooperative extension educator for the latest pesticide controls

Additional Species, Cultivars, or Varieties P. × 'Mohave', created at the U.S. National Arboretum, is 9 to 12 feet tall and has semi-evergreen foliage and brilliant orange-red fruits; it is free from fireblight and scab infections.

My Personal Favorite

NAME	SPECIAL CHARACTERISTICS
'Rutgers' Firethorn	A low-growing hybrid, 2 to 3 feet tall / proven to be completely free of scab and fireblight / superior substitute for 'Loboy'

Highbush Blueberry

Vaccinium corymbosum

Preferred Zones	Sun Preferences	Additional Benefits
3 to 8		

> *The dark blue-green leaves of Highbush Blueberry in summer, which change to bright-yellow, bronze, rich-orange, or scarlet-red combinations in fall, make for one of the most colorful shrubs in the landscape. I've seen a large planting on the leeward side of a sand dune when they were in color, and wow, what a show. Highbush Blueberry (you pick the cultivar) has two positive attributes. The plants make attractive fillers in a foundation planting, and when planted in the Tri-State area in groups of three, they will produce many quarts of rather tart edible blue-black berries, up to one-half inch in diameter, during July and August. (Let me know when you bake your first blueberry pie or muffins and I'll be there! They also make a delicious addition to buckwheat pancakes topped with a maple syrup sweetener.) I've grown Highbush Blueberry for years and have found it is most productive after a summer drought the previous year. The stress of heat and lack of water apparently trigger the abundant production of flowers, which means more fruit the following year.*

Bloom Period and Color White flowers bloom in mid-spring.

Mature Height × Spread 8 feet × 8 to 12 feet

When and How to Plant Plant in early spring. Planting two or three of a single cultivar is acceptable for fruiting, but for best pollination, plant more than one cultivar. Whatever cultivars you select, make sure they flower at the same time. Check with your county cooperative extension educator or Master Gardener for cultivars that grow best in your specific area. There is a big difference between the growing environments of Atlantic City, New Jersey; Old Lime, Connecticut; and upstate New York.

Sun and Soil Preferences Highbush Blueberry's native environment is a swampy soil. It also does well in full sun to partial shade in a well-drained, acid soil of pH 4.5 to 5.5. If planted balled-and-burlapped or container-grown, it flourishes extremely well in sandy soil like that found near the coast.

Moisture Requirements Mulch newly planted Highbush Blueberries with organic mulch, like pine needles or well-rotted compost, to continue an acid soil pH and to help retain moisture during dry periods. Water thoroughly after planting. Although somewhat drought-tolerant, Highbush Blueberry produces best if kept slightly moist.

Fertilizing Apply plant food for acid-loving plants annually in spring.

Pruning and Care If pruning becomes necessary, prune immediately after harvesting the fruits in August.

Pests and Diseases There are no serious pests when it is grown as an ornamental. In intensive agriculture, there are several insects and diseases which must be managed.

Additional Species, Cultivars, or Varieties 'Rubel', a native Northern Highbush Blueberry discovered in New Jersey in 1912, is famous for making it through late spring frosts at the Geneva Experiment Station of Cornell University in Geneva, New York.

My Personal Favorite

NAME	SPECIAL CHARACTERISTICS
'Jersey'	An old favorite / late-fruiting cultivar / extremely hardy in the Tri-State region / another cultivar famous for making it through late spring frosts in Geneva, New York

Inkberry Holly

Ilex glabra

Preferred Zones	Sun Preferences	Additional Benefits
4 to 9	☼ ☽ ☀	

If you see dark-green, lustrous broadleaf evergreens with black fruits in a landscape planting, chances are they are Inkberry. These Hollies are excellent choices, especially the cultivars, for planting as hedges, mass plantings, or accent plants in a foundation planting. For use as a seashore plant, tuck Inkberry into the landscape with other plants to shield the foliage from winterburn. I planted Ilex glabra 'Compacta' in full sun at the side of steps leading to a raised deck. The evergreen foliage hides most of the quarter- inch black fruits that remain on the plant from September through April. The mother plant, the one I planted, has begun to produce underground stems, and now suckers are emerging, creating an even more dense plant. I don't hesitate to recommend this plant for your landscape, too.

Bloom Period and Color White flowers bloom late May to early June.

Mature Height × Spread 6 to 8 feet × 8 to 10 feet

When and How to Plant Plant Inkberry Holly in spring, summer, or fall as long as water is available for the first growing season. If planting in a bed, work well-rotted compost or milled sphagnum peat moss into the parent soil to a depth equal to the depth of the root mass. This will help retain moisture throughout the year and encourage the roots of the shallow Inkberry to spread. The roots of a rootbound container-grown Inkberry must be spread into the backfill at planting time. Balled-and-burlapped and container-grown specimens should be planted no deeper than the depth of the root mass.

Sun and Soil Preferences Plant in full sun to full shade. Whether balled-and-burlapped or from container-grown stock, Inkberry Holly is easily established in moist, acid soils.

Moisture Requirements Water newly planted Inkberry Holly thoroughly the day of planting and again the following day. Then water as needed to keep the soil only slightly moist.

Fertilizing An application of a plant food for acid-loving shrubs encourages stronger growth and better fruit production. Follow label directions.

Pruning and Care Annual pruning keeps Inkberry and its cultivars in fine stead with dense foliage if pruned as new growth appears in the spring. Clipping the tip of the branch breaks apical dominance, forcing multiple shoots to emerge from the branch.

Pests and Diseases Inkberry Holly is quite pest-resistant.

Additional Species, Cultivars, or Varieties 'Ivory Queen' and 'Leuco-carpa', to 8 feet tall, are rather unusual white-fruited cultivars with lustrous non-spiny green foliage; *Ilex × meserveae* 'Blue Girl', 4 to 5 feet tall, has glossy, spiny, evergreen foliage with large red berries in the fall; to produce fruits on 'Blue Girl', plant 'Blue Boy' in a nearby location. 'China Boy', a pollinator for 'China Girl', grows to 10 feet in height and spread; and 'China Girl', which also grows to 10 feet in height and spread, produces an exceptionally heavy berry set. Both have spiny foliage.

My Personal Favorite

NAME	SPECIAL CHARACTERISTICS
'Compacta'	Dwarf / female clone / produces black berrylike fruits / 6 feet tall / introduced by Princeton Nursery, Princeton, New Jersey

Japanese Black Pine

Pinus thunbergii

Preferred Zones	Sun Preference		Additional Benefits
5 to 10	☀		

For years, the Japanese Black Pine has been the traditional needled evergreen for planting in the buffer strips along the New York, Connecticut, and New Jersey shorelines. When the Interstate Highway System reached completion, there must have been hundreds of thousands of Black Pines growing as screens and dividers. You can also plant Black Pine as a feature in the landscape. It is remarkably tolerant of salt spray, and its naturally contorted, windswept appearance makes it the most picturesque specimen plant along the ocean shore. Because of its freeform expression, the Japanese Black Pine is much sought-after for bonsai, as well as for use in containers and above-ground planters. One summer I did an estate planting of over 1000 gallon-size transplants, eighteen to twenty-four inches tall, in order to create a Black Pine forest. This was along the southern shore of Long Island, and we lost only three plants.
Note: *Male flower parts, anthers, produce great quantities of yellow pollen in spring. Oh, what a mess if you park a dark-colored car nearby!*

Bloom Period and Color "Pollen producers" appear in spring.

Mature Height × Spread 25 to 35 feet × 20 to 35 feet

When and How to Plant Large balled-and-burlapped or smaller container-grown specimens may be planted any time the soil is workable. For mass plantings, set plants 10 to 20 feet apart. In heavy-wind locations, trees larger than 3 to 4 feet tall will need to be staked for the first two years; use a collar of old garden hose to keep the guy wire from cutting into the trunk. Take care not to crack the ball or damage the roots when planting.

Sun and Soil Preferences Plant Japanese Black Pine in full sun in soil with good drainage and a pH as high as 8.0.

Moisture Requirements Provide moisture for the first growing season after planting; after that, the plant is drought-tolerant.

Fertilizing General plant food for evergreens on an annual schedule each spring is appreciated by the plants, but not absolutely necessary.

Pruning and Care Depending on the desired look, Black Pine can be grown as a single-trunk plant or one with multiple stems. To create a multi-stemmed specimen, clip the leader candle as it starts to elongate in early spring. This clipping breaks the apical dominance in the stem and promotes multiple shoots. It's natural for needled evergreens to drop last year's needles as the current season's needles mature in the fall. Don't panic at the sight of the dying needles. A gentle wind will come through, the yellowed needles will fall, and that will be the end of the problem.

Pests and Diseases Japanese Black Pine is susceptible to several insects like Maskell scale, adelgids, sawfly larvae, and pine shoot moths. New shoots of Japanese Black Pine are highly susceptible to *Diplodia* tip blight. Contact your county cooperative extension educator or Master Gardener for recommended controls.

Additional Species, Cultivars, or Varieties *P. nigra* Austrian Pine is similar to Japanese Black Pine but has a straighter single trunk; it tolerates salt but is highly susceptible to *Diplodia* tip blight.

My Personal Favorite

NAME	SPECIAL CHARACTERISTICS
'Thunderhead'	A compact tree / 5- to 7-inch-long twisted needles in groups of two / distinctive white candles in the spring

Little Bluestem
Schizachyrium scoparium

Preferred Zones	Sun Preferences	Additional Benefits
3 to 10		

Little Bluestem, seen growing in open fields from Canada to Florida and from the East Coast to as far west as Utah, is effective when used as a naturalized large-scale ground cover or as an unmown transition planting between a more formal landscape and a woodland setting. It's also good for erosion control on slopes. The fluffy plumes of ripening seedheads are produced from July through September in the Tri-State area. Lit by the low angle of early-morning or late-afternoon sun, the half-inch-wide leaves, standing up to sixteen inches tall, sway in coastal breezes. In fall, the grassy leaves and stems take on a beautiful bronze-to-flaming-orange color, which lasts well into winter. I'm not sure how it got its name, as Little Bluestem is not really blue, except that it does have a blue cast at the base of its stem. Create a native North American grass garden by planting clumps of Little Bluestem, Switch Grass Panicum virgatum, *Cotton Grass* Eriophorum latifolium, *and Ribbon Grass, or Grandmother's-Garters* Phalaris arundinacea var. picta. **Note:** *If you can't find* Schizachyrium scoparium, *look for* Andropogon scoparius, *another botanical name sometimes used for the same plant.*

Other Names Prairie Beard Grass / Broom Sedge

Bloom Period and Color Fluffy plumes appear July through September.

Mature Height × Spread 2 to 5 feet × 12 to 15 inches (clumping)

When and How to Plant Plant in early spring. Mother Nature has been spreading the North American native grass Little Bluestem by seed for as far back as who knows. For garden use, propagate by planting divided clumps. For container culture, plant Little Bluestem clumps in a sandy mix blended with well-rotted compost.

Sun and Soil Preferences Site in full sun to very light shade. Plant in sandy, well-drained, alkaline-to-neutral soil.

Moisture Requirements Organic matter helps hold moisture on sunny, dry days. Little Bluestem is drought-tolerant when established and even tolerates the oppressive humidity of the Northeast in summer. Newly planted clumps should be watered regularly.

Fertilizing Apply a slow-release turf-type fertilizer in early spring.

Pruning and Care Cut back the dried, winterworn stems to just above the grassy crown in late winter or early spring. No other care is needed.

Pests and Diseases This grass has no known pest or disease problems.

Additional Species, Cultivars, or Varieties The species of Little Bluestem stands alone with one exception (see below).

My Personal Favorite

NAME	SPECIAL CHARACTERISTICS
'Blaze'	Provides an alternate to the species S. s. / outstanding fall and winter color changing from pinkish-orange to russet or reddish-purple

Montauk Daisy

Nipponanthemum nipponicum

Preferred Zones	Sun Preference		Additional Benefit
5 to 9	☀		🌼

Although traffic is guaranteed to be heavy, get in line with other sightseers on a sunny afternoon during September or October (right up to killing frost), and drive to the Montauk area of Long Island, New York. When you see a rather large, strangely shaped flowering perennial, almost shrublike, covered with three-inch-diameter white blooms, you'll want to pull over and take a closer look at Nipponanthemum nipponicum. This flower's common name is Montauk Daisy, from its Long Island home of Montauk. Over many decades it has naturalized in open fields and along the beaches and has found its way into many perennial gardens. For a real seaside look, plant Montauk Daisy with such companions as Russian Olive, Bearberry, Shore Rose, Shore Juniper, and American Beachgrass. When you plant Montauk Daisy in your perennial garden, give it plenty of room. My Montauk Daisy, with its almost succulent foliage and rather woody stem, got bigger and bigger until it covered an area of almost eight square feet. **Note:** *If you can't find Nipponanthemum nipponicum, look for Chrysanthemum nipponicum, another botanical name sometimes used for the same plant.*

Other Name Nippon Daisy

Bloom Period and Color White ray florets with yellow disk centers bloom September through November.

Mature Height × **Spread** 2 to 5 feet × 8 feet (or wider)

When and How to Plant Plant rooted cuttings grown in 3-inch pots or larger plants from gallon-size nursery cans during spring or summer. Fall-planted Montauk Daisies often do not overwinter, as they do not get rooted into the soil before winter.

Sun and Soil Preferences Plant in full sun in well-drained average-to-rich soil.

Moisture Requirements For best growth, water regularly until established.

Fertilizing Feed with a plant food formulated for flowering plants, but at half the strength called for on the label.

Pruning and Care An older, well-established, unpruned Montauk Daisy takes on the look of a giant candelabra, with its natural "out-and-up" growth habit. To restore an overgrown Daisy, prune the woody stems back to about 1 foot above the ground in early spring. Severe pruning encourages new stems to sprout from the woody tissue at the base or crown of the plant. Newly planted container-grown stock and the sprouts from the severely pruned established plant should be pinched several times, beginning as new growth appears in spring. Stop pinching by midsummer so there will be time for flower bud formation by fall. Each pinch forces new branching, generally growing outward and upward to recreate the look of the candelabra.

Pests and Diseases Aphids often appear on new growth in late spring and early summer. A heavy infestation causes wilting of new growth and distorted leaves, as the aphid pierces and sucks the sap from the plant tissue. Apply insecticidal soap according to the label directions.

My Personal Favorite

NAME	SPECIAL CHARACTERISTICS
'Montauk Daisy'	*N. nipponicum*, the species / large, shrub-like perennial / 3-inch diameter white blooms

Privet

Ligustrum species

Preferred Zones	Sun Preferences	Additional Benefits
3 to 8		

Hardly any new or old community in the Tri-State area was without a hedge grown from the semi-evergreen or deciduous shrub Ligustrum vulgare, or Common Privet. That is, not until anthracnose twig blight, Glomerella cingulata, invaded the species. This disease manifests itself by drying out the foliage, blighting the stems, and developing canker. Don't despair, though: there are other species recommended for screening and hedging. California Privet (zones 5 to 7) and Amur Privet (zones 3 to 7) are the two best alternatives to Common Privet in our region. In every community along the southern coast of Long Island and down the shore of New Jersey you'll see many property lines outlined by one of these species planted as hedges. Privet seems to recover from the salt spray that accompanies the occasional hurricane. Instead of planting balled-and-burlapped or container plants for a hedge planting, start with bare-root transplants in early spring, and you'll save a ton of money.

Bloom Period and Color White flowers bloom late May to mid-June.

Mature Height × Spread 15 feet × 8 feet

When and How to Plant The most popular and least expensive method for establishing a Privet hedge is to purchase bare-root plants in early spring. Balled-and-burlapped or container-grown specimens may be planted any time the soil is workable. Just dig the hole (for a hedge, make it a trench), adding no amendments, spread out the roots, add unamended backfill, pack the soil around the roots, and water. Scraggly bare-root transplants should be clipped back by half to initiate multiple stems. Plant bare-root plants 12 inches apart for hedge use.

Sun and Soil Preferences Site in partial shade to full sun, and plant in a neutral to slightly acid soil. Privet is not fussy about soil type.

Moisture Requirements Water thoroughly at planting time. Create a water well around each plant, whether bare-root, balled-and-burlapped, or container grown, for future watering.

Fertilizing Provide a spring application of a slow-release or organic plant food for trees and shrubs at rates recommended on the label.

Pruning and Care Clip the hedge in an "A" frame shape (narrower at the top and slightly wider at the bottom). If the foliage receives direct light from top to bottom, the shrub will hold its leaves from top to bottom; if left unpruned, it becomes wider in the middle and drops its lower leaves. To tidy up a Privet in the Tri-State area, prune at any time except during mid-August through September—pruning at this time of year will force new growth that will not harden-off before the first killing frost. Got overgrown Privet with no foliage on the bottom half? Don't despair. Take a chance. "Close your eyes" and prune it to the ground in March.

Pests and Diseases There are no serious pest problems.

Additional Species, Cultivars, or Varieties *L. amurense* Amur Privet has rather dull, dark-green leaves with creamy white flowers in late May to early June.

My Personal Favorite

NAME	SPECIAL CHARACTERISTICS
L. ovalifolium California Privet	The most popular Privet / grows as a large, vigorous semi-evergreen shrub forming a dense thicket of erect stems

Rock Cotoneaster
Cotoneaster horizontalis

Preferred Zones	Sun Preferences	Additional Benefits
5 to 8	☀ ☀	

" *One of the many Cotoneaster species is sure to fill the bill for almost any landscape need, whether to cover a gentle slope, to add color to a foundation planting, or as an accent to a landscape feature like steps.* Cotoneaster horizontalis *Rock Cotoneaster is the most widely grown species, as it is particularly hardy in a seashore environment. The bright-red clusters of fruits, produced from late August through October in the Tri-State area, are accented with glossy green deciduous leaves. I've seen Rock Cotoneaster planted alongside a winding terraced walkway with steps built of pressure-treated land-scape timbers, a single plant set at the corner of each step. One homeowner positioned low-voltage night lights in the center of each plant, which not only lit each step but made the shiny, dark-green foliage and bright-red fruits almost glitter. C. microphyllus 'Emerald Spray' Little-leaf Cotoneaster, with very dense growth, is an excellent ground cover for seaside planting. The name Cotoneaster, often mispronounced as "cotton easter" (say "kuh-TOE-nee-ass-ter"), is derived from the Latin words* cotoneum, *"the quince," and* aster, *a suffix that means "inferior."* "

Other Name Rockspray Cotoneaster

Bloom Period and Color Tiny white flowers bloom in spring.

Mature Height × Spread 3 feet × 5 to 8 feet

When and How to Plant Plant container-grown or balled-and-burlapped plants as soon as the soil warms in spring right up to the time the soil starts to freeze in winter. Container-grown plants will likely be rootbound, so butterflying (cutting into the root mass and spreading it out) will be necessary. Fill the hole with unamended backfill; water and back off and watch it grow.

Sun and Soil Preferences Plant in full sun to light shade. It will flourish in almost any type of soil, from sandy to clay, with a wide pH range.

Moisture Requirements For best performance, water only moderately during the growing season.

Fertilizing Cotoneaster needs little extra nutrition; don't feed.

Pruning and Care If you've selected the right species of Cotoneaster for the location, it should not be pruned, for it will lose its natural grace. If wayward branches should appear, they may be pruned at any time of year. If chlorosis should show in the foliage (the yellow look of the tissue between the veins), apply iron chelate according to the label directions.

Pests and Diseases Fireblight, lace bug, scales, spider mites, or webworm may be a problem. Consult your county cooperative extension educator for the latest recommended control for your area and problem. Symptoms of fireblight in Rock Cotoneaster appear as though the stems and leaves have been burned by a flame. Prune out infected stems immediately when noticed.

Additional Species, Cultivars, or Varieties *C. apiculata* Cranberry Cotoneaster is similar to *C. horizontalis* in growth habit, but has larger fruit. *C. congestus* Pyrenees Cotoneaster grows as an evergreen tight mound. *C. dammeri* 'Coral Beauty' with rich, glossy, evergreen foliage grows with long trailing branches, making it ideal for spreading as a ground cover.

My Personal Favorite

NAME	SPECIAL CHARACTERISTICS
C. adpressus precox Creeping Cotoneaster	Very dwarf, compact, 1- to 1½-foot-high plant / roots where the branches touch the ground / deciduous

Rugosa Rose

Rosa rugosa

Preferred Zones	Sun Preference	Additional Benefits
2 to 8	☀	🦋 🍐 🧴 🫒 🌿 🌼 🐝 🪺

Rosa rugosa, *commonly called Shore Rose in the Tri-State area, particularly along the New Jersey, Long Island, and Connecticut shorelines, is a valuable plant for difficult sites. Plant it along sand dunes with American Beachgrass, Russian Olive, and Beach Plum, and you've created a naturalized landscape that will put up with almost anything, including salt spray and winter winds off the ocean. Throw in a few clumps of 'Silver Mound' Artemisia to complete the picture. The fruits (rose hips), brick-red in color when they mature, stand out against the dark-green foliage; they are high in Vitamin C and make some of the finest-tasting rose hip jelly. There's another name for Shore Rose I picked up from a seafaring Long Islander. I mentioned Shore Rose and he said in a very gruff voice, "It's Saltspray Rose. You know. The one that grows in salt water!" I know it grows in pure beach sand because I planted 100 bare-root* Rosa rugosa *within 100 feet of the Atlantic Ocean . . . but it also grows well in inland soil because it grows at my home.*

Other Names Shore Rose / Saltspray Rose

Bloom Period and Color Rose-purple to white flowers bloom June to October.

Mature Height × Spread 6 feet × 4 to 6 feet

When and How to Plant Plant seedlings and bare-root clumps in early spring, before budbreak, to take advantage of spring rains. Container-grown plants can be planted at any time from spring to fall, as long as water is available. When it comes to planting along the beach, there is nothing to it. If you have experienced digging in inland clay soils, what a joy it is to dig a hole in a sand dune! The inland gardener should dig an extra-wide hole to the depth of the root mass, incorporate organic matter into the backfill, spread out the roots if planting bare-root or seedlings, and fill the hole.

Sun and Soil Preferences The Shore Rose prefers a full-sun exposure, well-drained soil that is slightly acid, and well-rotted compost blended into the backfill at planting time.

Moisture Requirements Organic matter increases the moisture- and nutrient-holding capacities of the sand. Water thoroughly, and back off and watch it grow. During extreme drought, an occasional deep watering will encourage flowering, even in hot weather.

Fertilizing Shore Rose appreciates an annual feeding with a slow-release or organic plant food for flowering plants in early spring.

Pruning and Care Just let it grow. You'll find the species *Rosa rugosa* one of the most trouble-free roses.

Pests and Diseases Aphids, Japanese beetles, borers, scale, thrips, mites, powdery mildew, blackspot, various cankers—the list goes on and on. If confronted with one or more problems, consult your county cooperative extension educator for the latest recommended controls.

Additional Species, Cultivars, or Varieties 'Belle Poitevine' is an old cultivar dating back to 1894; it has slightly fragrant, semi-double, light mauve-pink flowers and is highly resistant to blackspot and powdery mildew.

My Personal Favorite

NAME	SPECIAL CHARACTERISTICS
'Albo-plena'	A selected mutation of *R. rugosa* 'Alba' / produces double, pure-white, fragrant flowers / dark-green foliage / up to 4 feet tall

Russian Olive

Elaeagnus augustifolia

Preferred Zones	Sun Preference	Additional Benefits
3 to 8	☼	🐝 🪺

Russian Olive, with silver-gray foliage, is an open, globular-shaped deciduous tree of rapid growth, particularly when planted in a sandy seaside location. Allowed to grow into shrub form, Elaeagnus plants are often used in highway plantings and parking lot islands, or it can be clipped into a more formal border. Create a landscape using Russian Olive as the focal point. Companion plantings for the seashore environment might be Shore Rose, Montauk Daisy, Silver Mound, and Black Pine. On the south side of Long Island, New York, you'll see Elaeagnus angustifolia planted along the winding highway called Dune Road; in some spots it has virtually naturalized into a Russian Olive forest or grove. Pull into the parking lot of a small shopping center and you'll likely see it too. Long Islanders have even used it for plantings in reclamation areas. The reason for the widespread use of the Elaeagnus is its resistance to and tolerance of salt spray from the ocean and from salt use on roads and parking lots during winter. It's a hardy rascal.

Bloom Period and Color Flowers that are silver to white outside and yellow inside bloom in May.

Mature Height × Spread 20 feet × 15 to 20 feet

When and How to Plant To allow maximum time for rooting-in before winter, plant balled-and-burlapped and container-grown Russian Olive in spring as new growth starts. Planting depth is not critical in a sandy soil. No amendments to the soil are recommended.

Sun and Soil Preferences Plant in a sunny location in soil with the best drainage. A sandy, salty soil, as found along the shore, is ideal for Russian Olive.

Moisture Requirements To help retain moisture for the first growing season, apply a 2- to 3-inch layer of organic mulch, such as shredded hardwood bark, at the time of planting, and give the rootball a thorough soaking. Water generously during the first season.

Fertilizing No supplemental nutrition is necessary, as the Russian Olive root system fixes atmospheric nitrogen from the soil.

Pruning and Care Prune the leader to restrict leggy growth, and clip lateral branches to create bushiness; otherwise, a rather scraggly canopy will develop.

Pests and Diseases Verticullium wilt, seen as random wilted stems and leaves, deadly to this species, has no control. Cut an entire stem from the suspect plant showing the wilt and consult your county cooperative extension educator for positive identification of this wilt disease.

Additional Species, Cultivars, or Varieties Autumn Elaeagnus, *Elaeagnus umbellata* 'Cardinal', a Soil Conservation Service introduction, is a shrub-type Autumn Olive that grows to 12 feet tall and equally as wide. If left unattended, it becomes a weedy shrub; it is a heavy seed producer, loved by the birds. *E. commutata* or Silverberry is a smaller shrub with bright silvery foliage. *E. umbellata*, the Autumn Olive, with green and silver leaves, grows into a shrubby thicket.

My Personal Favorite

NAME
Russian Olive

SPECIAL CHARACTERISTICS
E. augustifolia, the species / silver-gray foliage / rapid growth / tolerates salt spray

Thornless Honeylocust

Gleditsia triacanthos var. *inermis*

Preferred Zones
4 to 9

Sun Preference

Additional Benefits

Gleditsia triacanthos *Honeylocust—often called the Three-Thorned Acacia because of its armament of 4-inch-long, branched, needle-sharp thorns protruding in masses from the trunk, branches and twigs—grows natively throughout New York, New Jersey, and Connecticut. Luckily, the Tri-State gardener can use the thornless version of the Honeylocust, G. t. var. inermis Thornless Honeylocust, which comes in several varieties. My favorite, which I've seen up and down the coasts of all three states, is 'Shademaster'. It has ascending branches, with spread to thirty-five feet and almost podless, and is rated as a fast grower (a foot or more per year). The reason I like the Thornless Honeylocust best is that, in the fall, the leaflets, one-third to one-and-a-half inches long and up to five-eighths inch wide, drop to the ground and almost disappear. The first fall breeze literally takes care of their disposal. If you plant 'Shademaster' for patio shade, there will be no raking at all, other than using a broom to sweep away a few leaves.*

Bloom Period and Color Yellow flowers with pleasant fragrance bloom in spring.

Mature Height × Spread 70 feet × 50 feet

When and How to Plant Plant any time the soil is workable, spring, summer, or fall. Plant balled-and-burlapped specimens of any size in a hole no deeper than the depth of the rootball.

Sun and Soil Preferences Plant in full sun, in average, well-drained soil.

Moisture Requirements Immediately after planting and again the next day, thoroughly soak the rootball and backfill with water. Continue to water as needed for the first growing season, about 1 inch per week including rainfall.

Fertilizing Fertilize annually with a slow-release plant food for trees in early spring. If planted in the lawn, the turf fertilizer will be all that is needed. Do not use a weed-and-feed type of turf food within the drip zone, as the herbicide may damage the shallow roots of the tree.

Pruning and Care Grafted or budded selections are grown on rootstock of G. t., so care should be taken to remove any shoots which might sprout from the base—they will exhibit the thorns of the parent.

Pests and Diseases Select disease-resistant varieties. Insect pests include spider mites, aphids, webworms, and midge pod gall. Consult your county cooperative extension educator for the latest recommended controls.

Additional Species, Cultivars, or Varieties 'Sunburst' Thornless Honeylocust, 75 feet tall by 50 feet wide, is often found growing on parking lot islands, providing dappled shade for cars.

My Personal Favorite

NAME	SPECIAL CHARACTERISTICS
'Shademaster'	Generally fruitless / spreading canopy is ideal for patio shade because of the foliage which provides light shade and the non-interfering deep root system (in a lawn area, grass can be grown right up to the tree trunk in the filtered, light shade)

Tree of Heaven

Ailanthus altissima

Preferred Zones	Sun Preferences		Additional Benefits
5 to 10	☀	☀	

> It's often been said in Brooklyn, "If you can't grow the Tree of Heaven, you can't grow anything." This deciduous shade tree has been known to sprout from cracks of sidewalks, along street curbs, and in trash and rubble piles, under less-than-ideal cultural conditions. It withstands extreme heat, bitter cold, hard soils that are wet or dry, and salty, dusty, or polluted air. It's for these reasons that the Tree of Heaven will survive in virtually any urban environment—but many horticulturists still classify it as a weed tree. It is admired by some city dwellers, but scorned by others for the offensive odor of its male flowers. The male and female trees produce insignificant yellow-green flowers that, on the female, turn into large, drooping clusters of appealing reddish-brown winged seeds that are easily scattered by the wind. If pollinated by the male, new Trees of Heaven will emerge. The tree also travels by underground roots that push up new trees at considerable distance from the parent. Ailanthus, a native of China, does more than grow in sidewalk cracks and dirt piles in Brooklyn: it's used to feed wild silkworms in China.

Other Name "The Tree That Grows in Brooklyn"

Bloom Period and Color Small green male and female flowers are produced on separate trees at the tips of the branches in spring.

Mature Height × Spread 60 feet × 35 to 50 feet

When and How to Plant Plant before budbreak in spring. Seed gathered in the fall may be scattered in a compost pile in the fall for springtime germination. The smaller and younger the seedling, the easier and more successful the transplant; seedlings are generally not available commercially. Set transplants no deeper than the soil line on the stem and gently backfill with unamended soil. The soil line will show as the point on the plant where darker tissue above ground and lighter colored tissue where the stem was in the ground meet.

Sun and Soil Preferences Although they will grow in the shade of a tall building, plant seedlings of Tree of Heaven in full sun in well-drained, moist soil.

Moisture Requirements Provide water for establishment; then the tree is drought-resistant.

Fertilizing No extra nutrition is needed.

Pruning and Care Grow Tree of Heaven as a single leader tree. Prune back lateral branches to develop strong, sturdy branches. To reduce suckering: When suckers no more than 2 inches long sprout from the trunk, put on a pair of leather gloves, grab hold of the sprouts, and "yank" them off. Don't prune them off or multiple suckers will sprout from the same spot.

Pests and Diseases No pests and diseases of this tree are particularly serious.

My Personal Favorite

NAME

Tree of Heaven

SPECIAL CHARACTERISTICS

A. altissima, the species / survives virtually any environment

Washington Hawthorn

Crataegus phaenopyrum

Preferred Zones	Sun Preference	Additional Benefits
4 to 8	☀	

Washington Hawthorn, native to the East Coast, has long been regarded as one of the most colorful flowering trees in the landscape. In our Tri-State area of New York, New Jersey, and Connecticut, C. phaenopyrum Washington Hawthorn has been planted to landscape the median of many of the parkways. It's at home in a naturalized setting along the coast where wildlife abounds, and it's deer-resistant, at least with the herd that comes through my property each day. (I hope your deer can read this.) This ornamental with needle-like thorns up to three inches long produces plentiful clusters of small white blossoms in spring, followed by glossy berries. The berries turn bright red as they ripen in fall and persist through much of the winter, at least until the birds eat them. The foliage emerges as reddish purple, changing to dark green in summer, to scarlet, red, orange, and purple in fall. C. phaenopyrum *and its cultivars that have limited disease and pest resistance are recommended for windy seashore locations as well as for urban plantings.* **Caution:** *This tree is not recommended for planting where children play.*

Bloom Period and Color White blooms appear in spring.

Mature Height × **Spread** 35 feet × 20 to 25 feet

When and How to Plant Plant balled-and-burlapped or container-grown Washington Hawthorn specimens in spring or fall; a balled-and-burlapped specimen can even be planted in summer if water is available to keep the soil moist. Plant in a hole no deeper than the depth of the rootball. Bare-root plants must be planted while dormant in late winter or early spring and watered thoroughly to settle the soil around the bare roots.

Sun and Soil Preferences Plant in full sun, in any type of soil, even sandy beach soil or heavy clay soil with poor drainage.

Moisture Requirements Provide adequate water to keep the soil moist, not wet. Do not depend on nature for watering-in bare-root plants.

Fertilizing No soil amendments or fertilizer are necessary.

Pruning and Care When left unpruned, Washington Hawthorn has an almost shrublike appearance with multiple lower branches touching the ground. This growth characteristic makes an ideal impenetrable hedge. To make a tree form, care must be taken to remove lower branches to a height of at least 7 feet. The thorns, as long as 3 inches, are impossible to forget when one makes contact with them; they are worse than sticking your finger with a barbed fishing hook.

Pests and Diseases Tent caterpillars, aphids, lace bugs, leaf skeletonizer spider mites, powdery mildew, fireblight, rust, leaf spot, scab, and so on, may be problems. Tent caterpillars and leaf skeletonizers devour the new green foliage of spring and summer. If one or more of these pests invade your Washington Hawthorn, consult with your county cooperative extension educator for the latest recommended controls.

Additional Species, Cultivars, or Varieties *Crataegus phaenopyrum* Washington Hawthorn is the species most commonly planted in our area.

My Personal Favorite

NAME	SPECIAL CHARACTERISTICS
C. virdis 'Winter King'	30 feet tall by 25 feet wide / bears larger fruits and has fewer thorns than the Washington Hawthorn

Wintergreen Barberry

Berberis julianae

Preferred Zones	Sun Preferences		Additional Benefits
5 to 8	☼	☀	

> Broad-leaved evergreen Wintergreen Barberry is rated the hardiest of the evergreen Barberries by many horticulturists, but some leaf scorch may be seen after extreme cold and wind. April brings an abundance of yellow flowers, followed by one-third-inch-long bluish-black oval fruits. Winter foliage is an attractive bronze or wine-red. The deciduous B. thunbergii 'Aurea' exhibits bright-yellow foliage, and 'Atropurpurea' Red Japanese Barberry produces leaves of red to purplish-red. Visit Skylands Botanical Gardens, Ringwood, New Jersey, to see Barberry, wildflower gardens, bogs, heather, naturalized areas, and miles of woodland paths. For those on Long Island, Planting Fields Arboretum, Oyster Bay, New York, presents an alphabetically arranged shrub collection of over 400 species. **Caution:** The lustrous green foliage hides one-and-a-half-inch needle-like thorns, so plant, prune, and maintain this plant with care. (I would not grow it where children or forgetful adults tend to gather.)

Bloom Period and Color In April, yellow, 1/4- to 1/2-inch flowers appear in clusters.

Mature Height × Spread 35 feet × 20 to 25 feet

When and How to Plant Plant in spring, summer, or fall. Carefully, because of the thorns, plant balled-and-burlapped or container-grown Wintergreen Barberry in a hole no deeper than the depth of the rootball. Water thoroughly to settle the soil and moisten the roots after planting.

Sun and Soil Preferences Plant in full sun to partial shade in moist, well-drained, slightly acidic soil.

Moisture Requirements If planted during the heat of summer, provide extra water, particularly during the hottest part of the day. Mulch newly planted Barberry with organic mulch, like pine bark mini-nuggets or wood chips, to conserve moisture and keep down the weeds.

Fertilizing No extra nutrition is recommended.

Pruning and Care Prune immediately after flowering to develop a compact, well-branched plant. (Remember: Barberry is prickly!) Rabbit-ear growth (random shoots growing from the interior of the plant) can be pruned off during late summer without harming next spring's bloom. If you have a tired-looking, overgrown, scraggly Wintergreen Barberry, don't give up. In early spring, prune the entire plant to within 6 to 12 inches of ground level to promote complete rejuvenation.

Pests and Diseases There are no particular pest problems.

Additional Species, Cultivars, or Varieties 'Nana', a dwarf form to 3 feet tall, has a mounded growth habit. *B. thunbergii* 'Aurea', 5 feet tall by 5 feet wide, is deciduous, with bright yellow foliage. The dwarf 'Bonanza Gold', half the size of 'Aurea', develops best color in full sun. Deciduous *B. thunbergii* 'Atropurpurea' Red Japanese Barberry, 6 feet tall and wide, produces leaf color of red to purplish-red.

My Personal Favorite

NAME	SPECIAL CHARACTERISTICS
Wintergreen Barberry	A standard-size plant in the landscape design, or for small-space gardens

Shrubs *for the Tri-State*

Flowering shrubs can be major features in a landscape, they can be used to tie the landscape together, or they can create a colorful wall or backdrop.

Plan Before You Plant

One secret for successful use of flowering shrubs is to know when they bloom and in what colors. Before planting, draw a plan. (No, you don't have to be an artist or landscape architect.) Get out the old box of crayons from the front parlor desk and color squares or slips of paper the colors of flowering shrubs. You'll find moving a colored piece of paper, which represents a plant, to be much easier than actually digging a hole, setting the plant, and finding out when it's too late that you have positioned the plant in the wrong place.

Another thing to consider before planting time is the ultimate size of the shrub. Of course, most flowering shrubs can be pruned to keep them in bounds—you just need to know when they bloom and how much can be pruned off.

The Important Rules of Pruning

A rule of pruning: Plants that bloom in June or earlier (spring bloomers) are plants that bloom on last year's growth, so they should be pruned right after bloom.

Rhododendron, Azaleas, Laurel, and Andromeda are spring bloomers.

With the exception of *Rhododendron maximum*, which blooms in early July, plants that bloom after June, like Rose of Sharon and Butterfly Bush, are plants that bloom on new growth; they should be pruned in early spring to initiate new blooming stems for summer and fall.

When to Plant

Many deciduous flowering shrubs are available in early spring as bare-root plants. Forsythia, Rose of Sharon, Spirea, Viburnum, Hydrangea, and Roses are often planted bare-root. Just remember to provide water as needed, and they should be in the ground before budbreak. Container-grown and balled-and-burlapped flowering shrubs have a much longer planting period; they can be planted from spring well into fall as long as water is available.

Preparing the Soil

A point of consideration that even the most experienced gardener may overlook is to check the drainage before planting. Dig a hole eighteen to twenty-four inches deep and fill it with water. (Be sure to cover it so no one accidentally steps in it.) Check it after twenty-four hours. If water is still in the hole, you have a potential drainage problem. If there is no water, you're ready to plant.

Loosened soil with added organic matter encourages much better spread and penetration by the new roots. For singly planted shrubs, loosen the soil two to three feet out from the planting hole, and incorporate organic matter in the form of well-rotted compost or milled sphagnum peat moss. For a planting bed that will have many shrubs, spade or till the organic matter into the entire bed before planting.

Grooming and Nutrition

A little grooming pays off as well. Pinch or prune out spent flower heads before seed forms. Most summer-flowering shrubs will continue flower production if not allowed to produce seed. For general nutrition, feed the bed of flowering shrubs or individual plants with a 5-10-5 or equivalent at the rate of three to five pounds per 100 square feet. Do this in early spring and again in late fall.

Azalea

Rhododendron spp. and hybrids

Preferred Zones	Sun Preferences		Additional Benefits
4 to 9	☀	☀	

*That pure-white, fire-engine-red, or shocking-pink flowering shrub you saw in your neighbor's landscape last spring was more than likely an evergreen Azalea. You too can have Azaleas in bloom in your garden from March through June. In most cases, selecting Azaleas from a local nursery or garden center will assure they are hardy in your area. I say "in most cases" because some mass merchandisers may ship questionable stock to your region. What I am saying is that not all Azaleas are hardy in your area. If you plan before you plant, you can successfully grow Azaleas. It's a really good idea to check with your county cooperative extension educator for specific varieties that are good for your area. When purchasing plants at your local nursery, select them while they are in blossom so you can be assured of bloom time and color. **Note:** Botanically, Azaleas are a subdivision of the larger Rhododendron group.*

Bloom Period and Color White, red, pink, purple, salmon, yellow, orange, and bicolor flowers bloom April to June.

Mature Height × Spread 6 feet × 6 or more feet

When and How to Plant Plant in spring or fall. To plant a single Azalea, dig an extra-wide hole no deeper than the rootball. A rootbound container-grown Azalea must have its root system butterflied at planting time or the roots will not leave the root mass to spread into the parent soil. A balled-and-burlapped specimen should be planted no deeper than the depth of the rootball. Containerized Azaleas on a sunny deck or patio should be double-potted in light-colored containers to reflect the heat generated from sunlight. To avoid overheating the roots, set the pots on 2-inch-high spacers to allow air movement underneath the container—and don't forget to water.

Sun and Soil Preferences Plant in partial sun to full shade in an acidic soil improved with decomposed organic matter. The evergreen species of Azalea appreciates direct morning sunlight followed by afternoon shade, moist-but-not-wet soil, and extra care at planting time to ensure the roots do not dry out.

Moisture Requirements Amend the backfill with well-rotted compost or milled sphagnum peat moss; organic matter holds precious moisture and encourages fragile surface roots to spread with little resistance. To keep the soil moist and cool, mulch newly planted Azaleas with a 2- to 3-inch-deep layer of organic mulch like pine bark mini-nuggets or wood chips.

Fertilizing Use an organic iron-rich plant food formulated for acid-loving plants, following the label directions. Never apply lime where Azaleas or their relatives are to live.

Pruning and Care To maintain shape, prune after bloom. Drastic pruning is done only in early spring (March) in the Tri-State area.

Pests and Diseases Watch for spider mites during hot, dry weather. Apply insecticidal soap as a thorough drench of the entire plant. Read the label. Mealybugs may be controlled with the same pesticide.

Additional Species, Cultivars, or Varieties The most popular of ever-green Azaleas for landscape use include 'Hino-Crimson', bright scarlet; 'Delaware Valley White', snow white; 'Blaauw's Pink', salmon-pink; 'Blue Danube', bluish-violet; and 'Rosebud', rose-pink.

My Personal Favorite

NAME	SPECIAL CHARACTERISTICS
'Hershey Red'	Deep-red blooms

Burning Bush

Euonymus alatus

![Burning Bush shrub]

Preferred Zones	Sun Preferences		Additional Benefits
3 to 9	☀	◑	

> Burning Bush is an ideal deciduous shrub that has fall and winter interest. When growing in full sun, it produces some of the most brilliant red foliage in the fall. As the foliage drops in late fall, this plant's other common names become apparent: "Corky" winged branches are exposed for viewing during the winter, making it "Winged" Euonymus. There are two types of Burning Bush available: the standard Euonymus alatus, which grows easily to fifteen feet tall with an equal spread, and the other, compact variety, Euonymus alatus 'Compactus', which is easily maintained at six feet or less in height and spread. I have a compact Burning Bush featured with my Peony collection. In addition to the color and wings, the outreaching branches make the center of the plant look like a giant bird's nest. I clip the tips of the branches in spring to keep the bush fat and full. Pruning the entire plant in early spring by as much as one-half, and four to five inches of each stem again by midsummer, can easily keep a Dwarf Burning Bush within four feet tall and wide.

Other Names Winged Euonymus / Cork Bark Euonymus

Bloom Period and Color Flowers are insignificant. (Foliage turns red in fall; after leaf drop in fall, red-orange fruits become exposed for winter color.)

Mature Height × **Spread** 6 to 15 feet × 6 to 15 feet

When and How to Plant If you have a bare-root specimen, plant Burning Bush in early spring before growth starts. If your plant is container grown or balled and burlapped, plant at any time the ground is workable, from early spring to late fall. Plant no deeper than the rootball in a hole that is two to three times the rootball's width. Use unamended backfill.

Sun and Soil Preferences Plant in a location with direct sun to partial shade (the more sun, the brighter fall color will be). Burning Bush is not particular about soil type as long as it drains well.

Moisture Requirements Bare-root plants must be watered immediately after planting to settle the soil. Continue watering into summer and fall, depending on natural rainfall. An average of 1 inch of water per week is usually sufficient for establishing this shallow-rooted species.

Fertilizing Feed with an organic plant food for trees and shrubs as soil warms in spring.

Pruning and Care Overgrown *E. alatus* may be pruned severely in March to reduce leggy growth, followed by light clipping in early July to increase density of growth.

Pests and Diseases There are no serious pests or diseases, and never any deer damage. Not even a nibble. Aphids will occasionally appear on soft, new growth; apply insecticidal soap.

Additional Species, Cultivars, or Varieties *E. alatus* is the full-sized Burning Bush, with brilliant crimson to scarlet-red foliage in fall. *E. atropurpureus* Eastern Wahoo, or Burning Ash, is easy to recognize; it has off-pink or washed-out red foliage in fall, and its slightly winged stem is visible after leaf drop through winter.

My Personal Favorite

NAME	SPECIAL CHARACTERISTICS
'Compactus'	Known as Dwarf Burning Bush / compact growth to 6 feet / ideal variety for small-space gardens and landscapes

Butterfly Bush
Buddleia davidii

Preferred Zones
5 to 9

Sun Preference

Additional Benefits

Would you like to attract butterflies, hummingbirds, and honeybees to your garden? They're automatic visitors if you plant a combination of Butterfly Bush (Buddleia), Butterfly Weed, and Crocosmia, though the continuous bloom of the Buddleia will make it the winner. Buddleia attracts many species of butterflies, including monarch and swallowtail. All three species of plants are quite compatible and grow well together. A short story about my Buddleia: I planted three Butterfly Bushes to the west of my water garden in 1994. Each spring I pruned, and pruned hard. I pruned one of the plants to one foot above the ground, the second plant to eighteen inches, and the third to two feet. The shortest grew to at least eight feet tall, the eighteen-incher to ten to twelve feet high and wide, and the third stretches upward and outward from fifteen to eighteen feet. Now that's success. I tell you this because I know many beginning gardeners are afraid to do any drastic pruning.

Other Name Summer Lilac

Bloom Period and Color Purple, blue, violet, pink, and white flowers bloom summer to late fall.

Mature Height × Spread 6 to 12 feet × 6 to 12 or more feet

When and How to Plant Plant a container-grown or balled-and-burlapped Butterfly Bush in early spring or fall. Plant in a hole no deeper than the rootball and two to three times its width. Use unamended backfill.

Sun and Soil Preferences Plant in full sun, in a well-drained soil with a neutral to slightly acid pH.

Moisture Requirements Water generously for the first growing season to establish the roots. Once established, the *Buddleia* is quite drought-tolerant.

Fertilizing An application of a blossom-buster plant food (one with a high middle number) in late spring will encourage better bloom in summer and fall.

Pruning and Care As the Butterfly Bush blooms on new wood, the entire plant should be pruned back to between 6 and 12 inches above the ground in late winter or early spring. Be patient—the new sprouts may not emerge until late May or early June in the Tri-State area. Deadhead spent blossoms to encourage continuous bloom right up to frost. The plant may freeze to the ground in severe winters if there is no snow cover. Don't panic. Prune back dead stems, and wait for new sprouts that will likely emerge from the ground by early June.

Pests and Diseases Aphids may appear on new, tender growth. Apply insecticidal soap as a thorough drench to foliage and stems.

Additional Species, Cultivars, or Varieties 'White Bouquet' produces sparkling white flowers with orange throats. 'Pink Delight' bears long panicles of sweetly scented, pure-pink flowers.

My Personal Favorite

NAME	SPECIAL CHARACTERISTICS
'Black Knight'	The most popular cultivar / the most vigorous grower / long panicles of sweetly scented, dark purple-violet blossoms

Common Lilac

Syringa vulgaris

Preferred Zones	Sun Preference		Additional Benefits
4 to 7	☼		

> *Want to experience fragrances second to none? Take a trip in May to the Institute of Ecosystem Studies, Mary Flagler Cary Arboretum, Millbrook, New York, where the Howard Taylor Lilac Collection, featuring sixty-nine varieties, will be in bloom. Or visit Highland Park in Rochester, New York, which was dubbed America's Flower City in the late 19th century—every May, Rochester hosts a weeklong Lilac festival where you will find the largest collection of Lilacs in the country, 1200 shrubs representing 500 varieties! Visit either collection and I guarantee you'll do as I did. (I went home and planted a white, a purple, and a pink variety.) I now have my own collection, albeit small, and every spring when my Lilacs bloom, the air is filled with the sweet perfume of their blossoms. (And because they are mine, I can cut a few branches and bring the perfume indoors!) For the sunny landscape there are hundreds if not thousands of S. v. varieties from which to choose. Their color is often described with names like 'Blue Skies' and 'Lavender Lady'. 'Sensation' florets are purplish-red, edged with white, and 'President Lincoln' is pure blue. 'Mont Blanc' is white, and 'Primrose' is yellow.*

Bloom Period and Color Lilac, pink, blue, and white fragrant flowers bloom in spring.

Mature Height × Spread 20 feet × 9 to 10 feet

When and How to Plant Plant bare-root plants in early spring before budbreak, or plant container-grown or balled-and-burlapped specimens any time during the growing season. The secret to Lilac culture is full sun and great air circulation. Without either, Lilacs bloom sparsely if at all and become infected with mildew on the foliage.

Sun and Soil Preferences Plant in full sun in well-drained neutral to alkaline soil—no wet feet.

Moisture Requirements Water generously during the first growing season to establish the shallow, fibrous root system. Apply supplemental water only during extreme drought.

Fertilizing To encourage annual blooms, apply a blossom-booster plant food according to the label directions.

Pruning and Care Patience is a virtue when growing Lilacs. Leave the pruning shears in the toolshed for the first five to seven years, as it often takes that long to bring Lilacs into bloom after planting. They bloom on last-year's growth; deadhead spent flowers immediately after bloom to prevent seed production and to direct energy into next season's bloom. For that stubborn Lilac that refuses to bloom, sweeten the soil. In the Tri-State region, scatter a handful of lime around the root zone each fall to encourage better bloom the following year.

Pests and Diseases Powdery mildew is often a problem. Apply a fungicide for powdery mildew as a preventative. Read the label.

Additional Species, Cultivars, or Varieties The Littleleaf Lilac, *S. microphylla*, grows to 6 to 8 feet tall and 8 feet wide; its lilac-colored flower plumes are recommended for that sunny small-space garden.

My Personal Favorite

NAME	SPECIAL CHARACTERISTICS
Common Lilac	*S. vulgaris*, the species / fragrant blooms in spring / multistemmed with colorful flowers

English Boxwood

Buxus sempervirens

Preferred Zones	Sun Preferences	Additional Benefits
5 to 8	☀ ◐	🧴 🐝

Some years back, I worked with the owners of a large estate in Greenwich, Connecticut, and every Thanksgiving weekend I met with the grounds superintendent to discuss winter protection of the evergreen shrubs planted in front of the stone façade. These were giant English Boxwoods B. sempervirens, a plant often used with English architecture. When protected, both dwarf and standard English Boxwood are fantastic landscape evergreens; in a hostile location (under the eve, as these were), they are easily damaged by snow and ice and burned by winter wind. We constructed a "cage," a wooden frame around each plant to support snow fencing over the top to protect against chilling winter winds. Then we wrapped the cage with burlap. These plants had been there over seventy-five years, and constructing this protection was a yearly ritual. If you see any home with its front landscape plants wrapped in brown burlap over winter, chances are it has English Boxwood planted as foundation shrubs. English Boxwood and its relatives are much-sought-after plants to be used with Colonial architecture. Shop around, as even the tiniest plants are quite expensive.

Other Names Old English Boxwood / Common Boxwood

Bloom Period and Color Spring blooms are not showy.

Mature Height × Spread 10 to 20 feet (spread equal or greater)

When and How to Plant Plant in spring as new growth starts, and up to and during fall. Don't site the shrubs under the eve where snow will slide off and crush the plants. Plant each plant of container-grown or balled-and-burlapped stock in a hole no deeper than the depth of the rootball but two to three times its width.

Sun and Soil Preferences Site in full sun to partial shade. Since Boxwood is sensitive to winterburn in the Tri-State area, plant in well-drained soil amended with organic matter like milled sphagnum peat moss, well-rotted compost, or leaf mold.

Moisture Requirements Water thoroughly at planting time, and continue watering throughout the first growing season.

Fertilizing Make a spring application of an organic slow-release plant food for broadleaf evergreens.

Pruning and Care For the first winter, fall-planted Boxwood should be protected with a burlap screen or an antidesiccant spray according to label directions. To keep Boxwood in hedge form, prune lightly in early spring and again by midsummer. Do not prune Boxwood during late August through early October, as new, tender, frost-sensitive growth may be stimulated at that time.

Pests and Diseases Canker, twig blight, scale, mealybugs, boxwood leaf miner, and boxwood mite may present problems. Contact your county cooperative extension educator for the latest controls.

Additional Species, Cultivars, or Varieties Hybrid Little Leaf Boxwood (*B. microphylla* 'Winter Green' and 'Green Beauty'), which grows 3 to 4 feet tall, is a good choice for colder climates. *B. microphylla koreana* 'Korean Little Leaf Boxwood', standing 1½ feet high, is another good choice.

My Personal Favorite

NAME	SPECIAL CHARACTERISTICS
B. sempervirens 'Suffruticosa' Dwarf English Boxwood	Grows very slowly / 3 feet tall by 3 feet wide / produces a very dense plant / ideal for a clipped hedge or border / use in plantings around formal gardens, flower beds, and lawn borders, and along walks

Forsythia 'Spectabilis'

Forsythia × intermedia

Preferred Zones	Sun Preferences	Additional Benefit
4 to 8	☼ ◑	🌼

   Witchhazel, 'King Alfred' Daffodils, purple Crocus, and pure-white Snowdrops are all signs of spring, but if you really want to know when to start spring gardening projects, especially when to apply pre-emergent crabgrass controls, watch for that yellow-blooming shrub called Forsythia—for me, it is the flowering shrub that officially announces spring has arrived in my area. The bright-yellow blooms of F. × intermedia 'Spectabilis', Showy Border Forsythia, cover eight- to ten-foot-long, gracefully cascading branches for about three weeks every spring. From Atlantic City, New Jersey, to Torrington, Connecticut, there is often as many as three weeks' difference in bloom time; to Albany, New York, there may be four weeks' difference. To enjoy a breath of spring while the snow is still on the ground, cut a few Forsythia branches from last year's growth, place them in a vase of water indoors, and you'll have yellow blooms in just a few days. Except for occasionally harvesting a branch in late winter or early spring to bring indoors for forcing blooms, I allow Forsythia to grow in its natural form.

Other Names Showy Border Forsythia / Golden Bells

Bloom Period and Color Rich, golden-yellow flowers bloom early to mid-spring.

Mature Height × Spread 6 to 8 feet × 10 to 12 feet

When and How to Plant Plant Forsythia as bare-root whips in early spring before growth starts, or as container-grown or balled-and-burlapped transplants at any time of year when the ground is not frozen. Balled-and-burlapped or container-grown plants should be planted no deeper than their rootballs, using unamended backfill.

Sun and Soil Preferences Plant in full sun to partial shade in ordinary garden soil.

Moisture Requirements Apply a 2- to 3-inch layer of organic mulch like pine bark nuggets or wood chips to conserve moisture. Water frequently in the first growing season, then water only during extreme drought periods.

Fertilizing Feed with a balanced plant food for flowering plants according to the label directions.

Pruning and Care Prune immediately after flowering to encourage new, juvenile stems with more blooms for the following spring. Older, well-established Forsythia appreciates thinning. Prune out one-third of the oldest stems each spring, immediately after bloom.

Pests and Diseases There are no serious pest problems.

Additional Species, Cultivars, or Varieties 'Spring Glory' has bright-yellow flowers on stems that grow to 6 feet tall. *Forsythia* 'Arnold Dwarf' and *F.* × *viridissima* 'Bronxensis' are both 2 to 3 feet tall with a 6-foot spread, and each is usable as a living ground cover for an expansive area as well as single, dwarf flowering shrubs. For early bloom, *F. mandschurica* is the most flowerbud-hardy type for colder areas. It grows to 6 feet tall with a 10-foot spread.

My Personal Favorite

NAME	SPECIAL CHARACTERISTICS
'Lynwood Gold'	Butter-gold or pale-yellow flowers

Glossy Abelia
Abelia × grandiflora

Preferred Zones
5 to 9

Sun Preferences

Additional Benefit

In the Tri-State area, it's hard to believe there is a semi-evergreen shrub that starts blooming in late May and continues right up to the first killing frost of fall, but there is, and if I've figured right, that's close to twenty weeks. Glossy Abelia with its shiny semi-evergreen leaves and pink tubular or bell-shaped flowers is an attractive addition to a planting of spring-flowering broadleaf evergreens like Rhododendrons, Azaleas, and Andromeda. To brighten and extend the flowering period of a landscape border, plant Abelia within the planting. As the spring bloomers finish their show, Glossy Abelia just keeps right on blooming. Another landscape use of Abelia is to plant it with nonflowering evergreens like Mugo Pine, Taxus, Boxwood, and Small-leaf Holly. Since Glossy Abelia grows eight feet tall by five feet wide and its manner is to gracefully arch, you could set several plants in full sun as a screen. In winter, the purple-tinted foliage adds a hint of color.

Bloom Period and Color Pink-tinted white flowers bloom from spring to frost in fall.

Mature Height × Spread 6 to 10 feet × 4 to 6 feet

When and How to Plant Plant at any time throughout the growing season. Glossy Abelia is easily established from balled-and-burlapped or container-grown stock. Plant no deeper than the depth of the rootball, and use unamended backfill.

Sun and Soil Preferences Plant container-grown or balled-and-burlapped plants in full sun to partial shade in an organically rich soil with good drainage. Abelia thrives in the same acidic soil in which Rhododendrons, Azaleas, and many other evergreens thrive.

Moisture Requirements Water well for the first season of growth. Apply a 2- to 3-inch layer of organic mulch like pine bark mini-nuggets or wood chips to conserve moisture and keep down the weeds. During excessively dry summers, deep watering as needed will encourage better leaf color during the following winter.

Fertilizing An annual application of a plant food for acid-loving plants in early spring will stimulate blooms throughout the summer well into fall; apply according to label directions.

Pruning and Care If left unpruned, Abelia grows into a graceful shrub with wispy, cascading branches. As the plant matures, prune out a few of the oldest stems each year to renew growth from the base of the shrub.

Pests and Diseases There are no serious pest problems.

Additional Species, Cultivars, or Varieties In addition to the species, you may select from the cultivars 'Edward Goucher' with its lavender-purple to dark-red large tubular flowers from July through September, and 'Sherwood', a 3- to 4-feet mound of glossy foliage with drooping pinkish-white flowers climaxing with a purple tint of wintertime foliage.

My Personal Favorite

NAME	SPECIAL CHARACTERISTICS
Glossy Abelia	A. × *grandiflora*, the species / bronze-red foliage during winter

Harry Lauder's Walking Stick

Corylus avellana 'Contorta'

Preferred Zones	Sun Preferences		Additional Benefit
4 to 8	☼	◐	🌿

Harry Lauder was a famous Scottish entertainer and singer who carried a grotesquely gnarled and twisted walking stick as part of his act. Corylus avellana 'Contorta', known as Harry Lauder's Walking Stick, is a curled and twisted shrub with contorted stems. It was discovered in a hedgerow in 1863 at Frocester, in Gloucestershire, England, and has since become an architect's delight and an artist's envy. I'm not sure when it arrived in the Tri-State area, but I am glad it did. Plant a specimen where you can enjoy the twisted, almost corkscrew-like branches against winter snow. If you'd like to grow this conversation piece on a patio, terrace or rooftop garden, you can: all you need is a large (whiskey half-barrel size or larger) wooden container with drainage holes, a standard potting mix, and a grafted specimen on a standard or straight trunk. You'll enjoy growing this deciduous shrub year-round. (I'd like to be the mouse in the corner and listen to the comments from your visitors when they first see this plant.) Ask any flower arranger about Harry Lauder's Walking Stick and you will strike up a conversation for hours. It's amazing how plants make friends of humans.

Other Names Filbert / Corkscrew Hazel

Bloom Period and Color Male fruits of yellow catkins appear in March.

Mature Height × **Spread** 8 to 10 feet × 8 feet

When and How to Plant Container-grown Harry Lauder's Walking Sticks, available from many specialty nurseries in the Tri-State area as grafts on the species as a rootstock, can be planted at any time the ground is workable from spring to fall. The most economical way to get started is to purchase bare-root transplants from mail-order nurseries in early spring, for planting just before new growth starts. Plant a container-grown or balled-and-burlapped specimen in a hole no deeper than the rootball but two to three times its width; the wide hole allows for better root penetration as the plant becomes established.

Sun and Soil Preferences For best growth, plant in full sun to partial shade in well-drained, loamy, rich soil with a pH of 5.5 to 7.5.

Moisture Requirements Provide even moisture for the first two years of growth or until the plant is well established. Mulch newly planted specimens or rooted cuttings with an organic material such as pine bark mini-nuggets or shredded hardwood bark, to a depth of 3 to 4 inches.

Fertilizing Apply an organic plant food in early spring according to the label directions.

Pruning and Care Prune anytime you would like a twisted branch for a decorative arrangement. As straight sucker growth often sprouts from the rootstock, keep a careful eye on the base of the plant and prune it out. As it becomes well established, Harry Lauder's Walking Stick will become a tangled mess if it is not thinned.

Pests and Diseases This plant is relatively pest-free.

Additional Species, Cultivars, or Varieties The cultivar 'Pendula' has strongly pendulous branches; if grafted high on the species understock, it creates a handsome weeping specimen as a focal point in the garden.

My Personal Favorite

NAME	SPECIAL CHARACTERISTICS
'Contorta'	Stems are curled and twisted / male catkins dangle from contorted branches

Honeysuckle

Lonicera species

Preferred Zones	Sun Preferences	Additional Benefits
3 to 8		

You will know it if anyone in the neighborhood has Honeysuckle in the landscape. On a summer evening, the sweet fragrance from L. japonica, one of the sweetest smells in the garden, will waft through the air. Plant Hall's Honeysuckle, Lonicera japonica 'Hallinia', which has cream-to-yellow flowers on plants to thirty feet high, for bloom in July and August. Winter Honeysuckle, L. fragrantissima, has very fragrant cream-white blooms in late March to April. Tatarian Honeysuckle, once considered the "best" of the Honeysuckles because of its many cultivars, needs a little help. Without a pruning program, it will become a weed; and watch for the Russian aphids feeding on the new, succulent spring growth. You'll never stop the aphid invasion permanently, but you can certainly work to suppress a population by using yellow sticky cards to trap the adults and then spraying the plants with insecticidal soap. The name Lonicera was given to the plant to commemorate the German physician and naturalist, Adam Lonicer or Lonitzer, who died in 1586. The genus consists of 200 species, many hybrids, and improved cultivars.

Bloom Period and Color Bloom period, scent, and color are dependent upon the species.

Mature Height × **Spread** To 30 feet × variable

When and How to Plant Plant from the time the soil thaws in spring right up to the time the ground freezes in winter. Plant container-grown or balled-and-burlapped Honeysuckle at any time the soil is workable; plant bare-root stock while dormant in early spring. Container-grown stock should be set no deeper than the root mass.

Sun and Soil Preferences You may plant in full sun to partial shade, but for maximum bloom, plant in full sun. Honeysuckle prefers moist, organically rich soil that drains well.

Moisture Requirements Just water thoroughly to settle the soil.

Fertilizing Honeysuckle will appreciate an annual application of a plant food for flowering shrubs in early spring.

Pruning and Care Prune as needed to retain compactness of growth, but only after bloom. Remember this rule of pruning: A plant that blooms in June, or before, is a plant that blooms on last year's growth, so prune immediately after bloom. The new growth that sprouts after pruning will produce stems that contain next spring's bloom. Plants that bloom after June are ones that bloom on new growth, so prune these in spring.

Pests and Diseases There are no serious pest problems other than aphids—apply insecticidal soap.

Additional Species, Cultivars, or Varieties Recommended Honeysuckle for the Tri-State area include *Lonicera tatarica* 'Hack's Red', with red-purple flowers; 'Alba' with white flowers; and 'Rosea', with rosy-pink flowers. All three bloom prolifically during mid-spring; flowers are not scented. *Lonicera* × *brownii*, Scarlet Trumpet Honeysuckle, is sometimes semi-evergreen, climbs to 15 feet high, and produces unscented orange-scarlet blossoms in early summer and again in late summer. *L.* × *b.* 'Dropmore Scarlet' produces scarlet-red flowers with a longer blooming period.

My Personal Favorite

NAME	SPECIAL CHARACTERISTICS
Lonicera tatarica 'Alba'	Pure-white flowers / grows to 12 feet high with a 10-foot spread

Japanese Andromeda

Pieris japonica

Preferred Zones	Sun Preferences	Additional Benefit
6 to 8	☀ ☀	🐝

Pieris japonica *has long been described as Lily-of-the-valley in shrub form, and without a doubt, that is the best description of an Andromeda in bloom. As a single flowering shrub in a shaded foundation landscape, as a mass planting at woods' edge, or as a companion to Rhododendron, Azalea, and Mountain Laurel, Andromeda's Lily-of-the-valley–like blossoms take over the show. As the blossoms fall to the ground, new bronze-pink-to-red leaves sprout from the tips of the branches, setting the plant afire for spring. Some twenty years ago I planted four balled-and-burlapped specimens behind a raised retaining wall on the shady side of my driveway. These Andromeda have developed rather interesting characteristics, taking on a layered, almost tiered look. I never pruned these specimens and they are now at a height of seven to eight feet.*

Other Name Japanese Pieris

Bloom Period and Color Tiny, showy, white, urn-shaped blossoms bloom early to mid-spring.

Mature Height × **Spread** 8 feet × 6 feet

When and How to Plant Balled-and-burlapped specimens may be planted anytime after the soil thaws in the spring, through summer and right into late fall. This shallow-rooted plant should be planted no deeper than the depth of the rootball in a hole that is two to three times its width. Use unamended backfill for filling the hole.

Sun and Soil Preferences Japanese Andromeda insists on partial to full shade and moist but well-drained, organically rich acidic soil.

Moisture Requirements Water thoroughly immediately after planting. In a woodland setting, use wood-chip mulch or other organic material to conserve moisture. Apply water during extended drought.

Fertilizing Apply a plant food containing chelated iron for acid-loving plants, following the label directions.

Pruning and Care After the flower "bells" shatter (the ground will look like snow), stop seed production by pinching out the seedheads. This pruning should be all that is necessary to keep Japanese Andromeda a well-formed, fully clothed, evergreen shrub. Pinching out the spent blossoms puts energy into next year's flowerbud production. If drastic pruning becomes necessary, do it in March. Japanese Andromeda stems contain many adventitious buds that will break through the older bark if they are encouraged to emerge before hot, dry weather sets in.

Pests and Diseases Lace bugs, so called because of their lace-like wings, are the bane of Japanese Andromeda foliage. They suck the life right out of the glossy green leaves. Apply insecticidal soap according to the label directions, beginning in late May in the Tri-State area.

Additional Species, Cultivars, or Varieties 'Dorothy Wycoff' has deep-pink buds and pale-pink flowers; 'Mountain Fire', with white flowers, has unusual new foliage that is fiery red.

My Personal Favorite

NAME	SPECIAL CHARACTERISTICS
'White Cascade'	Improved, profusely flowering Japanese Andromeda / offers white blossoms up to 4 weeks longer than the species

Juniper

Juniperus chinensis 'Hetzii'

Preferred Zones	Sun Preference		Additional Benefits
4 to 9	☀		🐝 🔺

Take a drive through suburbia anywhere in the Tri-State area and what will you see? Junipers, Junipers, and more Junipers! They're planted along sunny foundations of commercial buildings, under south-facing windows of high ranch homes, along sunny property lines to screen out objectionable views, or in mass plantings to divide parking lots. Many are of the medium-sized species Juniperus chinensis. *With their color combinations and vigorous-growing, semi-erect, spreading branches, Junipers are a popular plant. In fact, the family of Junipers is the most widely used landscape plant in America. I planted J. c. 'Gold Coast', a compact, spreading form with new golden-yellow growth, next to my compact Burning Bush. What a fall show! Fire-engine red leaves on one and green-and-gold needles on the other . . . If you want evergreen boughs for holiday decorations, put on a pair of gloves, get out your pruners, and cut branches from Junipers. They'll outlast the holidays with their freshness.*

Bloom Period and Color Spring blooms are not showy.

Mature Height × **Spread** 12 to 15 feet × 12 to 15 feet

When and How to Plant Plant anytime during the growing season. The planting hole should be no deeper than the rootball and two to three times its width. Container-grown Junipers are often rootbound—butterfly the roots, and plant with unamended backfill.

Sun and Soil Preferences The most important growing condition is sunlight. The more the plant gets (six hours or more), the better it will grow. Plant container-grown or balled-and-burlapped Junipers in almost any type of soil, from sandy to clay. The pH can vary from acid to alkaline—the only soil condition they don't like is "wet feet."

Moisture Requirements Water newly planted Junipers immediately after planting. Mulch with pine bark nuggets, wood chips, or shredded hardwood bark to a depth of 3 to 4 inches to conserve moisture. Once established, Junipers need little water, and they are one of families recommended for water-efficient gardening.

Fertilizing Like junipers native to the Tri-State area, *J. chinensis* requires little or no extra nutrition, although it will benefit from an annual application of an organic plant food for evergreens in early spring as the soil warms.

Pruning and Care Prune as needed to retain shape or spread.

Pests and Diseases Keep down the weeds with mulch. Phomopsis tip blight, which kills new shoots, is prevalent in spring and during excessively wet weather. Wet foliage equals tip blight. To reduce susceptibility to this disease, plant Junipers in a location where they will dry off from overnight dew or rain as soon as the sun rises. Contact your county cooperative extension educator for the latest fungicide control.

Additional Species, Cultivars, or Varieties 'Gold Coast', 6 feet tall with a compact, spreading form, has golden-yellow new growth that persists and deepens in cold winter. 'Sea Green', 4 feet tall, has mint-green foliage. If you want an evergreen wall, plant 'Hetzi Columnaris'; it's an unusual dense column of bright-green needles, 15 to 20 feet tall.

My Personal Favorite

NAME	SPECIAL CHARACTERISTICS
'Hetzii'	Rapid growing upright spreader / branches in all directions

Korean Spice Viburnum

Viburnum carlesii

Preferred Zones	Sun Preferences		Additional Benefits
6 to 9	☀ ☼		

" *During late April through May, a visit to the New York Botanical Garden, Bronx, New York, would not be complete without a stroll through the Viburnum collection located just south of the Enid A. Haupt Conservatory, when the hillside is abloom with white, fragrant to extremely fragrant blossoms. In your garden, everyone for blocks around will know when your Viburnums are in bloom. I have planted* Viburnum carlesii *Korean Spice Viburnum, with pink to reddish flowerbuds opening to white, releasing a fragrance second to none. Over the past few years there has been a change in bloom-time. I noticed that this Viburnum bloomed a little earlier than normal, blossoming in mid- to late April instead of early May. I'm not complaining, as the timing corresponds with other fragrant plants in my garden, such as Lilacs, early Lilies, Peonies, and Honeysuckle, ending with Mock Orange in late May to early June.* **Note:** *Michael A. Dirr says in his Manual of Woody Landscape Plants, "A garden without a Viburnum is akin to life without music and art." Select and grow a fragrant species for your garden and you'll agree.* "

Bloom Period and Color White flowers bloom May to June.

Mature Height × Spread 7 feet × 8 feet

When and How to Plant Large balled-and-burlapped specimens are available for spring planting, and container-grown plants are available both spring and fall. Plant in a hole no deeper than the rootball but two to three times its width.

Sun and Soil Preferences Plant Viburnum in full sun to light shade, in an organically rich, moist soil that drains well.

Moisture Requirements Maintain organic mulch, such as pine bark or shredded hardwood, over the root system to retain moisture without keeping the soil too wet.

Fertilizing Apply an organic plant food for flowering shrubs annually in early spring at the rate prescribed on the label.

Pruning and Care In a natural border, prune carefully to maintain that natural appearance. If necessary, 'Mohawk', a spicy clove-scented Viburnum which is a cross between *V. burkwoodii* × *V. carlesii,* may be sheared to form a hedge, but do this pruning immediately after flowering. Viburnum blooms on last year's growth, so avoid shearing or drastic pruning late in the fall or in the spring before bloom.

Pests and Diseases There are a host of insect and disease problems that plague Viburnum such as leaf spot, powdery mildew, rust, garden beetles, borers, and scale. But don't despair! Contact your county cooperative extension educator for information on control of those that are prevalent in your area. The fragrances of the blooms will be your reward.

Additional Species, Cultivars, or Varieties *V. rhytidophyllum* Leatherleaf Viburnum, 12 feet tall and 8 feet wide, produces tiny yellowish-white flowers in 5- to 6-inch clusters; its evergreen, wrinkled, leatherlike foliage sets off abundant red berries. Prune right after bloom. *V. macrocephalum* Chinese Snowball is an attention-getter in May with its spectacular 6- to 10-inch snowball blooms.

My Personal Favorite

NAME	SPECIAL CHARACTERISTICS
Korean Spice Viburnum	*V. carlesii*, the species / grows to 7 feet high with a spread of 8 feet / pink buds open to white flowers / very fragrant

Mock Orange

Philadelphus × virginalis

Preferred Zones	Sun Preferences		Additional Benefits
4 to 8	☀	☀	

For those of you who have visited Florida and enjoyed the sweet smell of orange blossoms, and would like the same sweet fragrance in your Tri-State garden, I suggest you plant a Mock Orange as part of a shrub or mixed border. Because the lower portion of Mock Orange is often bare of foliage, set it back in the border, placing smaller shrubs (possibly a collection of evergreen Azaleas) to the front. Whenever you plant the Mock Orange, try to position it in a location where the prevailing breezes will help send the sweet orange-blossom fragrance in the direction you can enjoy most often. I planted a multistemmed balled-and-burlapped specimen of Mock Orange just outside the kitchen. While this deciduous shrub is in bloom, in late spring and early summer, the sweet smell of orange blossoms fills the morning and evening air. My wife dearly loves it. Want to share the fragrance of Mock Orange with a neighbor? Dig a clump in early spring before growth starts and have your neighbor plant it immediately.

Bloom Period and Color Single white flowers with pleasing fragrance bloom late spring to early summer.

Mature Height × **Spread** 8 to 10 feet × by 10 feet

When and How to Plant Mock Orange is easy to grow when starting from bare-root transplants or divisions dug from well-established plants. Start in early spring, before new growth starts. Container-grown or balled-and-burlapped nursery stock can be planted at any time of the year. Plant in unamended backfill.

Sun and Soil Preferences Plant in full sun, or in partial shade if there is at least a half-day of sun, in ordinary soil with good drainage.

Moisture Requirements To ensure establishment of its spreading root system, water generously the first season. Spread a permanent 2- to 3-inch layer of organic mulch, like pine bark nuggets or wood chips, over the root system to conserve precious moisture during periods of drought.

Fertilizing An application of a plant food for flowering shrubs will be appreciated in early spring.

Pruning and Care Prune Mock Orange immediately after flowering to stimulate new growth for bloom the following spring. Once a year, thin well-established plants by pruning the oldest stems to the ground. Division of older plants is simple. With a sharp spade, cut out a section of stems or sprouts (while dormant) from the ground. Be sure to include the roots. Replant at the same depth in the new location and water-in immediately.

Pests and Diseases There are no serious pest problems.

Additional Species, Cultivars, or Varieties 'Dwarf Minnesota Snowflake', a 4-foot-tall by 4-foot-wide shrub with white, double, fragrant blossoms, is ideal for small-space gardens.

My Personal Favorite

NAME	SPECIAL CHARACTERISTICS
Mock Orange	*P.* × *virginalis*, the species / sweet scent of orange wafts in morning and evening

Mountain Laurel

Kalmia latifolia

Preferred Zones	Sun Preferences		Additional Benefits
5 to 9	◐	☀	Ⓝ 🐝 🍃

In 1907, the Mountain Laurel was designated Connecticut's state flower. It is native to North America and grows in huge masses in rural woodland environments of the Tri-State area. When allowed room to grow, Mountain Laurel tends to be a rounded evergreen shrub that can grow six to twelve feet high and wide. The bell-shaped blossoms are large clusters of white. As the plant ages, it takes on a rather interesting, architecturally layered look, the upper, newest section of the plant appearing to grow out of the older one below. Enjoy a Sunday drive through the hillsides of the Tri-State area from May through June to see hundreds, if not thousands, of Mountain Laurel in bloom with white-to-rose blossoms. For continuing color, plant Mountain Laurel along with other broadleaf evergreens from the same family like white Andromeda, which offers April bloom; pink Rhododendrons, early-May bloom; and fire-engine-red Azaleas, late-May bloom. What a show!

Bloom Period and Color White-to-rose flowers with inside purple markings bloom May to June.

Mature Height × Spread 6 to 12 feet × 6 to 12 feet

When and How to Plant Plant any time in spring or early fall. Summer planting for balled-and-burlapped and container-grown plants is acceptable with adequate moisture. Plant at a depth no deeper than the rootball.

Sun and Soil Preferences Plant in partial to full shade, in a moist, acidic, well-drained, richly organic soil.

Moisture Requirements Organic matter increases the soil's moisture-holding capacity and lowers the pH. When setting plants into a landscape or garden bed with other Ericaceous plants, like Azalea, Leucothoe, and Rhododendron, incorporate generous amounts of well-rotted compost or milled sphagnum peat moss to a depth of 10 or more inches. To help retain moisture and keep soil cool, mulch newly planted specimens. During periods of heat and drought, an occasional deep watering will moisten the mulch and keep the shallow roots cool. Water is most beneficial if applied during flowerbud set in late summer and early fall.

Fertilizing As the soil warms in early spring, apply an organic plant food formulated for acid-loving plants. This will enhance bloom the following year.

Pruning and Care Remove spent blossoms immediately after they fade to prevent seed formation and to direct energy into next season's bud development. Deadheading reduces legginess, a perennial problem of Mountain Laurel. In the Tri-State growing area, overgrown Mountain Laurel and those at which the deer have been nibbling may be pruned drastically in late winter to early spring. New sprouts will emerge from the base.

Pests and Diseases Leaf spot, whitefly, lace bug, stem borer, and scale may present problems. Contact your county cooperative extension educator for recommended controls. Read and follow label directions.

Additional Species, Cultivars, or Varieties In addition to the native Mountain Laurel, you can select from other cultivars, including 'Alba', white blossoms; 'Elf', a dwarf with blush-white flowers; 'Nipmuck', bright-red buds opening to pale-pink blossoms; 'Pink Star', dark-pink, star-shaped flowers; and 'Sarah', red flowers maturing to rosy-red.

My Personal Favorite

NAME	SPECIAL CHARACTERISTICS
Mountain Laurel	*K. latifolia*, the species / clusters of perfectly-formed white to rose flowers

Red Twig Dogwood

Cornus sericea

Preferred Zones	Sun Preferences	Additional Benefits
3 to 7		

The Red Twig Dogwood, one of the most unappreciated and underused plants in the landscape, is beginning to gain some recognition in the Tri-State area. I've been talking about it on my Garden Hotline® radio program, telling listeners to look for it in the wetlands along the New York State Thruway, along the Merritt Parkway in Connecticut, along Interstate Route 80 in New Jersey, or just about any other sunny, swampy area. In winter, they will see bright-red twigs, eight to ten feet tall, standing upright through the snow—this is last season's new growth of Red Twig Dogwood. The red changes to gray as new stems sprout in spring, so prune them out after bloom in May and early June. A companion to Red Twig Dogwood is Yellow Twig Dogwood, C. sericea 'Lutea'. You can create your own winter postcard: Plant a grouping of Red Twig and Yellow Twig Dogwood, backdropped by dark-green evergreens such as Canadian Hemlock or Black Pine. When the cardinals and blue jays fly in, get out your camera with color film to record the beauty of it all. **Note:** *If you can't find* Cornus sericea, *look for* Cornus stolonifera, *another botanical name sometimes used for the same plant.*

Bloom Period and Color White flowers bloom late May to early June.

Mature Height × Spread 6 to 7 feet × 10 or more feet

When and How to Plant Since Red Twig Dogwood is a deciduous spring bloomer, it may be planted in early spring, before new growth emerges, or in the fall after leaf drop. Bare-root plants can be set out before new growth starts in spring. Plant a container-grown or balled-and-burlapped specimen in a hole no deeper than the rootball and at least two to three times its width.

Sun and Soil Preferences Plant in full sun to partial shade. Red Twig Dogwoods are easily established in moist, acid soil that is high in organic content.

Moisture Requirements Water the plants regularly until they become established. A single plant will soon develop into a shrubby clump as the dark-red stems spread by means of underground stolons.

Fertilizing Provide a springtime application of a balanced plant food for Red Twig Dogwood on an annual schedule.

Pruning and Care To capture and encourage the bright-red twigs for winter's landscape, practice pruning in favor of juvenile wood. Immediately after the late-spring bloom, prune the two-year-old stems to the ground. They will be easy to identify, as they will have lost their bright-red color. The current season's growth provides the brilliant red juvenile twigs for the coming winter.

Pests and Diseases Twig blight (canker) and bagworms may be problems. Contact your county cooperative extension educator for controls.

Additional Species, Cultivars, or Varieties *C. alba* 'Sibirica' Siberian Dogwood, 8 to 10 feet tall by 5 to 10 feet wide, has brilliantly red stems in winter. *Cornus alba* 'Argento Marginata' ('Elegantissima'), a variegated Red Twig Dogwood, is 8 to 10 feet tall and wide. *C. sericea* 'Lutea' Yellow Twig Dogwood, 6 to 7 feet tall, has bright-yellow stems in winter. *C. s.* 'Flaviramea', another variety 7 to 9 feet tall by 8 to 10 feet wide, has bright-yellow twigs in winter after leaf drop.

My Personal Favorite

NAME	SPECIAL CHARACTERISTICS
'Cardinal'	Known as Cardinal Redosier Dogwood / 7 to 9 feet tall by 8 to 10 feet wide

Rhododendron

Rhododendron spp. and hybrids

Preferred Zones	Sun Preferences	Additional Benefits
4 to 8	☀ ◐ ☀	

" Roseum elegans, Roseum elegans, Roseum elegans—*sounds repetitive, doesn't it?
You can't miss it. Roseum elegans is the most overused variety of Rhododendron in
the Tri-State area. It's that pinkish-red evergreen shrub you see in almost everyone's
landscape, more often than not obscuring the picture window! (Someone may have
forgotten that "from little plants often come great big plants.") If not pruned as needed,
it won't be many years before the view from the picture window is a thing of the past.
There are so many other Rhododendron species and varieties available from garden
centers and nurseries. I have a collection of some ninety-two species and hybrid
varieties in my landscape nursery and landscape, blooming from late March into
July. That's almost five months of bloom! With a little planning you, too, can have
Rhododendrons other than Roseum elegans in your landscape. (Oh, yes, I also have
Roseum elegans.)* "

Bloom Period and Color Flowers in shades of red, pink, white, lilac, purple, and yellow bloom early spring to early summer, depending on variety.

Mature Height × Spread 2 to 8 feet × 2 to 8 feet

When and How to Plant Whether planting balled-and-burlapped or container-grown Rhododendron, plant absolutely no deeper than the depth of the rootball. Keep a 2- to 3-inch layer of organic mulch over the spreading roots at all times to reduce soil compaction and weed growth.

Sun and Soil Preferences Depending on species and cultivar, it may be planted with exposure to full sun to deep shade. Plant in acid (4.5 to 6.5 pH), well-drained soil that holds moisture without remaining wet.

Moisture Requirements Mulch to retain moisture. During drought periods, deep watering is essential.

Fertilizing Feed Rhododendrons annually with a complete balanced plant food for acid-loving plants. The formula should include trace elements as well.

Pruning and Care The shallow roots are easily damaged by cultivation, so take care. Immediately after flowering, break out (deadhead) spent blossoms.

Pests and Diseases Rhododendron weevil, stem borers, and grubs may present problems. Consult with your county cooperative extension educator for the latest controls.

Additional Species, Cultivars, or Varieties H1, H2, and H3 are names of groups relating to the hardiness of Rhododendrons. H1 hybrids, for zones 4 to 7, include 'P.J.M.', which produces small dark-green leaves that turn reddish in fall and small bright-lavender-to-pink flowers in late April. H2 hybrids, for zones 5 to 8, include 'Chionoides', a low, broad Rhododendron that has white flowers with yellow centers. *Rhododendron* 'Catawbiense Album', Catawba Rhododendron, with pure-white flowers with yellowish throats, is very hardy and a prolific bloomer in May. Our native Rhododendron, *Rhododendron maximum*, which grows in the wild, is a magnificent species with light-pink to white blooms in early July; it can reach 20 feet tall with a 20-foot spread.

My Personal Favorite

NAME	SPECIAL CHARACTERISTICS
'Cheer'	Pink florets and purple throat / blooms prolifically in May and, often to the surprise of the gardener, again in late September through October with approximately 30 percent of the traditional spring bloom / H3 Hybrid

Rose of Sharon

Hibiscus syriacus

Preferred Zones	Sun Preference	Additional Benefits
5 to 8	☀	🦋 🐦 🌼 🐝

As a specimen in the sunny landscape, as a hedge along a border, or as a single plant in a large container—Rose of Sharon, a deciduous flowering shrub or tree, provides some of the most enjoyable, colorful flowers during the hottest, driest times of summer. Early one spring I was visiting friends when a question came up from Herb and Lucille about their Rose of Sharon. Herb wanted to prune back drastically the over-grown plant, and Lucille wanted no part of it. Pressed for an answer, I said, "Severely." "Severely?" Herb queried. "Yes," I replied, "severely—by as much as six or eight feet." Lucille turned her back and walked away in disgust, and I was sure I had lost a friend. That fall I got a call from the happy couple. With some relief in his voice, Herb informed me that their Rose of Sharon had produced literally thousands of blossoms all summer long.

Other Name Shrub Althea

Bloom Period and Color White, pink, crimson, purple, or bicolor flowers bloom July through early October, right up to frost.

Mature Height × **Spread** 8 to 12 feet × 6 to 8 feet

When and How to Plant Plant container-grown or balled-and-burlapped specimens no deeper than the rootball in spring or fall. Bare-root transplants may be set while dormant anytime the ground is thawed from late fall to late winter (November through February in the Tri-State area). Seedlings from your Rose of Sharon can be dug in late spring, potted in a well-drained soil, and used to make a new friend.

Sun and Soil Preferences Plant in full sun in well-drained, slightly acid (5.5 to 7.0 pH), rich soil.

Moisture Requirements Water-in all transplants (bare-root, container-grown, or balled-and-burlapped) immediately after planting. An occasional watering during periods of prolonged drought will encourage better flowering.

Fertilizing Feed annually with a plant food for flowering trees and shrubs, a 5-10-5 or equivalent.

Pruning and Care Springtime pruning pays off, as drastic pruning not only keeps Rose of Sharon in bounds but also promotes more bloom. This plant blooms on new growth each season. For plants that fail to bloom, check the light exposure—they need full sun. Rose of Sharon can be grown in either shrub or tree form. To create a shrub, leave the pruning tools in the shed; to grow a tree, prune as a single-stemmed plant.

Pests and Diseases Aphids on young, tender growth can be controlled with insecticidal soap.

Additional Species, Cultivars, or Varieties Seedless, triploid hybrids introduced by the United States National Arboretum include 'Helene', a white flower with deep-purple eye; 'Aphrodite', a rose-pink flower with dark-red eye; and 'Diana', my favorite. Another triploid USDA introduction includes 'Minerva', which produces magnificent lavender-pink blossoms with reddish-purple eyes. 'Red Heart', which has single white flowers with scarlet-red eyes, is an outstanding standard.

My Personal Favorite

NAME	SPECIAL CHARACTERISTICS
'Diana'	Pure white / 4-inch blossoms remain open at night

Slender Deutzia
Deutzia gracilis

Preferred Zones	Sun Preferences	Additional Benefits
4 to 8	☀ ☀	🌼 🐝

I have a single Slender Deutzia planted next to a bright-red Peony, and wow, what a show! Slender Deutzia, a deciduous flowering shrub in white or pink, is one of the heaviest bloomers in the landscape. In the Tri-State garden, its branches literally droop with thousands of blossoms in mid-May. The one-half- to three-quarter-inch flowers are borne in clusters up and down the stem with such profusion that they literally hide the rest of the branch. (I don't know of another flowering shrub that has more blooms.) One Deutzia in a foundation planting will steal the show. When planted as a border along a walkway, passersby will pause to look. As an informal hedge at two to four feet high, the profusion of bloom will lead your eye down the row. Use several plants as a filler in a large landscape garden—Deutzia in bloom will add character to spring cut-flower bouquets. The erect pink or pure-white flowers complement a vase filled with Giant Peonies and colorful tall Bearded Iris. Visit the Brooklyn Botanic Garden, Brooklyn, New York, in mid-May, and you'll find specimens of Slender Deutzias planted through-out the garden.

Other Name Spreading Deutzia

Bloom Period and Color Pure-white flowers bloom late spring to early summer.

Mature Height × Spread 2 to 4 feet × 2 to 4 feet

When and How to Plant Slender Deutzia, whether container grown or balled and burlapped, can be planted from early spring to late fall. When planting, take care to spread the roots of container-grown plants, as they tend to be rootbound. Plant no deeper than the rootball. Bare-root plants, primarily available by mail order, must be planted and watered-in as soon as the soil is workable in early spring, before new growth buds expand.

Sun and Soil Preferences Plant in full sun to partial shade, in acidic soil that drains well.

Moisture Requirements Make sure adequate moisture is provided for establishment during the first year. Mulch newly planted Deutzia with organic mulch such as pine bark nuggets, and renew the mulch annually.

Fertilizing If you've planted it in a bed with other flowering plants, you may provide the same fertilizer.

Pruning and Care Deutzia blooms on last season's growth, so prune as soon as flowers drop to stimulate new growth for next season's buds. Periodic thinning of the oldest stems encourages juvenile shoots for better bloom.

Pests and Diseases There are no serious pest problems.

Additional Species, Cultivars, or Varieties In addition to the species, recommended cultivars include 'Nikko', which has white blossoms on arching branches and burgundy foliage color in fall, and 'Pink', which has pink blossoms on arching branches. Other Deutzia species are *Deutzia crenata* 'Nikko', a 1- to 2-foot dwarf hardy to zone 6 that produces attractive burgundy foliage in the fall; *Deutzia × lemoinei* Lemoine Deutzia, a 5- to 7-foot-tall species recommended for its tolerance to cold; and *D. × magnifica* Showy Deutzia, a large shrub that grows 10 feet tall and is very prolific, with white double-flower blooms for about three weeks in late spring.

My Personal Favorite

NAME	SPECIAL CHARACTERISTICS
Slender Deutzia	*D. gracilis*, the species / covered with pure-white flowers for about 2 weeks in spring

Spirea

Spirea japonica

Preferred Zones
4 to 9

Sun Preferences

Additional Benefit

The most common Spirea, the classic 'Vanhoutte', with upright-arching branches covered with clusters of tiny white blossoms in late May, should not be overlooked. You'll find 'Vanhoutte' planted as a flowering shrub around many of the older homes that were built from the '30s through the '60s in the Tri-State area. My neighbor has several of these classics planted along the railing of an expansive, raised, old-fashioned wooden porch. Visit Mohonk Mountain House, New Paltz, New York, where you'll find classic Spireas as well as some 100 other older varieties of trees and shrubs, including such favorites as Deutzia, Viburnum, Shrub Honeysuckle, Mock Orange, Old-fashioned Lilacs, Weigela, and Hydrangea. But in today's modern landscape, the smaller-growing, deep-pink Bridal Wreath, 'Anthony Waterer', excites the gardener more. Not only does it have pink to rosy-pink flowers in May, it has the added benefit of spring foliage tinged with pink turning to purplish-red in fall.

Other Name Bridal Wreath Spirea

Bloom Period and Color Depending upon the species, pink to rose-pink flowers bloom all summer, or white flowers bloom in spring.

Mature Height × Spread 3 to 4 feet × 3 to 4 feet

When and How to Plant Plant balled-and-burlapped or container-grown Spirea at any time in spring, summer, or fall. Container-grown plants are often rootbound, requiring butterflying of the root mass at planting time. Plant no deeper than the rootball. Use unamended backfill.

Sun and Soil Preferences Although Spirea may be planted in full sun to partial shade, the more sun, the more prolific the bloom. Plant in any average, slightly acidic soil.

Moisture Requirements Water thoroughly immediately after planting, and then water only during extremely dry periods.

Fertilizing Feed Spirea in early spring, according to label directions, with a granular plant food formulated for flowering trees and shrubs.

Pruning and Care To encourage compactness, clip stem tips in early spring just before new growth starts. After flowering, deadhead blossoms to encourage more blossoms. If plants become too woody and overgrown, every few years you can cut back old stems to the ground early in spring to begin a new plant.

Pests and Diseases During excessively warm, dry weather, watch for spider mites. The stippled, bleached-out appearance of the leaves is a clue. Apply insecticidal soap or hot pepper wax spray according to the label directions.

Additional Species, Cultivars, or Varieties 'Gold Flame' is unique, with foliage of bronze-gold in spring, yellow-green in summer, and copper-orange in fall; it has 3- to 5-inch clusters of crimson flowers in summer. 'Alpina' is probably the smallest of Spirea, growing to only 2 feet tall and 2½ feet wide; it's ideal for a small-space garden of perennials and landscape evergreens. *Spirea thunbergii* Thunberg Spirea, a reliable "old standby," has white blossoms in early spring.

My Personal Favorite

NAME	SPECIAL CHARACTERISTICS
Spirea × arguta Bridal Wreath Spirea	A profusion of white flowers on slender arching stems / blooms early spring to mid-spring / reaches to 6 to 8 feet high and wide

Star Magnolia

Magnolia stellata

Preferred Zones	Sun Preferences	Additional Benefits
4 to 8	☀ ◑	🐝 🌿

M. stellata *Star Magnolia, a deciduous shrub, exhibits dark-green, showy leaves that turn copper-yellow in the fall. The fragrant white or pink flowers often open in spring just before the last frost, a frost that may cause the entire plant to wake up the next morning looking something like a huge chocolate ice-cream cone. In late March to early April, observe the two* M. stellata *that are planted near the Administration Building at the New York Botanical Garden, Bronx, New York. I've been passing by these two specimens every spring for thirty-four years, but only about ten of those years did I ever notice them with the "chocolate-ice-cream-cone" look, undoubtedly because they are in a protected location. If you have a somewhat protected area for planting where there is little chance of late frost, I wouldn't hesitate to try growing Star Magnolia. For extra protection, integrate it into a foundation planting.*

Bloom Period and Color White flowers bloom early to mid-spring.

Mature Height × Spread 10 to 15 feet × 10 to 15 feet

When and How to Plant Plant before new growth starts in spring. Plant a balled-and-burlapped or container-grown plant in a hole no deeper than the rootball and two to three times its width. Small container-grown plants can be planted at any time as long as water is available during the first growing season. Once it is established, leave Star Magnolia in place. It does not take to transplanting.

Sun and Soil Preferences Plant in full sun to dappled shade, in rich, slightly acid (6.0 to 6.5 pH) soil that drains well.

Moisture Requirements Water thoroughly at planting. To prevent stress due to heat and drought and scorch of the dark-green foliage, spread an organic mulch like pine bark mini-nuggets or shredded hardwood bark over the root system immediately after planting, and renew the mulch every year.

Fertilizing Feed each spring with an organic plant food formulated for acid-loving flowering plants.

Pruning and Care To create the tree form, simply prune out the multiple stems as they sprout from the base.

Pests and Diseases Star Magnolia is basically trouble-free.

Additional Species, Cultivars, or Varieties Available cultivars worthy of planting include 'Waterlily', which has pink buds opening to white flowers with pink on the backsides of the petals; 'Rubra' Red Star Magnolia, with large, purplish to pink flowers; 'Rosea', the Pink Star Magnolia, with pale-pink blossoms; and 'Royal Star'. If late frost is common in your garden, plant one of the 'Little Girl' Hybrids, which include 'Ann', 'Betty', 'Jane', 'Judy', 'Randy', 'Ricki', and 'Susan'. They flower later than the species *M. stellata*. **Note:** Star Magnolia, hardiest of the Magnolia family, recently went through a taxonomic change and is now listed as *M. kobus* var. *stellata*.

My Personal Favorite

NAME	SPECIAL CHARACTERISTICS
'Royal Star'	Produces exceptionally large, white flowers on an almost treelike shrub / blooms late, reducing the risk of late frost damage

Weigela

Weigela florida

Preferred Zones	Sun Preference	Additional Benefit
4 to 8	☀	🐝

> While driving around the neighborhood at any time other than late spring to early summer, you might overlook Weigela, one of the most underrated flowering shrubs in the Tri-State landscape—without bloom, it's only a graceful, unobtrusive deciduous shrub with arching branches. Variegated Weigela, however, with its creamy-white leaf margins, will definitely catch your eye during bloom time. Depending on the variety, the arching branches are clothed with tubular blossoms with wide-open trumpets in colors ranging from pure white to pink to red. The sizes range from plants that are six to ten feet tall and wide, to compact cultivars only two to three feet tall and wide. A few cut branches in bloom will add charm to spring flower arrangements. I saw a hillside on Long Island covered with Weigela in bloom from late spring into early summer. There must have been fifty or more individual plants. What a show-stopper!

Bloom Period and Color White, rose, or pink (depending on cultivar) flowers bloom from May to June.

Mature Height × Spread 6 to 9 feet × 12 feet

When and How to Plant Plant before new growth starts in early spring. Weigela is one of the easiest plants to establish. Dig the hole twice as wide as the spread of the bare roots (loosen the soil below for bare-root transplants only). Container-grown and balled-and-burlapped Weigela is plantable in spring or fall: dig the hole no deeper than the depth of the rootball but twice as wide. Use unamended backfill. *Weigela florida* reaches 10 feet tall and wide, so should be planted in an area where there is room to grow.

Sun and Soil Preferences Plant in a full-sun environment, in a fertile soil that drains well and has a neutral to slightly acid pH.

Moisture Requirements Provide water at planting time, and continue watering as needed for the first growing season, particulary during drought. Following summer drought with excessive heat in the Tri-State area, it is not uncommon for Weigela to open a few flowers in fall. The stress of heat and drought trigger a false dormancy in the current season's growth, allowing buds of next year's growth to open in fall.

Fertilizing An early-spring application of an organic plant food for flowering shrubs on a annual schedule will benefit Weigela.

Pruning and Care Pruning is just about the only task required for Weigela. Overgrown plants can be pruned severely, right after bloom. For normal maintenance, just cut out a few of the oldest stems each year immediately following bloom. Weigela flowers on last year's wood; the new growth encouraged from pruning sets flowerbuds for the following spring.

Pests and Diseases There are no serious pest problems.

Additional Species, Cultivars, or Varieties 'Bristol Ruby', with ruby-red flowers, and 'Mont Blanc', with pure-white flowers, are both much smaller than the species, reaching 5 or 6 feet tall. 'Variegated Nana', a very dwarf variety only 2 to 3 feet tall, has yellow-edged foliage and produces fountains of deep-rose flowers.

My Personal Favorite

NAME	SPECIAL CHARACTERISTICS
Weigela	*W. florida*, the species / old-fashioned favorite / arching branches touch the ground / a bonus: it may bloom in fall

Witchhazel

Hamamelis × intermedia

Preferred Zones	Sun Preferences		Additional Benefits
3 to 8			

Do you want a flowering shrub that will get you out in the garden in winter? Plant a variety of Witchhazel, which has spiderlike blooms that last for weeks on end, seemingly unaware of the temperature. The very pleasant fragrance released from these winter gems will penetrate the winter air, so plant a Witchhazel near a window or door so you can enjoy the fragrance without getting a chill. If you notice a sweet fragrance in the air in February or early March, you can rest assured it's coming from a Witchhazel. There is no other plant with Witchhazel's blooming potential in the Tri-State area. Visit the Highland Botanical Park, Rochester, New York, during the chilly days of winter and you're guaranteed to see blooming Witchhazel, even in the bitter cold. Planning a fragrance garden? Plant Witchhazel and its many cultivars for winter, Viburnum carlesii for spring, and Old-fashioned Roses to carry you through the summer.

Bloom Period and Color Depending on the species and cultivar, yellow, gold, lemon-yellow, orange-red, and red flowers bloom November through March.

Mature Height × Spread 10 feet × 12 feet

When and How to Plant Large balled-and-burlapped specimens establish themselves easily if planted in early spring or early fall, but may go out of bloom for three to four years after transplanting. Bare-root transplants are planted before going into leaf in early spring. Plant Witchhazel in a hole two to three times the diameter of the rootball but no deeper than the root mass. Container-grown Witchhazel tends to be massively rootbound—to prevent girdling, cut away any circling roots and spread the remaining roots into the backfill.

Sun and Soil Preferences Plant in full sun to dappled shade in average to poor garden soil.

Moisture Requirements Water thoroughly immediately after planting, and continue watering as needed until the plant is well established. Water during extreme drought periods will be beneficial.

Fertilizing Mulch newly planted Witchhazel with organic mulch such as pine bark mini-nuggets or wood chips, replenishing the mulch annually. As the mulch becomes humic acid (the end product of decaying matter), it will provide nutrients for growth. No other fertilizing is necessary.

Pruning and Care Sucker growth originating from the base of grafted hybrids should pruned out as soon as it appears.

Pests and Diseases There are no serious pest problems.

Additional Species, Cultivars, or Varieties Common Witchhazel *H. virginiana*, native to the northeast, blooms in later fall and early winter. *H. japonica* Japanese Witchhazel, blooms in February to March and has yellow flowers. *H. mollis* Chinese Witchhazel has fragrant yellow flowers with rich red-brown calyx eyes; it blooms Feburary to March.

My Personal Favorite

NAME	SPECIAL CHARACTERISTICS
Witchhazel	*H. × intermedia*, the species / a hybrid between *H. japonica* and *H. mollis* / produces many cultivars showing red, yellow, and orange flowers / blooms from late January into March

Small Flowering Trees

There is probably nothing more satisfying than planting a beautiful tree, nurturing it for a few seasons, then watching it come into bloom for the first time. A double-flowering, pink Kwansan Cherry tree may be planted as a special feature in the landscape. Eastern White Dogwood may be planted as focal points along a winding drive. Eastern Redbud may be planted to complete the framing of a landscape bed at the corner of the house. A Weeping Cherry might be just the plant to go next to the patio. The disappointing part of planting a flowering tree is that it may take up to five years or more to bloom.

Selecting Your Flowering Tree

When purchasing a flowering tree, buy the best. Look for specimens with symmetrical form. There is always a good side and a better side for trees. The branch structure

should be typical of the species. The vase-shaped Kwansan Cherry should be growing in that form from the beginning. The Weeping Cherry should have a natural weep. Check the bark on the trunk of the tree; look for bruises or cuts that might have resulted from handling and transporting. Balled-and-burlapped specimens must be intact. A cracked ball of earth diminishes the chance of planting success, or can greatly affect the time it takes to get into bloom. A cracked ball is almost equivalent to a bare-root plant.

Whatever species of flowering tree you choose, always investigate its hardiness for your region. The Tri-State area extends from Hardiness Zone 3a (-35 to -40 Fahrenheit average minimum temperature) to Hardiness Zone 7b (+10 to +5 average minimum temperature). This means that trees selected for the Atlantic City, New

for the Tri-State

Jersey, area may not survive in the coldest upstate New York landscape, or even in Connecticut near the Long Island Sound.

Planting Tips

Don't forget to remove any artificial burlap (plastic or nylon) from a balled-and-burlapped plant before completing the planting process. Thoroughly moisten the rootball, carefully set the plant into the hole, then remove the artificial burlap by sliding it from underneath the ball. Don't take it off before positioning the plant in the hole, as the soil may fall off the roots.

A container-grown flowering tree must come out of the can before planting, even if it is in a "plantable" pot. The organic matter of the pressed fiber or paper pots does not deteriorate or decay fast enough to allow penetration of the parent soil by the new tree's roots. Thoroughly water the soil and roots in the container before trying to remove the plant from the container. Water acts as a lubricant, making it much easier to slip the plant from its container.

A Final Tip for Growing Success

In spring, flowering trees in the nursery or garden center will likely be budded up for bloom— they've been growing in an ideal environment. But if you can bring yourself to do it, pinch off the flower buds before they open. By removing the buds/flowers for the first season, you will make sure energy is directed toward the development of a good root system. This stronger root system will help establish a tree with more blooms in years to come. Remember that it is not unusual for a newly planted flowering tree to wait three to five years after being planted before reestablishing a blooming cycle.

Eastern Redbud
Cercis canadensis

Preferred Zones	Sun Preferences	Additional Benefits
5 to 9		

When I drive down the gravel road leaving my home in spring, I don't have to go far to see one of nature's wonders: the flowering characteristic of the Eastern Redbud. I see the specimen's "blooming" branches stretched out over a stone wall. Tiny clusters of flowers, spaced at regular intervals around an entire branch, paint an appearance that suggests the woody stem is actually a bloom (which it is not). Michael A. Dirr, in the Manual of Woody Landscape Plants, *refers to the Eastern Redbud as "a native tree with a touch of class." Eastern Redbud becomes an outstanding specimen when planted as part of a spring-blooming perennial border filled with bright-yellow large-trumpeted King Alfred Daffodils, or as a single focal point in a landscape bed of Creeping Junipers. C. c. 'Alba' produces white flowers with just as much class. Cercis chinensis Chinese Redbud, which grows to ten feet in zone 5, is covered with masses of showy pink pealike flowers in April. Its compact growth creates an ideal plant for the small-space landscape.*

Bloom Period and Color Purple-pink buds open to rose-pink flowers in mid-spring (April to early May).

Mature Height x Spread 20 to 30 feet x 25 to 35 feet

When and How to Plant Plant in late fall after leaf drop or in very early spring before buds begin to expand. Bare-root plants, available by mail order, should be set while dormant in winter as long as the soil is not frozen. Plant nursery-grown container or balled-and-burlapped specimens absolutely no deeper than the rootball in a hole two to three times the diameter of the rootball. Do not amend the backfill—use the native natural soil.

Sun and Soil Preferences Plant in full sun to partial shade, in well-drained moist soil with a pH of 5.5 to 7.5.

Moisture Requirements Water-in all newly planted Redbuds immediately after planting and again the following day. The second watering ensures a thorough soaking of the rootball as well as the backfill.

Fertilizing No additional nutrition is necessary for this native species.

Pruning and Care After planting, and for general care, apply a 3- to 4-inch layer of organic mulch on the soil surface around the tree. The bark tissue of Redbud is very sensitive to frost damage. If mulched to a depth of 3 to 4 inches around the trunk, pull the mulch from the bark in late August through October to allow the bark tissue to harden and dry for winter. The mulch can be replaced for winter.

Pests and Diseases There are no pest problems.

Additional Species, Cultivars, or Varieties Varieties for planting in the Tri-State garden and landscape include 'Flame', with double-flowered red-purple blossoms; 'Wither's Pink Charm', with clear-pink blossoms; and 'Alba', with pure-white blossoms.

My Personal Favorite

NAME	SPECIAL CHARACTERISTICS
'Forest Pansy'	Single-flowered red-purple blossoms and purple foliage

Flowering Crab Apple

Malus spp. and hybrids

Preferred Zones	Sun Preference	Additional Benefits
4 to 9	☀	🍒 🐝 🪺 🍃

Flowering Crab Apples offer an abundance of spring flowers, varying from pure white to soft- and bright-pink to red, either single or double, followed by brilliantly colored fall and winter fruit. They are a popular deciduous flowering tree in the Tri-State landscape, although the fruit can cause a mess. A homeowner who has planted a Flowering Crab Apple as a feature in the front lawn or next to the patio for light shade may call in to my radio show and ask the question: "We love the tree, but can we eliminate the fruit?" The answer is "Yes." I have successfully used a product called Florel Brand Fruit Eliminator manufactured by Monterey Lawn and Garden Products, Inc., P.O. Box 5317, Fresno, CA 93755. The key to eliminating fruit is the timing of the application of the spray. Read the label and follow the manufacturer's recommended rates and directions. I also suggest making a crab apple jelly from the fruits, but I'm not sure how many callers take that advice.

Bloom Period and Color Showy pink, red, and white flowers with pleasing fragrance bloom in spring.

Mature Height x Spread 10 to 25 feet x 10 to 25 feet

When and How to Plant Plant balled-and-burlapped or container-grown specimens at any time during the growing season, no deeper than the root-ball in a hole two to three times its width. Plant bare-root 4- to 5-foot whips before new growth emerges in early spring, in a hole no deeper than the root flare at the base of the stem.

Sun and Soil Preferences Plant in full sun in well-drained, slightly acidic soil. Flowering Crab Apples thrive in a wide range of soils, wet to dry, sand to clay.

Moisture Requirements Water generously at planting time to settle the soil. Water as needed to keep the soil surface slightly moist during hot, dry periods of summer and fall. A deep watering may be necessary, particularly during a drought.

Fertilizing Feed with a plant food for flowering and fruiting plants, following label directions.

Pruning and Care Prune newly planted Crab Apple trees to produce strong structural branches. Remove sucker growth from the trunk of a tree before the sprouts reach no more than 2 inches long: don a pair of leather gloves, grab hold of the sprouts, and yank. A small piece of bark will be dislodged with the sucker, but the wound will heal and no more sprouts will emerge from that spot.

Pests and Diseases Select scab-resistant varieties. If a fungicide becomes necessary for apple scab, check with your county cooperative extension educator for the latest control.

Additional Species, Cultivars, or Varieties M. *baccata* 'Columnaris' (Columnaris Siberian Crab Apple), 25 feet tall with a spread of 8 to 10 feet, is a white-flowered, narrow, upright grower. M. × 'Donald Wyman' (Donald Wyman Crab Apple), 25 feet tall by 20 to 25 feet wide, develops clear-white flower bloom from rich-red buds; it has small, glossy, bright-red fruits that remain on the tree well into winter.

My Personal Favorite

NAME	SPECIAL CHARACTERISTICS
M. *atrosanguinea* 'Royalty'	Produces bright-red foliage all summer long / covered with fragrant royal-red flowers in early spring

Flowering Dogwood
Cornus florida

Preferred Zones	Sun Preferences	Additional Benefits
5 to 9		

*Take a drive in any direction in the Tri-State area during the three- to four-week period when the white blossoms of the Flowering Dogwood (also called Eastern Dogwood) are in their prime, and you will know that spring has arrived. It's not unusual to see an entire hillside covered with these white blooms. Later, when the Dogwood foliage turns a brilliant red color, you can rest assured that fall has arrived, with winter not far behind. I'm saddened by the disease which is attacking these Flowering Dogwoods in the Tri-State area—Discula destructiva, which causes Dogwood anthracnose, can be deadly. I'm thankful for the six Stellar cultivars, however, created by Elwin Orton over the past twenty-five years at Rutgers University. With a little help from God and Mr. Orton, we'll still have Flowering Dogwoods, albeit a different species, in our landscapes. **Note:** The common name Dogwood has no relationship to the canine species. It is a concoction of the old name* dagwood *or* dagger wood—*daggers for skewering meat were made from the wood of some of these trees.*

Bloom Period and Color Pure-white flowers bloom in spring.

Mature Height × Spread 20 to 30 feet × 20 to 30 feet

When and How to Plant Plant *Cornus florida* in early spring, as the roots are sensitive to transplant shock. Dig the hole no deeper than the rootball. Set the tree into the hole; untie and fold back the burlap. Carefully scrape away excess soil to expose the trunk's flare. The planting depth should be measured at that level.

Sun and Soil Preferences Plant balled-and-burlapped *Cornus florida* in moist, well-drained, richly organic soil, in full sun to partial shade. The more sun, the more prolific the bloom.

Moisture Requirements Spread a 2- to 3-inch layer of organic mulch over the root zone to conserve moisture and reduce soil compaction.

Fertilizing Water transplants immediately after planting with a bio-soil activator such as Roots®, Organica Plant Growth Activator®, or PHC BioPak Biostimulant™, which helps convert soil nutrients into consumables for root pickup.

Pruning and Care Remove sucker growth from branches and trunk before they reach more than 3 inches long. Do not prune—pull (yank) them off. Prune out dead twigs immediately upon observance. If a living ground cover is planted within the root zone, provide extra water during drought periods.

Pests and Diseases Dogwood anthracnose is proving to be deadly for the Eastern species. Plant resistant varieties, some of which are named below.

Additional Species, Cultivars, or Varieties Other varieties include Cherokee Sunset™, with deep-red flowers; Red Beauty®, 20 feet tall and wide, with dark-red flowers on a compact tree; and 'Cherokee Chief', my favorite. *C. kousa* Kousa Dogwood, 30 feet tall and wide, has pure-white blossoms in late spring to early summer, and is resistant to anthracnose. Six Stellar cultivars created by Elwin Orton are hybrids of *Cornus kousa* and *Cornus florida*. They are resistant to the destructive dogwood borer and *Discula destructiva*, which causes dogwood anthracnose. They include 'Rutlan' Ruth Ellen®, 'Rutfan' Stardust®, 'Rutcan' Constellation®, 'Rutdan' Celestial®, 'Rutban' Aurora®, and 'Rutgan' Stellar Pink®, all hardy in zones 5 to 8.

My Personal Favorite

NAME	SPECIAL CHARACTERISTICS
'Cherokee Chief'	Pure-white blossoms in spring / 30 feet tall and wide

Japanese Pagoda Tree

Sophora japonica

Preferred Zones	Sun Preference	Additional Benefits
4 to 8	☀	🦋 🐦 ✿ 🐝 💧

The Japanese Pagoda, also called Scholar Tree, is a tree for the homeowner who has patience. Literature says the tree must be at least ten years of age before it even thinks of blooming, even though you'll also find references to heavy flowering and fruiting within three to five years. Whatever the time frame, it's worth the wait, for when it does bloom (mid- to late summer), the Pagoda will be the talk of the neighborhood. The white-to-light-yellow Wisteria-like flowers are followed by showy three- to eight-inch-long yellow peapods in the fall (the peapods often stay on the tree over winter). Plant the Japanese Pagoda tree in a large, open landscape, surrounded with turf, or as the feature tree in a buffer planting. If you are interested in dyeing wool or tie-dyeing, I'm told a yellow dye can be extracted from the flowers by baking them until brown and then boiling them in water. **Note**: The name Sophora is directly related to the tree's peapod-like fruits. It is an adaptation of the Arabian word sophero, a name for a tree with pealike flowers and fruit.

Bloom Period and Color Creamy-white flowers appear in late summer, resulting in beanlike pods that hang in clusters into fall.

Mature Height × Spread 50 to 70 feet × 50 to 70 feet

When and How to Plant Plant Japanese Pagoda tree while it is small, long before the development of the taproot, during spring or early fall. Plant balled-and-burlapped or container-grown plants in a hole two to three times the diameter of the root mass but only as deep as the ball. Once planted, leave it alone. Established plants should not be transplanted, as digging severs the taproot and damages future growth.

Sun and Soil Preferences The planting site should be in full sun with fertile, slightly acidic, well-drained soil. The tree tolerates polluted city conditions along with heat and drought.

Moisture Requirements Water newly planted Japanese Pagoda trees thoroughly immediately after planting and again the following day. Little additional watering is required after establishment.

Fertilizing An annual feeding with a slow-release plant food for flowering trees will benefit a newly planted Scholar Tree.

Pruning and Care With the exception of having to prune away lower branches interfering with pedestrian traffic or the person on the riding lawn mower, the Pagoda tree needs pruning only to develop a strong central structure. Prune lower aggressive branches to force growth of the upper canopy.

Pests and Diseases There are no particular pest problems.

Additional Species, Cultivars, or Varieties 'Princeton Upright' has a compact upright branching system. It is taller than wide at maturity, making it ideal for a narrow street. It is very urban-tolerant. 'Regent' (my favorite) thrives exceptionally well under harsh city conditions and is a candidate for the small-space city garden.

My Personal Favorite

NAME	SPECIAL CHARACTERISTICS
'Regent'	Grows faster than the species / blooms at a younger age

Japanese Stewartia

Stewartia pseudocamellia

Preferred Zones	Sun Preferences	Additional Benefits
5 to 7		

*Japanese Stewartia foliage emerges in early spring with a bronze-purple tone that turns to medium green. The fall foliage turns orange, red, and bronze. When the tree is planted as a focal point in the landscape, its peeling bark becomes a point of interest with shades of gray, orange, and reddish-brown in winter. The real show is the many white Camellia-like blossoms that open in mid- to late summer and continue in bloom for many weeks. If you can't locate a Stewartia in your local area, take a drive to the Morris Arboretum at the University of Pennsylvania in Philadelphia or to the Case Estates in Weston, Massachusetts (a facility of the Arnold Arboretum at Jamaica Plain, Massachusetts). I know you'll find Stewartia at both gardens because I've seen them in bloom in July. I'm sure there are specimens in the Tri-State area, but the drive will be enjoyable on a warm summer's day. **Note:** Stewartia is related to Franklinia, Camellias, and Gordonia, all members of the Tea family Theaceae. The name commemorates John Stuart, Earl of Bute, an eighteenth-century patron of botany.*

Bloom Period and Color White flowers with yellow centers bloom mid- to late summer.

Mature Height × **Spread** 20 to 40 feet × 20 to 40 feet

When and How to Plant Plant anytime the soil is ready for planting in spring to late fall. Set a balled-and-burlapped specimen or container-grown stock in a hole no deeper than the rootball but two to three times its width; the wide hole allows for spread of the roots with little resistance. Backfill with unamended soil.

Sun and Soil Preferences Plant balled-and-burlapped Japanese Stewartia specimens in full sun to partial shade, in acidic soil with a pH of 5.5 to 6.5 and rich in organic matter.

Moisture Requirements Water generously after planting, and continue regular watering during the first growing season. Apply a 2- to 3-inch layer of mulch like pine bark nuggets, shredded hardwood bark, or wood chips over the planting area to conserve moisture and to reduce heat stress during drought periods.

Fertilizing Use the same plant food you would for Azaleas and Camellias to maintain soil acidity. Never allow lime applied to the lawn with a broadcast spreader to drift within 2 feet of the dripline of the tree or shrub. Japanese Stewartia trees don't like lime.

Pruning and Care Patience is a virtue when it comes to realizing the full potential of Stewartia bloom. It is not unusual to take three to five years for the establishment of a full-blooming plant. Maintain the mulch layer to prevent weeds.

Pests and Diseases There are no particular pest problems.

Additional Species, Cultivars, or Varieties *S. koreana* Korean Stewartia, a smaller species, is often used in small-space gardens and urban backyards.

My Personal Favorite

NAME	SPECIAL CHARACTERISTICS
Japanese Stewartia	*S. pseudocamellia*, the species / white blossoms / when planted as a single specimen, it's a showpiece

Smoketree

Cotinus coggygria

Preferred Zones	Sun Preference	Additional Benefits
5 to 9	☀	🌿🐝🪹✦

The Smoketree or Smokebush (the form is dependent on pruning practices) is appro-priately named. When in bloom in May and June in the Tri-State area, this deciduous tree's tiny pinkish-gray to purplish flowers in eight-inch many-branched panicles look like puffs of smoke. When planted in a visible location, with a backdrop of dark-green foliage such as that produced on Taxus or Ilex, a tree or shrub covered with "puffs of smoke" becomes the conversation of the neighborhood. I've seen many singly planted Smokebushes in bloom in my area. When planted individually, one is quite a show—but to really make a statement, plant in groups of three or more. When caught unaware occasionally, you may even wonder where the fire is. If growing a specimen as a tree, provide a tall evergreen backdrop or an uncluttered horizon or clear blue sky to show it off. Once established, Smoketrees or Smokebushes become prime plants for a xeriscape landscape. They endure long summer droughts.

Bloom Period and Color Pinkish-gray to purplish flowers bloom in May and June with a smoky look that can last to late summer.

Mature Height × Spread 10 to 12 feet × 8 to 12 feet

When and How to Plant Plant container-grown or balled-and-burlapped specimens in spring to early summer as long as water is available. Plant no deeper than the depth of the rootball in a hole two to three times its width. Backfill with unamended soil and water thoroughly to settle the backfill. Repeat watering the following day to ensure a deep and thorough watering of rootball and backfill.

Sun and Soil Preferences The Smoketree or Smokebush, a real sun-lover, grows well in any well-drained soil, tolerating a wide range of pH levels.

Moisture Requirements Continue watering well for the first growing season.

Fertilizing Provide a general feeding of a flowering tree and shrub plant food in early spring on an annual schedule.

Pruning and Care Prune immediately after flowering in June to encourage new stems for setting "smoke" plumes for the following year. The Smoketree or Smokebush blooms on last year's growth. *Cotinus coggygria* may be grown as a shrub or a small tree. To create a tree form, prune to a single-stemmed plant; for a shrub form, prune to force multiple stems.

Pests and Diseases There are no particular pest problems.

Additional Species, Cultivars, or Varieties 'Pendulus', with drooping branches, has dark-red flowers and leaves of the deepest purple; 'Purpureus' has flowers and leaves in the same colors. 'Royal Purple' starts with new red foliage in spring, which then matures to a deep purple, almost black, holding the color until leaf drop.

My Personal Favorite

NAME	SPECIAL CHARACTERISTICS
'Nordine'	Hardiest form in zones 4 to 10 / holds its purplish-red leaves well into fall

Weeping Higan Cherry

Prunus subhirtella

Preferred Zones	Sun Preference	Additional Benefits
5 to 8	☼	🐝 🪺

Weeping Higan Cherry 'Pendula', America's most popular of all weeping ornamentals, grows to thirty feet tall and blossoms profusely with deep-pink flowers. It is usually grafted on a six-foot-tall understock. For colder, exposed environments, however, it is recommended that you select a Cherry that is not grafted. Select a seedling from 'Pendula'. You can't visit a botanical garden or arboretum in the Tri-State area in April without seeing this graceful plant in bloom. Luckily, I need only walk out the front door onto my deck to see a forty-foot specimen lavishly flowered with delicate pink blooms. I planted that tree in 1980 when it was only a six-foot-tall understock with a few stubbed grafts at the top. In twenty years it has grown thirty-five feet and has a spread of twenty feet of gracefully arching, pendulous branches that sweep to the ground. When it's time for petals to drop, light breezes create a fairyland snowstorm of floating elegance. Allow the pendulous branches of the Weeping Cherry to sweep the ground. As the breezes of spring, summer, fall, and winter blow, the thin branches will continue to swing and sway like an old-fashioned straw broom or Hawaiian grass skirt.

Bloom Period and Color Pink blooms appear in spring.

Mature Height × Spread 35 feet × 25 feet

When and How to Plant This tree is best planted in spring for maximum root growth before winter, but it can be planted in fall if water is available to settle the soil and thoroughly wet the rootball. Plant nursery-grown balled-and-burlapped grafted stock in well-drained soil, in a hole no deeper than the rootball and two to three times its width. Backfill with unamended natural soil taken from the hole.

Sun and Soil Preferences Plant nursery-grown balled-and-burlapped grafted stock in well-drained soil, in a full-sun exposure for maximum bloom.

Moisture Requirements Spread organic mulch, like shredded pine bark or pine bark mini-nuggets, over the planting area to reduce weeds, conserve moisture, and to conceal surface roots. An evergreen ground cover, such as Pachysandra, is a good alternative to bark mulch. If a living ground cover is planted underneath, provide supplemental water during extended drought.

Fertilizing Feed with a plant food for flowering trees and shrubs in early spring on an annual schedule.

Pruning and Care Roots protrude at the soil surface, making it impossible to mow grass underneath the tree, so maintain a 2- to 3-inch layer of mulch, like bark chips, out to the edge of the canopy. Do not prune new leaders as they sprout and grow in an upward direction unless you want to maintain a particular height—these new leaders will eventually weep as they grow.

Pests and Diseases Spring canker worms and eastern tent caterpillars may present problems. Control with a biological pesticide (B.t., *Bacillus thuringiensis*). Read the label and follow directions.

Additional Species, Cultivars, or Varieties 'Pendula' Snow Fountain, a smaller plant 8 to 15 feet tall, has white flowers that provide a fountain of bloom. 'Yae-shidare-higan' has deep-pink flowers on pendulous branches; that last longer than those of 'Pendula'. *Prunus serrulata* Japanese Flowering Cherry offers upright growers, typically vase-shaped, that are available in white, greenish yellow, pink, rose pink, and light pink in double and semi-double blossoms; cultivars include 'Mt. Fuji', 'Amanogawa', 'Fugenzo', and 'Shogetsu', but the deep-pink *P. serrulata* 'Kwanzan' is the most popular.

My Personal Favorite

NAME	SPECIAL CHARACTERISTICS
'Pendula'	Graceful, cascading, long weeping branches that touch the ground

Winter King Hawthorn
Crataegus viridis 'Winter King'

Preferred Zones
4 to 7

Sun Preference

Additional Benefits

*Winter King Hawthorn, a species often grafted on the roots of Washington Hawthorn, is the most attractive variety of Hawthorn, with year-round appeal. Whether grown as a single-stem tree or as a shrub with multiple stems, when given a chance in the Tri-State landscape this deciduous flowering tree grows almost like a weed. Plant in the tree form for shade in the small-space garden; in the shrub form, use for screening or as tall hedges. It's not unusual to see a hedge of Winter King Hawthorn planted and maintained as a property line divider. The inch-long thorns are far less a hazard than those of its relative, C. phaenopyrum, which has three-inch thorns, but 'Winter King' still provides an impenetrable barrier against neighborhood trespassers. The single white flowers in spring are followed by small green berry fruits, which turn an attractive orange-red color later in the summer. The fruits are quickly consumed by birds when winter sets in. Birds also enjoy the protection of the thorns (sharp-spined branches) when building nests. Another important reason for choosing 'Winter King' is its resistance to fireblight disease. **Note:** It is not recommended for areas frequented by children.*

Bloom Period and Color White flowers bloom in April, followed by masses of colorful orange-red fruits in late summer and fall.

Mature Height × Spread 20 to 30 feet × 20 to 35 feet

When and How to Plant Plant anytime after the ground thaws in spring right up to early fall. Plant a balled-and-burlapped or container-grown specimen in a hole no deeper than the rootball but two to three times its width. Do not amend the backfill. Use the natural soil for the planting mix.

Sun and Soil Preferences Plant young container-grown or balled-and-burlapped tree or shrub-form Winter King Hawthorn in well-drained soil in full sun. Soil acidity can range from 5.5 to 7.5 pH.

Moisture Requirements Water immediately after planting to settle the soil and to thoroughly wet the rootball. Water as needed for the first season. If planted in fall, continue watering until the ground freezes. To ensure the colorful yellow-to-red foliage of fall and orange-red fruits for winter, provide sustained moisture during extreme drought.

Fertilizing Apply a slow-release plant food for flowering trees in early spring or late fall.

Pruning and Care Apply a 2- to 3-inch layer of organic mulch under the tree or shrub out to the end of the branches. This will stop maintainers from having to mow or tend weeds underneath the tree. If suckers emerge from the rootstock, prune them out immediately—do not let them develop.

Pests and Diseases Hawthorn is a member of the Rose family; select resistant varieties not prone to having pests of roses.

Additional Species, Cultivars, or Varieties *C. laevigata* 'Crimson Cloud' English Hawthorn, a Princeton Nurseries introduction has red, single flowers and is resistant to leaf blight. *C. phaenopyrum*, Washington Hawthorn, grows to 25 to 30 feet with a 20- to 25-foot spread with fall foliage color of orange to scarlet to purple. 'Fastigiata', a columnar type, has white flowers followed by bright red fruit.

My Personal Favorite

NAME	SPECIAL CHARACTERISTICS
'Winter King'	Loved by the birds / produces orange-to-red fruits following its April white bloom

Trees *for the Tri-State*

Remember: If you are considering planting a large, slow-growing tree in your landscape, the tree you plant may not be fully enjoyed by you, but by others. Plant a ten-foot-tall Weeping Willow and in ten years it may be fifty feet tall with a fifty-foot spread. Plant a ten-foot-tall Red Oak, however, and in ten years it may only be twenty feet tall with a fifteen-foot spread. From small plants often come great big plants, and that ten-foot-tall Oak will probably be ninety to a hundred feet tall in a hundred years or so.

When planting a tree you are, in effect, investing in the future. Just think of the improvement in the environment if every resident in the Tri-State area planted only one tree each year for the next ten years. Why, that would equal more than 90,000,000 trees!

How to Buy a Shade Tree

You don't just call a nursery and ask for a shade tree. First consider the kind of shade you need. Is the tree for summer shade? If so, is the tree to provide filtered shade like that needed for a patio, or is dense shade needed for cooling the house? Filtered

shade is provided by Thornless Honeylocust, like 'Shademaster' or 'Sunburst'. Dense shade is provided by trees in the Maple family. It has been proven that a shade tree properly placed in the landscape can and will lower your energy bill. When planted to the southwest corner of a house, the Sugar Maple, Red Maple, or even the Norway Maple provides a canopy of dense shade during the hottest part of the day in summer and fall.

The Uses of Evergreens

Evergreen trees provide cooling both in summer and in winter, so don't plant them too close to the house if you are depending on winter sun to warm your home. Consider planting an evergreen tree, or trees, as a barrier or windbreak against those bitter cold winds of winter that we know so well in the Tri-State area. The Norway or Blue Spruce provides dense needle coverage from top to bottom, making these trees ideal for barrier plantings in an exposed area. For best results, plant them on the north and west sides of whatever you are protecting. To screen out an objectionable view, you can't beat a planting of evergreen trees like Canadian Hemlock, Eastern White Pine, or Leyland Cypress. They also hold their foliage from top to bottom, which is an important requirement for screening. If you are looking for a focal point, plant Blue Atlas Cedar or Weeping Hemlock. You can let them stand as individual specimens on an open lawn or at the corner of the house, or you can feature them in the landscape by planting low-growing shrubs and ground covers at their base.

Plan Before You Plant

If the electrical service to your home is aboveground, or if there are power lines strung on poles running along the curb, check with your local power company for street tree planting recommendations and pruning requirements to keep them out of the power lines. And before digging the hole along the curb or where there is any potential of underground utilities, call the toll-free number for locating underground utilities. It's in the front of every phone book. A little thought before planting can save you a lot of trouble.

American Holly

Ilex opaca

Preferred Zones
5 to 9

Sun Preferences

Additional Benefits

What a grand sight to see this evergreen tree or shrub in any landscape planting: two giant conical evergreens growing side by side, one with shiny, dark-green, prickly leaves and the other covered with bright-red berries. Of course they are a pair of American Hollies, one male (without the berries) and the other female (with the red fruits). I see such a pair when I walk out my front door. They were each six feet tall when I planted them fifteen feet apart twenty-five years ago. It took the female three years to produce her first berries and she has never missed a year since. Both trees are now over thirty-five feet tall, each with a spread of twelve feet or more. (Of course I wish I had planted them farther apart, but that's 20-20 hindsight.) Every Christmas my Hollies give up branches to make various holiday decorations for our home. To keep the leaves fresh and shiny, spray them with an antidesiccant spray as you would for reducing outdoor winterburn.

Bloom Period and Color Flowers are not showy.

Mature Height × **Spread** 45 feet × 25 to 30 feet

When and How to Plant Plant in spring, summer, or fall. Plant a balled-and-burlapped specimen or container-grown stock in a hole no deeper than the depth of the rootball and a minimum of two to three times its diameter. Use unamended backfill.

Sun and Soil Preferences Plant in full sun to partial shade, in a slightly acidic, loose organic soil.

Moisture Requirements The shallow compact root system transplants with little damage as long as the root mass is watered thoroughly the day of planting and again the day after. Continue watering as needed through the first complete growing season, right up to the time the ground starts to freeze.

Fertilizing Provide an annual application of a plant food for broadleaf flowering evergreens in early spring.

Pruning and Care Little pruning if any is required. Mulch the soil surface around the tree with organic mulch such as pine needles, pine bark, or shredded hardwood bark. If berries are the goal, plant both male and female plants within 20 feet of each other, and let the bees do the pollinating. Remember: the female Holly is the fruit producer. To reduce winterburn of the foliage on fall-planted Holly (and on those planted in wind exposure), apply an antidesiccant before cold weather sets in for the winter. There are many antidesiccant brands available at local garden-supply stores. Read the label and follow the manufacturer's directions, paying particular attention to night temperature precautions on the label.

Pests and Diseases Holly leaf miner, a larva which lives inside the leaf tissue making visible squiggly tunnels, is a common pest. Contact your county cooperative extension educator for insecticide recommendations. Timeliness in the application of the control is essential.

Additional Species, Cultivars, or Varieties There are literally hundreds of cultivars of American Holly, varying in leaf size and shape, tree form, and fruit color. 'Croonenburg' is superior to the species, as it is self-pollinating, producing fruit on a single plant.

My Personal Favorite

NAME	SPECIAL CHARACTERISTICS
'Greenleaf'	Called Greenleaf American Holly / popular cultivar / more compact than the species / sets red berries at a younger age

Atlas Cedar

Cedrus atlantica

Preferred Zones	Sun Preference	Additional Benefits
6 to 9	☀	NA

A feature at the main entryway to the Queens Botanical Garden, Flushing, New York, is the handsome Cedrus atlantica 'Glauca' Blue Atlas Cedar. Standing over thirty feet tall, this maturing evergreen tree provides a visual treat at all times, especially when it produces the barrel-shaped, two- to three-inch-round cones on the upper branches. These cones, bluish when young, turn pale green, then brown as they ripen. The cones mature and open in the second or third year after forming. This silvery-bluish evergreen is tolerant of air pollutants, making it a great specimen for city environs—the wax coating on needles of blue conifers provides protection from air pollution. The two most popular Atlas Cedars used in landscaping in the Tri-State landscape are Cedrus atlantica 'Glauca' Blue Atlas Cedar and C. a. 'Glauca Pendula' Weeping Blue Atlas Cedar. When planting either variety, start small—no more than two feet tall. This is a species where bigger is not better.

Bloom Period and Color Flowers are not showy.

Mature Height × Spread 60 feet × 30 to 40 feet

When and How to Plant Set transplants in early spring before budbreak. A successful planting of Atlas Cedar starts with a small container-grown specimen, no more than 2 feet tall, in a hole no deeper than the rootball and two to three times its width—transplanting a larger tree would damage its root system, which is very sensitive and slow to recover (if it recovers at all).

Sun and Soil Preferences Although this *Cedrus* will survive in almost any soil (proof of this is the landfill, soggy, clay-type soil in which the Blue Atlas Cedar at the Queens Botanical Garden now grows), for maximum growth plant Atlas Cedar in a full-sun exposure.

Moisture Requirements Water thoroughly after planting, and continue watering to keep the soil slightly moist during the first growing season.

Fertilizing Fertilize with a slow-release organic plant food for evergreens in early spring on an annual schedule.

Pruning and Care Other than pruning a few misdirected branches, there is little to do for the Atlas Cedar. Leave its dropped needles beneath the tree to act as mulch.

Pests and Diseases Tip blight, browning back of new tip growth, may appear during wet, humid weather. Consult your county cooperative extension educator for the latest fungicide recommendation. This tree has no significant insect problems in the Tri-State area.

Additional Species, Cultivars, or Varieties In addition to the species *Cedrus atlantica*, cultivars to choose from include 'Glauca Pendula' Weeping Blue Atlas Cedar, a specialized grafted form that must be staked or supported on a trellis to develop its height and weep and *C. deodara aurea* Golden Deodara Cedar, an 80- to 100-foot-tall tree with yellowish foliage that is spectacular in spring as new growth emerges (provide adequate room for growth). Two other evergreens with a blue-green or blue color are *Picea pungens glauca* Colorado Blue Spruce and *Abies concolor* White Fir.

My Personal Favorite

NAME	SPECIAL CHARACTERISTICS
'Glauca'	Known as Blue Atlas Cedar / potentially grows to 60 feet tall

Canadian Hemlock

Tsuga canadensis

Preferred Zones	Sun Preferences	Additional Benefits
3 to 7		

The evergreen tree Canadian Hemlock has long been a staple of landscapes in the Tri-State area of New York, New Jersey, and Connecticut. Whether planted in shade or full sun, Hemlocks have been dependable plants for use in screening or hedging, or as features in the landscape. Birds love to make their nests in a Hemlock hedge. Many landscapers are not recommending the planting of Canadian Hemlock, mostly because of the hemlock woolly adelgid problem. I hope that entomologists will soon have a control for this pest since this exotic insect, brought into our environment where there are no natural controls, pierces and sucks the life from the tree. The entomologists of the Departments of Agriculture of New Jersey and Connecticut are researching and raising for release a special friendly, tiny lady beetle that they hope will just love to eat woolly adelgid. For chemical controls, check with your local cooperative extension educator.

Bloom Period and Color   Flowers are not showy.

Mature Height × Spread   70 feet × 25 to 35 feet

When and How to Plant   Plant during the coolest part of the planting season, early spring or late fall. Plant a balled-and-burlapped or container-grown specimen in a hole no deeper than the rootball and two to three times its width. Use unamended backfill for filling the hole. Water immediately after planting, and repeat the watering the second day.

Sun and Soil Preferences   Plant in full sun to full shade, in well-drained, fertile, moist, acidic soil.

Moisture Requirements   Provide even moisture while the Hemlock is becoming established, then water during drought only.

Fertilizing   Provide an annual application of an organic slow-release plant food for broadleaf evergreens. Follow the label directions for rates of application.

Pruning and Care   To thicken the foliage density when growing as a hedge, clip Hemlock in early spring just as the new buds emerge. Clip again as needed in summer to remove rabbit-ear growth. Avoid pruning in August or September, as this would stimulate new growth that will not harden off before the first killing frost.

Pests and Diseases   Start Hemlock care in late winter by applying a dormant oil spray to suppress overwintering insect, mite, and scale pests. Follow the recommended rates and directions. Hemlocks growing in full sun are susceptible to spider mites during hot, dry summer weather. Apply a miticide according to the label directions. Maintain a watchful eye for the telltale characteristics of the woolly adelgid: white, cottony blobs on needles and stems.

Additional Species, Cultivars, or Varieties   'Sargentii', a dwarf 10 to 15 feet tall by 20 to 30 feet wide in a spreading weeping form, works well in group plantings; it responds to pruning when sheared to hedge form or a small specimen. 'Pendula Sargentii' Sargent's Weeping Hemlock, a cultivar of *T. c.*, is 12 feet tall and 25 feet wide.

My Personal Favorite

NAME	SPECIAL CHARACTERISTICS
Canadian Hemlock	*T. canadensis*, the species / dependable for use as screening, as hedging, or as features in the landscape

Eastern White Pine
Pinus strobus

Preferred Zones	Sun Preference	Additional Benefits
3 to 7	☀	

When set in the right environment, Eastern White Pine is one of the most stately, picturesque, needled evergreen trees in the Tri-State area. In a group planting, preferably with twenty feet between each plant, these trees create an attractive wall of green color. White Pine is fast-growing, as much as three feet per year, ultimately reaching eighty feet tall. The soft blue-green-to-green needles, in bundles of five, are three to five inches long. The fruits of the White Pine are six- to eight-inch elongated cones, which are absolutely wonderful for use in dried-plant arrangements and holiday decorations. In the spring of 1975, I planted a six-foot-tall, balled-and-burlapped Eastern White Pine on the north edge of my front yard. It's now sixty feet tall with a spread of forty feet. (I didn't know it at the time, but I planted this Pine in the leach field area of the septic tank, an area generally loaded with nutrients and beneficial bacteria.) A visit to the Bayard Cutting Arboretum, Great River, Long Island, New York, will treat you to one of the finest collections of Pinus in the Tri-State region. In addition to the Pine collection, you'll find Spruce, Fir, Cypress, Taxus, and Hemlock. It's well worth the trip.

Bloom Period and Color Flowers that bloom in spring are not showy, but produce lots of pollen.

Mature Height × Spread 80 feet × 40 feet

When and How to Plant In the Tri-State area, White Pine may be planted as soon as soil thaws in spring and right up to the time soil begins to freeze in early winter. Plant either balled-and-burlapped or container-grown plants. The depth of the planting hole should be absolutely no deeper than the depth of the root mass. Use unamended backfill. The growing environment should be one of clean air, and it should be salt-free. Do not plant White Pine along the curb if your community spreads salt on the street.

Sun and Soil Preferences Plant in full sun in well-drained, moist, slightly acidic soil.

Moisture Requirements To establish White Pine, water thoroughly throughout the first growing season, and continue watering during drought periods.

Fertilizing A White Pine planted in the lawn will benefit from the application of a slow-release turf fertilizer as long as it reaches the expansive root zone. Care should be exercised when applying weed-and-feed combinations: do not allow weedkillers to reach the shallow root zone of White Pine. Read and follow the label directions.

Pruning and Care No pruning is required unless lower branches need to be removed for clearance from the ground. Prune in early spring. If multiple leaders develop, prune out all but one while they are still small.

Pests and Diseases White pine weevil and, in some cases, the woolly adelgid may present problems. Consult with your county cooperative extension educator for the latest controls.

Additional Species, Cultivars, or Varieties 'Blue Shag' offers a dwarf shrubby growth habit and bluish needles; 'Fastigiata' starts columnar as a young upright tree and becomes somewhat wider with age; and 'Pendula', is a graceful weeping White Pine 8 to 10 feet tall. Other species add to the collection. *P. cembra* Swiss Stone Pine, 30 feet tall by 10 feet wide, is slow-growing and tolerates wind and salt spray. *P. c* 'Glauca' and 'Silver Sheen' have needles that are bluer than those of other plants in the species.

My Personal Favorite

NAME	SPECIAL CHARACTERISTICS
Eastern White Pine	*P. strobus*, the species / soft, flexible, light-to-bluish green needles / 6- to 8-inch-long cones

European Beech
Fagus sylvatica

Preferred Zones	Sun Preference	Additional Benefits
3 to 9	☀	🐝 ⭕

Take a Sunday drive by many of the grand old estates of Long Island, New York, and coastal Connecticut, and you will discover ancient green and copper Beech trees, deciduous shade trees that were planted many, many years ago in the middle of finely manicured turf lawns. These large specimens, some as large as eighty feet tall and sixty feet wide, extend their green-leaved branches outward like cantilevered awnings, each domed canopy so dense that it creates a roomlike area beneath. Little or no sunlight, which is necessary for leaf growth, ever reaches the inside of Fagus sylvatica European Beech—the inner foliage simply matures and drops off. In days gone by, it was quite relaxing to rest under the umbrella-like foliage of one of these behemoths. If you want to use such a setting as your outdoor living room, level the area under the tree with two or three inches of wood chip mulch, which will help you avoid tripping over exposed roots.

Bloom Period and Color A three-winged nut, not showy, appears late April to mid May.

Mature Height × Spread 80 feet × 60 feet

When and How to Plant Plant container-grown or balled-and-burlapped specimens in early spring, before new growth starts. Planting a European Beech requires a large open space to achieve its potential, along with many years of time. Plant in a well-drained soil in a hole no deeper than the depth of the rootball and two to three times its width. Do not amend the backfill.

Sun and Soil Preferences Plant in full sun, in an acidic soil (pH 5.0 to 6.5) with excellent drainage. Like its American cousin, European Beech will not tolerate wet or compacted soil.

Moisture Requirements Water thoroughly immediately after planting, and again the following day.

Fertilizing Apply an organic plant food for trees and shrubs in early spring on an annual schedule.

Pruning and Care Prune in summer or early fall if needed. The density of the canopy and the shallow surface roots of the European Beech make it impossible to grow turf and most shrubs underneath the tree. For springtime color, plant bulbs, such as small drifts of Grape Hyacinths, dwarf Daffodils, Crocus, Scilla, and others, in pockets of soil between the exposed roots. For summer and fall color, consider using planters of shade-loving Impatiens, Non-stop Begonias, or Fibrous-rooted Begonias.

Pests and Diseases There are no significant insect problems.

Additional Species, Cultivars, or Varieties For specialty landscapes, plant 'Asplenifolia' Fernleaf Beech, the weeping form 'Pendula', and the purple-leaved 'Purpurea Pendula'. 'Fastigiata' is an upright narrowly columnar form for the small-space garden (zones 5 to 7). 'Atropunices' Purple European Beech produces attractive dark-purple foliage. *Fagus grandifolia* American Beech is another good selection for a large landscape.

My Personal Favorite

NAME	SPECIAL CHARACTERISTICS
European Beech	*F. sylvatica*, the species / at least one of the cultivars 'Asplenifolia', 'Fastigiata', 'Pendula', or 'Riversii' will blend into any landscape

Ginkgo

Ginkgo biloba

Preferred Zones	Sun Preference	Additional Benefits
4 to 9	☼	🍐 🐝 🪺 🌿

" *Picturesque, exotic, stately, ancient . . . these are all words that can be used to describe the tree that produces foliage shaped like that of a Maidenhair Fern. A deciduous shade tree tolerant of atmospheric pollution and city conditions, the Ginkgo dates back to the days when huge dinosaurs roamed the earth, 175 to 200 million years ago. The 1- to 2¾-inch-long stalked fan-shaped leaves, notched at the apex, are unlike those found on any other species. The fan-shaped green foliage matures to a bright yellow in fall. Visit the New York Botanical Garden, Bronx, New York, next autumn, and you can view these prehistoric specimens. You won't have to go far, because female Ginkgo trees were planted as shade trees for the parking lot. If you should visit when the fruits of the tree have ripened and fallen to the ground, beware, and watch your step. To say that the fruits of the Ginkgo are fragrant might be misleading. They stink!* "

Other Name Maidenhair Tree

Bloom Period and Color Blooms are not showy.

Mature Height × **Spread** 50 to 80 feet × 30 to 40 feet

When and How to Plant Large specimens can be safely transplanted with great success in spring or fall. Bare-root stock may be planted while dormant in late winter to early spring. Prepare a planting hole by digging no deeper than the depth of the rootball and two to three times its width. Use the soil taken from the hole as is, without amending for backfill. Purchase only male trees. Ginkgo may be propagated by seeds, although this is not recommended, as there is no way to tell whether the tree is female or male until it reaches fruit-production age at twenty years old. It may also be propagated by rooted cuttings, or grafting onto seedlings under greenhouse conditions in spring.

Sun and Soil Preferences *Ginkgo biloba* is adaptable to almost any environment. Plant in full sun in any fertile, well-drained soil.

Moisture Requirements Provide water immediately after planting. Generally no extra water is needed except during extreme drought periods.

Fertilizing Apply a slow-release organic plant food for trees on an annual schedule each spring.

Pruning and Care Other than pruning to remove lower branches as the tree reaches to the sky, no pruning is needed. If sucker growth emerges from the rootstock, prune out the sprouts immediately—there has no way to ensure that the sprouts are not from female stock.

Pests and Diseases Ginkgo is virtually disease- and insect-resistant.

Additional Species, Cultivars, or Varieties 'Autumn Gold', a male variety, has outstanding golden fall color and a handsome symmetrical broad conical form. 'Fairmount', a male variety, has an upright, narrow, pyramidal form.

My Personal Favorite

NAME	SPECIAL CHARACTERISTICS
Princeton Sentry®	Grafted, male variety / narrow, upright-growing type for city streets and confined backyards

Golden Weeping Willow

Salix alba 'Tristis'

Preferred Zones	Sun Preference	Additional Benefits
5 to 9	☼	🐝 🪹

When the Golden Weeping Willow comes into conversation, the mind's eye may immediately focus on that magnificent, graceful, grand tree, hanging branches swaying over the pond's edge tickling the surface, a gaggle of geese silently paddling about, and water lilies in bloom. On the other side of the pond are cattails and rushes backdropped by an expansive, closely mown turf extending water's edge. Well, yes, this is a personal image from my childhood. The Golden Weeping Willow was my hideout with a treehouse built from old orange crates. (That was a long time ago, when crates were made of wooden slates, not plastic or cardboard.) I had ropes tied high in the tree so I could swing like Tarzan from branch to branch. Ah, yes. Wouldn't it be nice if every child could experience such fun? All it takes is a pond and a Golden Weeping Willow . . . **Caution:** Do not plant Weeping Willows near underground water sources such as sewer lines or septic tank drain fields. The roots are notoriously aggressive and will cause significant damage. **Note:** Salix alba is often listed as S. babylonica by mistake.

Other Name Niobe Weeping Willow

Bloom Period and Color Male and female upright catkins appear in spring.

Mature Height × **Spread** 70 feet × 70 feet

When and How to Plant Set out bare-root plants while dormant in early spring; plant a balled-and-burlapped or container-grown Willow spring, summer, or fall, in a hole no deeper than the rootball but two to three times its width. The number-one requirement is that it have lots of room. Use unamended backfill. Water immediately to settle the soil.

Sun and Soil Preferences Plant in full sun. Whether bare-root, balled-and-burlapped, or container-grown, the Weeping Willow can be grown in a wide range of soil conditions, including humusy, sandy, or clay, and acid or alkaline.

Moisture Requirements Water during establishment. As a Willow prefers moist soil, it's ideal for planting along streams and ponds, although it will also grow in drier soil if given water during periods of drought.

Fertilizing Generally, no extra nutrition is required or recommended.

Pruning and Care The canopy creates a graceful, sweeping action of drooping branches under which nothing else will grow; use a 2- to 3-inch layer of decorative mulch to cover the bare soil. Prune to remove broken branches and develop good structure. This is one of our fastest-growing trees, with weak, brittle wood, so you may find many broken branches on the ground after a heavy winter storm.

Pests and Diseases Powdery mildew, tar spot, leaf blight, black canker, crown gall, cytospora canker, aphids, imported willow leaf beetle, basket willow gall, and so on, may cause problems. Sounds bad, but growing a Willow is worth the effort. It is much too large for you to spray—contact a professional arborist or tree service for advice and application of both fungicides and insecticides.

Additional Species, Cultivars, or Varieties *S.* × *babylonica* Babylon Weeping Willow, 30 to 40 feet tall and 30 to 40 feet wide, is a very graceful tree with a broad, rounded crown of weeping branches sweeping the ground.

My Personal Favorite

NAME	SPECIAL CHARACTERISTICS
'Tristis' Niobe Weeping Willow	Also known as the Golden Weeping Willow / 50 to 70 feet tall with an equal spread / most popular species

Hinoki False Cypress

Chamaecyparis obtusa

Preferred Zones	Sun Preferences		Additional Benefit
4 to 8	☀	☼	🐝

If allowed to grow in unrestricted form, Chamaecyparis obtusa *becomes a giant in the landscape in time (and I mean a long time). The twisted, gnarled, rich-green foliage makes a luxurious evergreen backdrop or a feature in a garden, and the dense growth of a grouping can provide excellent screening. This dense pyramidal conifer is easy to maintain, and Hinoki's many cultivars can bring the plant down to a manageable size for almost any garden. When we bought our home in the early 1970s, we found a twenty-foot-tall Hinoki False Cypress growing next to a brick stairway on the north side of our front porch. We realized that we could not use the stairway where it was, due to winter icing, and so we moved it—but not the Hinoki. It now stands some twenty-five feet tall and is the stateliest of twisted centenarians.*
Note: *The name* Chamaecyparis *comes from the Greek word* chamai, *which means "dwarf," and* kyparissos, *which means "cypress." It alludes to the growth habit of some of these trees.*

Bloom Period and Color Blooms are not showy.

Mature Height × **Spread** 50 to 70 feet × 20 feet

When and How to Plant Plant at any time during the growing season. Hinoki False Cypress and its cultivars are very slow-growing, so start with a substantial plant. Small plants are available container-grown, while larger, much older specimens are available balled-and-burlapped. Plant in a hole no deeper than the rootball and two to three times its width.

Sun and Soil Preferences Plant Hinoki False Cypress in moist, well-drained soil, in full sun to partial shade. These trees love the humid weather of the summers in the Tri-State area.

Moisture Requirements Hinoki False Cypress prefers moist soil throughout the year. Water during extensive drought periods.

Fertilizing Apply a balanced slow-release plant food for evergreens on an annual schedule each spring.

Pruning and Care Branches droop as the tree grows; unless a broken branch should appear, leave the pruning shears in the toolshed. If growing False Cypress as a hedge, however, pruning will be necessary to create a solid green wall.

Pests and Diseases There are no significant pest problems.

Additional Species, Cultivars, or Varieties In addition to the giant Hinoki False Cypress *Chamaecyparis obtusa* used in a landscape planting, there are a great number of cultivars that are ideal for containers on decks, patios, rooftop gardens, or small-space gardens. Selections include 'Crippsii' Golden Hinoki Cypress, which grows to 10 feet tall, with dense pyramidal, evergreen, brilliant golden foliage; 'Gracilis Compacta', an irregular pyramidal form that grows to 20 feet tall, with green foliage; and 'Nana' Dwarf Hinoki Cypress, an extremely slow grower that grows to only 4 feet tall. *C. pisifera* 'Boulevard' Blue Moss Cypress, which grows to 15 feet tall in thirty years, exhibits silvery-green foliage in summer, blue-gray in winter. *C. p.* 'Filifera Aurea' Golden Thread Cypress, 15 feet tall in thirty years, produces golden yellow, threadlike, nodding branches on pyramidal plants.

My Personal Favorite

NAME	SPECIAL CHARACTERISTICS
Hinoki False Cypress	*C. obtusa*, the species / foliage of shining dark green above and whitish markings below / reddish-brown bark sheds in long narrow strips

Leyland Cypress

Cupressocyparis leylandii

Preferred Zones	Sun Preferences	Additional Benefit
6 to 10		

"Some adjectives that can be used to describe Leyland Cypress are wispy, featherlike, flexible, willowy, graceful, fine-textured, tall, pyramidal . . . it is recommended for use as a single specimen or as part of an evergreen screen. Once established, this rapidly growing tree can put on as much as three to four feet in one growing season, ultimately reaching a height of forty to fifty feet. It is often recommended for coastal landscapes with salt-spray exposure. If you want to plant a Leyland Cypress in your zone-6-or-warmer landscape, visit a Tri-State nursery in early spring. The supply is often limited, and the growers of Leyland Cypress don't dig them once the new growing season is under way. Visit the Bayard Cutting Arboretum, Great River, New York, and you can view an extensive collection of Cypresses, as well as Pines, Firs, Spruces, Hemlocks, Yews, and lesser known conifers that grow on Long Island."

Bloom Period and Color Blooms are not showy.

Mature Height × Spread 50 feet × 25 feet

When and How to Plant Plant balled-and-burlapped and container-grown Leyland Cypress in early spring before new growth begins. This will allow the plant a full growing season to become rooted into the parent soil. Plant a container-grown specimen in a hole no deeper than the rootball and at least two to three times its width. A balled-and-burlapped specimen that has been properly root-pruned before digging may be planted in the same way.

Sun and Soil Preferences Plant in full sun to partial shade. It is adaptable to sandy or organic soil conditions, with variations from acid to slightly alkaline.

Moisture Requirements Water generously the first season, and apply a 3- to 4-inch organic mulch like pine bark nuggets or shredded hardwood bark. Renew the mulch annually.

Fertilizing Apply an organic plant food for evergreens on an annual schedule in early spring.

Pruning and Care Provide support for specimen plants taller than 8 feet for the first growing year. This reduces the possibility the root system will be shaken loose by wind and summer storms. Multiple-stemmed plants are susceptible to breakage from ice and snow loads in winter in the Tri-State area; maintain a single-leader plant by pruning out a multiple-stemmed *C. leylandii*.

Pests and Diseases There are no serious pests and diseases.

Additional Species, Cultivars, or Varieties Leyland Cypress *Cupressocyparis leylandii* is a hybrid from *Cupressus macrocarpa* Monterey Cypress and *Chamaecypris nootkatensis* Alaska Cedar, and gives rise to outstanding cultivars. 'Castlewellan' is a pyramidal compact plant with gold-tipped leaves; 'Leighton Green' has a symmetrical columnar form; 'Haggerston Gray' has sage-green foliage; and 'Silver Dust', with a wide-spreading, oval form, has blue-green foliage marked with white variegations. Upright evergreens used as alternates to Leyland Cypress are *Thuja plicata* 'Hogan', *Juniperus chinensis* 'Spartan', and *Thuja occidentalis* 'Lutea' (American Arborvitae) with golden-yellow foliage.

My Personal Favorite

NAME	SPECIAL CHARACTERISTICS
Leyland Cypress	*C. leylandii*, the species / fine-textured bluish-green feathery foliage / columnar to pyramidal form

Littleleaf Linden
Tilia cordata Greenspire®

Preferred Zones
3 to 7

Sun Preference

Additional Benefits

I often marvel at the problems created by planting too many of the same species of plant in any given area. Years ago we experienced the Dutch Elm disease and lost most of our grand old American Elms, trees that lined almost every small-town boulevard and shaded a great many of our university campuses. To replace them we planted Pyrus calleryana Callery Pear and its cultivars; you'll see these white-flowering street trees in almost every development in the Tri-State area, zones 5 to 8. We are now planting pollution-tolerant Greenspire Linden Tilia cordata and other cultivars, as deciduous street and shade trees for city and suburban environs. In the autumn this cultivar's dark-green heart-shaped leaves turn a magnificent bright-yellow color. Have we learned from the past? I hope so. If there are too many of one species being planted in your neighborhood, start planting different species at your own home. **Note:** *As a shade tree for the urban patio, Littleleaf Linden can be grown in standard potting soil in a large planter constructed from treated lumber with drainage holes.*

Bloom Period and Color Yellowish fragrant flowers bloom late June to early July.

Mature Height × Spread 40 feet × 20 to 30 feet

When and How to Plant Plant any time the ground is workable, even during the dormant periods before leaf growth in spring and after leaf drop in fall. Plant in a hole no deeper than the depth of the rootball but two to three times its width; use unamended backfill. To reduce the potential of damage from lawn mowers and string trimmers, simply plant an evergreen ground cover, such as Vinca or Pachysandra, under the tree.

Sun and Soil Preferences Plant in full sun, in moist, well-drained, fertile soil.

Moisture Requirements Water immediately after planting to settle the soil. To reduce the watering needs of both landscape and container-planted Lindens, spread 2 to 3 inches of organic mulch, like pine bark mini-nuggets, over the soil surface. Although the soil can be allowed to dry considerably between waterings, never let it dry completely.

Fertilizing When used as a shade tree, the normal lawn fertilizer will be adequate for nutrition; otherwise, apply a slow-release fertilizer for flowering trees and shrubs according to label directions.

Pruning and Care Little or no pruning is needed unless lower branches need to be removed or the tree is being grown as a hedge.

Pests and Diseases Aphids and Japanese beetle adults may present problems. Apply insecticidal soap for the aphids and milky spore disease for the Japanese beetle grubs. If you have chewing damage from Japanese beetle adults, contact your county cooperative extension educator for the latest insecticide recommendation.

Additional Species, Cultivars, or Varieties *T. americana* 'Redmond' (Redmond American Linden) is a tough, hardy tree that grows 80 feet tall by 20 to 40 feet wide, with large dark-green leaves.

My Personal Favorite

NAME	SPECIAL CHARACTERISTICS
Littleleaf Greenspire® Linden	Fast-growing cultivar / glassy dark-green leaves with silvery undersides / highly recommended

Norway Spruce

Picea abies

Preferred Zones	Sun Preference		Additional Benefits
2 to 7	☀		

Norway Spruce is ideal for use as a living Christmas tree, and may be planted after the holidays in a landscape setting. Check with your favorite nurseryperson for directions on hardening-off plants that have been indoors. As one of our fastest-growing evergreens, this plant that grows up to forty feet wide must have room to grow. When using as a screen, plant on a staggered basis, leaving twenty or more feet between plants if at all possible. Norway Spruce makes a grand, stately specimen tree in any sunny landscape. Lyndhurst, in Tarrytown, New York, on the east bank of the Hudson River just south of the Tappan Zee Bridge, is home to some of the most magnificent specimens of Norway Spruce. The sixty-seven-acre grounds provides plenty of room for these Spruce to grow. You'll also find Japanese Maples in all twists and shapes, Magnolias, and a rose garden with 127 varieties. The annual Christmas tree at Rockefeller Center in New York City is a Norway Spruce. After the holidays, this tree continues its service when it is chipped and used as landscape mulch.

Bloom Period and Color Blooms are not showy.

Mature Height × **Spread** 40 to 100 feet × 40 feet

When and How to Plant Plant balled-and-burlapped or container-grown specimens any time of the year when the soil is workable, in a hole no deeper than the rootball. Stake large specimens during the first two growing seasons to reduce wind damage to the roots. Use unamended backfill, and water thoroughly to wet the rootball and backfill.

Sun and Soil Preferences Plant in full sun, in a moderately moist, acid, sandy, well-drained soil. Norway Spruce tolerates dry soils and windy conditions.

Moisture Requirements Apply a 2- to 3-inch layer of shredded hardwood or pine bark mulch over the root system at planting time to conserve moisture.

Fertilizing A normal turf fertilizing will benefit a Spruce planted as a specimen in the lawn. For a Spruce in a landscape bed, apply a slow-release organic plant food annually in spring.

Pruning and Care Want to grow grass under the Norway Spruce? Forget it. The fine, massive root system of the Spruce grows too close to the soil surface for that.

Pests and Diseases Spruce gall, red spider, bagworm, and borers may present problems. Consult your county cooperative extension educator for the latest controls. If the gall produced by the spruce gall aphid should appear at the tip of new growth in late spring, remove it by pruning. Red spider, a predominant pest during hot, dry weather, leaves a fine webbing on the new growth and gives a stippled or bleached-out look to the needles. Apply insecticidal soap as a thorough drench of the entire plant.

Additional Species, Cultivars, or Varieties 'Acrocona', an irregular-shaped shrub form of Norway Spruce, has reddish cones at the tips of its branches. *P. a.* 'Cupressina', a narrow, upright Norway Spruce, is often recommended for planting in cities and confined landscapes. 'Columnaris', also narrow and upright, is somewhat wider than 'Cupressina'. 'Gregoryana', a very dwarf, 18-by-18-inch compact evergreen tree, is ideal for container and rock garden culture.

My Personal Favorite

NAME	SPECIAL CHARACTERISTICS
Norway Spruce	*P. abies*, the species / bright green needles changing to lustrous dark green as they mature in summer

Red Buckeye

Aesculus pavia

Preferred Zones	Sun Preferences	Additional Benefits
4 to 8		

> *A drive down the Palisades Interstate Parkway from New York into New Jersey in late April into early May will reward the driver with an unusual sight. Tucked in the tree-lined parkway plantings are Red Buckeye trees in full bloom, with showy red panicles standing upright like candelabras on the tips of every branch. The fruits in the fall, which come from pear-shaped pods, are shiny, somewhat knobby, brown seeds called "lucky buckeyes." My father always carried a lucky buckeye in his pocket, and he showed it to me one time when we were hunting quail in southern Illinois. (It was interesting, but not lucky, I thought, because we didn't get a single bird.) Other trees that produce fruits called lucky buckeyes are A. glabra Ohio Buckeye and A. × carnea Red Horse Chestnut (an old hybrid of A. hippocastanum and A. pavia). I don't know which "lucky" buckeye my father carried.*

Bloom Period and Color Red flowers bloom in spring.

Mature Height × **Spread** 10 to 20 feet × 8 to 15 feet

When and How to Plant Plant in early spring, or in late fall after leaf drop. Plant balled-and-burlapped or container-grown specimens in a hole no deeper than the depth of the rootball and at least two to three times its width; the roots need room to spread. Do not amend the backfill.

Sun and Soil Preferences Plant in moist, well-drained acid soil rich in organic matter while the tree is dormant, in full sun to partial shade.

Moisture Requirements During periods of drought, soak the root system regularly to alleviate the condition known as leaf scorch. Cover the soil under the tree out to the drip line with an organic mulch, such as pine bark mini-nuggets or bark chips, to reduce competition from turf, weeds, and the extremely shallow feeder roots of the tree. As the tree grows, expand the mulched area to include the spreading feeder roots.

Fertilizing Feed with an organic slow-release plant food for flowering trees according to the label directions in spring, on an annual schedule.

Pruning and Care To maintain a strong structure, prune out crossing branches and remove weak, minor limbs in early spring. Sucker growth should be pruned off when first observed on the trunk.

Pests and Diseases There are no significant insect pests. During extremely humid weather, powdery mildew may develop on the foliage; apply a powdery mildew fungicide according to label directions. Leaf scorch, a physiological disorder, appears as brown, curled leaf margins; there is no control available.

Additional Species, Cultivars, or Varieties *Aesculus flava* Yellow Buckeye, with yellow flowers, grows to 50 feet tall. Related species of interest for landscapes in the Tri-State area are *A. glabra* Ohio Buckeye and *A.* × *carnea* Red Horse Chestnut, an old hybrid of *A. hippocastanum* and *A. pavia*.

My Personal Favorite

NAME	SPECIAL CHARACTERISTICS
Red Buckeye	*A. pavia*, the species / ideal for small-space gardens / spreads to only 8 to 15 feet

Red Maple

Acer rubrum

Preferred Zones	Sun Preference	Additional Benefits
4 to 9	☼	

If you're looking for a deciduous shade tree with beautiful fall foliage color that will make your property the talk of the neighborhood, select and plant one of the cultivars of Acer rubrum, the Red Maple. Position this tree at the southwest corner of the house and its shade will be an air-conditioner on hot, sunny summer afternoons. The canopy of foliage for summer shade changes in color from green to yellow to orange to bright red, over an eight-week period into the fall. My favorite cultivar, October Glory®, introduced by Princeton Nursery of New Jersey, produces foliage that turns brilliant orange to red in fall. Red Sunset® starts with orange and goes to a brilliant red about two weeks earlier than October Glory. A bonus with October Glory is that it holds its brilliant-orange foliage for about two weeks longer than do other Red Maples.

Other Name Scarlet Maple / Swamp Maple

Bloom Period and Color Although not showy, red flowers appear in late March to early April.

Mature Height × **Spread** 50 to 70 feet × 50 feet

When and How to Plant Plant balled-and-burlapped or container-grown stock in spring, summer, or fall, as long as water is available. Bare-root transplants must be planted while dormant in early spring. Plant the top of the rootball an inch or so above soil level so the flare of the roots at the base of the tree trunk is slightly exposed at the surface. A nursery-grown plant is often dug and balled with extra soil around the base of the trunk. Grass will be difficult to grow under the Red Maple due to the shade and surface roots of the tree; spread a decorative mulch of pine bark nuggets or wood chips, 2 to 3 inches thick, or plant Pachysandra or Vinca to provide an evergreen blanket beneath the tree.

Sun and Soil Preferences Plant in full sun, in slightly acid soil.

Moisture Requirements Water a newly planted tree thoroughly immediately after planting to settle the backfill, and follow again the second day with an equally large watering to ensure a thorough soaking of the rootball. Once established, no extra watering is needed.

Fertilizing Provide an organic plant food for trees and shrubs in early spring according to label directions, on an annual schedule.

Pruning and Care Little pruning is required except for crossing branches. Avoid pruning in early spring when the sap is flowing.

Pests and Diseases This tree has few pest problems in the Tri-State area. Spring canker worms may chew holes in a few leaves. Apply *B.t.*, the natural biological control *Bacillus thuringiensis*. Read the label.

Additional Species, Cultivars, or Varieties Red Sunset® shows off orange-red foliage in early fall. 'Armstrong', growing to 60 feet tall with a narrow spread of only 30 to 40 feet, has bright-red fall foliage; it is particularly suitable for narrow streets or limited city plantings.

My Personal Favorite

NAME	SPECIAL CHARACTERISTICS
October Glory®	Retains its leaves longer, which extends nature's colorful season / brilliant red-orange fall foliage

Red Oak

Quercus rubra

Preferred Zones	Sun Preference	Additional Benefits
4 to 7	☼	

Red Oak is often a cache for animal friends. When acorns ripen in early fall, they become choice morsels for friendly squirrels, turkeys, and other wildlife, and deer nibble at the tips of low-growing branches. Quercus rubra *Red Oak* (also identified as Quercus borealis maxima), when positioned where it has room to grow, is a stately tree in the Tri-State area. It's not unusual to see mature trees attain a height of seventy-five feet, with an equally wide canopy. This Red Oak is the official tree of the state of New Jersey, and I can understand why. Spring foliage emerges with a bronze-red color, maturing to a dark green throughout the summer, and then to a brilliant red in fall. A relative, Quercus alba *White Oak* (also know as Charter Oak), grows to a height of ninety-five feet and a width of eighty feet, and produces rich orange-red-to-purple foliage in fall. Quercus alba *White Oak* is the state tree of Connecticut. In some years, the foliage of White Oak turns to a rich, reddish-purple-to-wine color that lasts for long periods of time.

Other Name Northern Red Oak

Bloom Period and Color Blooms are not showy.

Mature Height × Spread 60 to 75 feet × 60 to 75 feet

When and How to Plant Ideally, plant Red Oak in early spring. This species does not develop a significant taproot, and balled-and-burlapped specimens are easier to establish than Oaks that do develop a taproot (disturbed taproots do not reestablish well). Red Oak makes an ideal plant for the city gardener, as it tolerates air pollution and grows substantially faster than do other Oak species. Young seedlings may be taken as bare-root transplants if dug before buds swell in spring. Plant with unamended backfill in a hole no deeper than the depth of the rootball and two to three times its width.

Sun and Soil Preferences Plant in full sun, in acidic well-drained but moist soil.

Moisture Requirements Although the Red Oak is drought-tolerant and recommended for water-efficient gardens, a newly planted tree must be well watered and will appreciate soakings throughout the first year after planting.

Fertilizing This tree generally requires no extra nutrition when planted in average soil in the Tri-State area. As a shade tree in the lawn, annual turf feeding will benefit the tree, but care must be taken not to expose the tree roots to weed-and-feed combinations.

Pruning and Care Pruning is best done while the tree is dormant in late winter, or in midsummer after spring growth has hardened off.

Pests and Diseases As with all Oaks, watch for invasions of gypsy moth caterpillars in spring. The Oak is the preferred diet of this destructive critter. Apply the biological control *Bacillus thuringiensis*, known as *B.t.*, according to the label directions.

My Personal Favorite

NAME	SPECIAL CHARACTERISTICS
Red Oak	*Q. rubra*, the species / russet-red to bright red foliage color in fall

Sugar Maple

Acer saccharum

Preferred Zones
4 to 8

Sun Preferences

Additional Benefits

Are you looking for a tall, spreading shade tree with dark-green summer foliage followed by brilliant fall colors of burnt orange, red, and yellow for your lawn? You need look no further than the native New York state tree, Acer saccharum Sugar Maple, also know as Hard Maple. The Sugar Maple is a slow grower when compared to other Maples, one reference stating that a tree grows twenty-three feet in twenty-eight years. (Now that's slow!) Another reference suggested a growth of twenty-three feet high and wide in just ten years. Most of the maple syrup we all love at breakfast is the end product of the sap from this native tree. The sap must be concentrated, boiled down— it takes forty gallons to make one gallon of syrup for your pancake, French toast, or waffle breakfast. Oh, what a treat! Today, special instruments measure sugar content in the sap in order to select the best-producing trees. Take a trip to Vermont in late winter and enjoy maple sugar time. **Note:** *To avoid the damage to the surface roots of a Sugar Maple that might occur when mowing grass, plant an evergreen ground cover such as Pachysandra or Vinca under the tree.*

Other Name Hard Maple

Bloom Period and Color Blooms are not showy.

Mature Height × Spread 50 to 80 feet × 30 to 50 feet

When and How to Plant Plant in spring before new leaves emerge, in summer after new growth has hardened off, or in fall as the tree changes color. Bare-root seedlings, available by mail order only, can be planted while dormant in early spring. Plant a balled-and-burlapped specimen in a hole no deeper than the rootball and two to three times its width. For summer planting, reduce the rate of transpiration by applying an antitranspirant spray to the foliage to reduce transplant shock. When planted where the surface roots can spread without restriction, this hardwood tree will grow about one foot per year.

Sun and Soil Preferences Plant in full sun to partial shade in moist, well-drained soil. The tree tolerates a wide range of soil pH.

Moisture Requirements Water all newly planted Maple trees immediately after planting, and continue to water as needed for the first growing season. During periods of drought, a slow soaking with water will benefit the Maple as well as the ground cover beneath.

Fertilizing If planted as a shade tree in the lawn, the normal lawn feeding will suffice for the Maple. Otherwise, fertilize annually with a tree and shrub fertilizer such as 10-6-4 according to the label directions.

Pruning and Care No pruning is generally required other than the imme-diate removal of storm-damaged branches.

Pests and Diseases Verticillium wilt disease may be a problem, but there is no control. Provide water during extreme drought to reduce susceptibility. Spring canker worms (inchworms) can be controlled with *B.t.* Read the label.

Additional Species, Cultivars, or Varieties Bonfire™, which grows to 50 to 70 feet tall, is a rapid grower with good heat tolerance. It was intro-duced by Princeton Nursery. 'Temple's Upright', 4 to 10 feet wide with a pole-like growth habit, is ideal for a small-space garden.

My Personal Favorite

NAME	SPECIAL CHARACTERISTICS
Green Mountain®	Introduced by Princeton Nursery / 50 to 75 feet tall / particularly hardy to -40 degrees Fahrenheit

Glossary

Acid soil: soil with a pH lower than 7.0; also referred to as sour soil.

Adventitious: originating from an unusual or unexpected position.

Alkaline soil: soil with a pH greater than 7.0; also referred to as sweet soil. It lacks acidity, often because it has limestone in it.

All-purpose fertilizer: powdered, liquid, or granular fertilizer with a balanced proportion of the three key nutrients—nitrogen (N), phosphorus (P), and potassium (K). It is suitable for maintenance nutrition for most plants.

Annual: a plant that lives its entire life in one growing season. It is genetically determined to germinate, grow, flower, set seed, and die the same year.

Apical bud: the bud located at the tip of a branch or stem.

Apical dominance: the tendency of a leader or central shoot with an apical bud to inhibit the development of side shoots on a stem or plant.

Balled-and-burlapped: describes a tree or shrub, usually field grown, whose soilball was dug and wrapped with protective burlap and twine for sale or transplanting. "Balled-and-burlapped" is commercially referred to as B&B.

Bare root: describes plants that have been dug without any soil around their roots. (Often young, dormant shrubs and trees are purchased through the mail; they arrive with their exposed roots covered with moist peat or sphagnum moss, sawdust, or similar material, and wrapped in plastic.) "Bare root" is commercially referred to as BR.

Barrier plant: a plant that has intimidating thorns or spines and is sited purposely to block foot traffic or other access to the home or yard.

Beneficial insects: insects or their larvae that prey on pest organisms and their eggs. They may be flying insects, such as ladybugs, parasitic wasps, praying mantids, and soldier bugs, or soil dwellers such as predatory nematodes, spiders, and ants.

Berm: a narrow raised ring of soil around a newly planted tree or shrub, used to hold water so it will be directed to the root zone. (Also a mound of soil used to create an elevated landscape effect for planting of trees and shrubs.)

Bract: a modified leaf structure on a plant stem near its flower that resembles a petal. Often it is more colorful and visible than the actual flower, as in Dogwood.

Bud union: the point at which the top scion or bud of a plant was grafted to the rootstock; usually refers to roses and ornamental trees.

Butterfly: the process of scoring (cutting vertically into the root mass) the solid mass of roots of a rootbound plant in order to spread them out for planting.

Canopy: the overhead branching area of a tree, usually referring to its extent including foliage.

Cold hardiness: the ability of a perennial plant to survive the winter cold in a particular area.

Composite: a flower that is actually composed of many tiny flowers. Typically, they are flat clusters of tiny, tight florets, sometimes surrounded by wider-petaled florets. Composite flowers are highly attractive to bees and beneficial insects.

Compost: organic matter that has undergone progressive decomposition by microbial and macrobial activity until it is reduced to a spongy, fluffy texture. Added to soil of any type, it improves the soil's ability to hold air, water, and nutrients and to drain well.

Corm: the swollen energy-storing structure, analogous to a bulb, under the soil at the base of the stem of plants such as Crocus and Gladiolus.

Crown: the base of a plant at, or just beneath, the surface of the soil where the roots meet the stems.

Cultivar: a CULTIvated VARiety. It is a naturally occurring form of a plant that has been identified as special or superior and is purposely selected for propagation and production.

Cure: to dry or heat fresh cuts of corms, rhizomes, stolons, and tubers. Time required varies from a few hours to several days.

Deadheading: a pruning technique that removes faded flower heads from plants to improve their appearance, abort seed production, and stimulate further flowering.

Deciduous plants: unlike evergreens, these trees and shrubs lose their leaves in the fall and releaf the following growing season.

Desiccation: drying out of foliage tissues, usually due to drought, or wind, or in the case of seashore plantings, to salt spray.

Division: the practice of splitting apart perennial plants to create several smaller-rooted segments. The practice is useful for controlling the plant's size and for acquiring more plants; it is also essential to the health and continued flowering of certain species.

Dormancy: the period, usually the winter, when perennial plants temporarily cease active growth and rest. **Go dormant** is the verb form, as used in this sentence: *Some plants, like spring-blooming bulbs, go dormant in the summer.*

Endophyte: a naturally occurring fungus (found in certain species of grasses) that improves drought-resistance and resistance to some aboveground feeding insects.

Establishment: the point at which a newly planted tree, shrub, or flower has become adapted to its new growing conditions. This may be indicated by the production of new growth, either foliage or stems, and may indicate that the roots have recovered from transplant shock and have begun to grow and spread.

Evergreen: describes perennial plants that do not lose their foliage annually with the onset of winter. Needled or broadleaf foliage will persist and continues to function on a plant through one or more winters, aging and dropping unobtrusively in cycles of two or more years.

Fall: the drooping lower flower petal of an Iris.

Flare: the point where roots begin to spread from the base of the stem or trunk.

Floret: a tiny flower, usually one of many forming a cluster, that comprises a single blossom.

Foliar: of or about foliage—usually refers to the practice of spraying foliage, as in foliar feeding or treating with insecticides and fungicides.

Germinate: to sprout. Germination is a fertile seed's first stage of development.

Girdling: the growth of a root in a strangulating manner around the base of a shrub or tree trunk. The root can physically strangle the plant by cutting off the flow of manufactured food to the roots.

Graft (union): the point on the stem of a woody plant with sturdier roots where a stem scion or bud from a highly ornamental plant is inserted so it will join with it. Roses are commonly grafted.

Hardscape: the permanent, structural, nonplant part of a landscape, such as walls, sheds, pools, patios, arbors, and walkways.

Herbaceous: describes plants having fleshy or soft stems that die back with frost; the opposite of **woody.**

Humic acid: the end product of decaying matter. The black liquid which acts as cement to hold soil particles together as well as apart, gives soil its dark color, improves its nutrient-holding capacity, and improves aeration and drainage.

Hybrid: a plant that is the result of intentional or natural cross-pollination between two or more different kinds of plants of the same species or genus.

Leader candle: the central, upright growing main stem of a single trunk tree.

Low-water-demand: describes plants that tolerate dry soil for varying periods of time. Typically, they have succulent, hairy, or silvery-gray foliage and tuberous roots or taproots.

Melting-out: the physiological dieback of turfgrass, usually during summer, caused by heat, drought, oppressive humidity, and certain diseases.

Mulch: a covering over the surface of the soil used to reduce compaction, conserve moisture, reduce runoff of water, prevent erosion, stop weed growth, and reduce soil temperature fluctuation. It may be inorganic (gravel, plastic, fabric) or organic (wood chips, bark, pine needles, chopped leaves, etc.).

Naturalize: (a) to plant seeds, bulbs, or plants in a random, informal pattern as they would appear in their natural habitat; (b) to adapt to and spread throughout adopted habitats (a tendency of some nonnative plants).

Nectar: the sweet fluid produced by glands on flowers that attracts pollinators such as hummingbirds and honeybees for whom it is a source of energy.

Organic material, organic matter: any material or debris that is derived from plants. It is carbon-based material capable of undergoing decomposition and decay.

Peat moss: organic matter from peat sedges (United States) or sphagnum mosses (Canada), often used to improve soil texture and as bulk in soilless potting mixes. The acidity of sphagnum peat moss makes it ideal for boosting or maintaining soil acidity while also improving its moisture-holding capacity and drainage.

Perennial: a flowering plant that lives over two or more seasons. Many die back with frost, but have roots that survive the winter and generate new shoots in the spring.

Petiole: the stalk of a leaf.

pH: a measurement of the relative acidity (low pH) or alkalinity (high pH) of soil or water based on a scale of 0 to 14, 7 being neutral. Individual plants require soil to be within a certain range so that nutrients can dissolve in moisture and be available to them.

Pinch: to remove tender stems and/or leaves by pressing them between thumb and forefinger. This pruning technique encourages branching, compactness, and flowering in plants, or it removes aphids clustered at growing tips.

Pollen: the often yellow, powdery grains produced by the anthers (male parts of the flower). They are transferred to the female flower parts by means of wind or animal pollinators to facilitate fertilization and seed production.

Raceme: an arrangement of single stalked flowers along an elongated, unbranched axis.

Rhizome: a swollen energy-storing stem structure, similar to a bulb, that lies horizontally in the soil, with roots emerging from its lower surface and growth shoots from a growing point at or near its tip, as in Bearded Iris.

Root flare: the transition at the base of a tree trunk where the bark tissue begins to differentiate and roots begin to form just before entering the soil. This area should not be covered with soil when planting a tree.

Rootbound (or potbound): the condition of a plant that has been confined in a container too long, its roots having been forced to wrap around themselves and even swell out of the container. Successful transplanting or repotting requires untangling and trimming away of some of the matted roots.

Root-prune: to cut outwardly spreading roots of a tree or shrub in preparation for transplanting.

Scarify: (a) to scratch or nick the seed coat (outer covering) of a seed to facilitate penetration of water and free oxygen for germination; (b) to immerse seed in acid, bleach, or hot water.

Self-seeding: the tendency of some plants to sow their seeds freely around the yard. It creates many seedlings the following season that may or may not be welcome.

Semi-evergreen: tending to be evergreen in a mild climate but deciduous in a rigorous one.

Shearing: the pruning technique whereby plant stems and branches are cut uniformly with long-bladed pruning shears (hedge shears) or powered hedge trimmers. It is used when creating and maintaining hedges and topiary.

Slow-release fertilizer: fertilizer that is water-insoluble and therefore releases its nutrients gradually as a function of soil temperature, moisture, and related microbial activity. Typically granular, it may be organic or synthetic.

Standard: (a) one of the erect central petals of an Iris flower; (b) a plant grown with a round, bushy top or head of branches atop a single, upright stem.

Stolon: an aboveground stem growing on the soil surface from which roots and new plants are produced at intervals along its length.

Succulent growth: the sometimes undesirable production of fleshy, water-storing leaves or stems that results from overfertilization and/or excessive moisture.

Sucker: a new growing shoot. Underground plant roots produce suckers to form new stems and spread by means of these suckering roots to form large plantings, or colonies. Some plants produce root suckers or branch suckers as a result of pruning or wounding.

Transpiration: the giving off of water vapor and liquid water through the aerial parts of the plant. It is the cooling system for a living plant.

Tuber: a type of underground storage structure in a plant root or stem, analogous to a bulb. It generates roots below and stems above ground (example: Dahlia).

Variegated: having various colors or color patterns. The term usually refers to plant foliage that is streaked, edged, blotched, or mottled with a contrasting color, often green with yellow, cream, or white.

Whip: a young seedling or sapling or grafted tree without lateral branches.

White grubs: fat, off-white, wormlike larvae of Japanese and other kinds of beetles. They reside in the soil and feed on plant (especially grass) roots until pupation, when they emerge as beetle adults to feed on plant foliage and flowers.

Wings: (a) the corky tissue that forms edges along the twigs of some woody plants such as Winged Euonymus; (b) the flat, dried extension of tissue on some seeds, such as Maple, that catch the wind and help them disseminate.

Xeriscape gardening: water-efficient gardening that makes use of drip irrigation and drought-adaptable plants.

Public Gardens in Connecticut, New Jersey, and New York

For many gardeners there is nothing more enjoyable than a visit to a botanical garden or arboretum. Go on a crisp, sunny spring day when the Tulips, Daffodils, and Flowering Cherries are in bloom. Sit in the shade of a giant Oak tree on a hot, humid summer's afternoon. Or stroll through landscapes as the Maple, Hawthorn, and Ginkgo leaves exhibit their palette of fall colors.

Plan a family visit to one of the public gardens listed below, but call first to ask about any admission charges and to determine what is currently in bloom. As the seasons change, so does the show. You can visit the same garden or arboretum several times a year and each time see something different in bloom. Enjoy your visit.

Connecticut

Caprilands Herb Farm, 534 Silver Street, North Coventry, CT 06238, Phone: (860) 742-7244

Elizabeth Park Rose Garden, Prospect and Asylum Avenue, West Hartford, CT 06119,
    Phone: (860) 242-0017

The Gertrude Jekyll Garden at the Glebe House Museum, Hollow Road, Woodbury, CT
    06798, Phone: (203) 263-2855

The Sundial Herb Garden, 59 Hidden Lake Road, Higganum, CT 06441,
    Phone: (860) 345-4290

University of Connecticut, Bartlett Arboretum, 151 Brookdale Road, Stamford, CT
    06903-4199, Phone: (203) 322-6971

New Jersey

Duke Gardens, US Route 206 South, Somerville, NJ 08876, Phone: (908) 722-3700

Felinghuysen Arboretum, 53 East Hanover Avenue, Morristown, NJ 07962,
    Phone: (201) 326-7600

Presby Memorial Iris Gardens, 474 Upper Mountain Avenue, Upper Montclair, NJ 07043,
    Phone: (973) 783-5974

Rudolf W. van der Goot Rose Garden Colonial Park, Mettler's Road, East Millstone, NJ
    08873, Phone: (908) 234-2677

Skylands Botanical Garden, Ringwood State Park, Ringwood, NJ 07456, Phone: (973) 962-7527

Willowwood Arboretum, Pottersville Road, Chester, NJ (Morris County Park Commission,
    PO Box 1295, Morristown, NJ 07962, Phone: (201) 326-7600

New York State

Brooklyn Botanic Gardens, 1000 Washington Avenue, Brooklyn, NY 11225,
Phone: (718) 622-4433

Buffalo and Erie County Botanical Gardens, South Park Avenue and McKinley Parkway,
Buffalo, NY 14128, Phone: (716) 828-1040

Conservatory Garden in Central Park, Fifth Avenue at 105th Street, Manhattan, NY
10021, Phone: (212) 360-2766

Cornell Plantations, One Plantations Road, Ithaca, NY 14850, Phone: (607) 255-3020

Highland Park, 180 Reservoir Avenue, Rochester, NY 14620, Phone: (716) 244-8079

Mohonk Mountain House Gardens, 100 Mountain Rest Road, New Paltz, NY 12561,
Phone: (845) 255-1000

New York Botanical Gardens, 200th Street and Southern Blvd., Bronx, NY 10458,
Phone: (718) 817-8700

Old Westbury Gardens, 71 Old Westbury Road, Old Westbury, Long Island, NY
11568, Phone: (516) 333-0048

Planting Fields Arboretum State Historic Park, Planting Fields Road, Oyster Bay, Long
Island, NY 11771, Phone: (516) 922-9200

Queens Botanical Garden, 43-50 Main Street, Flushing, NY 11355,
Phone: (718) 886-3800

Sonnenberg Gardens, 151 Charlotte Street, Canandaigua, NY 14424,
Phone: (716) 394-4922

Wave Hill, The Bronx, West 249th Street and Independence Avenue, New York, NY
10471, Phone: (718) 549-3200

Mail-Order Seed and Plant Resources

In addition to the many fine garden centers, plant shops, and nurseries in the Tri-State, you may wish to try some mail-order suppliers of seeds, plants, and garden supplies. Write or call for their latest catalogs.

W. Atlee Burpee & Co.
300 Park Avenue
Warminster, PA 18974
Phone: 215-674-4900

Ferry Morse Seeds
P.O. Box 488
Fulton, KY 42041-0488
Phone: 800-283-3400

Harris Seeds
60 Saginaw Drive
P.O. Box 22960
Rochester, NY 14692-2960
Phone: 716-442-0410

Jackson and Perkins
1 Rose Lane
Medford, OR 97501-0702
Phone: 541-776-2145

J.W. Jung Seed Co.
335 S. High Street
Randolph, WI 53957-0001
Phone: 920-326-3121

Ledden Brothers
195 Center Street
Sewell, NJ 08080
Phone: 856-468-1002

Mellinger's Nursery
2310 W. South Range Road
North Lima, OH 44452
Phone: 216-246-1020

E. J. Miller Nurseries
5060 West Lake Road
Canandaigua, NY 14424
Phone: 800-836-9630

Monticello Thomas Jefferson
    Center for Historic Plants
P.O. Box 316
Charlottesville, VA 22092
Phone: 804-984-9816

Oliver Nurseries
1159 Bronson Road
Fairfield, CT 06430
Phone: 203-259-5609

George W. Park Seed Co.
Cokesbury Road
Greenwood, SC 29647-0001
Phone: 800-845-3369

Roslyn Nursery
211 Burrs Lane
Dix Hills, NY 11746
Phone: 516-643-9347

Spring Hill Nurseries
110 West Elm Street
Tipp City, OH 45371
Phone: 800-582-8527

Stokes Seed Inc.
Box 548
Buffalo, NY 14240-0548
Phone: 800-396-9238

Territorial Seed Company
P.O. Box 157
Cottage Grove, OR
    97424-0061
Phone: 541-942-9547

Thompson & Morgan, Inc.
P.O. Box 1308
Jackson, NJ 08527-0308
Phone: 800-247-7333

K. Van Bourgondien & Sons
245 Route 109, P.O. Box 1000
Babylon, NY 11702-9004
Phone: 800-552-9916

Wayside Gardens
1 Garden Lane
Hodges, SC 29695-0001
Phone: 800-845-1124

White Flower Farm
P.O. Box 50
Litchfield, CT 067759-0050
Phone: 800-503-9624

Bibliography

Armitage, Allan M. *The Educated Gardener.* Compact Disc, ISBN 1-890354-02-3, PlantAmerica, Locust Valley, NY, 1998.

Brickell, Christopher (editor), et al. *The American Horticultural Society Encyclopedia of Gardening.* London, England: Dorling Kindersley Limited, 1993.

Clausen, Ruth Rogers and Nicholas H. Ekstron. *Perennials for American Gardens.* New York, NY: Random House, 1989.

Dirr, Michael A. *Manual of Woody Landscape Plants.* Champaign, IL: Stipes Publishing Co., 1990.

Ellis, Barbara W. *Taylor's Guide to Annuals.* Boston, MA: Houghton Mifflin Company, 1999.

Everett, Thomas H. *The New York Botanical Garden Illustrated Encyclopedia.* Vol 1 through 10, New York, NY: Garland Publishing, Inc., 1980.

Gilman, E.F., R.F. Lyons. *Horticopia A to Z.* Compact Disc, ISBN 1-887215-07-7, Purcellville, VA: Horticopia, Inc., 1999.

Greenlee, John. *The Encyclopedia of Ornamental Grasses.* Emmaus, PA: Rodale Press Books, 1992.

Hillier Nurseries. *The Hillier Manual of Trees & Shrubs,* sixth edition. Trowbridge, Great Britain: David & Charles, 1995.

Joyce, David (John Elsley, U.S. Consultant). *The Perfect Plant.* New York, NY: Stewart, Tabori, & Chang, 1998.

Lyons, Robert E. *Horticopia Perenials and Annuals,* edition II. Compact Disc, ISBN 1-887215-03-4, Purcellville, VA: Horticopia, Inc., 1997.

MacKenzie, David S. *Perennial Ground Covers.* Portland, OR: Timber Press, 1997.

Marinelli, Janet (Series Editor). *Growing Conifers, 21st-Century Gardening Series.* Brooklyn, NY: Brooklyn Botanic Garden, 1997.

——. *Starting from Seed, 21st-Century Gardening Series.* Brooklyn, NY: Brooklyn Botanic Garden, 1998.

Martin, Tovah. *Heirloom Flowers.* New York, NY: Simon & Schuster, 1999.

Mulligan, William C. *The Complete Guide to North American Gardens: The Northeast.* Boston, MA: Little, Brown and Company, 1991.

Proctor, Rob (Editor). *The Cutting Garden.* Boston, MA: Houghton Mifflin Company, 2000.

Reilly, Ann. *Park's Success with Seeds.* G. W. Park Seed Company, Inc., Greenwood, SC, 1978.

Schneider, Peter (Editor). *Taylor's Guide to Roses,* revised edition. Boston, MA: Houghton Mifflin Company, 1995.

Tenenbaum, Frances (Editor). *Taylor's Master Guide to Gardening.* Boston, MA: Houghton Mifflin Company, 1994.

Tenenbaum, Frances (Series Editor). *Taylor's 50 Best Perennials for Shade.* Boston, MA: Houghton Mifflin Company, 1999.

——. *Taylor's 50 Best Perennials for Sun.* Boston, MA: Houghton Mifflin Company, 1999.

——. *Taylor's 50 Best Roses.* Boston, MA: Houghton Mifflin Company, 1999.

——. *Taylor's 50 Best Shrubs.* Boston, MA: Houghton Mifflin Company, 1999.

——. *Taylor's 50 Best Trees.* Boston, MA: Houghton Mifflin Company, 1999.

Turgeon, A.J. *Turfgrass Management,* fifth edition. Saddle River, NJ: Prentice Hall, 1999.

Wyman, Donald. *Shrubs & Vines for American Gardens.* New York, NY: Macmillan Publishing Co., Inc., 1977.

Yang, Linda. *The City & Town Gardener.* New York, NY: Random House, Inc., 1990.

Additional References

Bissett Nursery Corp., 470 Deer Park Avenue, Dix Hills, NY 11746.

Cornell Cooperative Extension, Caroline T. Kiang. Seashore Plantings. Suffolk County, Oakdale, New York, 1998.

Park Seed Company, Flowers and Vegetables 2000. Greenwood, SC, 2000.

Princeton Nurseries, P.O. Box 185, Allentown, NJ 08501.

Professional Lawn Care Association of America, 1000 Johnson Ferry Road, NE, Suite C-135, Marietta, GA 30068.

Sea Grant, New York and Cornell Cooperative Extension of Suffolk County, Marine Program. American Beach Grass. Riverhead, NY, 1999.

Wayside Gardens, The Complete Wayside Garden Catalog. Hodges, SC, 2000.

White Flower Farms, 50th Anniversary Edition, Spring 2000. Litchfield, CT, 2000

Photography Credits

Sources for the photography in this book are as follows:

Thomas Eltzroth

Pages: Front Cover, 5, 18, 22, 24, 28, 30, 32, 34, 36, 38, 40, 44, 46, 56, 57, 62, 68, 70, 78, 84, 86, 88, 89, 90, 92, 98, 122, 124, 126, 130, 132, 134, 136, 148, 150, 153, 155, 156, 158, 162, 164, 166, 168, 170, 171, 172, 176, 182, 184, 188, 190, 192, 194, 196, 198, 200, 202, 208, 212, 220, 222, 226, 228, 230, 233, 236, 238, 242, 247, 250, 256, 272, 286, 298, 314, 332, 334, 336, 340, 344, 348, 352, 362, 364, 366, 368, 372, 378, 380

Liz Ball and Rick Ray

Pages: 11, 12, 13, 14, 19, 20, 42, 48, 50, 54, 58, 60, 72, 74, 76, 80, 82, 94, 100, 104, 108, 110, 112, 116, 118, 120, 128, 131, 140, 142, 144, 146, 174, 178, 186, 204, 206, 210, 216, 218, 224, 234, 246, 252, 254, 260, 264, 266, 268, 270, 276, 278, 280, 282, 284, 288, 290, 295, 296, 300, 302, 308, 310, 320, 322, 324, 326, 328, 330, 338, 341, 342, 350, 354, 358, 359, 360, 370, 374, 382, 384

Ralph Snodsmith

Pages: 6, 9, 64, 66, 102, 138, 180, 214, 231, 244, 294, 306, 318, 346

Pamela Harper

Pages: 248, 258, 274, 292, 304, 312, 316, 356, 376, 386, 388

Lorenzo Gunn

Pages: 26, 52, 96, 106, 114, 232, 262

Photo Reproduced Courtesy of the Scott's Seed Company

Page: 160

Bruce Asakawa

Page: 240

Index

About the Author

Ralph Snodsmith is best known as the host of the "Garden Hotline®" radio show, where he has answered gardening questions for more than 35 years. Television viewers will recognize Snodsmith as the congenial host of "Flower Time with Ralph Snodsmith," broadcast on Long Island's Newsday Cable channel from 1983 through 1986. From 1987 through 1995, Ralph worked as the garden editor for ABC TV's "Good Morning America."

Snodsmith shares his gardening wisdom in numerous articles for local and national publications. He has written a monthly garden column for *1001 Home Ideas* magazine and *Trees* magazine. He has contributed to the *Americana Encyclopedia* yearbooks every year since 1984, and he writes and publishes the *Garden Hotline® Newsletter*. In addition to authoring *The Tri-State Gardener's Guide,* published by Cool Springs Press, he is the author of *Tips from the Garden Hotline,* and the author and publisher of *Ralph Snodsmith's Fundamentals of Gardening.* Gardeners can find Snodsmith's advice on the Internet at three different websites: wor710.com, radiorockland.com, and gardenhotline.com.

Snodsmith has received numerous awards and honors from prestigious organizations. He received the Cornell Cooperative Extension "Friend of the Year" for 1999. He has also received the "Ramshorn Award" from SUNY Farmingdale, the "Master Gardener's Perennial Garden Award" from Cornell Cooperative Extension of Rockland County, the "Man of the Year" award from the Planting Fields Arboretum, the "Gold Medal Award" from Wayside Gardens, the "Gold Leaf" award from the New York State Arborist, ISA chapter, the "Garden Communicator Award" from the American Association of Nurserymen, the "Gold Medal of Horticulture" award from the New York Nurserymen's Association, the "Founder's Award" from the Marigold Society of America, and many others. Snodsmith currently resides in Suffern, NY.